SYNGRESS®

Ethereal®
Packet Sniffing

Angela Orebaugh

with

Greg Morris
Ed Warnicke
Gilbert Ramirez   Technical Editor

KEY	SERIAL NUMBER
001	HGY63D5HNO
002	92KJE32D5F
003	8292HCM9OP
004	CHI92W2W2R
005	49IMPO9U7N
006	CZXW32I8K7
007	KOLL6245BN
008	298KHBCFT4
009	IJW379OMNV
010	IMWQ295T6T

PUBLISHED BY
Syngress Publishing, Inc.
800 Hingham Street
Rockland, MA 02370

Ethereal Packet Sniffing

Printed in the United States of America
    6 7 8 9 0
ISBN: 1-932266-82-8

Acquisitions Editor: Christine Kloiber
Technical Editor: Gilbert Ramirez
Page Layout and Art: Patricia Lupien

Cover Designer: Michael Kavish
Copy Editor: Amy Thomson
Indexer: Julie Kawabata

Distributed by O'Reilly & Associates in the United States and Jaguar Book Group in Canada.

Acknowledgments

We would like to acknowledge the following people for their kindness and support in making this book possible.

Many thanks to Gerald Combs and the rest of the Ethereal development team for creating and mainatining a tool as dynamic and innovative as Ethereal, and for all of their support for this book.

Syngress books are now distributed in the United States by O'Reilly & Associates, Inc. The enthusiasm and work ethic at ORA is incredible and we would like to thank everyone there for their time and efforts to bring Syngress books to market: Tim O'Reilly, Laura Baldwin, Mark Brokering, Mike Leonard, Donna Selenko, Bonnie Sheehan, Cindy Davis, Grant Kikkert, Opol Matsutaro, Lynn Schwartz, Steve Hazelwood, Mark Wilson, Rick Brown, Leslie Becker, Jill Lothrop, Tim Hinton, Kyle Hart, Sara Winge, C. J. Rayhill, Peter Pardo, Leslie Crandell, Valerie Dow, Regina Aggio, Pascal Honscher, Preston Paull, Susan Thompson, Bruce Stewart, Laura Schmier, Sue Willing, Mark Jacobsen, Betsy Waliszewski, Dawn Mann, Kathryn Barrett, and to all the others who work with us.

The incredibly hard working team at Elsevier Science, including Jonathan Bunkell, AnnHelen Lindeholm, Duncan Enright, David Burton, Rosanna Ramacciotti, Robert Fairbrother, Miguel Sanchez, Klaus Beran, and Rosie Moss for making certain that our vision remains worldwide in scope.

David Buckland, Wendi Wong, Daniel Loh, Marie Chieng, Lucy Chong, Leslie Lim, Audrey Gan, and Joseph Chan of STP Distributors for the enthusiasm with which they receive our books.

Kwon Sung June at Acorn Publishing for his support.

Jackie Gross, Gayle Voycey, Alexia Penny, Anik Robitaille, Craig Siddall, Iolanda Miller, Jane Mackay, and Marie Skelly at Jackie Gross & Associates for all their help and enthusiasm representing our product in Canada.

Lois Fraser, Connie McMenemy, Shannon Russell, and the rest of the great folks at Jaguar Book Group for their help with distribution of Syngress books in Canada.

David Scott, Tricia Wilden, Marilla Burgess, Annette Scott, Geoff Ebbs, Hedley Partis, Bec Lowe, and Mark Langley of Woodslane for distributing our books throughout Australia, New Zealand, Papua New Guinea, Fiji Tonga, Solomon Islands, and the Cook Islands.

Winston Lim of Global Publishing for his help and support with distribution of Syngress books in the Philippines.

To all the folks at Malloy who have made things easy for us and especially to Beth Drake and Joe Upton.

Author

Angela Orebaugh (CISSP, GCIA, GCFW, GCIH, GSEC, CCNA) has worked in information technology for 10 years. She is currently an Associate at Booz Allen Hamilton in the Washington, DC metro area. Her focus is on perimeter defense, secure architecture design, vulnerability assessments, penetration testing, and intrusion detection. Angela is an expert in many commercial and Open Source intrusion detection and analysis tools including: Ethereal, Snort, Nessus, and Nmap. She is a graduate of James Madison University with a masters in computer science, and she is currently pursuing her PhD with a concentration in information security at George Mason University. Her GCFW practical received honors recognition and was used as a case study in the book *Network Perimeter Security: The Definitive Guide to Firewalls, VPNs, Routers, and Network Intrusion Detection* by Stephen Northcutt (ISBN: 0735712328). Angela is a researcher, writer, and speaker for the SANS Institute, where she has helped to develop and revise SANS course material and also serves as the Senior Mentor Coach for the SANS Local Mentor Program.

Contributors

Greg Morris (5-CNA, 5-CNE, 3-MCNE, Linux+, LPIC-1) is a Senior Resolution Engineer for Novell Technical Services in Provo, UT. Originally from Oklahoma, Greg has spent over 25 years in the computer industry. Although Greg has a degree in management, his passion is to be creative. This is what the software development process provides. His vast experience includes hardware and software troubleshooting on mainframe, midrange, and PC computers. Greg's early roots in software development was in database technologies, dabbling in C and assembly, but mostly working with a language called Clipper by Nantucket. Greg's work on Ethereal began in November of 2000. Since that time he has made a significant number of contributions to the Ethereal project. This would include new dissectors (NCP, NDS, NDPS) as well as new features (Extended Find capabilities). Greg has made a number of modifications to many other dissectors and is currently developing Novell Modular Authentication Services (NMAS), Novell SecretStore Services (SSS), Novell International Cryptographic Infrastructure (NICI), and a host of other Novell specific decodes. Greg has actively developed customer and internal training programs for a number of different Novell products. One of his most unique programs was developed to teach internal users the skills necessary to analyze packet traces. Greg started working with packet traces many years ago with Novell's LANalyzer product. From there Greg migrated to Network Associates Sniffer product. But, since working with Ethereal to add complete Novell NCP/NDS packet support, Greg would use nothing else. He currently develops on Windows 2000 with Microsoft's Visual C++, but has plans to move to SuSe Linux and the GNU compiler for future Ethereal development.

Ed Warnicke (CCIE #9466) has worked for almost four years at Cisco Systems doing network testing. Prior to joining Cisco he worked as the acting Senior Systems Administrator for the physics department at Rutgers University. Ed holds a masters degree in physics from Rutgers University and bachelors degrees in physics and mathematics from Purdue University where he holds the record for the largest number of credit hours successfully completed in a single semester: 34. Prior to attending college Ed dropped out of high school in a fit of boredom. Ed has contributed code to the Ethereal project and he also performed the last revision of the Ethereal User's guide.

Technical Editor and Contributor

Gilbert Ramirez was the first contributor to Ethereal after it was announced to the public and is known for his regular updates to the product. He has contributed protocol dissectors as well as core logic to Ethereal. He is a systems engineer at a large company with network-related products, where he works on tools and software build systems. Gilbert is a family man, a want-to-be chef, and a student of tae kwon do. His degree is in linguistics, but his first love is programming computers, which he has been doing since childhood.

Series Editor

Jay Beale is a security specialist focused on host lockdown and security audits. He is the Lead Developer of the Bastille project, which creates a hardening script for Linux, HP-UX, and Mac OS X, a member of the Honeynet Project, and a core participant in the Center for Internet Security. A frequent conference speaker and trainer, Jay speaks and trains at the Black Hat and LinuxWorld conferences, among others. A senior research scientist with the George Washington University Cyber Security Policy and Research Institute, Jay makes his living as a security consultant through the DC-based firm Intelguardians, LLC. Jay wrote the Center for Internet Security's Unix host security tool, currently in use worldwide by organizations from the Fortune 500 to the Department of Defense. He maintains the Center's Linux Security benchmark document and, as a core participant in the non-profit Center's Unix team, is working with private enterprises and US agencies to develop Unix security standards for industry and government.

Aside from his CIS work, Jay has written a number of articles and book chapters on operating system security. He is a columnist for Information Security Magazine and previously wrote a number of articles for SecurityPortal.com and SecurityFocus.com. He authored the Host Lockdown chapter in *Unix Unleashed*, served as the security author for *Red Hat Internet Server*, and co-authored *Snort 2.0 Intrusion Detection* (Syngress Publishing, ISBN: 1-931836-74-4). In addition, he is the editor of the "Jay Beale Open Source Security Series" from Syngress. Jay is currently finishing a Linux lockdown book focused on Bastille entitled, 'Locking Down Linux.' Formerly, he served as the Security Team Director for MandrakeSoft, helping set company strategy, design security products, and pushing security into the third largest retail Linux distribution. He now works to further the goal of improving operating system security. To read Jay's past articles and learn about his past and future conference talks, take a look at his site at www.bastille-linux.org/jay.

Technical Reviewer

Robert J. Shimonski (TruSecure TICSA, Cisco CCDP, CCNP, Symantec SPS, NAI Sniffer SCP, Nortel NNCSS, Microsoft MCSE, MCP+I, Novell Master CNE, CIP, CIBS, CNS, IWA CWP, DCSE, Prosoft MCIW, SANS.org GSEC, GCIH, CompTIA Server+, Network+, Inet+, A+, e-Biz+, Security+, HTI+) is a Network Manager for a leading manufacturing company, Danaher Corporation. At Danaher, Robert is responsible for leading the IT department within his division into implementing new technologies, standardization, upgrades, migrations, high-end project planning and designing infrastructure architecture. Robert is also part of the corporate security team responsible for setting guidelines and policy for the entire corporation worldwide. In his role as a Lead Network Engineer, he has designed, migrated, and implemented very large-scale Cisco- and Nortel-based networks. In addition, Robert maintains a role as a part time technical trainer at a local computer school, teaching classes on networking and systems administration whenever possible.

Robert is also a part-time author who has worked on over 25 book projects as both an author and technical editor. He has written and edited books on a plethora of topics with a strong emphasis on network security. Robert has designed and worked on several projects dealing with cutting edge technologies for Syngress Publishing, including the only book dedicated to the Sniffer Pro protocol analyzer, *Sniffer Pro Network Optimization & Troubleshooting Handbook* (Syngress, ISBN: 1-931836-57-4).

Contents

Foreword   xix

Chapter 1 Introducing Network Analysis   **1**
Introduction   2
What is Network Analysis and Sniffing?   2
Who Uses Network Analysis?   5
    How are Intruders Using Sniffers?   6
    What does Sniffed Data Look Like?   8
    Common Network Analyzers   9
How Does It Work?   14
    Explaining Ethernet   14
    Understanding the OSI model   16
    CSMA/CD   20
    Hardware: Taps, Hubs, and Switches, Oh My!   21
    Port Mirroring   24
    Defeating Switches   25
Detecting Sniffers   27
Protecting Against Sniffers   31
Network Analysis and Policy   33
Summary   34
Solutions Fast Track   35
Frequently Asked Questions   37

**Chapter 2 Introducing Ethereal: Network
Protocol Analyzer**   **39**
Introduction   40
What is Ethereal?   40
    History of Ethereal   41
    Compatibility   43
    Supported Protocols   44

Ethereal's User Interface   46
Filters   48
Great Resources!   52
Supporting Programs   54
Tethereal   54
Editcap   57
Mergecap   57
Text2pcap   58
Using Ethereal in Your Network Architecture   59
Using Ethereal for Network Troubleshooting   64
Summary   69
Solutions Fast Track   69
Frequently Asked Questions   71

Chapter 3 Getting and Installing Ethereal   73
Introduction   74
Getting Ethereal   75
Platforms and System Requirements   76
Packet Capture Drivers   78
Installing libpcap   80
Installing libpcap Using the RPMs   80
Installing libpcap from the Sun packages   83
Installing libpcap from the source files   85
Installing WinPcap   87
Installing Ethereal on Windows   91
Installing Ethereal on UNIX   99
Installing Ethereal from the RPMs   99
Installing the Solaris Ethereal Package   104
Building Ethereal from Source   108
Installing Ethereal from Source on Red Hat Linux   108
Installing the Dependencies   109
Building Ethereal   115
Enabling and Disabling features via *configure*   118
Summary   121
Solutions Fast Track   121
Frequently Asked Questions   123

Chapter 4 Using Ethereal   125
Introduction   126
Getting Started with Ethereal   126
Exploring the Main Window   127
  Summary Window   128
  Protocol Tree Window   130
  Data View Window   132
Other Window Components   134
  Filter Bar   134
  Information Field   136
Exploring the Menus   136
  File   136
    Open   138
    Save As   140
    Print   141
  Edit   147
    Find Packet   149
    Go To Packet   151
    Time Reference Submenu   151
    Preferences   153
  View   154
    Display Options   155
    Apply Color Filters   156
    Show Packet in New Window   160
  Capture   161
    Capture Options   162
    Edit Capture Filter List   169
  Analyze   171
    Edit Display Filter List   172
    Match and Prepare Submenus   175
    Enabled Protocols   176
    Decode As   177
    Decode As: Show   179
    Contents of TCP Stream   179
    TCP Stream Analysis Submenu   181
    Summary   192

Protocol Hierarchy Statistics   192
Statistics Submenu   194
Help   194
Contents   195
Supported Protocols   196
About Plugins   196
About Ethereal   197
Pop-up Menus   197
Summary Window Pop-up Menu   197
Protocol Tree Window Pop-up Menu   198
Data View Window Pop-up Menu   200
Using Command Line Options   200
Capture and File Options   201
Filter Options   202
Other Options   202
Summary   203
Solutions Fast Track   203
Frequently Asked Questions   205

Chapter 5 Filters   **207**
Introduction   208
Writing Capture Filters   209
Tcpdump Syntax Explained   209
Host Names and Addresses   210
Hardware Addresses (MAC Addresses)   211
Ports   212
Logical Operations   212
Protocols   213
Protocol Fields   215
Bitwise Operators   221
Packet Size   223
Examples   224
Using Capture Filters   225
Writing Display Filters   227
Writing Expressions   229
Integers   231
Booleans   234

Floating Point Numbers   234
Strings   234
Byte Sequences   236
Addresses   237
Time Fields   239
Other Field Types   240
Ranges   241
Logical Operations   244
Multiple Occurrences of Fields   244
Hidden Fields   247
Filter List Dialog Boxes   249
Filter Expression Dialog Box   254
Summary   257
Solutions Fast Track   257
Frequently Asked Questions   259

Chapter 6 Other Programs Packaged with Ethereal   261
Introduction   262
Tethereal   262
Tethereal Statistics   271
Editcap   281
Mergecap   287
Text2pcap   293
Summary   299
Solutions Fast Track   299
Frequently Asked Questions   301

Chapter 7 Integrating Ethereal with Other Sniffers   303
Introduction   304
Reading Capture Files with Ethereal   304
Saving Capture Files with Ethereal   306
Ethereal Integration   308
Tethereal   308
Capturing and Saving Data With Tethereal   310
Reading Ethereal Files With Tethereal   312
TCPDump   313
Capturing and Saving Data With TCPDump   314

Reading Ethereal Files With TCPDump   316
WinDump   317
    Capturing and Saving Data With WinDump   318
    Reading Ethereal Files With WinDump   319
Snort   320
    Capturing and Saving Data With Snort   322
    Reading Ethereal Files With Snort   325
Snoop   326
    Capturing and Saving Data With Snoop   329
    Reading Ethereal Files With Snoop   330
Microsoft Network Monitor   333
    Capturing and Saving Data With Network Monitor   334
    Reading Ethereal Files With Network Monitor   336
WildPackets EtherPeek   336
    Capturing and Saving Data With EtherPeek   336
    Reading Ethereal Files With EtherPeek   338
Network Associates' Sniffer Technologies Netasyst   339
    Capturing and Saving Data With Netasyst   340
    Reading Ethereal Files With Netasyst   341
HP-UX's nettl   342
    Capturing and Saving Data with nettl   345
    Reading Ethereal Files with nettl   347
Summary   350
Solutions Fast Track   350
Frequently Asked Questions   352

Chapter 8 Real World Packet Captures   353
Introduction   354
Scanning   354
    TCP Connect Scan   355
    SYN Scan   356
    Xmas Scan   357
    Null Scan   358
Remote Access Trojans   359
    SubSeven Legend   360
    NetBus   361
    RST.b   363

Dissecting Worms   365
    SQL Slammer Worm   365
    Code Red Worm   367
    Ramen Worm   371
Summary   376
Solutions Fast Track   376
Frequently Asked Questions   378

Chapter 9 Developing Ethereal   379

Introduction   380
Prerequisites for Developing Ethereal   381
    Skills   382
    Tools/Libraries   383
Ethereal Design   387
    aclocal–fallback and aclocal–missing   388
    debian   388
    doc   388
    epan   389
    gtk   389
    help   390
    image   390
    packaging   390
    plugins   391
    tools   392
    wiretap   392
Developing a Dissector   392
    Step 1 Copy the Template   393
    Step 2 Define the *Includes*   395
    Step 3 Create the Function to Register   397
    Step 4 Instruct Ethereal   400
    Step 5 Create the Dissector   401
    Step 6 Pass Payloads   408
    Running a Dissector   409
    The Dissection Process   410
Advanced Topics   412
    Dissector Considerations   413
        Creating Sub-trees   413

Bitfields   415
Unicode Strings   417
Conversations   418
Packet Retransmissions   419
Passing Data Between Dissectors   420
Saving Preference Settings   421
Packet Fragmentation   422
Value Strings   422
The Ethereal GUI   424
The Item Factory   424
Using GTK   425
TAPS   429
Plug-ins   429
Summary   430
Solutions Fast Track   431
Frequently Asked Questions   434

Appendix Supported Protocols   **437**
About the CD   **449**
Index   **451**

Foreword

When Syngress proposed Ethereal as the first book in my Open Source Security series, my first thought was "a whole book on Ethereal? Isn't it just a sniffer?" At the time, I didn't realize the scope of this program.

However, as we began developing the chapters, I saw exactly why Ethereal warranted an entire book. It has a tremendous number of useful features and included tools that most people never explore because it is so simple to use for day-to-day sniffing. Along these lines, chapter 6 (Other Programs Packaged with Ethereal) brings up less-often highlighted tools like *mergecap*, which many an IDS analyst or network forensics expert has used to read packet data from multiple sources and write that data out in the format of their choice. I recently spoke to an IDS expert who had never used *text2pcap*, (another tool covered by chapter 6) that he and I both found immensely useful in creating pcap packet captures from text-based hex-dumps. Chapter 7 (Integrating Ethereal with other Sniffers) offers an excellent treatment on how to interoperate Ethereal with a multitude of other free and commercial sniffers. Chapter 9's (Developing Ethereal) coverage of how to expand and build on Ethereal will prove useful for anyone who manages to find a protocol for which it doesn't yet have specific decoding functionality. And, I loved that chapter 5 (Filters) describes an undocumented feature in Ethereal so effectively and completely.

Most of all, I found chapter 8 (Real World Packet Captures) the most exciting. It demonstrates how to use Ethereal to dissect and understand attacks, allowing you to follow along by using Ethereal on the packet captures included on the accompanying CD-ROM. While the SQL Slammer and Ramen worm hands-on material was very interesting, I especially enjoyed following the Code Red analysis.

What comes out of reading these chapters is the realization that Ethereal is no run-of-the-mill freeware network sniffer. Ethereal offers more protocol decoding and reassembly than any free sniffer out there and ranks pretty well among the commercial tools. We've all used tools like tcpdump or windump to examine individual packets (and always will), but Ethereal makes it easier to make sense of a stream of ongoing network communications. Ethereal not only makes network troubleshooting work far easier, but also aids greatly in network forensics, the art of finding and examining an attack, by giving a better "big picture" view. Finally, when you're trying to find, isolate, and understand anomalous traffic, its expandable-tree view of your network traffic is invaluable.

I hope that you'll find this book just as invaluable. Ethereal has the ability to be a simple, single-purpose tool that you use without thinking about when you need to look at packets, or it can be the backbone of your security toolkit. This book gives you the information you need to take Ethereal to whatever level of performance you want.

—*Jay Beale*

## Chapter 1

Introducing
Network Analysis

Solutions in this Chapter:

- What is Network Analysis and Sniffing?
- Who Uses Network Analysis?
- How Does it Work?
- Detecting Sniffers
- Protecting Against Sniffers
- Network Analysis and Policy

☑ Summary

☑ Solutions Fast Track

☑ Frequently Asked Questions

Introduction

"Why is the network slow?" "Why can't I access my e-mail?" "Why can't I get to the shared drive?" "Why is my computer acting strange?" If you are a systems administrator, network engineer, or security engineer you have probably heard these questions countless times. Thus begins the tedious and sometimes painful journey of troubleshooting. You start by trying to replicate the problem from your computer. Sure enough, you can't get to anything on the local network or the Internet either. Now what? Go to each of the servers and make sure they are up and functioning? Check that your router is functioning? Check each computer for a malfunctioning network card?

What about this scenario: you go to your main access switch, or border router, and configure one of the unused ports for port mirroring. You plug in your laptop, fire up your network analyzer, and see thousands of User Datagram Protocol (UDP) packets destined for port 1434 with various, apparently random, Internet Protocol (IP) addresses. You immediately apply access filters to block these packets from entering or exiting your network until you do more investigating. A quick search on the Internet holds the answer. The date is January 25, 2003, and you have just been hit with the SQL Slammer worm. You were able to contain the problem relatively quickly thanks to your knowledge and use of your network analyzer.

What is Network Analysis and Sniffing?

Network analysis is the process of capturing network traffic and inspecting it closely to determine what is happening on the network. A network analyzer decodes, or dissects, the data packets of common protocols and displays the network traffic in human-readable format. Network analysis is also known by several other names: traffic analysis, protocol analysis, sniffing, packet analysis, and eavesdropping to name a few. Sniffing tends to be one of the most popular terms in use today. However, as you will see later in this chapter, due to malicious users it has had a negative connotation in the past.

A network analyzer can be a standalone hardware device with specialized software, or it can simply be software that you install on your desktop or laptop computer. Network analyzers are available both free and commercially. Differences between network analyzers tend to depend on features such as the number of supported protocol decodes, the user interface, and graphing and statistical capabilities. Other differences include inference capabilities, such as expert analysis features, and the quality of packet decodes. Although several network analyzers all decode the same protocols, some may decode better than others.

> **NOTE**
>
> Sniffer (with a capital "S") is a trademark owned by Network Associates referring to its Sniffer product line. However, it has become common industry usage that a "sniffer" (with a lower case "s") is a program that captures and analyzes network traffic.

Figure 1.1 shows the Ethereal Network Analyzer display windows. A typical network analyzer displays the captured traffic in three panes:

- **Summary** This pane displays a one line summary of the capture. Fields usually include date, time, source address, destination address, and the name and information about the highest-layer protocol.

- **Detail** This pane provides all of the details for each of the layers contained inside the captured packet in a tree-like structure.

- **Data** This pane displays the raw captured data both in hexadecimal and ASCII format.

Figure 1.1 Example Network Analyzer Display

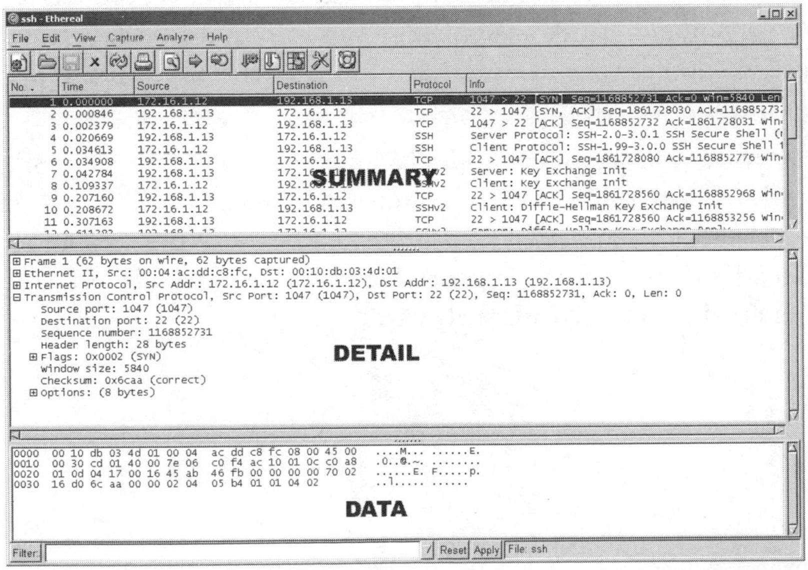

A network analyzer is a combination of hardware and software. Although there are differences in each product, a network analyzer is composed of five basic parts:

- **Hardware** Most network analyzers are software-based and work with standard operating systems (OSs) and network interface cards (NICs). However, there are some special hardware network analyzers that offer additional benefits such as analyzing hardware faults including: Cyclic Redundancy Check (CRC) errors, voltage problems, cable problems, jitter, jabber, negotiation errors, etc. Some network analyzers only support Ethernet or wireless adapters, while others support multiple adapters and allow users to customize their configuration. Sometimes you will also need a hub or a cable tap to connect to the existing cable.

- **Capture driver** This is the part of a network analyzer that is responsible for actually capturing the raw network traffic from the cable. It will also filter out the traffic that you want and store the data in a buffer. This is the core of a network analyzer and you cannot capture data without it.

- **Buffer** This component stores the captured data. Data can be stored in a buffer until it is full, or in a rotation method such as "round robin" where the newest data replaces the oldest data. Buffers can be disk-based or memory-based.

- **Real-time analysis** This feature analyzes the data as it comes off the cable. Some network analyzers use this to find network performance issues, and network intrusion detection systems do this to look for signs of intruder activity.

- **Decode** This component displays the contents of the network traffic with descriptions so that it is human-readable. Decodes are specific to each protocol, so network analyzers tend to vary in the number of decodes they currently support. However, new decodes are constantly being added to network analyzers.

NOTE

Jitter is a term used to describe the random variation in the timing of a signal. Electromagnetic interference and crosstalk with other signals can cause jitter. *Jabber* is when a device is improperly handling electrical signals, thus affecting the rest of the network. Faulty network interface cards can cause jabber.

Who Uses Network Analysis?

System administrators, network engineers, security engineers, system operators, even programmers, all use network analyzers. Network analyzers are invaluable tools for diagnosing and troubleshooting network problems. Network analyzers used to be dedicated hardware devices that were very expensive. New advances in technology have allowed for the development of software network analyzers. This makes it more convenient and affordable for administrators to effectively troubleshoot a network. It also brings the capability of network analysis to anyone who wishes to perform it.

The art of network analysis is a double-edged sword. While network, system, and security professionals use it for troubleshooting and monitoring of the network, intruders can also use network analysis for harmful purposes. A network analyzer is a tool, and like all tools they can be used for both good and bad intentions.

The following list describes a few reasons why administrators use network analyzers:

- Converting the binary data in packets to human-readable format
- Troubleshooting problems on the network
- Analyzing the performance of a network to discover bottlenecks
- Network intrusion detection
- Logging network traffic for forensics and evidence
- Analyzing the operations of applications
- Discovering a faulty network card
- Discovering the origin of a Denial of Service (DoS) attack

- Detecting spyware
- Network programming to debug in the development stage
- Detecting a compromised computer
- Validating compliance with company policy
- As an educational resource when learning about protocols
- For reverse-engineering protocols in order to write clients and supporting programs

How are Intruders Using Sniffers?

When used by malicious individuals, sniffers can represent a significant threat to the security of your network. Network intruders often use network sniffing to capture valuable, confidential information. The terms sniffing and eavesdropping have often been associated with this practice. However, sniffing is now becoming a non-negative term and most people use the terms sniffing and network analysis interchangeably.

Using a sniffer in an illegitimate way is considered a passive attack. It does not directly interface or connect to any other systems on the network. However, the computer that the sniffer is installed on could have been compromised using an active attack. The passive nature of sniffers is what makes detecting them so difficult. We will discuss the methods used to detect sniffers later in this chapter.

The following list describes a few reasons why intruders are using sniffers on the network:

- Capturing clear-text usernames and passwords
- Compromising proprietary information
- Capturing and replaying Voice over IP telephone conversations
- Mapping a network
- Passive OS fingerprinting

Obviously, these are illegal uses of a sniffer, unless you are a penetration tester whose job it is to find these types of weaknesses and report them to an organization.

For sniffing to occur, an intruder must first gain access to the communication cable of the systems that are of interest. This means being on the same shared network segment, or tapping into the cable somewhere between the path of communications. If the intruder is not physically present at the target system or communications access point, there are still ways to sniff network traffic. These include:

- Breaking into a target computer and installing remotely controlled sniffing software.

- Breaking into a communications access point, such as an Internet Service Provider (ISP) and installing sniffing software.

- Locating/finding a system at the ISP that already has sniffing software installed.

- Using social engineering to gain physical access at an ISP to install a packet sniffer.

- Having an insider accomplice at the target computer organization or the ISP install the sniffer.

- Redirecting communications to take a path that includes the intruder's computer.

Sniffing programs are included with most *rootkits* that are typically installed on compromised systems. Rootkits are used to cover the tracks of the intruder by replacing commands and utilities and clearing log entries. They also install other programs such as sniffers, key loggers, and backdoor access software. Windows sniffing can be accomplished as part of some RAT (Remote Admin Trojan) such as SubSeven or Back Orifice. Often intruders will use sniffing programs that are configured to detect specific things, such as passwords, and then electronically send them to the intruder (or store them for later retrieval by the intruder). Vulnerable protocols for this type of activity include telnet, FTP, POP3, IMAP, SMTP, HTTP, rlogin, and SNMP.

One example of a rootkit is T0rnKit, which works on Solaris and Linux. The sniffer that is included with this rootkit is called t0rns and is installed in the hidden directory /usr/srec/.puta. Another example of a rootkit is Lrk5 (Linux Rootkit 5), which installs with the linsniff sniffer.

Intruders commonly use sniffer programs to control back doors. One method is to install a sniffer on a target system that listens for specific information. Then, backdoor control information can be sent to a neighboring system. The sniffer picks this up, and acts appropriately on the target computer. This type of backdoor control is often hard for investigators to detect, since it looks like the innocent neighbor system is the compromised target.

cd00r is an example of a backdoor sniffer that operates in non-promiscuous mode, making it even harder to detect. Using a product like Nmap to send a series of Transmission Control Protocol (TCP) SYN packets to several predefined ports will trigger the backdoor to open up on a pre-configured port. More information about Cdoor can be found at www.phenoelit.de/stuff/cd00r.c.

NOTE

A *rootkit* is a collection of trojan programs that are used to replace the real programs on a compromised system in order to avoid detection. Some common commands that get replaced are *ps, ifconfig,* and *ls*. Rootkits also install additional software such as sniffers.

NOTE

Nmap is a network scanning tool used for network discovery and auditing. It can send raw IP packets to destination ports on target systems.

What does Sniffed Data Look Like?

We have done a lot of talking about sniffers and what they are used for, but the easiest way to grasp the concepts previously discussed is watching a sniffer in action. Figure 1.2 shows a capture of a simple FTP session from a laptop to a Sun Solaris system. The two highlighted packets show you just how easy it is to sniff the username and password. In this case, the username is "root" and the password is "password". Of course, allowing root to FTP into a system is a very poor security practice; this is just for illustration purposes!

Figure 1.2 Example of Sniffing a Connection

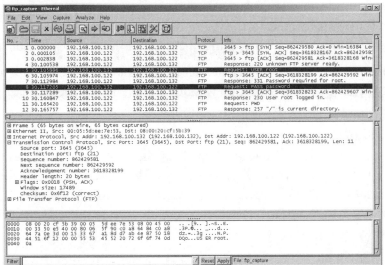

Common Network Analyzers

A simple search on SecurityFocus (www.securityfocus.org/tools/category/4) shows the diversity and number of sniffers available. Some of the most prominent ones are:

- **Ethereal** Of course, this one is the topic of this book! Ethereal is obviously one of the best sniffers available. It is being developed as a free commercial quality sniffer. It has numerous features, a nice graphical user interface (GUI), decodes for over 400 protocols, and it is actively being developed and maintained. It runs on both UNIX-based systems and Windows. This is a great sniffer to use, even in a production environment. It is available at www.ethereal.com.

- **WinDump** This is the Windows version of tcpdump available at http://windump.polito.it. It uses the WinPcap library and runs on Windows 95/98/ME/NT/2000/XP.

- **Network Associates Sniffer** This is one of the most popular commercial products available. Now marketed under McAfee Network Protection Solutions, Network Associates has an entire Sniffer product line for you to peruse at www.nai.com.

- **Windows 2000/NT Server Network Monitor** Both Windows 2000 Server and NT Server have a built-in program to perform network analysis. It is located in the Administrative tools folder, but is not installed by default, so you may have to add it from the installation CD.

- **EtherPeek** This is a commercial network analyzer by WildPackets. There are versions for both Windows and Mac, as well as other network analysis products that can be found at www.wildpackets.com.

- **Tcpdump** This is the oldest and most common network sniffer. The Network Research Group (NRG) of the Information and Computing Sciences Division (ICSD) at Lawrence Berkeley National Laboratory (LBNL) developed tcpdump. It is command line-based and runs on UNIX-based systems. It is being actively developed and maintained at www.tcpdump.org.

- **Snoop** This command line network sniffer is included with the Sun Solaris operating system. It is especially competent at decoding Sun-specific protocols.

- **Sniffit** This network sniffer runs on Linux, SunOS, Solaris, FreeBSD and IRIX. It is available at http://reptile.rug.ac.be/~coder/sniffit/sniffit.html.

- **Snort** This is a network intrusion detection system that uses network sniffing. It is actively developed and maintained at www.snort.org. For more information, refer to *Snort 2.0:Intrusion Detection* (Syngress Publishing, ISBN: 1-931836-74-4)

- **Dsniff** This is very popular network sniffing package. It is a collection of programs to sniff specifically for interesting data such as passwords, and to facilitate the sniffing process such as evading switches. It is actively maintained at www.monkey.org/~dugsong/dsniff.

- **Ettercap** This sniffer is designed specifically to sniff in a switched network. It has built-in features such as password collecting, OS fingerprinting, and character injection. It runs on several platforms including Linux, Windows, and Solaris. It is actively maintained at http://ettercap.sourceforge.net.

- **Analyzer** This is a free sniffer for the Windows OS that is being actively developed by the makers of WinPcap and WinDump at

Politecnico di Torino. It can be downloaded from
http://analyzer.polito.it.

- **Packetyzer** This is a free sniffer for the Windows OS that uses
  Ethereal's core logic. It tends to run a version or two behind the current
  release of Ethereal. It is actively maintained by Network Chemistry at
  www.networkchemistry.com/products/packetyzer/index.html.

Notes from the Underground...

Carnivore or Vegetarian?

No talk about network analyzers would be complete without the mention of Carnivore. While certainly not a commonly used network analyzer, it has created a lot of talk in the security world as well as the media. Carnivore is the code name for the FBI's network analyzer. It is used to monitor relevant communications among selected individuals as part of a criminal investigation. Its name has been changed to DCS100 in an attempt to obscure its image and to calm the public's fear of its misuse. When necessary, federal agents will arrive at a suspect's ISP with a "black box", which is merely a dedicated server running Windows 2000 or NT and the FBI's Carnivore software preloaded. The server is placed on the ISP's trunk to read header information for any traffic going to or coming from the suspect. This was rather common at numerous ISPs after September 11, 2001.

Many people have been concerned about the use of Carnivore and its ability to intercept all traffic, mostly due to privacy issues. They are concerned about how Carnivore works, how it could be misused by law enforcement, and the privacy debate over cable taps in general.

Carnivore is an Internet wiretap designed by the U.S. Federal Bureau of Investigation (FBI). It is designed with the special needs of law enforcement in mind. For example, some court orders might allow a pen-register monitoring of just the From/To e-mail addresses, whereas other court orders might allow a full capture of the e-mail. A summary of Carnivore's features can be seen within the configuration program shown in Figure 1.3.

Continued

Figure 1.3 Carnivore Configuration Program

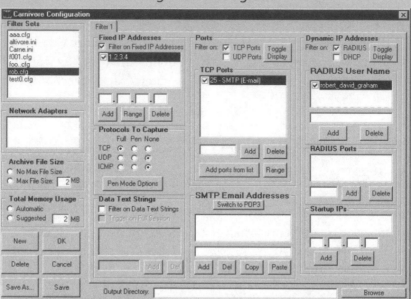

The features are:

- **Filter sets** The settings are saved in configuration files; the user can quickly change the monitoring by selecting a different filter set.

- **Network adapters** A system may have multiple network adapters; only one can be selected for sniffing at a time.

- **Archive file size** A limit can be set on how much data is captured; by default, it fills up the disk.

- **Total memory usage** Network traffic may come in bursts faster than it can be written to disk; memory is set aside to buffer the incoming data.

- **Fixed IP address** All traffic to/from a range of IP addresses can be filtered. For example, the suspect may have a fixed IP address of 1.2.3.4 assigned to their cable modem. The FBI might get a court order allowing them to sniff all of the suspect's traffic.

Continued

- **Protocols to capture** Typically, a court order will allow only specific traffic to be monitored, such as SMTP over TCP. In Pen mode, only the headers are captured.

- **Data text strings** This is the Echelon feature that looks for keywords in traffic. A court order must specify exactly what is to be monitored, such as an IP address or e-mail account. Such wide-open keyword searches are illegal in the United States. The FBI initially denied that Carnivore had this feature.

- **Ports** A list of TCP and UDP ports can be specified. For example, if the FBI has a court order allowing e-mail capture, they might specify the e-mail ports of 25 (SMTP), 110 (POP3), and 143 (IMAP).

- **SMTP e-mail addresses** A typical scenario is where Carnivore monitors an ISPs e-mail server, discarding all e-mails except those of the suspects. An e-mail session is tracked until the suspect's e-mail address is seen, then all the packets that make up the e-mail are captured.

- **Dynamic IP addresses** When users dial up the Internet, they are logged in via the RADIUS protocol, which then assigns them an IP address. Normally, the FBI will ask the ISP to reconfigure their RADIUS servers to always assign the same IP address to the suspect, and will then monitor all traffic to/from that IP address. Note: if you are a dial-up user and suspect the FBI is after you, check to see if your IP address is the same every time you dial up. Sometimes this isn't possible. Carnivore can be configured to monitor the RADIUS protocol and dynamically discover the new IP address assigned to the suspect. Monitoring begins when the IP address is assigned, and stops when it is unassigned.

The FBI developed Carnivore because other existing utilities do not meet the needs of law enforcement. When an e-mail is sent across the wire, it is broken down into multiple packets. A utility like mailsnarf will reassemble the e-mail back into its original form. This is bad because the suspect's defense attorneys will challenge its accuracy: Did a packet get dropped somewhere in the middle that changes the meaning of the e-mail? Did a packet from a different e-mail somehow get inserted into the message? By capturing the raw packets rather than reassembling

Continued

them, Carnivore maintains the original sequence numbers, ports, and timestamps. Any missing or extra packets are clearly visible, allowing the FBI to defend the accuracy of the system.

Another problem that the FBI faces is minimization of the sniffed data. When the FBI wiretaps your line, they must assign an agent to listen in. If somebody else uses your phone (like your spouse or kids), they are required to turn off the tape recorders. In much the same way, Carnivore is designed to avoid capturing anything that does not belong to the suspect. A typical example would be using Carnivore to monitor the activities of a dial-up user. Carnivore contains a module to monitor the RADIUS traffic that is used by most ISPs to authenticate the user and assign a dynamic IP address. This allows Carnivore to monitor only that user without intercepting any other traffic.*

The following websites have more information on Carnivore:

- www.fbi.gov
- www.robertgraham.com/pubs/carnivore-faq.html
- www.stopcarnivore.org

*Excerpt from Robert Graham's chapter in *Hack Proofing Your Network, Second Edition*. Syngress Publishing 1-928994-70-9.

How Does It Work?

This section provides an overview of how all of this sniffing takes place. It gives you a little background on how networks and protocols work; however, there are many excellent resources out there that fill entire books themselves! The most popular and undoubtedly one of the best resources is Richard Stevens' "TCP/IP Illustrated, Vol. 1 – 3".

Explaining Ethernet

Ethernet is the most popular protocol standard used to enable computers to communicate. A protocol is like speaking a particular language. Ethernet was built around a principle of a shared medium where all computers on the local network segment share the same cable. It is known as a *broadcast* protocol because when a computer has information to send, it sends that data out to all other computers on the same network segment. This information is divided up into manageable chunks called packets. Each packet has a header, which is like an envelope containing the addresses of both the destination and source computers. Even though this information is sent out to all computers on a segment, only the computer with the matching destination address will respond. All of the other computers on the network still see the packet, but if they are not the intended receiver they will disregard and discard it, unless a computer is running a sniffer. When you are running a sniffer, the packet capture driver that we mentioned earlier will put the computer's NIC into what is known as promiscuous mode. This means that the sniffing computer will be able to see all of the traffic on the segment regardless of who it is being sent to. Normally computers run in non-promiscuous mode, listening for information only designated for themselves. However, when a NIC is in promiscuous mode it can see conversations to and from all of its neighbors.

Ethernet addresses are known as Media Access Control (MAC) addresses, hardware addresses, or sometimes just Ethernet addresses. Since many computers may share a single Ethernet segment, each must have an individual identifier. These identifiers are hard-coded on to the NIC. A MAC address is a 48-bit number, also stated as a 12-digit hexadecimal number. This number is broken down into two halves, the first 24-bits identify the vendor of the Ethernet card, and the second 24-bits is a serial number assigned by the vendor.

The following steps will allow you to view your NIC's MAC address:

- **Windows 9x** Access **Start | Run**, and type **winipcfg.exe**. The MAC address will be listed as "Adapter Address".

- **Windows NT/2000/XP** Access the command line and type **ipconfig /all**. The MAC address will be listed as "Physical Address".

- **Linux and Solaris** Type **ifconfig −a** at the command line. The MAC address will be listed as "HWaddr" on Linux and "ether" on Solaris.

You can also view the MAC addresses of other computers that you have communicated with recently, by using the command **arp −a**. More will be discussed about this in the "Defeating Switches" section.

MAC addresses are unique, and no two computers should have the same one. However, this is not always the case. Occasionally there could be a manufacturing error that would cause more than one network interface card to have the same MAC address, but mostly, people will change their MAC addresses on purpose. This can be done with a program, such as ifconfig, that will allow you to fake your MAC address. Faking your MAC address is also called *spoofing*. Also, some adapters allow you to use a program to reconfigure the runtime MAC address. And lastly with the right tools and skill you can physically re-burn the address into the network interface card.

> **NOTE**
>
> Spoofing is the altering of network packet information such as the IP source address, MAC address, or even an e-mail address. This is often done to masquerade as another device in order to exploit a trust relationship, or to make tracing the source of attacks difficult. Address spoofing is also used in denial of service (DoS) attacks, such as Smurf, where the return address of network requests are spoofed to be the IP address of the victim.

Understanding the OSI model

The International Standards Organization (ISO) developed the Open Systems Interconnection (OSI) model in the early 1980's to describe how network protocols and components work together. It divides network functions into seven layers, and each layer represents a group of related specifications, functions, and activities.

The layers of the OSI model are:

- **Application layer** This topmost layer of the OSI model is responsible for managing communications between network applications. This layer is not the application program itself, although some applications may have the ability and the underlying protocols to perform application layer functions. For example, a Web browser is an application, but it is the underlying Hypertext Transfer Protocol (HTTP) protocol that provides the application layer functionality. Examples of application layer protocols include File Transfer Protocol (FTP), Simple Network Management Protocol (SNMP), Simple Mail Transfer Protocol (SMTP), and Telnet.

- **Presentation layer** This layer is responsible for data presentation, encryption, and compression.

- **Session layer** The session layer is responsible for creating and managing sessions between end systems. The session layer protocol is often unused in many protocols. Examples of protocols at the session layer include NetBIOS and Remote Procedure Call (RPC).

- **Transport layer** This layer is responsible for communication between programs or processes. Port or socket numbers are used to identify these unique processes. Examples of transport layer protocols include: TCP, UDP, and Sequenced Packet Exchange (SPX).

- **Network layer** This layer is responsible for addressing and delivering packets from the source computer to the destination computer. The network layer takes data from the transport layer and wraps it inside a packet or datagram. Logical network addresses are generally assigned to computers at this layer. Examples of network layer protocols include IP and Internetwork Packet Exchange (IPX). Devices that work at this layer are routers and Layer 3 switches.

- **Data link layer** This layer is responsible for delivering frames between NICs on the same physical segment. Communication at the data link layer is generally based on MAC addresses. The data link layer wraps data from the network layer inside a frame. Examples of data link layer protocols include Ethernet, Token Ring, and Point-to-Point Protocol (PPP). Devices that operate at this layer include bridges and switches.

- **Physical layer** This layer defines connectors, wiring, and the specifications on how voltage and bits pass over the cabled or wireless media. Devices at this layer include repeaters, concentrators, hubs, and cable taps. Devices that operate at the physical layer do not have an understanding of network paths.

NOTE

The terms *frame* and *packet* tend to be used interchangeably when talking about network traffic. However, the difference lies in the various layers of the OSI model. A frame is a unit of transmission at the data link layer. A packet is a unit of transmission at the network layer, however many people use the term packet to refer to data at any layer.

The OSI model is very generic and can be used to explain virtually any network protocol. Various protocol suites are often mapped against the OSI model for this purpose. A solid understanding of the OSI model aids tremendously in network analysis, comparison, and troubleshooting. However, it is also important to remember that not all protocols map nicely to the OSI model. For example, TCP/IP was designed to map to the U.S. Department of Defense (DoD) model. In the 1970s, the DoD developed its four-layer model. The core Internet protocols adhere to this model.

The DoD model is merely a condensed version of the OSI model. Its four layers are:

- **Process layer** This layer defines protocols that implement user-level applications such as mail delivery, remote login, and file transfer.

- **Host-to-host layer** This layer handles the connection, data flow management, and retransmission of lost data.

- **Internet layer** This layer is responsible for delivering data from source host to destination host across a set of different physical networks that connect the two machines.

- **Network access layer** This layer handles the delivery of data over a particular hardware media.

Notes from the Underground...

The TCP/IP Protocols

You will be seeing a lot of references in this book to TCP/IP and its associated protocols, specifically IP, TCP, and UDP. TCP/IP, developed by the Defense Advanced Research Projects Agency (DARPA), is the most widely used routed protocol today. IP is a Layer 3 protocol that contains addressing and control information that allows packets to be routed. IP is a connectionless protocol; therefore, it provides unreliable best-effort packet delivery service. Since IP only provides best-effort delivery, a packet may be discarded during transmission. All IP packets consist of a header and a payload (data from upper layers).

At the transport layer of the TCP/IP stack, the two commonly used protocols are TCP and UDP. The headers for both of these protocols

Continued

include a source and destination port number, which are used to determine the application or process that the TCP segment or UDP datagram originate from and destined to. TCP is a connection-oriented protocol, and UDP is a connectionless protocol. The TCP header includes sequence and acknowledgment numbers for reliable delivery. When IP needs reliable, guaranteed transfers it depends on TCP to provide this functionality.

Since TCP is a connection-oriented protocol it creates a dialog between the two communicating hosts to establish a connection. This is known as the three-way handshake. It starts by Host A sending a *SYN* packet to Host B letting it know that it wants to talk. Host B then responds with a *SYN/ACK*, saying that it is available to talk. Host A then finalizes the connection with an ACK.

TCP can also use the sliding window principle. The sliding window algorithm allows a buffer to be placed between the application program and the network data flow. Data received from the network is placed into this buffer until the application is ready to read it. The window is the amount of data that can be fetched into the buffer before an acknowledgment must be sent. Examples of applications that use TCP include FTP, Telnet, Network File System (NFS), SMTP, HTTP, Domain Name System (DNS), and Network News Transfer Protocol (NNTP). Examples of applications that use UDP include DNS, Routing Information Protocol (RIP), NFS, SNMP, and Dynamic Host Configuration Protocol/Boot Protocol (DHCP/BOOTP). As you can see, some applications (such as DNS and NFS) can use both protocols.

Notes from the Underground...

Writing Your Own Sniffer

There is an excellent paper titled "Basic Packet-Sniffer Construction from the Ground Up" by Chad Renfro located at www.unixgeeks.org/security/newbie/security/sniffer/sniffer_construction.txt. In this paper he presented a very basic 28-line packet sniffer written in C, called sniff.c. Even if you aren't a programmer, Chad explains the program line by line in an

Continued

easy to understand manner. The program demonstrates the use of the RAW_SOCKET device to read TCP packets from the network and print basic header information to std_out. For simplicity, the program operates in non-promiscuous mode, so you would first need to put your interface in promiscuous mode by using the **ifconfig eth0 promisc** command.

There is also a header file that has to be copied into the same directory as sniff.c. It provides standard structures to access the IP and TCP fields. The structures identify each field in the IP and TCP header. It contains more information than what the sniff.c actually uses, but it least it is there to build upon.

To run the program, copy the sniff.c and headers.h into the same directory, and enter the command **gcc -o sniff sniff.c**. This will compile the program and create and executable file called sniff, which can be run by typing **./sniff**. The following text shows the output of the sniff program when I attempted a TELNET and FTP connection:

```
Bytes received :::    48

Source address ::: 192.168.1.1

IP header length ::: 5

Protocol ::: 6

Source port ::: 1372

Dest port   ::: 23

Bytes received :::    48

Source address ::: 192.168.1.1

IP header length ::: 5

Protocol ::: 6

Source port ::: 1374

Dest port   ::: 21
```

Once you are done capturing data, you can end the program by typing **CTRL-C**. You may also want to remove your interface from promiscuous mode by typing the command **ifconfig eth0 –promisc**.

CSMA/CD

Ethernet uses the Carrier Sense Multiple Access/Collision Detection (CSMA/CD) protocol for devices on the network to exchange data. The term *multiple access* refers to the fact that many network devices attached to the same segment have the opportunity to transmit. Each device is given an equal opportunity; no device has priority over any other. *Carrier sense* describes how an Ethernet interface on a network device listens to the cable before transmitting. The network interfacer ensures that there are no other signals on the cable before it transmits. An Ethernet interface also listens while transmitting to ensure that no other network device transmits data at the same time. When two network devices transmit at the same time, a *collision* occurs. Since Ethernet interfaces listen to the media while they are transmitting, they are able to identify the presence of others through their *collision detection* method. If a collision occurs, the transmitting device will wait a random amount of time before retransmitting. This function is known as *random backoff*.

Traditionally, Ethernet operation has been *half duplex*. This means that an interface may either transmit or receive data, but it cannot do both at the same time. If more than one network interface on a segment tries to transmit at the same time, a collision occurs, as per CSMA/CD. When a crossover cable is used to connect two devices or a single device is attached to a switch port, only two interfaces on the segment need to transmit or receive and no collisions occur. This is because the transmit (TX) of device A is connected to the receive (RX) of device B, and the TX of B is connected to the RX of A. The collision detection method is therefore no longer necessary, so interfaces can be placed in *full-duplex* mode of operation. This mode allows network devices to transmit and receive at the same time, thereby increasing performance.

Hardware: Taps, Hubs, and Switches, Oh My!

Cable taps are hardware devices that assist in connecting to the network cable. Tap stands for Test Access Point, and you can use this device to access any cable between computers, hubs, switches, routers, and other devices. Taps are available in full or half-duplex for 10, 100, and 1000 Mbps Ethernet links. They are also available in various multi-port sizes. Following is a list of some popular cable tap products:

- Net Optics carries several types of network taps for copper and fiber cables. They can be viewed at www.netoptics.com.

- The Century Tap family is available by Shomiti at www.shomiti.net/shomiti/century-tap.html. They offer a variety of taps for copper and fiber cables.

A hub is a device that allows you to connect multiple hosts together on a shared medium, such as Ethernet. When a computer sends information, it travels into the hub and the hub blindly forwards the information to all other computers connected to it. As we explained before with Ethernet, the computer that the information was intended for will recognize its own MAC address in the packet header and then accept the data. The area that the hub forwards all information to is known as a *collision domain*, or *broadcast domain*. A hub has only one collision domain for all of the traffic to share. Figure 1.4 shows a network architecture with collision domains related to hubs. Large collision domains not only makes sniffing easier, but also create performance issues like bandwidth hogging or excessive traffic on the hub.

Figure 1.4 Hub Collision Domains

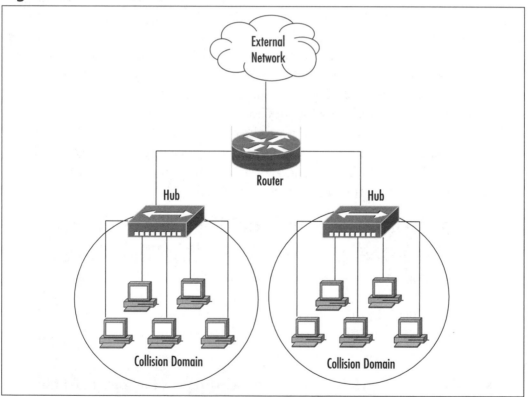

A switch operates very differently from a hub. It is also used to connect computers together on a shared medium; however, when a switch receives information from a computer it doesn't just blindly send it to all other computers. A switch will actually look at the packet header to locate the destination MAC address. A switch maintains a list of all MAC addresses and corresponding ports on the switch that the computers are connected to. It will then forward the packets to the specified port. This narrows the collision domain, or broadcast domain to a single port, as shown in Figure 1.5. This type of collision domain will also provide a definite amount of bandwidth for each connection rather than a shared amount on a hub. Since the price of switches has fallen dramatically in the last few years, there is no reason to not replace hubs with switches, or to choose switches when purchasing new equipment. Also, some of the more costly switches often include better technology to make them more resistant to sniffing attacks.

Figure 1.5 Switch Collision Domains

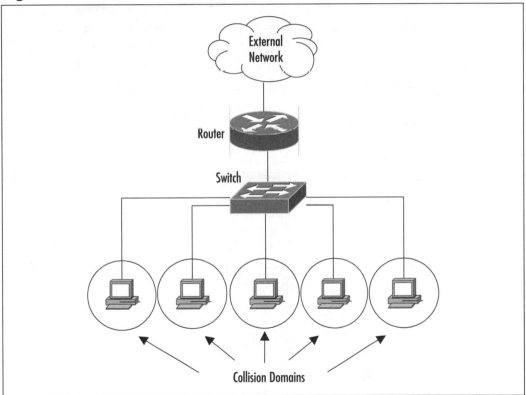

As you can see from the diagrams, hubs make sniffing easier, and switches make it more difficult. However, switches can be tricked, as discussed in the "Defeating Switches" section.

Port Mirroring

What if you are working in a network that uses switches and you want to perform network analysis legitimately? You are in luck, as most switches and routers come with a feature known as *port mirroring,* or *port spanning.* To mirror ports, you need to configure the switch to duplicate the traffic from a port you want to monitor to a port you are connected to with your network analyzer. This feature was designed just for this purpose, to analyze network traffic for troubleshooting.

Using port spanning does not interfere with the normal operation of switches, but you always want to check the documentation of the exact switch you are configuring and periodically check the device's logs. You won't affect the switch, but you will increase the amount of traffic on a specific destination port, so make sure your properly configured network analyzer is the destination port. Please consult the documentation for your specific switch to learn the exact command to enable port mirroring. Figure 1.6 shows the process of port mirroring. The switch is configured to mirror all port 1 traffic to port 5. The network analyzer will see any traffic to and from Computer A. Sometimes administrators will mirror the uplink port on a switch; that way they will see all traffic to and from the switch and all of its ports.

Figure 1.6 Port Mirroring

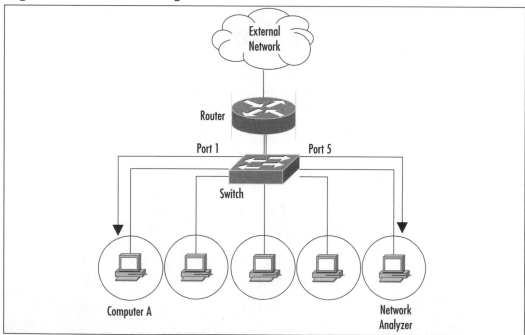

NOTE

Span means Switched Port ANalyzer. Cisco uses the word *span* to describe the concept of port mirroring. To span a port in Cisco terms is the same as mirroring a port.

Defeating Switches

We mentioned earlier that the use of switches in your network makes sniffing more difficult. In theory, on a switch you should only see traffic destined for you own computer. Notice we didn't say that switching eliminates sniffing. There are ways to trick a switch, or to get around its technology. The following list describes several ways in which a switch can be defeated:

- **Switch Flooding** Some switches can be made to act like a hub, where all packets are broadcast to all computers. This can be accomplished by overflowing the switch address table with all kinds of fake MAC addresses. This is known as a device *failing open*, thus removing all security provisions. Devices that *fail close* will incorporate some sort of security measure, such as shutting down all communications. The Dsniff package comes with a program called *macof* that is designed to perform switch MAC address flooding. It can be downloaded from http://monkey.org/~dugsong/dsniff.

- **ARP Redirects** When a computer needs to know the MAC address of another computer, it will send an ARP request. Each computer maintains an ARP table to store the MAC addresses of other computers that it has talked to. ARPs are broadcast on a switch, so all computers on that switch will see the request and the response. There are several methods that use ARP to trick a switch into sending traffic somewhere it shouldn't. First, an intruder can subvert a switch by sending out an ARP claiming to be someone else as the MAC address. An intruder can also send an ARP claiming to be the router, in which case computers will try to send their packets through the intruder's computer. Or, an intruder can send an ARP request just to one victim, claiming to be the router, at which point the victim will start forwarding packets to the intruder. All of these tricks will allow an intruder to see information that he/she is not supposed to see.

- **ICMP Redirect** Sometimes computers are on the same physical segment, the same switch, but different logical segments. This means they are in different IP subnets. When Computer A wants to talk to Computer B it will send its request through a router. The router knows that they are on the same physical segment, so it will send an ICMP Redirect to Computer A letting it know that it can send its packets directly to Computer B. An intruder, Computer X, could send a fake ICMP redirect to Computer A, claiming that it should send Computer B's packets to Computer X.

- **ICMP Router Advertisements** These advertisements inform computers of who the router is. An intruder could send these types of advertisements out claiming to be the router, and computers will start to forward all packets through the intruder.

- **MAC Address Spoofing** An intruder can pretend to be using a different computer by spoofing its MAC address. Sending out packets with the source address of the victim will trick the switch. The switch will enter the spoofed information into its table and begin sending packets to the intruder. But what about the victim, who is still on the switch and sending updates causing the switch to change the table back? This can be solved by taking the victim offline with some sort of DoS attack, then redirecting the switch and continuing with communications. The intruder could also broadcast out the traffic that he receives to ensure that the victim computer still receives the packets. Some switches have a countermeasure that will allow you to statically assign a MAC address to a port. This may be difficult to manage if you have a large network, but it will eliminate MAC spoofing.

  To spoof your MAC on Linux or Solaris when you are connected locally, you can simply use ifconfig as follows:

```
ifconfig eth0 down
ifconfig eth0 hw ether 00:02:b3:00:00:AA
ifconfig eth0 up
```

Register the MAC on all hosts by broadcast ping (and use Control C to close the ping): **ping –c 1 –b 192.168.1.255**

Now you can sniff all traffic to the computer that owns this MAC address.

- **Reconfigure port spanning on the switch** As we mentioned earlier, switch ports can be configured to see traffic destined for other ports. An intruder could perform this by connecting to the switch via Telnet or some other default backdoor. The intruder could also use SNMP if it is not secured.

- **Cable taps** As mentioned earlier, cable taps can be used to physically tap into the cable. Tapping into the uplink cable on a switch will show you all of the traffic entering and exiting that switch.

There are many methods of defeating switches, but this is contingent upon how a switch operates. Not all of the methods discussed will work, especially with newer, more technologically savvy switches. The Dsniff FAQ contains some good information for sniffing in a switched environment. It can be located at http://monkey.org/~dugsong/dsniff/faq.html.

Detecting Sniffers

Remember earlier that we said sniffers are a form of passive attack. They don't interact with any devices or transmit any information, thus making them very difficult to detect. Although tricky, detecting sniffers is possible. The easiest method is to check your network interfaces to see if they are in promiscuous mode. On UNIX-based systems the command **ifconfig –a** will list the network adapters on the system. Look for the PROMISC flag in the output, such as in the following example:

```
[root@localhost root]# ifconfig -a
eth0      Link encap:Ethernet  HWaddr 00:02:B3:06:5F:5A
          inet addr:192.168.1.2  Bcast:192.168.1.255  Mask:255.255.255.0
          UP BROADCAST RUNNING PROMISC MULTICAST  MTU:1500  Metric:1
          RX packets:204 errors:0 dropped:0 overruns:0 frame:0
          TX packets:92 errors:0 dropped:0 overruns:0 carrier:0
          collisions:0 txqueuelen:100
          RX bytes:46113 (45.0 Kb)  TX bytes:5836 (5.6 Kb)
          Interrupt:11 Base address:0x1800 Memory:e8120000-e8120038
```

If ifconfig is not detecting a sniffer that you know is currently installed and in promiscuous mode, you can try using the **ip link** command, a handy TCP/IP interface configuration and routing utility. The following example shows the output from the ip command:

```
[root@localhost root]# ip link
1: lo: <LOOPBACK,UP> mtu 16436 qdisc noqueue
    link/loopback 00:00:00:00:00:00 brd 00:00:00:00:00:00
2: eth0: <BROADCAST,MULTICAST,PROMISC,UP> mtu 1500 qdisc pfifo_fast qlen 100
    link/ether 00:02:b3:06:5f:5a brd ff:ff:ff:ff:ff:ff
```

Detecting promiscuous mode on Windows systems is more difficult because there are no standard commands that will list that type of information. However, there is a free tool called PromiscDetect, developed by Arne Vidstrom, that will detect promiscuous mode network adapters for Windows NT, 2000, and XP. It can be downloaded from http://ntsecurity.nu/toolbox/promiscdetect. The following example shows the output of PromiscDetect, the D-link adapter is in normal operation mode, but the Intel adapter has Ethereal running on it:

```
C:\>promiscdetect
PromiscDetect 1.0 - (c) 2002, Arne Vidstrom (arne.vidstrom@ntsecurity.nu)
                 - http://ntsecurity.nu/toolbox/promiscdetect/
Adapter name:
 - D-Link DWL-650 11Mbps WLAN Card
Active filter for the adapter:
 - Directed (capture packets directed to this computer)
 - Multicast (capture multicast packets for groups the computer is a member
of)
 - Broadcast (capture broadcast packets)
Adapter name:
 - Intel(R) PRO/100 SP Mobile Combo Adapter
Active filter for the adapter:
 - Directed (capture packets directed to this computer)
 - Multicast (capture multicast packets for groups the computer is a member
of)
 - Broadcast (capture broadcast packets)
 - Promiscuous (capture all packets on the network)
WARNING: Since this adapter is in promiscuous mode there could be a sniffer
         running on this computer!
```

Unfortunately some sniffers can cover their tracks by hiding the promiscuous flags. Also, if the sniffer was installed on a compromised system by using a rootkit, the intruder has most likely replaced commands like ifconfig. The following list describes several other methods that could be used to detect sniffers on the network:

- Monitor DNS reverse lookups. Some sniffers will perform DNS queries to resolve IP addresses to host names. Performing a network ping scan or pinging your entire network address space could trigger this activity.

- Send TCP/IP packets to all IP addresses on the same Ethernet segment, but with fake MAC addresses. Normally the network interface card will drop packets with the wrong MAC address. However, some systems, when in promiscuous mode, will answer with a reset packet (RST). This may also work in a switched environment since switches forward broadcast packets that they don't have MAC addresses listed for. Many newer sniffers have build in defenses for this technique by altering the way they handle MAC addresses.

- Carefully monitor hub ports. Ideally you would have a network diagram and your cables would be labeled. Then, if something unusual appeared, such as a new device or a newly active hub port, you would recognize it. However, in reality, wiring closets and cabling can be a nightmare. If your hubs are being monitored with a protocol such as SNMP via a network management system, you may be able to use this information to detect any unusual connects and disconnects.

- Remember how ARP is used to link IP addresses to MAC addresses. Normally an ARP is sent out as a broadcast to everyone. However, you could send out an ARP to a non-broadcast address, followed by a broadcast ping. No one should have your information in his or her ARP table except the sniffer because it was listening to all traffic, even the non-broadcast traffic. Therefore the computer with the sniffer would respond.

- Use a honeypot. A honeypot is a server that is set up to monitor the activity of intruders. It contains fake data and services. In this case you could create fake administrator or user accounts on the honeypot and then create connections across the network to it using clear text protocols such as Telnet or FTP. If there are sniffers monitoring for user

names and passwords they will see the honeypot and the intruder will
eventually try to log into it. Honeypots run intrusion detection software
to monitor activity, and special signatures can be added to trigger alerts
when the fake accounts are used.

■   Carefully monitor your hosts. This includes disk space, CPU utilization,
and response times. Sniffers gradually consume disk space each day as
they log traffic, and they can sometimes put a noticeable load on the
CPU. When the infected computer's resources become consumed it will
respond more slowly than normal.

There are several tools that can be used to detect sniffers on your network.
Many of them are outdated and no longer actively maintained, and sometimes
just hard to find. Also, newer sniffers have been rewritten to evade their detection. However, we want to take a moment to mention some of them.

■   **PromiScan Ver 0.27** This is a free program by Security Friday that is
up-to-date and actively maintained. It runs on Windows 2000 and XP
and requires the WinPcap driver. It can scan the local network looking
for remote promiscuous mode adapters, using ARP packets. It can be
downloaded from www.securityfriday.com/ToolDownload/
PromiScan/promiscan_doc.html.

■   **AntiSniff** This program was originally written by L0pht, but is no
longer supported or maintained. Archived Windows and UNIX versions
can be downloaded from http://packetstormsecurity.nl/sniffers/antisniff.

■   **Sentinel** This free program performs remote promiscuous detection,
and runs on various versions of BSD and Linux. It requires the libpcap
and libnet libraries to operate. It can be downloaded from www.packet-
factory.net/projects/sentinel.

■   **Neped** Network Promiscuous Ethernet Detector is a free UNIX-based
program originally written by the Apostols Group to remotely detect
promiscuous mode network interface cards on Linux computers. It only
detects on a subset of Linux systems with unpatched kernels before version 2.0.36. The Apostols website no longer exists and neped can be
difficult to find. Currently there is a version located at
www.dsinet.org/tools/network-sniffers/neped.c.

- **Check Promiscuous Mode (CPM)** This is a free UNIX-based program developed by CERT/CC in response to increased network sniffing. More information, including the program, can be obtained from www.cert.org/advisories/CA-1994-01.html.

- **Ifstatus** This is a free UNIX-based program to detect promiscuous mode interfaces on Solaris and AIX systems. It can be downloaded from ftp://ftp.cerias.purdue.edu/pub/tools/unix/sysutils/ifstatus.

- **Promisc.c** This is a free UNIX-based program to detect promiscuous mode interfaces on Linux and some SunOS systems. It can be downloaded from www.dsinet.org/tools/network-sniffers/promisc.c.

Protecting Against Sniffers

So far you have learned what sniffing is and how it works. You have also learned some of the tricks that can be used by intruders to sniff where they aren't supposed to, and some not-so-foolproof methods of detecting sniffers. None of this sheds much of a positive light on your plight to protect your network and data. Fortunately there are some methods that you can use on your network that offer protection against the passive attack known as sniffing.

We talked earlier about using switches on your network instead of hubs. However, we also learned the methods used to defeat switches. Using switches is a network best practice that will allow increased performance and security that should be used regardless of existing methods to evade them. While switches will present a barrier to casual sniffing, the best method of protecting your data is encryption. Encryption is the best form of protection against traffic interception, on public networks as well as your own internal networks. Intruders will still be able to sniff the traffic, but the data will appear unreadable. Only the intended recipient should be able to decrypt and read the data. Some methods of encryption still leave the headers in cleartext, so the intruder will be able to see the source and destination addresses and possibly map the network, but the data will be obscured. Other forms of encryption will also mask the header portion of the packet.

A virtual private network (VPN) uses encryption and authentication to provide secure communications over an otherwise insecure network. VPNs protect the transmission of data over the Internet, and even your internal network. However, if an intruder compromises either of the end nodes of a VPN, the protection is rendered useless. The following list describes some of the VPN methods in use today that will protect your data against sniffing:

- **Secure Shell (SSH)** SSH is an application-level VPN that runs over TCP to secure client-to-server transactions. This is often used for general logins and to administer servers remotely. It is typically used to replace Telnet, FTP, and Berkley Services "r" commands. However, since any arbitrary TCP protocol can be tunneled through an SSH connection, it can be used for numerous other applications. SSH provides authentication by RSA or DSA asymmetric key pairs. The headers in an SSH session are not encrypted, so an intruder will still be able to view the source and destination addresses.

- **Secure Sockets Layer (SSL)/Transport Layer Security (TLS)** SSL was originally developed by Netscape Communications to provide security and privacy to Internet sessions. It has been replaced by TLS as stated in RFC 2246. TLS provides security at the transport layer and overcomes some security issues of SSL. It is used to encapsulate the network traffic of higher-level applications such as LDAP, HTTP, FTP, NNTP, POP3, and IMAP. It provides authentication and integrity via digital certificates and digital signatures.

- **IP Security (IPSec)** IPSec is a network-level protocol that incorporates security into the IPv4 and IPv6 protocols directly at the packet level by extending the IP packet header. This allows the ability to encrypt any higher layer protocol. It is currently being incorporated into routing devices, firewalls, and clients for securing trusted networks to one another. IPSEC provides several means for authentication and encryption, supporting quite a few public key authentication ciphers and symmetric key encryption ciphers. It can operate in tunnel mode to provide a new IP header that will mask the original source and destination addresses.

One-time passwords (OTP) is another method to protect against sniffing. S/key, One-time Passwords In Everything (OPIE), and other one-time password techniques will protect against the collection and reuse of passwords. They operate by using a challenge-response method, and a different password is transmitted each time authentication is needed. The passwords that a sniffer collects will be useless since they are only used once. Smart cards are a popular method of implementing one-time passwords.

E-mail protection is a hot topic for both companies and individuals. Two methods of protecting e-mail, by encrypting it in transit and in storage, are Pretty

Good Privacy (PGP) and Secure Multipurpose Internet Mail Extensions (S/MIME). Each of these methods also provides authentication and integrity by the use of digital certificates and digital signatures.

Network Analysis and Policy

There is one very important topic that we would like to take time to address. Before cracking open your newly installed network analyzer at work, please read your company policy! A properly written and comprehensive "Appropriate Use" network policy will more than likely prohibit you from running network analyzers. Usually the only exception to this is if network analysis is in your job description. Also, just because you may provide security consulting services for company clients, does not mean that you can use your sniffer on the company network. However, if you are an administrator and are allowed to legitimately run a sniffer, you can use it to enforce your company's security policy. If your security policy prohibits the use of file sharing applications such as KaZaA, Morpheus, or messaging services such as Internet Relay Chat (IRC) or Instant Messenger, you could use your sniffer to detect this type of activity.

Also, if you provide security services for clients, such as an ethical hacker who performs penetration testing, be sure that the use of a sniffer is included in your Rules of Engagement. Be very specific about how, where, and when it will be used. Also provide clauses, such as Non-Disclosure Agreements, that will exempt you from the liability of learning confidential information.

Another word of caution: many ISPs prohibit the use of sniffers in their "Appropriate Use" policy. If they discover that you are using one while attached to their network, they may disconnect your service. The best place to experiment with a sniffer is on your own home network that is not connected to the Internet. All you really need is two computers with a crossover cable between them. You can use one as a client, and install server services on the other, such as Telnet, FTP, Web, and mail. Install the sniffer on one or both computers and have fun!

> **NOTE**
>
> You can also download packet traces from numerous websites and read them with your network analyzer to get used to analyzing and interpreting packets. The HoneyNet Project at http://project.honeynet.org has monthly challenges and other data for analysis.

Summary

Network analysis is the key to maintaining an optimized network and detecting security issues. Proactive management can help find issues before they turn into serious problems and cause network downtime or compromise confidential data. In addition to identifying attacks and suspicious activity, you can use your network analyzer data to identify security vulnerabilities and weaknesses and enforce your company's security policy. Sniffer logs can be correlated with IDS, firewall, and router logs to provide evidence for forensics and incident handling. A network analyzer allows you to capture data from the network, packet by packet, decode the information, and view it in an easy to understand format. Network analyzers are easy to find, often free, and easy to use; they are a key part of any administrator's toolbox.

We covered the basics of networking, Ethernet, the OSI model, and hardware that is used in a network architecture. Believe me, we only scratched the surface here. A good networking and protocols reference should be on every administrator's bookshelf. This will come in very handy when you discover some unknown or unusual traffic on your network.

As an administrator, you should also know how to detect the use of sniffers by intruders. You should keep up to date on the methods that intruders use to get around security measures that are meant to protect against sniffing. As always, you will also need to make sure that your computer systems are up to date with patches and security fixes to protect against rootkits and other backdoors.

We also covered a variety of methods used to protect your data from eavesdropping by sniffers. You should always remain up to date on the latest security technologies, encryption algorithms, and authentication processes. Intruders are constantly finding ways to defeat current security practices, thus more powerful methods are developed. A good example is the cracking of the DES encryption scheme and its subsequent replacement with Triple Data Encryption Standard (3DES).

Finally, remember the rule of network analysis—only do it if you have permission. A happy, curious, up-and-coming administrator could easily be mistaken as an intruder. Make sure you have permission or use your own private network to experiment.

Solutions Fast Track

What is Network Analysis and Sniffing?

☑ Network analysis is capturing and decoding network data.

☑ Network analyzers can be hardware or software, and are available both free and commercially.

☑ Network analyzer interfaces usually have three panes: summary, detail, and data.

☑ The five parts of a network analyzer are: hardware, capture driver, buffer, real-time analysis, and decode.

Who Uses Network Analysis?

☑ Administrators use network analysis for troubleshooting network problems, analyzing the performance of a network, and intrusion detection.

☑ When intruders use sniffers, it considered is a passive attack.

☑ Intruders use sniffers mostly to capture user names and passwords, collect confidential data, and map the network.

☑ Sniffers are a common component of a rootkit.

☑ Intruders are using sniffers to control backdoor programs.

How Does it Work?

☑ Ethernet is a shared medium that uses MAC, or hardware, addresses.

☑ The OSI model has seven layers and represents a standard for network communication.

☑ Hubs send out information to all hosts on the segment, creating a shared collision domain.

☑ Switches have one collision domain per port and keep an address table of the MAC addresses that are associated with each port.

☑ Port mirroring is a feature that allows you to sniff on switches.

☑ Switches make sniffing more difficult, however the security measures in switch architectures can be overcome by a number of methods, thus allowing the sniffing of traffic designated for other computers.

Detecting Sniffers

☑ Sometimes sniffers can be detected on local systems by looking for the promiscuous mode flag.

☑ There are several tools available that attempt to detect promiscuous mode by using various methods.

☑ Carefully monitoring your hosts, hub and switch ports, and DNS reverse lookups can assist in detecting sniffers.

☑ Honeypots are a good method to detect intruders on your network who are attempting to use compromised passwords.

☑ Newer sniffers are smart enough to hide themselves from traditional detection techniques.

Protecting Against Sniffers

☑ Switches offer some, but little protection against sniffers.

☑ Encryption is the best method of protecting your data from sniffers.

☑ SSH, SSL/TLS, and IPSEC are all forms of VPNs that operate at various layers of the OSI model.

☑ IPSec tunnel mode can protect the source and destination addresses in the IP header by appending a new header.

Network Analysis and Policy

☑ Make sure you have permission to use a sniffer on a network that is not your own.

☑ Read the appropriate use policies of your ISPs before using a sniffer.

☑ If you are hired to assess a computer network, and plan to use a sniffer, make sure you have some sort of non–disclosure agreements in place, because you may have access to confidential data.

☑ One-time passwords render compromised passwords useless.

☑ E-mail should be protected while in transit and storage with some type of data encryption method.

Frequently Asked Questions

The following Frequently Asked Questions, answered by the authors of this book, are designed to both measure your understanding of the concepts presented in this chapter and to assist you with real-life implementation of these concepts. To have your questions about this chapter answered by the author, browse to **www.syngress.com/solutions** and click on the **"Ask the Author"** form. You will also gain access to thousands of other FAQs at ITFAQnet.com.

Q: I ran a switch flooding program against my switch and it didn't do anything, why not?

A: Some newer switches are resilient to some of the older flooding tools.

Q: I have hubs daisy-chained through the floors of my company's building, is that all one collision domain?

A: Yes! Hubs do not have any intelligence built into them to know where to send data, so they will blindly forward it on to everyone. So every hub that is connected together is seeing traffic for all ports.

Q: When I run Ethereal on my Linux system, I don't see the PROMISC flag in the ifconfig –a output.

A: Ethereal uses the libpcap program to perform packet capturing and filtering. Some newer versions if libpcap use a different method of putting an interface into promiscuous mode that ifconfig cannot detect.

Q: Will adding encryption to my network decrease performance?

A: Yes, encrypting and decrypting data can be resource–intensive, depending on several factors including the type of encryption algorithm and length of the key. However, depending on your network architecture, end users may not notice the difference in performance.

Q: What if an attacker compromises a host that I am using a VPN client on?

A: Your VPN would basically offer a safe and secure environment for the attacker to run wild! For example, you connect your work laptop at home to the Internet over dial-up or high-speed Internet, and your system is compromised via a trojan. Your connections back to the office are secured via a VPN connection which gets enabled once you connect to your mail server or other protected work resources. The attacker then has the ability to access these resources that are otherwise protected by your VPN.

Q: I still don't understand how one-time passwords work.

A: Let me give you an example. You are provided with an RSA Secure ID hardware token. This is a small device that has a screen on it with some numbers that change every sixty seconds. These numbers are your responses to the RSA server challenges, i.e. your password. The token and the server are synchronized, so when you log in, the server presents you with a challenge, i.e. asks you your password, and you type in whatever number is showing on your Secure ID token screen at the time. You will be authenticated for this session, but next time you login it will be a different number, hence a one-time password.

## Chapter 2

Introducing Ethereal: Network Protocol Analyzer

Solutions in this Chapter:

- What is Ethereal?
- Supporting Programs
- Using Ethereal in Your Network Architecture
- Using Ethereal for Network Troubleshooting

☑ Summary

☑ Solutions Fast Track

☑ Frequently Asked Questions

Introduction

You probably picked up this book because you have already heard about Ethereal and its feature-rich graphical user interface (GUI). Maybe you read about it on the Internet, overheard a coworker talking about it, or heard about it at a security conference. However, if you are looking for a comprehensive guide to get you started and unleash the powers of Ethereal, you've come to the right place.

Ethereal is undoubtedly the best open source network analyzer available. And, the best part is: it's free! It is packed with features that are comparable to a commercial network analyzer, and with a large and diverse collection of authors, new enhancements are made everyday. Technically, the code is still considered beta, so there are still bugs. However, once these bugs are reported to the development team, they are quickly resolved. Because Ethereal is actively maintained, new releases tend to come out every few months, but we will be focusing on Ethereal version 0.10.0, since that is the current release at the time of writing this book. Ethereal version 0.10.0 contains many performance enhancements, especially when working with capture files. Several user interface enhancements have also been made, including the application menus, help windows, and capture progress window bar graphs. The source tar files and Linux RPMs have been replaced with version 0.10.0a due to some help file packaging issues.

In this chapter, you'll get an understanding of what Ethereal is, what its features are, and how to use it on your network architecture for troubleshooting. Additionally, you'll learn about the history of Ethereal, how it came to be such a popular network analyzer, and why it remains a top pick for administrators.

NOTE

Exactly how is Ethereal pronounced? Well, some people pronounce it with 3 syllables, and two distinct parts, "ether-real", like *real ether*, but backwards. Others pronounce it with 4 syllables "e-the-re-al", as in ghostly or otherworldly. Really, either way is acceptable.

What is Ethereal?

Simply put, Ethereal is a network analyzer. It reads packets from the network, decodes them, and presents them in an easy to understand format. We have already mentioned some of the most important aspects of Ethereal: that it is open source, actively maintained, and free. Let's take a moment to mention some of the other important aspects of Ethereal:

- It is maintained under the GNU General Public License (GPL).

- It works in promiscuous and non-promiscuous modes.

- It can capture data from the network or read from a capture file.

- It has an easy to read, and very configurable GUI.

- It has rich display filter capabilities.

- It supports Tcpdump format capture filters.

- It has a nice feature that reconstructs a TCP session and displays it in ASCII or Extended Binary Coded Decimal Interchange Code (EBCDIC), hexadecimal dump, or C arrays.

- It is available in precompiled binaries and source code.

- It runs on over 20 platforms, both UNIX-based and Windows.

- It supports over 480 protocols, and because it is open source, new ones are contributed very frequently.

- It can read capture files from over 20 different products.

- It can save capture files in a variety of formats including libpcap, Network Associates Sniffer, Microsoft Network Monitor, and Sun snoop.

- It can capture data from a variety of media including Ethernet, Token-Ring, 802.11 Wireless, and more.

- It includes a command line version of the network analyzer called *tethereal*.

- It includes a variety of supporting programs such as *editcap*, *mergecap*, and *text2pcap*.

- Output can be saved or printed as plain text or PostScript.

History of Ethereal

Gerald Combs first developed Ethereal in 1997 because he was expanding his knowledge of networking and needed a tool for network troubleshooting. The first version, 0.2.0, was released in July 1998. A development team, including Gilbert

Ramirez, Guy Harris, and Richard Sharpe, quickly formed to provide patches, enhancements, and additional dissectors. Dissectors are what allow Ethereal to decode individual protocols and present them in readable format. Since then, a large number of individuals have contributed specific protocol dissectors that they needed and other enhancements to Ethereal. This continues to be a great way to become involved, so if you need support for a particular protocol, start writing a dissector for it! This will not only benefit the project, but yourself and other users as well. You can view the list of authors at www.ethereal.com/introduction. html#authors. Because of the overwhelming development support and the large user base, Ethereal's capabilities and popularity continue to grow every day.

Notes from the Underground...

The GNU General Public License

The GNU Project (pronounced "guh-NEW") was originally developed in 1984 to provide a free Unix-like operating system. This operating system is known as a "GNU/Linux" system because it uses the GNU utilities and a Linux kernel. The GNU Project is run and sponsored by the Free Software Foundation (FSF). Richard Stallman wrote the GNU General Public License (GPL) in 1989, for the purpose of distributing programs released as part of the GNU project. It is a copyleft, free software license and is based on similar licenses used for early versions of GNU Emacs. It has become one of the most widely used free software licenses due to its purpose of giving the public more freedom instead of less.

Copyleft became a term from the phrase "Copyleft—all rights reversed". It is the application of copyright law to ensure public freedom to manipulate, improve, and redistribute a work of authorship and all derivative works. This means that the copyright holder grants an irrevo-cable license to all recipients of a copy, permitting the redistribution and sale of possibly further modified copies, under the condition that all those copies carry the same license and are made available in a form which also facilitates modification. This is a key feature in free and open source software to keep the work free and open. There are legal conse-quences to face if a licensee fails to distribute the work under the same license. If the licensee distributes copies of the work, the source code and modification must be made available. Sure you can make private modifications to GPL software, just don't distribute it to anyone!

Continued

> The GPL software license itself cannot be modified. You can copy and disitribute it as much as you want, but don't change the text of the GPL. Other licenses created by the GNU project include the GNU Lesser General Public License and the GNU Free Documentation License.
>
> There remains an ongoing dispute about the GPL and whether or not non-GPL software can link to GPL libraries. Although derivative works of GPL code must abide by the license, it is not clear whether an executable that links to a GPL library is considered a derivative work. The FSF states that such executables are derivatives to the GPL work, but others in the software community disagree. To date, there have not been any court decisions to resolve this conflict.

Compatibility

As we previously stated, Ethereal can read and process capture files from a number of different products including other sniffers, routers, and network utilities. Because Ethereal uses the popular libpcap-based capture format, it interfaces easily with other products that use libpcap. It also has the capability of reading captures in a variety of other formats as well. Ethereal can automatically determine what type of file it is reading and can also uncompress gzip files. The following list shows the products from which Ethereal can read capture files:

- Tcpdump
- Sun snoop and atmsnoop
- Microsoft Network Monitor
- Network Associates Sniffer (compressed or uncompressed) and Sniffer Pro
- Shomiti/Finisar Surveyor
- Novell LANalyzer
- Cinco Networks' NetXRay
- AG Group/WildPackets EtherPeek/TokenPeek/AiroPeek
- RADCOM's WAN/LAN analyzer
- Visual Networks' Visual UpTime
- Lucent/Ascend router debug output
- Toshiba's ISDN routers dump output

- Cisco Secure IDS iplog

- AIX's iptrace

- HP-UX nettl

- ISDN4BSD project's i4btrace output

- pppd logs (pppdump-format)

- VMS's TCPIPtrace utility

- DBS Etherwatch VMS utility

- CoSine L2 debug

- Accellent's 5Views LAN agent output

- Endace Measurement Systems' ERF capture format

- Linux Bluez Bluetooth stack "hcidump −w" traces

- Network Instruments Observer version 9

Supported Protocols

When a network analyzer reads data from the network it needs to know how to interpret what it is seeing and display the output in an easy to read format. This is known as protocol decoding. Often, the number of protocols a sniffer can read and display determines its strength, thus most commercial sniffers can support several hundred protocols. Ethereal is very competitive in this area with its current support of over 480 protocols. New protocols are constantly being added by various contributors to the Ethereal project. Protocol decodes, also known as dissectors, can be added directly into the code or included as plugins. The following list shows the 483 protocols that are currently supported at the time of this writing, no doubt by the time you read this there will be more:

802.11 MGT, AAL1, AAL3_4, AARP, ACAP, ACN, AFP, AFS (RX), AH, AIM, AJP13, ALCAP, ANS, ANSI BSMAP, ANSI DTAP, ANSI IS-637-A Teleservice, ANSI IS-637-A Transport, ANSI IS-683-A (OTA (Mobile)), ANSI MAP, AODV, ARCNET, ARP/RARP, ARTNET, ASAP, ASF, ASN1, ASP, ATM, ATM LANE, ATP, ATSVC, Auto-RP, AVS WLANCAP, BACapp, BACnet, BEEP, BFD Control, BGP, BICC, Boardwalk, BOFL, BOOTP/DHCP, BOOTPARAMS, BOSSVR, BROWSER, BSSAP, BSSGP, BUDB, BUTC, BVLC, CCSDS, CDP, CDS_CLERK, cds_solicit, CFLOW, CGMP, CHDLC, CLDAP,

CLEARCASE, CLNP, CLTP, CONV, COPS, COSEVENTCOMM, CoSine, COSNAMING, COTP, CPFI, CPHA, cprpc_server, CUPS, Data, DCCP, DCE_DFS, dce_update, DCERPC, DDP, DDTP, DEC_STP, DFS, DHCPv6, Diameter, DISTCC, DLSw, DNS, DNSSERVER, DOCSIS, DOCSIS BPKM-ATTR, DOCSIS BPKM-REQ, DOCSIS BPKM-RSP, DOCSIS DSA-ACK, DOCSIS DSA-REQ, DOCSIS DSA-RSP, DOCSIS DSC-ACK, DOCSIS DSC-REQ, DOCSIS DSC-RSP, DOCSIS DSD-REQ, DOCSIS DSD-RSP, DOCSIS MAC MGMT, DOCSIS MAP, DOCSIS REG-ACK, DOCSIS REG-REQ, DOCSIS REG-RSP, DOCSIS RNG-REQ, DOCSIS RNG-RSP, DOCSIS TLVs, DOCSIS UCC-REQ, DOCSIS UCC-RSP, DOCSIS UCD, DOCSIS VSIF, DRSUAPI, DSI, DTSPROVIDER, DTSSTIME_REQ, DVMRP, EAP, EAPOL, ECHO, EDONKEY, EIGRP, ENC, ENIP, ENTTEC, EPM, EPM4, ESIS, ESP, ETHERIP, Ethernet, FC, FC ELS, FC FZS, FC-dNS, FC-FCS, FC-SB3, FC-SP, FC-SWILS, FC_CT, FCIP, FCP, FDDI, FIX, FLDB, FR, Frame, FTP, FTP-DATA, FTSERVER, FW-1, GIOP, GMRP, GNUTELLA, GPRS NS, GRE, Gryphon, GSM BSSMAP, GSM DTAP, GSM MAP, GSM RP, GSM SMS, GSS-API, GTP, GVRP, H.261, H.263, H1, H225, H245, H4501, HCLNFSD, HPEXT, HSRP, HTTP, HyperSCSI, IAPP, IB, ICAP, ICL_RPC, ICMP, ICMPv6, ICP, ICQ, IEEE 802.11, IGAP, IGMP, IGRP, ILMI, IMAP, INITSHUTDOWN, IP, IPComp, IPFC, IPMI, IPP, IPv6, IPX, IPX MSG, IPX RIP, IPX SAP, IPX WAN, IRC, ISAKMP, iSCSI, ISDN, ISIS, ISL, iSNS, ISUP, IUA, Jabber, KADM5, KLM, Kpasswd, KRB5, KRB5RPC, L2TP, LACP, LANMAN, LAPB, LAPBETHER, LAPD, Laplink, LDAP, LDP, LLAP, LLC, LMI, LMP, LPD, LSA, LSA_DS, Lucent/Ascend, LWAPP, LWAPP-CNTL, LWAPP-L3, LWRES, M2PA, M2TP, M2UA, M3UA, Malformed packet, MAPI, MDS Header, MEGACO, Messenger, MGCP, MGMT, MIPv6, MMSE, Mobile IP, Modbus/TCP, MOUNT, MPEG1, MPLS, MRDISC, MS Proxy, MSDP, MSNIP, MSNMS, MTP2, MTP3, MTP3MG, MySQL, NBDS, NBIPX, NBNS, NBP, NBSS, NCP, NDMP, NDPS, NetBIOS, NETLOGON, NFS, NFSACL, NFSAUTH, NIS+, NIS+ CB, NLM, NLSP, NMPI, NNTP, NSPI, NTLMSSP, NTP, Null, OAM AAL, OSPF, OXID, PCLI, PCNFSD, PER, PFLOG, PFLOG-OLD, PGM, PIM, POP, Portmap, PPP, PPP BACP, PPP BAP, PPP CBCP, PPP CCP, PPP CDPCP, PPP CHAP, PPP Comp, PPP IPCP, PPP IPV6CP, PPP LCP, PPP MP, PPP MPLSCP, PPP PAP, PPP PPPMux, PPP PPPMuxCP, PPP VJ, PPPoED, PPPoES,

PPTP, Prism, Q.2931, Q.931, Q.933, QLLC, QUAKE, QUAKE2, QUAKE3, QUAKEWORLD, RADIUS, RANAP, Raw, Raw_SIP, RDM, REMACT, REP_PROC, RIP, RIPng, Rlogin, RMCP, RMI, RMP, roverride, RPC, RPC_BROWSER, RPC_NETLOGON, RPL, rpriv, RQUOTA, RS_ACCT, RS_ATTR, RS_BIND, rs_misc, RS_PGO, RS_PLCY, rs_prop_acct, RS_REPADM, RS_REPLIST, RS_UNIX, rsec_login, RSH, RSTAT, RSVP, RSYNC, RTCFG, RTCP, RTMP, RTNET, RTP, RTP Event, RTSP, RWALL, RX, SADMIND, SAMR, SAP, SCCP, SCCPMG, SCSI, SCTP, SDLC, SDP, SEBEK, SECIDMAP, Serialization, SES, sFlow, SGI MOUNT, Short frame, SIP, SKINNY, SLARP, SliMP3, SLL, SMB, SMB Mailslot, SMB Pipe, SMPP, SMTP, SMUX, SNA, SNA XID, SNAETH, SNMP, Socks, SONMP, Spnego, SPNEGO-KRB5, SPOOLSS, SPRAY, SPX, SRVLOC, SRVSVC, SSCOP, SSH, SSL, STAT, STAT-CB, STP, STUN, SUA, SVCCTL, Syslog, T38, TACACS, TACACS+, TAPI, TCAP, TCP, TDS, TELNET, TEREDO, TFTP, TIME, TKN4Int, TNS, Token-Ring, TPCP, TPKT, TR MAC, TSP, TZSP, UBIKDISK, UBIKVOTE, UCP, UDP, UDPENCAP, Unreassembled fragmented packet, V.120, Vines ARP, Vines Echo, Vines FRP, Vines ICP, Vines IP, Vines IPC, Vines LLC, Vines RTP, Vines SPP, VLAN, VRRP, VTP, WBXML, WCCP, WCP, WHDLC, WHO, WINREG, WKSSVC, WSP, WTLS, WTP, X.25, X.29, X11, XDMCP, XOT, XYPLEX, YHOO, YMSG, YPBIND, YPPASSWD, YPSERV, YPXFR, ZEBRA, ZIP

Ethereal's User Interface

Ethereal's graphical user interface is very configurable and easy to use. We will be covering the interface in detail in Chapter 4, however we want to touch on some of the highlights here. Like other network analyzers, Ethereal displays capture information in three main window panes. Figure 2.1 shows what a typical Ethereal capture looks like in each of its panes. Each of the panes is adjustable in size by clicking on the row of dots between the panes and dragging up or down. The upper-most pane is the summary pane that displays a one–line summary of the capture. Ethereal's default fields include: packet number, time, source address, destination address, and the name and information about the highest-layer protocol. These columns are configurable and new ones can be added under Preferences. You can also click on the column heading to sort ascending and descending by each field.

The middle pane is the protocol detail view. This pane provides all of the details for each of the layers contained inside the captured packet in a tree-like structure. Clicking on various parts of the protocol tree will highlight corresponding hexadecimal and ASCII output in the bottom pane. The bottom displays the raw captured data both in hexadecimal and ASCII format. Clicking on various parts of this data will also highlight the corresponding fields in the protocol tree in the middle pane. Figure 2.1 shows the Ethereal interface and an example of a network SYN scan. Notice that highlighting the source MAC address in the middle, protocol view pane, automatically highlights that portion of the hexadecimal dump in the bottom data pane.

Figure 2.1 Ethereal's GUI

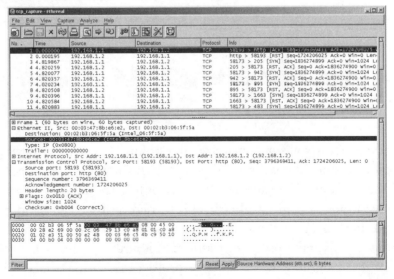

One of the coolest features of Ethereal is its ability to reassemble all of the packets in a TCP conversation and display the ASCII in a very easy to read format. It can also be viewed in EBCDIC, Hex dump, and C arrays. This data can then be saved or printed. A good use for this can be to reconstruct a web page. Just follow the stream of the HTTP session and save the output to a file. You should then be able to view the reconstructed HTML offline, without graphics of course, in a web browser. Figure 2.2 shows the TCP stream output of a Telnet session. Notice how easy it is to read the username and password in cleartext. Some text, such as "root" and "exit" includes double letters because it is displaying the sending of the character and the ACK response of the character from the server. This is a good example of why you would never want to Telnet as root!

Figure 2.2 Follow the TCP Stream

Filters

Filtering packets helps you find what you are looking for without sifting through numerous other distracting packets. Ethereal has the ability to use both capture filters and display filters. The capture filter syntax follows the same syntax that Tcpdump uses from the libpcap library. This is used on the command line or in the Capture Filter dialog box to capture certain types of traffic. Display filters provide a powerful syntax to sort on traffic that is already captured. As the number of protocols grows, the number of protocol fields for display filters grow as well. However, not all protocols that Ethereal currently supports have display filters. Also, some protocols provide display filter field names for some of their fields, but not all of their fields. Hopefully as the product matures and users contribute to the development process this will change. Table 2.1 shows an example of a supported protocol and its display filters:

Table 2.1 IP Display Filters

Internet Protocol (IP)		
Field	**Name**	**Type**
ip.addr	Source or Destination Address	IPv4 address
ip.checksum	Header checksum	Unsigned 16-bit integer
ip.checksum_bad	Bad Header checksum	Boolean
ip.dsfield	Differentiated Services field	Unsigned 8-bit integer
ip.dsfield.ce	ECN-CE	Unsigned 8-bit integer
ip.dsfield.dscp	Differentiated Services Codepoint	Unsigned 8-bit integer
ip.dsfield.ect	ECN-Capable Transport (ECT)	Unsigned 8-bit integer
ip.dst	Destination	IPv4 address
ip.flags	Flags	Unsigned 8-bit integer
ip.flags.df	Don't fragment	Boolean
ip.flags.mf	More fragments	Boolean
ip.frag_offset	Fragment offset	Unsigned 16-bit integer
ip.fragment	IP Fragment	Frame number
ip.fragment.error	Defragmentation error	Frame number
ip.fragment.multipletails	Multiple tail fragments found	Boolean
ip.fragment.overlap	Fragment overlap	Boolean
ip.fragment.overlap. conflict	Conflicting data in fragment overlap	Boolean
ip.fragment. toolongfragment	Fragment too long	Boolean
ip.fragments	IP Fragments	No value
ip.hdr_len	Header Length	Unsigned 8-bit integer
ip.id	Identification	Unsigned 16-bit integer

Continued

Table 2.1 IP Display Filters

Internet Protocol (IP)		
Field	**Name**	**Type**
ip.len	Total Length	Unsigned 16-bit integer
ip.proto	Protocol	Unsigned 8-bit integer
ip.reassembled_in	Reassembled IP in frame	Frame number
ip.src	Source	IPv4 address
ip.tos	Type of Service	Unsigned 8-bit integer
ip.tos.cost	Cost	Boolean
ip.tos.delay	Delay	Boolean
ip.tos.precedence	Precedence	Unsigned 8-bit integer
ip.tos.reliability	Reliability	Boolean
ip.tos.throughput	Throughput	Boolean
ip.ttl	Time to live	Unsigned 8-bit integer
ip.version	Version	Unsigned 8-bit integer

Once you have implemented a display filter, all of the packets that meet this requirement are displayed in the packet listing in the summary pane. You can use the filters to compare fields within a protocol against a value, such as ip.src == 192.168.1.1, or to compare fields to fields, such as ip.src == ip.dst, or just to check the existence of specified fields or protocols. Filters are also used by statistical features and to colorize the packets.

Suppose you would like to create a simple filter to search for a certain protocol or field. For example, if you want to see all of the HTTP packets, simply type **http**. To see just HTTP request packets, such as GET, POST, and HEAD, type **http.request**. Filter fields can also be compared against values, such as **http.request.method=="GET"**, to see just the HTTP GET requests. . The comparison operators can be expressed using the following abbreviations or symbols:

Equal: eq, ==

Not equal: ne, !=

Greater than: gt, >

Less Than: lt, <

Greater than or Equal to: ge, >=

Less than or Equal to: le, <=

Display and capture filters are explained in detail in Chapter 5. We just wanted to give you an overview of just how powerful this Ethereal feature is. As you can see, filters offer a great deal of flexibility when troubleshooting network problems or trying to pinpoint issues. Anything that makes the administrator's job easier is certainly welcomed!

NOTE

Ethereal supports many different types of media, such as Ethernet, Token Ring, Wireless, and asynchronous transfer mode (ATM). You may want to check the "Supported Capture Media" table at www.ethereal.com/media.html to ensure that you are using a compatible OS and media. You will notice that Linux supports just about all media types. You will also notice that Ethernet is supported on all operating systems.

Notes from the Underground…

The CVS System

The Concurrent Version System (CVS) is a versioning system that allows many developers to work on the same project simultaneously, while keeping track of what changes have been made, who made them, and most importantly, what versions exist and keeping them separated. You will generally find many versions of a project in a CVS tree.

You will find that CVSs exist on many websites for almost every open-source project. For example, SourceForge (www.sourceforge.net) has CVS repositories for all of the projects it contains. To browse most CVS trees, you will need a CVS client application. However, SourceForge has a Web interface for browsing as well, which is a nice feature if you need to quickly get some information or code from a CVS tree. Here are a couple of GUI applications for CVS:

Continued

- If you would like a CVS front-end app for Linux, VisualCVS (www.scentech.ch/products/visualcvs) is a client worth checking out.

- If you would like a CVS application for Windows, WinCVS (www.wincvs.org) is a pretty good client.

The Ethereal CVS listing is maintained at www.ethereal.com/development.html. There are several ways to obtain the CVS source code for Ethereal:

- **Command line** You can use the CVS command line client (www.cvshome.org) to anonymously log in and download the development source.

- **Nighly snapshots** You can also download gzipped tarballs containing nightly snapshots of the development source tree.

- **CVS Web Interface** You can download the source tree via the Ethereal web interface. Here you can view each file and differences between versions of each file.

- **CVSGrab** You can use the Java CVS client that uses the ViewCVS web interface to download the latest versions of each file. This method tends to be slower than the others.

When using CVS versions of Ethereal or other open source products, remember that they are considered beta code and could have bugs. Also, these development versions tend to not be supported yet.

Great Resources!

Some of the best resources for Ethereal information and support include the five e-mail distribution lists. You can subscribe by visiting www.ethereal.com/lists and filling out the appropriate form. One thing to note is that the form asks for a password, which is occasionally e-mailed to you in cleartext. You don't want to pick the same password that you use for other valuable accounts, because anyone sniffing the network traffic can easily see the cleartext password when it is e-mailed! There are some great conversations on these lists, and a lot of good information is revealed about the source code, new developments, installation issues and more.

- *Ethereal-announce* includes announcements on new releases, bug fixes, and general issues about Ethereal. Any general Ethereal user should subscribe to this list to remain current on important topics. This list tends to be low-volume with just a few messages per month. To post a message, send an email to ethereal-announce@ethereal.com.

- *Ethereal-users* includes general information and help on using Ethereal. Any general Ethereal user should subscribe to this list to share ideas and suggestions. It contains moderate traffic, typically several messages per day. To post a message, send an e-mail to ethereal-users@ethereal.com.

- *Ethereal-dev* includes developer related information about Ethereal. This list contains a lot of information about the inner workings of Ethereal and is intended for those who are interested in contributing to the development of Ethereal. Even if you aren't the programmer type, this list has lots of great information. Be prepared, however, because this list receives a higher volume of traffic with many messages per day. To post a message, send an e-mail to ethereal-dev@ethereal.com.

- *Ethereal-doc* includes documentation-related information about Ethereal. It is intended for those who wish to be involved in the documentation development process. This list tends to be low-volume with just a few messages per month. To post a message, send an e-mail to ethereal-doc@ethereal.com.

- *Ethereal-cvs* includes developer-related information to monitor changes to the Ethereal source tree. It is useful for developers to know when changes are made, and what the changes are. The CVS repository sends e-mails to this list every time code is committed to the Ethereal CVS repository. It receives a higher volume of traffic with many messages per day. Users do not post directly to this list and replies to messages on this list should be sent to ethereal-dev@ethereal.com.

When subscribing to the mailing lists you can choose to have your e-mail batched in a daily digest. This is great for high volume lists, to cut down on the amount of traffic and messages. However, you won't get the attachments that may be included with the e-mails. All of the messages from the mailing lists are also archived on the Ethereal website, as well as a few mirror sites. Messages are categorized by month as far back as 1998. When troubleshooting a problem, a great strategy is to perform a search to see if someone else may have the answer already.

Another great source of information is the Ethereal User's Guide, by Richard Sharpe, located at www.ethereal.com/docs/user-guide. It is a bit outdated, based on version 0.9.7, but it still contains some great information. It is also available in PDF format at www.ethereal.com/distribution/docs/user-guide.pdf, however, this document seems to be based on version 0.8.19. Beware, when you print out the entire document, it is 454 pages! The first 102 pages include a great deal of good information about installing and using Ethereal. The rest of the document is a list of the hundreds of supported protocols and their associated display filter fields.

As always, the Ethereal web page, www.ethereal.com, has a lot of good information as well. The links page www.ethereal.com/links.html, has some great reference websites. This includes information on protocols, RFCs, networking, port spanning, and other tools. The sample captures page, www.ethereal.com/sample, contains packet traces of various network traffic that can be downloaded and viewed with Ethereal for analysis. This is a great way to learn to use Ethereal and its features, as well as learning about various protocols.

Supporting Programs

Most people who are familiar with Ethereal tend to use the Ethereal GUI. However, when Ethereal is installed it also comes with several other very handy supporting programs. The command line version of Ethereal, called *tethereal*, and three other programs to assist you in manipulating capture files. We won't go into too much detail here because these programs are covered in Chapter 6. However, we do want to give you an overview of these programs and why they are used.

Tethereal

Tethereal is the command line version of Ethereal. It can be used to capture live packets from the wire or to read saved capture files. By default, tethereal prints the summary line information to the screen. This is the same information contained in the top pane of the Ethereal GUI. The following shows the default tethereal output:

```
1.199008 192.168.100.132 -> 192.168.100.122 TCP 1320 > telnet [SYN]
Seq=1102938967 Ack=0 Win=16384 Len=0

1.199246 192.168.100.132 -> 192.168.100.122 TCP 1320 > telnet [SYN]
Seq=1102938967 Ack=0 Win=16384 Len=0

1.202244 192.168.100.122 -> 192.168.100.132 TCP telnet > 1320 [SYN, ACK]
Seq=3275138168 Ack=1102938968 Win=49640 Len=0
```

```
1.202268 192.168.100.132 -> 192.168.100.122 TCP 1320 > telnet [ACK]
Seq=1102938968 Ack=3275138169 Win=17520 Len=0

1.202349 192.168.100.132 -> 192.168.100.122 TCP 1320 > telnet [ACK]
Seq=1102938968 Ack=3275138169 Win=17520 Len=0
```

The **–V** option will cause tethereal to print the protocol tree view, like the middle pane in the Ethereal GUI. This will show all of the protocols in the packet and includes the data portion at the end of the list. The following shows the more detailed protocol tree tethereal output:

```
Frame 5 (74 bytes on wire, 74 bytes captured)
    Arrival Time: Nov  2, 2003 15:22:33.469934000
    Time delta from previous packet: 0.000216000 seconds
    Time relative to first packet: 1.349439000 seconds
    Frame Number: 5
    Packet Length: 74 bytes
    Capture Length: 74 bytes
Ethernet II, Src: 00:05:5d:ee:7e:53, Dst: 08:00:20:cf:5b:39
    Destination: 08:00:20:cf:5b:39 (SunMicro_cf:5b:39)
    Source: 00:05:5d:ee:7e:53 (D-Link_ee:7e:53)
    Type: IP (0x0800)
Internet Protocol, Src Addr: 192.168.100.132 (192.168.100.132), Dst Addr:
192.168.100.122 (192.168.100.122)
    Version: 4
    Header length: 20 bytes
    Differentiated Services Field: 0x00 (DSCP 0x00: Default; ECN: 0x00)
        0000 00.. = Differentiated Services Codepoint: Default (0x00)
        .... ..0. = ECN-Capable Transport (ECT): 0
        .... ...0 = ECN-CE: 0
    Total Length: 60
    Identification: 0x160c (5644)
    Flags: 0x00
        .0.. = Don't fragment: Not set
        ..0. = More fragments: Not set
    Fragment offset: 0
    Time to live: 128
    Protocol: ICMP (0x01)
    Header checksum: 0xda65 (correct)
```

```
    Source: 192.168.100.132 (192.168.100.132)
    Destination: 192.168.100.122 (192.168.100.122)
Internet Control Message Protocol
    Type: 8 (Echo (ping) request)
    Code: 0
    Checksum: 0x3c5c (correct)
    Identifier: 0x0500
    Sequence number: 0c:00
    Data (32 bytes)
0000  61 62 63 64 65 66 67 68 69 6a 6b 6c 6d 6e 6f 70   abcdefghijklmnop
0010  71 72 73 74 75 76 77 61 62 63 64 65 66 67 68 69   qrstuvwabcdefghi
```

Finally, the **−x** command will cause tethereal to print a hexadecimal and ASCII dump of the packet data with either the summary line or protocol tree. The following shows the hexadecimal and ASCII output with the summary line:

```
  9.463261 192.168.100.122 -> 192.168.100.132 TELNET Telnet Data ...
0000  00 05 5d ee 7e 53 08 00 20 cf 5b 39 08 00 45 00   ..].~S.. .[9..E.
0010  00 9a c3 8a 40 00 3c 06 30 84 c0 a8 64 7a c0 a8   ....@.<.0...dz..
0020  64 84 00 17 05 29 cd 5d 7d 12 4c 1d ea 76 50 18   d....).]}.L..vP.
0030  c1 e8 47 ca 00 00 4c 61 73 74 20 6c 6f 67 69 6e   ..G...Last login
0040  3a 20 53 75 6e 20 4e 6f 76 20 20 32 20 31 35 3a   : Sun Nov  2 15:
0050  34 34 3a 34 35 20 66 72 6f 6d 20 31 39 32 2e 31   44:45 from 192.1
0060  36 38 2e 31 30 30 2e 31 33 32 0d 0a 53 75 6e 20   68.100.132..Sun
0070  4d 69 63 72 6f 73 79 73 74 65 6d 73 20 49 6e 63   Microsystems Inc
0080  2e 20 20 20 53 75 6e 4f 53 20 35 2e 39 20 20 20   .   SunOS 5.9
0090  20 20 20 20 47 65 6e 65 72 69 63 20 4d 61 79 20       Generic May
00a0  32 30 30 32 0d 0a 23 20                           2002..#
```

When using tethereal to output to a file, by default it will output in the libpcap format. Tethereal can read the same capture files from other products that Ethereal can. Tethereal can also use display, also called *read*, filters and capture filters just like Ethereal. And finally, it can also decode the same protocols that Ethereal can. Basically, it has almost all of the powers of Ethereal, except the ones inherent to the GUI, in an easy to use command line version. Chapter 3 (Installation) will further elaborate on the **−x** and **−v** options.

Editcap

Editcap is a program used to remove packets from a file and to translate the format of capture files. It is similar to the Save As feature, but better. Editcap can read all of the same types of files that Ethereal can, and by default writes to libpcap format. Editcap can also write captures to standard and modified versions of libpcap, Sun snoop, Novel LANalyzer, NAI Sniffer, Microsoft Network Monitor, Visual Network traffic capture, Accellent 5Views capture and Network Instruments Observer version 9. It has the ability to specify all or just some of the packets to be translated. The following is an example of using editcap to translate the first five packets from a tethereal libpcap capture file called *capture* to a Sun snoop output file called *capture_snoop*:

```
C:\Program Files\Ethereal>editcap -r -v -F snoop capture capture_snoop 1-5
File capture is a libpcap (tcpdump, Ethereal, etc.) capture file.
Add_Selected: 1-5
Inclusive ... 1, 5
Record: 1
Record: 2
Record: 3
Record: 4
Record: 5
```

Mergecap

Mergecap is used to combine multiple saved capture files into a single output file. Mergecap can read all of the same types of files that Ethereal can, and by default writes to libpcap format. Mergecap can also write the output capture file to standard and modified versions of libpcap, Sun snoop, Novel LANalyzer, NAI Sniffer, Microsoft Network Monitor, Visual Network traffic capture, Accellent 5Views capture, and Network Instruments Observer version 9. By default, the packets from the input files are merged in chronological order based on each packets timestamp. If the **–a** option is specified, packets will be copied directly from each input file to the output file regardless of timestamp. The following is an example of using mergecap to merge four capture files (*capture1, capture2, capture3, and capture4*) into a single Sun snoop output file called *merge_snoop*, it will keep reading packets until the end of the last file is reached:

```
C:\Program Files\Ethereal>mergecap -v -F snoop -w merge_snoop capture1
capture2 capture3 capture4
mergecap: capture1 is type libpcap (tcpdump, Ethereal, etc.).
mergecap: capture2 is type libpcap (tcpdump, Ethereal, etc.).
mergecap: capture3 is type libpcap (tcpdump, Ethereal, etc.).
mergecap: capture4 is type libpcap (tcpdump, Ethereal, etc.).
mergecap: opened 4 of 4 input files
mergecap: selected frame_type Ethernet (ether)
Record: 1
Record: 2
Record: 3
Record: 4
Record: 5
Record: 6
Record: 7
Record: 8
Record: 9
Record: 10
output removed
```

Text2pcap

Text2pcap reads in ASCII hexadecimal dump captures and writes the data into a libpcap output file. It is capable of reading hexdumps with multiple packets in them, and building a capture file of multiple packets. Text2pcap can also read in hexdumps of application level data only, by inserting dummy Ethernet, IP, and UDP or TCP headers. The user can specify which of these headers to add. This way Ethereal and other sniffers can read the full data. The following is an example of the type of hexadecimal dump that text2pcap can recognize:

```
0000   00 05 5d ee 7e 53 08 00 20 cf 5b 39 08 00 45 00   ..].~S.. .[9..E.
0010   00 9a 13 9e 40 00 3c 06 e0 70 c0 a8 64 7a c0 a8   ....@.<..p..dz..
0020   64 84 00 17 05 49 0e a9 91 43 8e d8 e3 6a 50 18   d....I...C...jP.
0030   c1 e8 ba 7b 00 00 4c 61 73 74 20 6c 6f 67 69 6e   ...{..Last login
0040   3a 20 53 75 6e 20 4e 6f 76 20 20 32 20 31 37 3a   : Sun Nov  2 17:
0050   30 36 3a 35 33 20 66 72 6f 6d 20 31 39 32 2e 31   06:53 from 192.1
0060   36 38 2e 31 30 30 2e 31 33 32 0d 0a 53 75 6e 20   68.100.132..Sun
0070   4d 69 63 72 6f 73 79 73 74 65 6d 73 20 49 6e 63   Microsystems Inc
```

```
0080   2e 20 20 20 53 75 6e 4f 53 20 35 2e 39 20 20 20      .   SunOS 5.9
0090   20 20 20 20 47 65 6e 65 72 69 63 20 4d 61 79 20          Generic May
00a0   32 30 30 32 0d 0a 23 20                                  2002..#
```

The following is an example of using text2pcap to read the previously shown hexadecimal dump, hex_sample.txt, and output it to the libpcap_output file:

```
C:\Program Files\Ethereal>text2pcap hex_sample.txt libpcap_output
Input from: hex_sample.txt
Output to: libpcap_output
Wrote packet of 168 bytes at 0
Read 1 potential packets, wrote 1 packets
```

Using Ethereal in Your Network Architecture

In the previous chapter we talked about various network hardware devices that can be used to attach a sniffer to the network: cable taps, hubs, and switches. Now we will look at some network architectures and critical points to use Ethereal. Network placement is critical for proper analysis and troubleshooting. Most importantly, you need to make sure that you are on the proper network segment as the devices or problems that you are trying to troubleshoot. When you are troubleshooting network issues you may be moving between various wiring closets, or even different buildings. For this reason it is beneficial to run Ethereal on a laptop. It is also a good idea to keep a small hub and a few network cables, crossover and straight-through, with your laptop for a troubleshooting toolkit. Figure 2.3 shows an incorrect placement of Ethereal if you want to capture communication between the external client and the server. The Ethereal laptop, as well as the switch it is connected to, will never see traffic destined for the server because it will be routed over to the server's switch.

Figure 2.3 Incorrect Ethereal Placement

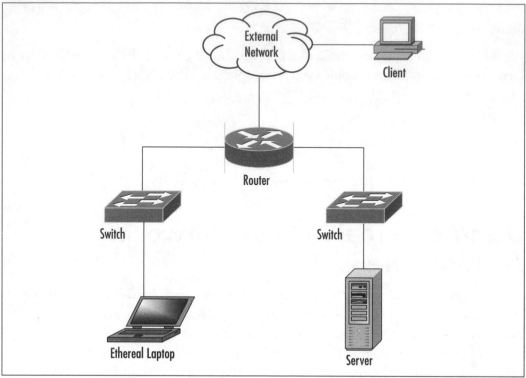

Figure 2.4 shows how to capture traffic from the external client to the server by using port spanning. The Ethereal laptop has to be connected to the same switch as the server. Next, port spanning has to be activated on the switch to mirror all traffic to and from the server's port to the port that Ethereal is plugged into. Using this method will not cause any disruption of traffic to and from the server.

Figure 2.4 Correct Ethereal Placement Using Port Spanning

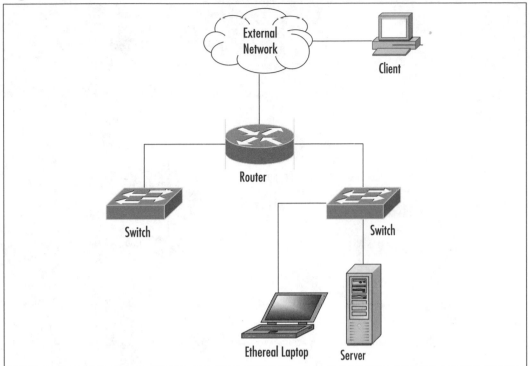

Figure 2.5 shows how to capture traffic from the external client to the server by using a hub. You can install a small hub between the server and the switch, and connect the Ethereal laptop to it. Ethereal will then see all traffic going to and from the server. Using this method will temporarily disrupt the traffic to and from the server while the hub is being installed and the cables connected.

Figure 2.5 Correct Ethereal Placement Using a Hub

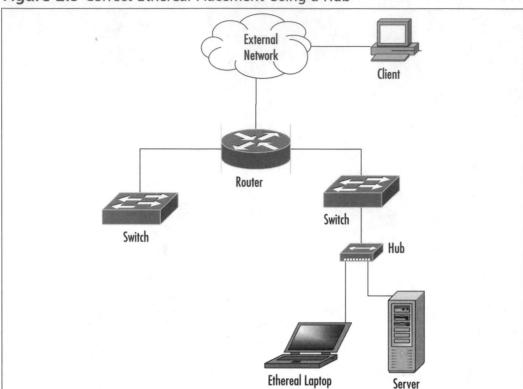

Figure 2.6 shows a network architecture that uses a permanent tap installed at the router. Some administrators use this method to have a permanent connection point at critical areas. The Ethereal laptop will then see all traffic going to and from the server, plus any other traffic on this segment. Using this method will not disrupt the traffic to and from the server if the tap is permanent installed and the cables are already connected through it. Taps can also be portable and used like the hub in Figure 2.5.

Figure 2.6 Ethereal Placement with a Cable Tap

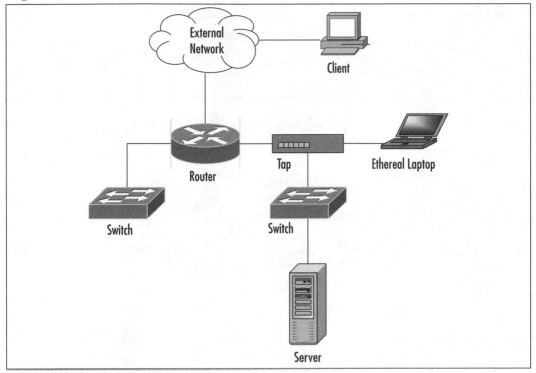

Most network architectures aren't as simple as the ones depicted in this section. However, these examples should give you a good idea of how to use Ethereal at various points in your network. Some architectures are very complicated and can be fully meshed and include redundancy, as shown in Figure 2.7. Also, network segments can branch out for several levels as your network is expanded to buildings, and even floors within buildings. You must have a good understanding of your network in order to make the most effective choices for sniffer placement.

Figure 2.7 Fully Meshed Network

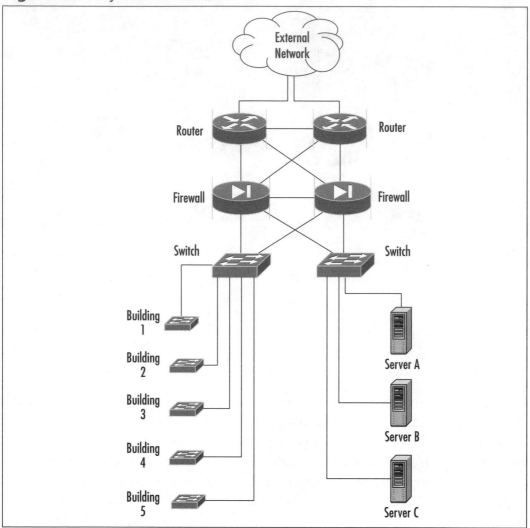

Using Ethereal for Network Troubleshooting

Every network administrator will have the unpleasant occurrence of being paged to solve a network problem. This can often result in a surge of emotions, panic, urgency, and maybe even a sense of heroism. The key to successfully troubleshooting a problem is knowing how your network functions under normal conditions. This will allow you to quickly recognize unusual and abnormal operations. One way to know how your network normally functions is to use your sniffer at various points in the network. This will allow you to get a sense of the protocols that are running on your network, the devices on each segment, and the top talkers (computers that are sending and receiving data most frequently). You may even find some things on your network that you didn't know about, such as an old printer server that no ones uses any more and is flooding the network with broadcasts.

Once you have an idea of how your network functions, you can develop a strategy for network troubleshooting. This way you can approach the problem methodically and resolve it with minimum disruption to customers. With the basic concept of troubleshooting, a few minutes spent evaluating the symptoms can save hours of time lost because you are tracking down the wrong problem. A good approach to network troubleshooting involves the following 7 steps:

1. Recognize the symptoms
2. Define the problem
3. Analyze the problem
4. Isolate the problem
5. Identify and test the cause of the problem
6. Solve the problem
7. Verify that the problem has been solved

The first step to network troubleshooting is to recognize the symptoms. Besides the annoying beep of your pager, you might also learn about a network problem from another user, network management station alerts, or you may be having trouble accessing the network yourself. The problem could be performance issues, connectivity issues, or other strange behavior. Compare this behavior to normal network operation. Was a change made to the network, or to a server right before the problem started? Did an automatic process, such as a scheduled backup, just begin? Is there a prescheduled maintenance window for this time period? Once you have answered these questions and spoken to the helpdesk or other users, the next step is to write down a clear definition of the problem.

Once the symptoms have been identified and the problem has been defined, the next step is to analyze the problem. You will need to gather data for analysis and narrow down the location of the problem. Is it at the core of the network, a single building, or a remote office? Is the problem related to an entire network segment, or a single computer? Can the problem be duplicated elsewhere on the network? You may need to test various parts of your network to narrow down the problem. You may be using your network analyzer a lot at this step; this is when having it installed on a laptop makes things easier.

Now that you have analyzed and found the problem, you can move onto the next step of isolating the problem. There are many ways you could do this. You may need to disconnect the computer that is causing problems, reboot a server, activate a firewall rule to stop some suspected abnormal traffic, or failover to a backup Internet connection.

The next step to network troubleshooting is to identify and test the cause of the problem. Now that you have a theory about the cause of the problem you will need to test it. Your network analyzer can come in handy here to see what is going on behind the scenes. Sometimes, at this point, you may be researching the problem on the Internet, contacting various hardware or software vendors, or contacting your ISP. You may also want to verify with www.cert.org or www.incidents.org, that this is not some wide spread issue.

Once you have determined a resolution to the problem, you will need to implement it. This could involve upgrading hardware or software, implementing a new firewall rule, reinstalling a compromised system, replacing failed hardware, or redesigning the segments of your network.

The last step to network troubleshooting is to verify that the problem has been resolved. You will also want to make sure that the fix for this problem did not create any new problems, or that the problem you solved is not indicative of a deeper underlying problem. Part of this step of the process includes documenting the steps you took to resolve the problem. This will assist in future troubleshooting efforts. If you find that you have not solved the problem you will need to repeat the process again from the beginning. The flowchart in Figure 2.8 depicts the network troubleshooting process:

Figure 2.8 Network Troubleshooting Methodology

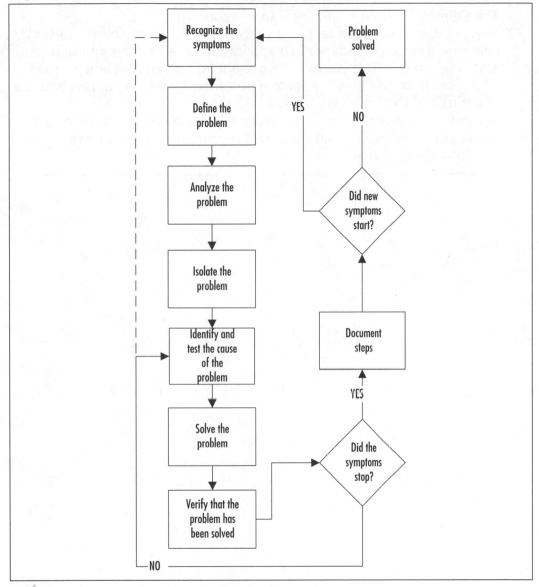

To be a successful network troubleshooter, you need a strong under-standing of network protocols. Understanding different protocols and their characteristics will help you recognize abnormal behavior when it occurs in your network.

NOTE

The Ethereal website maintains a spam report at www.ethereal.com/spamreport.html. The spam prevention effort uses a common gateway interface (CGI) application called Sugarplum that generates poisoned HTML pages for anyone that is trying to harvest email addresses from the site. The spam report lists the e-mail address and the IP address of the harvester. You can use this information to match against spam attempts in your mail logs. The website maintainers also list e-mail addresses so that they can't be automatically harvested, such as "author[AT]ethereal.com".

Summary

We have given you a pretty high-level overview of Ethereal, its various features, and supporting programs. We covered the history of Ethereal, its compatibility with other sniffers, and its supported protocols. We gave you a brief look into the Ethereal GUI and the filter capabilities, because these areas will be covered in detail in later chapters. We also covered the programs that come with Ethereal that add additional functionality by manipulating capture files.

We explored several scenarios for using Ethereal in your network architecture. Spend some time getting to know your network and the way it is connected. Knowing how your network is segmented will greatly help with placing Ethereal to capture the information you need.

Finally, we covered an example network troubleshooting methodology. It is good practice to use this methodology every time you troubleshoot a problem. Once again, spending time getting to know your network, and the protocols running on it will help make troubleshooting a lot easier.

Solutions Fast Track

What is Ethereal?

- ☑ Ethereal is a free and feature rich network analyzer that rivals commercial counterparts.

- ☑ Ethereal can decode more than 480 protocols (See Appendix).

- ☑ Ethereal is compatible with more than 20 other sniffers and capture utilities.

- ☑ Display and capture filters can be used to sort through network traffic.

- ☑ Ethereal mailing lists are a great resource for information and support.

Supporting Programs

- ☑ Ethereal also installs with supporting programs: tethereal, editcap, mergecap, and text2pcap.

- ☑ Tethereal is a command line version of Ethereal.

☑ Editcap is used to remove packets from a file and translate the format of capture files.

☑ Mergecap is used to merge multiple capture files into one.

☑ Text2pcap is used to translate ASCII hexadecimal dump captures into libpcap output files.

Using Ethereal in Your Network Architecture

☑ Correct placement of Ethereal in your network architecture is critical to capture the data you need.

☑ Taps, hubs, and switches with port spanning enabled, can all be used to connect Ethereal to your network.

☑ You should create a troubleshooting toolkit consisting of a small hub, small network tap, and extra straight-through and crossover cables.

☑ Installing Ethereal on a laptop makes troubleshooting at various locations easier.

Using Ethereal for Network Troubleshooting

☑ Following a methodical troubleshooting process can minimize the time it takes to solve the problem.

☑ Identifying and testing the cause of a problem often involves research on the Internet or support calls to hardware or software vendors.

☑ Sometimes, solving one problem could create another.

☑ Keeping detailed notes on how you solved the problem will assist in future troubleshooting efforts.

Frequently Asked Questions

The following Frequently Asked Questions, answered by the authors of this book, are designed to both measure your understanding of the concepts presented in this chapter and to assist you with real-life implementation of these concepts. To have your questions about this chapter answered by the author, browse to **www.syngress.com/solutions** and click on the **"Ask the Author"** form. You will also gain access to thousands of other FAQs at ITFAQnet.com.

Q: How do I know if someone is already working on a protocol dissector for a protocol that isn't supported yet by Ethereal?

A: Send an e-mail to the Ethereal developers mailing list. Mostly likely if someone is writing a dissector they are also part of this list.

Q: Will port spanning increase the load on my switch?

A: Yes, but how much depends on several factors, such as how many ports you are mirroring, and how much traffic is going through those ports. Newer switches can handle port spanning efficiently and the increased load will not be noticeable.

Q: I started using Ethereal on my network just to have a look and I couldn't believe how much traffic was out there! It was scrolling so fast I couldn't even make sense of it, what should I do?

A: This is common, especially on larger networks, or networks with large collisions domains. The best thing to do is to start capturing chunks of data and saving them to a file. Then you can use various display filters to sort out the data and make sense of what is going on.

Q: Do I need to use Editcap to translate capture files that are from different products to a common format before merging them with Mergecap?

A: No, Mergecap can automatically translate the files as it merges them. It will do this for all of the compatible products that Ethereal supports. It can even automatically uncompress gzip files if you compiled Ethereal with gzip support.

Q: When I am on call for network problems I follow a basic troubleshooting methodology and keep detailed notes, however my coworkers fail to do the same when they are on call. What should I do?

A: Get management's support on the necessity and benefits of documenting the troubleshooting process. You can even suggest that you start a "day after" e-mail report that will thoroughly document the problem and the resolution. This e-mail report can be used to update the upper level management and general users in the organization. Your coworkers would have more reason to comply with this policy when their names will be attached to something so public!

Q: I am using a hub to analyze network traffic, however I am still not seeing all of the traffic.

A: Some hubs have an "auto-sensing" or "dual speed" feature that will sense your network interface card speed and set the hub port to the appropriate speed, 10Mbps, or 100Mbps. Some of these types of hubs will only broadcast 10Mbps traffic to other 10Mbps ports, and 100Mbps traffic to other 100Mbps ports. So if you have mixed speed traffic on your hub you may be missing some if it. Linksys and Netgear have been known to have this issue, check with your hub vendor to see if this is documented for your product.

Q: Can I perform port spanning on switches other than Cisco?

A: Yes, port spanning is a Cisco term, but other products perform the same thing and call it port mirroring. These products include HP and Nortel switches, and some newer products are even coming with dedicated management ports built in.

Chapter 3

Getting and Installing Ethereal

Solutions in this Chapter:

- Getting Ethereal
- Packet Capture Drivers
- Installing Ethereal on Windows
- Installing Ethereal on UNIX
- Building Ethereal from Source

☑ Summary

☑ Solutions Fast Track

☑ Frequently Asked Questions

Introduction

In this chapter we will cover all of the steps necessary to complete a functioning installation of the Ethereal network analyzer. Due to the overwhelming amount of UNIX-based distributions available today, installation instructions can vary from distribution to distribution, and are beyond the scope of this chapter. For this reason we will be focusing on information specific to installation on the Red Hat 9.0 platform and the Solaris 9.0 platform. We have chosen Red Hat because it is the most commonly used Linux distribution in the world, and serves as a good starting point on which to base further installations. Most of what we cover here should apply to most other popular distributions without a large amount of modification; but if the instructions do vary, it will be minimal. We chose Solaris because of its common use in commercial and government environments, and for its ease of management and software installation process. For the Windows side we will be focusing on Windows 2000 Professional, due to its common use. However, since Windows XP is also a popular choice these days, we tested the installation process on it as well. Although it won't be covered in this book, the installation on Windows XP was exactly the same as Windows 2000.

For the installations in this chapter, we started with fresh installations of all three of the operating systems (OSs). For Red Hat 9.0 we chose the *workstation* install option so that the proper development libraries would be included. In the Solaris 9.0 install we used the *Entire Distribution* option. For the Windows 2000 Professional installation, we just accepted the default installation parameters. These types of installations often install needless software, and leave many security vulnerabilities wide open. There are a lot of best practices that you should follow when installing new systems, and subsequently applying operating system security procedures. These methods are beyond the scope of this book, but you should pick up a good reference for securing your particular operating system. Please make sure your operating system is current, patched, and secured. You will also need to verify that your networking is set up and functioning properly, or you might not be able to see any packets to analyze!

Let's take a moment to introduce you to the way we approached this chapter. When it comes to computers, networking, and security, some of you are beginners and some of you are pros. Based on the varying technical abilities of the target audience of the book, we tried to approach almost every subject as if we were learning it for the first time. Our only assumption is that you do have a basic understanding of the operating system and how to use it. Knowing that this can be redundant information for those of you who are already comfortable with the terminology and procedures, we made the step-by-step instructions for each installation easy to find and read. This chapter will serve as an excellent *skimming* reference for the more experienced reader. The only time we will have a lengthier explanation with the procedures is when there is possibly some pitfall to watch for, or during description of certain side notes that might be helpful. We keep all of our longer descriptions and discussions *outside* of the chapter installation instructions. So, let's start installing Ethereal!

Getting Ethereal

Ethereal is readily available, in both source and binary form, for download from a variety of sources. The most authoritative source for downloads is the Ethereal download website at www.ethereal.com/download.html. This web page contains a list of mirror sites and locations around the world to download binary distributions and ready-to-install packages for several platforms. It also contains the source code in *tar* archive format for downloading via Hypertext Transfer Protocol (HTTP) and File Transfer Protocol (FTP). Another source for obtaining Ethereal may be your OS CD-ROM. However these tend to be older versions and it is worth the time to download the latest versions. There are several requirements and dependencies to install Ethereal properly. These requirements depend on a variety of factors including the operating system platform and whether you are installing a precompiled binary or compiling from source. We will address these issues for several platforms throughout this chapter.

The packages you will need for installing Ethereal are available free of charge on the Internet at their respective web sites. We have also included the latest release (as of press time) of each package on the CD-ROM that accompanies this book to save you some effort when it comes time to build the programs. If you would like to download the latest version of the software before beginning, feel free to do so; just make sure to substitute package names when necessary. For example, if we reference the file ethereal-0.10.0a.tar.gz and you have ethereal-0.10.0.tar.gz, use your filename because it's newer.

Platforms and System Requirements

"On what operating system platforms can you install Ethereal?" The following list shows a number of platforms that have readily available Ethereal binaries:

- MacOS X
- BeOS
- Debian GNU/Linux
- FreeBSD
- Gentoo Linux
- Tru64 UNIX
- HP-UX
- AIX
- S/390 Linux
- Mandrake Linux
- Windows
- NetBSD
- OpenBSD
- PLD Linux
- Red Hat Linux
- ROCK Linux
- SCO
- Irix
- Solaris/Intel
- Solaris/SPARC
- Slackware Linux
- SuSE Linux

This list is constantly expanding as developers *port* the Ethereal source to new platforms. If your operating system is not listed, and you are feeling brave, go ahead and download the source code and begin building it for your system!

> **NOTE**
>
> Several of the Ethereal binary packages are available through The Written Word, www.thewrittenword.com. The Written Word provides pre-compiled binaries of open source software specifically for AIX, HP-US, IRIX, RedHat Linux, Solaris, and Tru64 UNIX. Releases can be purchased on a one-time basis, or as a subscription service.

System requirements vary depending on the platform and distribution that you use. When compiling from source code, the important packages to have include:

- **Libpcap** The packet capture library that is responsible for capturing the data off of the network.

- **GIMP Toolkit (GTK+)** The graphical user interface library.

- **Glib** The low-level core library for GTK+.

- **Zlib** The data compression library that allows Ethereal to read gzip-compressed files on the fly.

- **Perl** A high-level programming language used to build the Ethereal documentation.

- **Net-SNMP** The Simple Network Management Protocol (SNMP) library used to translate Object Identifiers (OIDs) to names and to decode variable bindings with the use of Management Information Base (MIB) files.

- **GNU adns** The asynchronous-capable Domain Name System (DNS) client library and utilities that allow Ethereal to perform faster name resolution.

- **PCRE** The Perl Compatible Regular Expressions (PCRE) library is a set of functions that implement regular expression pattern matching using the same syntax and semantics as Perl 5. This library is needed to use the "matches" display filter.

You may not need all of the prerequisites if you are installing a precompiled binary distribution on UNIX and Windows. For example, the Windows binary only depends on the WinPcap capture library. And it doesn't even need that if you are only using Ethereal to view saved capture files. We will cover these requirements in detail later in this chapter.

Packet Capture Drivers

When a computer is placed on a network, the network card is responsible for receiving and transmitting data to other hosts. Network applications use methods, like sockets, to establish and maintain connections, while the underlying operating system handles the low level details and provides protocol stacks for communications. Some programs, however, need direct access to handle the raw network data, without interference from protocol stacks. A packet capture driver provides exactly this; it has the ability capture raw network packets. Better than that, a packet capture driver can capture *all* data on a shared network architecture, regardless of the intended recipient. This is what allows a program like Ethereal to passively monitor network traffic.

Two very famous and widely used packet capture drivers are libpcap, and its Windows counterpart, WinPcap. Libpcap is a free, open source packet capture library originally developed at the Lawrence Berkeley National Laboratory in California. It is now maintained by a variety of authors at www.tcpdump.org. Not only does libpcap allow data to be captured, it also provides a mechanism for filtering the data based on user specifications before passing it to the application. WinPcap is maintained by a group of developers at http://winpcap.polito.it. It uses some of the code of libpcap as well as some newly added code. There are many other programs that use the libpcap and WinPcap libraries including, TCPDump, WinDump, Snort, Ettercap, Dsniff, Nmap, tcpflow, and TCPstat. Programs that use libpcap tend to be network monitors, protocol analyzers, traffic loggers, network intrusion detection systems, and various other security tools.

NOTE

TCPDump is another protocol analyzer, like Ethereal, that can be used to monitor network traffic. It is a command line application that runs on UNIX-based systems. The Windows version is called Windump.

SECURITY ALERT

CERT Advisory CA-2002-30 reports that several distributions of TCPDump and libpcap have an altered source code that contains malicious trojan code. Although this advisory was dated November 2002, there are still many altered copies floating around. The advisory can be found at www.cert.org/advisories/CA-2002-30.html. Please verify that you are downloading your distributions from trusted sources, and verifying the MD5 hashes.

Notes from the Underground...

Compression Utilities

As you are downloading software packages from the Internet, you will encounter numerous compression utilities. Many people are already familiar with the zip compression format that is used on both Windows and UNIX systems. In this chapter we discuss the tar format that is used for archiving files. The tar format does not provide compression, it merely packages files together into one single file. This single tar file will still take up the same amount of space, plus a little more, as the sum of all of the individual files. Tar files are typically compressed with other utilities such as gzip or bzip2.

Gzip is used to reduce the size of files, thus making it a great tool for compressing large packet captures. Gzip files are recognized by the .gz extension. Ethereal can automatically uncompress and read Gzip compressed files, even if they don't have the .gz extension. We have included both UNIX and Windows version of Gzip on the accompanying CD-ROM in the /syngress/gzip directory. Files can be compressed by typing the command gzip filename. Files can be uncompressed by using the commands gzip –d filename or gunzip filename.

Bzip2 is a newer file compression utility and is capable of greater compression ratios than gzip. Bzip2 files are recognized by the .bz2 extension. Files can be compressed by typing the command bzip2 filename. Files can be uncompressed by using the commands bzip2 –d filename or bunzip2 filename. At this time Ethereal cannot read bzip2 compressed files.

Installing libpcap

We are going to cover three methods of installing libpcap: the Red Hat Package Manager (RPM), the Sun Solaris packages, and building from source. Once you install libpcap (or WinPcap) you won't have to do anything else with it unless you are a developer. Ethereal will use the libpcap libraries to passively capture network data. Let's get started installing libpcap!

Installing libpcap Using the RPMs

Installing software from the RPM can be a very tricky process. Luckily the libpcap installation poses no problems. See the "Notes from the Underground" sidebar in this chapter for more details on RPMs. For now, this is how we install libpcap from the RPM. We have also included the libpcap RPM on the accompanying CD-ROM. Remember, there might be newer versions that have been released since the writing of this book, you can download the latest libpcap RPM from www.rpmfind.net. Make sure that you are getting the proper RPM for your system, Red Hat Linux 9.0 in our case. Before you begin, you will need to have root privileges to install an RPM. Make sure you are logged in as root, or switch to root by typing **su root**, press **Enter**, and type the appropriate root password.

1. Open a terminal window by right-clicking the **desktop** and choosing **New Terminal**.

2. Install the libpcap RPM by typing **rpm –ivh /mnt/cdrom/pcap/libpcap-0.7.2-7.1.i386.rpm** and press **Enter**.

3. Verify the installation by typing **rpm –qa | grep libpcap** and press **Enter**. If you see libpcap-0.7.2-7.1 listed, it is installed!

The following output shows how to install the libpcap RPM and then verify that it is installed:

```
[root@localhost root]# rpm -ivh /mnt/cdrom/pcap/libpcap-0.7.2-7.1.i386.rpm
Preparing...              ########################################### [100%]
   1:libpcap             ########################################### [100%]
[root@localhost root]# rpm -qa | grep libpcap
libpcap-0.7.2-7.1
```

Not too bad! Now that you have libpcap installed feel free to move on to the "Installing Ethereal on UNIX" section where you can continue with the RPM process or compile Ethereal from the source code.

NOTE

If your system does not have *automount* enabled, mount the accompanying CD-ROM by entering the command **mount /dev/cdrom /mnt/cdrom** and pressing **Enter**. The CD-ROM can be unmounted by typing **eject cdrom** and pressing **Enter**. Some versions of UNIX use different names for the location of the CD-ROM, instead of the standard */mnt*. Please check the documentation that came with your OS if the mount command is not working.

Notes from the Underground...

A Word about RPMs

The Red Hat Package Manager (RPM) is a powerful package management system capable of installing, uninstalling, verifying, querying, and updating Linux software packages. Finding RPMs is relatively easy, and www.rpmfind.net has a well-designed search and download system. However, since RPMs tend to be contributed by various individuals, they are often times a version or two behind the current source code release. They are created on systems with varying file structures and environments, which can lead to difficulties if your system does not match those parameters. Installing an RPM can sometimes be easier than compiling from source – provided there are no dependency problems.

The RPM system, while an excellent package management tool, is fraught with problems regarding dependencies. It understands and reports which specific files the package requires that you install, but is not yet capable of acquiring and installing the packages necessary to fulfill its requirements. If you are not familiar with the term, *dependencies* are packages and/or libraries required by other packages. The RedHat Linux OS is built on dependencies, which you can visualize as an upside-

Continued

down tree structure. At the top of the tree are your basic user-installed programs, such as Ethereal. Ethereal depends on libpcap to operate, and libpcap requires other libraries to function. This tree structure is nice, but it adds to the dependency problem. For example, you may want to install a new software package and receive an error stating that another library on the system needs to be updated first. OK, so you download that library and attempt to update it. But, now, that library has dependencies too that need to be updated! This can be a never ending and stressful adventure.

There are several ways to get information about RPMs:

- **rpm –q** (query) can be used to find out the version of a package installed, for example **rpm –q ethereal-base**.

- **rpm –qa** (query all) can be used to show a very long list of all of the packages on the system. To make this list shorter you can *pipe* the query into a *grep* to find what you are looking for: **rpm –qa | grep ethereal**.

- **rpm –ql** (query list) shows all of the files that were installed on the system with a particular package, for example **rpm –ql ethereal-base-0.10.0a-1.RH9**.

- **rpm –qf** (query file) can be used to find out which RPM a particular file belongs to, for example **rpm –qf /usr/sbin/ethereal**.

There are three choices when using the RPM utility to install software:

- **rpm –i** (install) installs a new RPM file, and leaves any previous installed versions alone.

- **rpm –u** (update) installs new software and removes any existing older versions.

- **rpm –f** (freshen) installs new software, but only if a previous version already exists. This is typically used for installing patches.

There is one way to uninstall an RPM from your system:

- **rpm –e** (erase) will remove an RPM from the system, for example **rpm –e ethereal-base-0.10.0a-1.RH9**.

Sometimes you can be successful by installing a package with the **–nodeps** option (notice there are two hyphens there). This causes the package to install regardless of the dependencies it calls for. This may, or

Continued

may not work, depending on whether the package you are installing really does need all of the dependencies to function. One final note, the **–force** option (once again two hyphens) might not be the best choice when you are tired, stressed, and angry at your computer. We used this to try and replace an old package with a new one no matter what, at all costs, and ended up crashing X windows, and when all was said and done, We had to reinstall the system. Not fun!

Installing libpcap from the Sun packages

Installing software from the Solaris packages is much like using the RPM method, and is sometimes much easier. We have included the libpcap Solaris package on the accompanying CD-ROM. Remember, there might be newer versions that have been released since the writing of this book, and you can download the latest versions from www.sunfreeware.com. Make sure that you are getting the proper package for your system, Solaris 9.0 for Sparc systems in our case. We will now step through the process of installing the libpcap package. Before you begin, you will need to have root privileges to install the packages. Make sure you are logged in as root, or switch to root by typing **su root**, press **Enter**, and type the appropriate root password.

1. Open a terminal window by right clicking the **desktop** and choosing **Tools | Terminal**.

2. Install the libpcap package by typing **pkgadd –d /cdrom/syngress/pcap/libpcap–0.7.2–sol9–sparc–local** and press **Enter**. Confirm the installation of the SMClpcap package by pressing **Enter**. If this is the first time you have installed a package, you may see a message requesting the creation of the /usr/local directory. To create the directory, type **y** and press **Enter**.

3. You should see a message stating that the installation completed success-fully and you are done!

Now that you have libpcap installed feel free to move on to the "Installing Ethereal on UNIX" section where you can continue with the Solaris package process or compile Ethereal from the source code.

The following output shows the process of installing the libpcap package:

```
# pkgadd -d /cdrom/syngress/pcap/libpcap-0.7.2-sol9-sparc-local

The following packages are available:
  1  SMClpcap      libpcap
```

```
                          (sparc) 0.7.2
Select package(s) you wish to process (or 'all' to process all packages).
(default: all) [?,??,q]: <enter>
Processing package instance <SMClpcap> from </cdrom/syngress/pcap/libpcap-
0.7.2-sol9-sparc-local>
libpcap
(sparc) 0.7.2
The Tcpdump Group
The selected base directory </usr/local> must exist before installation is
attempted.
Do you want this directory created now [y,n,?,q] y
Using </usr/local> as the package base directory.
## Processing package information.
## Processing system information.
## Verifying disk space requirements.
## Checking for conflicts with packages already installed.
## Checking for setuid/setgid programs.
Installing libpcap as <SMClpcap>
## Installing part 1 of 1.
/usr/local/doc/libpcap/CHANGES
/usr/local/doc/libpcap/CREDITS
/usr/local/doc/libpcap/CVS/Entries
/usr/local/doc/libpcap/CVS/Entries.Log
/usr/local/doc/libpcap/CVS/Repository
/usr/local/doc/libpcap/CVS/Root
/usr/local/doc/libpcap/CVS/Tag
/usr/local/doc/libpcap/FILES
/usr/local/doc/libpcap/INSTALL.txt
/usr/local/doc/libpcap/LICENSE
/usr/local/doc/libpcap/README
/usr/local/doc/libpcap/SUNOS4/CVS/Entries
/usr/local/doc/libpcap/SUNOS4/CVS/Repository
/usr/local/doc/libpcap/SUNOS4/CVS/Root
/usr/local/doc/libpcap/SUNOS4/CVS/Tag
/usr/local/doc/libpcap/SUNOS4/nit_if.o.sparc
/usr/local/doc/libpcap/SUNOS4/nit_if.o.sun3
/usr/local/doc/libpcap/SUNOS4/nit_if.o.sun4c.4.0.3c
```

```
/usr/local/doc/libpcap/TODO
/usr/local/doc/libpcap/VERSION
/usr/local/include/net/bpf.h
/usr/local/include/pcap-namedb.h
/usr/local/include/pcap.h
/usr/local/lib/libpcap.a
/usr/local/man/man3/pcap.3
[ verifying class <none> ]
Installation of <SMClpcap> was successful.
```

Installing libpcap from the source files

Installing libpcap from the source *tarball* is a relatively simple process. A tarball is a single file that can contain many other files, like a zip file. The tar format by itself does not provide compression like the zip format does, so it is customary to compress the tar file with either gzip or bzip2. See the sidebar for more information on using the gzip and bzip2 compression utilities. We will be extracting the contents of the tar file as well as compiling the source code. We will follow the common **configure | make | make install** format for building the package into the system. We have included the libpcap source tarball on the accompanying CD-ROM. It is standard practice NOT to build software as root, but to change to root to do the *make install* step. We will now step through the process of installing libpcap from the source files.

1.   Open a terminal window by right clicking the **desktop** and choosing **New Terminal**.

2.   Change to the /tmp directory by typing **cd /tmp** and pressing **Enter**.

3.   Extract the tarball by typing **tar –xvf /mnt/cdrom/pcap/libpcap-0.7.2.tar** and pressing **Enter**. This will create a new directory in /tmp called **libpcap-0.7.2**. You will see the extracted output displayed on the screen.

> **NOTE**
>
> Let's take a moment to define the typical variables used for the tar command: *-z, -x, -v,* and *-f* options.
>   The **-z** option specifies that the file must be processed through the *gzip* filter. You can tell if an archive was created with gzip by the *.gz* exten-

sion. The –z options is only available in the GNU version of tar. If you are not using the GNU version, you will have to unzip the tar file with a command such as **gunzip or gzip –dc filename.tar.gz | tar xvf -.**

The **-x** option indicates that you want the contents of the archive to be extracted. By default, this action will extract the contents into the current working directory unless otherwise specified.

The **-v** option stands for verbose, which means that tar will display all files it processes on the screen. This is a personal preference and is not critical to the extraction operation.

The **-f** option specifies the file that tar will process. For example, this could be libpcap-0.7.2.tar.gz. Sometimes it might be necessary to specify a full path if the file you want to work with is located in another directory.

4. Change directories by typing **cd libpcap–0.7.2** and pressing **Enter**.

5. Run the configure script by typing **./configure** and pressing **Enter**. The configure script will analyze your system to make sure that dependencies, environment variables, and other parameters are acceptable. You will see a question–and–answer type of analysis displayed on the screen.

6. When the *configure* process is complete, and the command prompt is displayed, make sure that there are no errors. If everything appears trouble-free, run the *make utility* simply by typing **make** and pressing **Enter**. This utility will compile the actual source code. You will see the output of the compilation on the screen.

7. The last step of the process is to distribute the executables and other files to their proper locations in the systems directories. We are going to switch to the root user to perform this step. If the *make* utility completes without errors, type **su root** and press **Enter**. Enter the password for root and press **Enter**. Next, type **make install** and press **Enter**. Once again you will see the output of this process on the screen.

8. After the *make install* process completes, the command prompt will be displayed once again. If everything looks error free, you are done! You can type **exit** to log out as the root user and return to your normal user shell.

Now that you have libpcap installed feel free to move on to the "Installing Ethereal on UNIX" section where you can continue with compiling Ethereal from the source code or choose one of the other processes.

The following output shows the whole process of installing the libpcap source code:

```
[testuser@localhost testuser]$ cd /tmp
[testuser@localhost tmp]$ tar -xvf /mnt/cdrom/pcap/libpcap-0.7.2.tar
[output reomoved]
[testuser@localhost tmp]$ cd libpcap-0.7.2
[testuser@localhost libpcap-0.7.2]$ ./configure
[output removed]
[testuser@localhost libpcap-0.7.2]$ make
[output removed]
[testuser@localhost libpcap-0.7.2]$ su root
Password: <password>
[root@localhost libpcap-0.7.2]# make install
[root@localhost libpcap-0.7.2]# exit
```

If at anytime during the installation process you receive errors, you will need to investigate the problem and resolve it before continuing. Most of the time dependency issues, software versions, or environment settings cause compiling errors. Compiling software from the source files offers the benefit of providing highly customized and optimized software for your system.

> **NOTE**
>
> Some UNIX distributions (such as Red Hat 9.0) have software like libpcap, Ethereal, and others preinstalled. It is worth the time and effort to install the latest versions of these packages. You will benefit from the increased stability, features, bug fixes, and speed of updated software.

Installing WinPcap

The latest WinPcap installation executable can be downloaded from http://win-pcap.polito.it. It will install on Windows 95, 98, ME, NT, 2000, and XP. This site also contains a developers' pack download and source code download, but we won't be covering those here. We have also included the WinPcap installation executable on the accompanying CD-ROM. To install WinPcap, you need to have the right to install new drivers to your system, and will need to be logged in as Administrator or have administrator rights. Now we will step through the process of installing the WinPcap 3.0 auto-installer on a Windows 2000 system.

1. Browse to the **/pcap** folder on the CD-ROM.

2. Begin the installation process by double-clicking on the installer, **WinPcap_3_0.exe**. The first screen that appears is show in Figure 3.1. This is a general welcome screen that informs you of what you are about to do, recommends that you exit other Windows programs, and warns you about the copyright law.

3. Click **Next** to continue.

NOTE

If you do not have WinPcap installed you will be able to open saved capture files, but you will not be able to capture live network traffic.

Figure 3.1 The WinPcap Installation Wizard

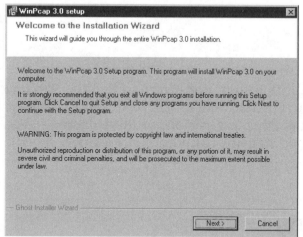

4. The next screen in Figure 3.2 displays information on the WinPcap license. You must click the box "**Yes, I agree with all the terms of this license agreement**" and click Next to accept the license and continue.

Figure 3.2 The WinPcap License Agreement

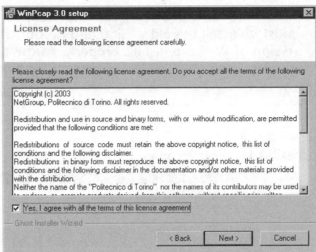

5. Figure 3.3 shows the Setup Status window. It lets you know which files are being copied and displays a progress bar. You might not see this window during the installation because it completes so quickly.

Figure 3.3 WinPcap Setup Status

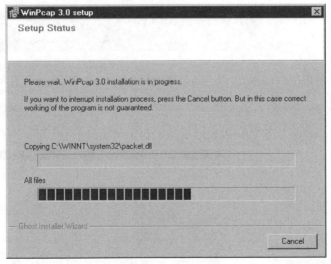

6. The next screen (Figure 3.4) warns you to reboot the system if an old version of WinPcap was already present. It is always good practice to uninstall an old version of WinPcap before installing a new version. Click **Next** to continue.

WARNING

If you have an older version of WinPcap and would like to install a new one, you must uninstall the old version and reboot. This will ensure that the new version of WinPcap installs properly. At the time of this writing, version 3.0 is recommended, as it supports multiprocessor machines and Windows XP.

Figure 3.4 WinPcap Readme Information

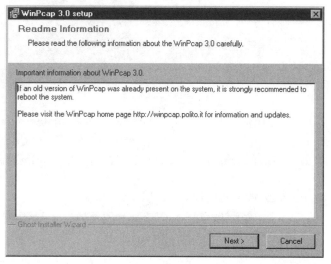

7. Finally installation is complete, as seen in Figure 3.5. Click **OK** to exit the setup.

Figure 3.5 WinPcap Installation Complete

WinPcap installs by default in C:\Program Files\WinPcap. This directory will contain *daemon_mgm.exe, npf_mgm.exe, rpcapd.exe, install.log,* and *Uninstall.exe.* Unless you are developing applications to use the WinPcap driver, you won't need to use the first three. If you need to uninstall WinPcap, please use the provided uninstall executable located in this directory. The setup copies the following to the C:\WINNT\system32 directory: *packet.dll, wpcap.dll,* and *pthreadVC.dll.* It also copies npf.sys to the C:\WINNT\system32\drivers directory and makes some registry changes for the uninstall program and the packet drivers. See how easy that was! Now let's move on to the Ethereal installation.

Installing Ethereal on Windows

The latest Ethereal Windows executable can be downloaded from the local archive at www.ethereal.com/download.html. It will install on a variety Windows platforms. We have also included the Ethereal executable on the accompanying CD-ROM. Note that you don't need administrator rights to install Ethereal. Now that WinPcap is installed, we will step through the process of installing Ethereal 0.10.0 on a Windows 2000 Professional system.

1. Browse to the **/ethereal/windows** folder on the CD-ROM.

2. Begin the installation process by double-clicking on the installer, **ethereal-setup-0.10.0.exe**. The first screen that appears is shown in Figure 3.6. This is the GNU General Public License Agreement that Ethereal uses. After reading and accepting the terms of the license, click **I Agree** to continue.

Figure 3.6 The Ethereal GNU License Agreement

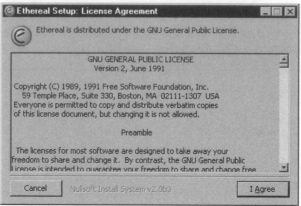

3. The next screen, shown in Figure 3.7, allows you to choose which Ethereal components to install. We will be discussing the other supporting programs that Ethereal includes in Chapter 6. Notice that the entire distribution requires 36.2MB of free space. Ethereal consumes 20.7MB and Tethereal uses 15.8MB of the total. The rest of the components are trivial in size. Of course you would want to have adequate free space for storing your capture files as well. Accept the default to install all components and click **Next** to continue.

Figure 3.7 Ethereal Installation Components

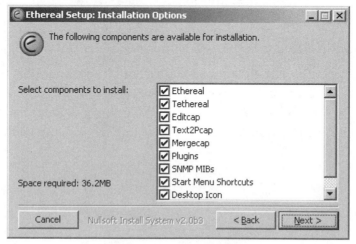

4. The next screen, shown in Figure 3.8, allows you to choose the folder where you would like to install Ethereal. Accept the default of C:\Program Files\Ethereal and click **Install** to begin the installation process.

Figure 3.8 Ethereal Installation Directory

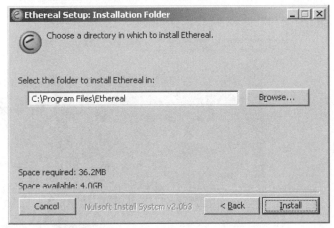

5. The next screen, shown in Figure 3.9, shows the status of the installation process. It gives line-by-line details of what is happening behind the scenes as well as an overall progress bar.

Figure 3.9 Ethereal Installation Status

6. All done! Figure 3.10 shows that Ethereal is installed and ready to go. It even puts a nice shortcut icon right on the desktop. Click **Close** to close the dialog box.

7. You can now double-click on the Ethereal desktop icon to open the Ethereal network analyzer GUI.

Figure 3.10 Ethereal Installation Completed

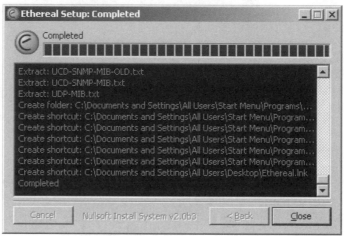

NOTE

A nice feature of the completed installation box shown in Figure 3.10 is the ability to save the installation log to a file. Simply right-click on one of the lines in the box and a small window will pop up that says "Copy Details To Clipboard". Select this option and paste the results into Notepad or your favorite text editor.

NOTE

The first time you execute a WinPcap-based application such as Ethereal after installation, you must be logged in as Administrator, or have administrator rights. This will allow the driver to be installed on the system and from then on every user will be able to use WinPcap applications.

By default Ethereal is installed in C:\Program Files\Ethereal. As you saw during the installation process, this can be changed. Several files are placed within the Ethereal directory. The following installation log output shows exactly what the setup was doing:

```
Output folder: C:\Program Files\Ethereal
Extract: wiretap-0.0.dll
Extract: iconv.dll
Extract: libglib-2.0-0.dll
Extract: libgmodule-2.0-0.dll
Extract: libgobject-2.0-0.dll
Extract: intl.dll
Extract: zlib1.dll
Extract: adns_dll.dll
Extract: pcre.dll
Extract: FAQ
Extract: README
Extract: README.win32
Extract: manuf
Extract: pcrepattern.3.txt
Output folder: C:\Program Files\Ethereal\diameter
Extract: dictionary.dtd
Extract: dictionary.xml
Extract: mobileipv4.xml
Extract: nasreq.xml
Extract: sunping.xml
Output folder: C:\Program Files\Ethereal
Created uninstaller: uninstall.exe
Output folder: C:\Program Files\Ethereal
Extract: ethereal.exe
Extract: ethereal.html
Extract: ethereal-filter.html
Extract: libgtk-0.dll
Extract: libgdk-0.dll
Output folder: C:\Program Files\Ethereal
Extract: tethereal.exe
Extract: tethereal.html
```

```
Output folder: C:\Program Files\Ethereal
Extract: editcap.exe
Extract: editcap.html
Output folder: C:\Program Files\Ethereal
Extract: text2pcap.exe
Extract: text2pcap.html
Output folder: C:\Program Files\Ethereal
Extract: mergecap.exe
Extract: mergecap.html
Output folder: C:\Program Files\Ethereal\plugins\0.10.0
Extract: acn.dll
Extract: artnet.dll
Extract: asn1.dll
Extract: docsis.dll
Extract: enttec.dll
Extract: coseventcomm.dll
Extract: cosnaming.dll
Extract: gryphon.dll
Extract: lwres.dll
Extract: megaco.dll
Extract: mgcp.dll
Extract: pcli.dll
Extract: rdm.dll
Extract: rtnet.dll
Output folder: C:\Program Files\Ethereal\snmp\mibs
Extract: AGENTX-MIB.txt
Extract: DISMAN-EVENT-MIB.txt
Extract: DISMAN-SCHEDULE-MIB.txt
Extract: DISMAN-SCRIPT-MIB.txt
Extract: EtherLike-MIB.txt
Extract: HCNUM-TC.txt
Extract: HOST-RESOURCES-MIB.txt
Extract: HOST-RESOURCES-TYPES.txt
Extract: IANA-ADDRESS-FAMILY-NUMBERS-MIB.txt
Extract: IANA-LANGUAGE-MIB.txt
Extract: IANAifType-MIB.txt
```

```
Extract:  IF-INVERTED-STACK-MIB.txt

Extract:  IF-MIB.txt

Extract:  INET-ADDRESS-MIB.txt

Extract:  IP-FORWARD-MIB.txt

Extract:  IP-MIB.txt

Extract:  IPV6-ICMP-MIB.txt

Extract:  IPV6-MIB.txt

Extract:  IPV6-TC.txt

Extract:  IPV6-TCP-MIB.txt

Extract:  IPV6-UDP-MIB.txt

Extract:  LM-SENSORS-MIB.txt

Extract:  MTA-MIB.txt

Extract:  NET-SNMP-AGENT-MIB.txt

Extract:  NET-SNMP-EXAMPLES-MIB.txt

Extract:  NET-SNMP-MIB.txt

Extract:  NET-SNMP-MONITOR-MIB.txt

Extract:  NET-SNMP-SYSTEM-MIB.txt

Extract:  NET-SNMP-TC.txt

Extract:  NETWORK-SERVICES-MIB.txt

Extract:  NOTIFICATION-LOG-MIB.txt

Extract:  RFC-1215.txt

Extract:  RFC1155-SMI.txt

Extract:  RFC1213-MIB.txt

Extract:  RMON-MIB.txt

Extract:  SMUX-MIB.txt

Extract:  SNMP-COMMUNITY-MIB.txt

Extract:  SNMP-FRAMEWORK-MIB.txt

Extract:  SNMP-MPD-MIB.txt

Extract:  SNMP-NOTIFICATION-MIB.txt

Extract:  SNMP-PROXY-MIB.txt

Extract:  SNMP-TARGET-MIB.txt

Extract:  SNMP-USER-BASED-SM-MIB.txt

Extract:  SNMP-VIEW-BASED-ACM-MIB.txt

Extract:  SNMPv2-CONF.txt

Extract:  SNMPv2-MIB.txt

Extract:  SNMPv2-SMI.txt
```

```
Extract: SNMPv2-TC.txt

Extract: SNMPv2-TM.txt

Extract: TCP-MIB.txt

Extract: TUNNEL-MIB.txt

Extract: UCD-DEMO-MIB.txt

Extract: UCD-DISKIO-MIB.txt

Extract: UCD-DLMOD-MIB.txt

Extract: UCD-IPFILTER-MIB.txt

Extract: UCD-IPFWACC-MIB.txt

Extract: UCD-SNMP-MIB-OLD.txt

Extract: UCD-SNMP-MIB.txt

Extract: UDP-MIB.txt

Create folder: C:\Documents and Settings\All Users\Start
Menu\Programs\Ethereal

Create shortcut: C:\Documents and Settings\All Users\Start
Menu\Programs\Ethereal\Ethereal.lnk

Create shortcut: C:\Documents and Settings\All Users\Start
Menu\Programs\Ethereal\Ethereal Manual.lnk

Create shortcut: C:\Documents and Settings\All Users\Start
Menu\Programs\Ethereal\Display Filters Manual.lnk

Create shortcut: C:\Documents and Settings\All Users\Start
Menu\Programs\Ethereal\Uninstall.lnk

Create shortcut: C:\Documents and Settings\All Users\Start
Menu\Programs\Ethereal\Ethereal Program Directory.lnk

Create shortcut: C:\Documents and Settings\All Users\Desktop\Ethereal.lnk

Completed
```

Notice that one of the files in C:\Program Files\Ethereal is uninstall.exe. You can use this executable to uninstall Ethereal if necessary. Some other important files to note are the five executables and their associated manual pages in HTML format: *ethereal.exe, tethereal.exe, editcap.exe, mergecap.exe*, and *text2pcap.exe*. These supporting programs will be discussed in detail in Chapter 6.

NOTE

If you are having trouble capturing packets with Ethereal, ensure that WinPcap is working properly by using Windump to try capturing packets. Windump can be downloaded from http://windump.polito.it/install/default.htm. The command **windump –D** will display a list of valid adapters that WinPcap is able to detect.

Installing Ethereal on UNIX

In this section we will cover two methods of installing Ethereal: the Red Hat Package Manager and the Sun Solaris packages. The next section will focus on building Ethereal from source. Now that libpcap is installed, we will step through the process of installing Ethereal 0.10.0a and 0.10.0 on two UNIX-based systems, Red Hat Linux 9.0 and Solaris 9.0, respectively. The Red Hat Linux version of Ethereal was repackaged as version 0.10.0a due to some problems with the help files. Let's get started installing Ethereal!

Installing Ethereal from the RPMs

Installing the Ethereal software from the RPM can be a very tricky process because of dependencies. Now that libpcap is installed, the step-by-step process below can be used to install Ethereal on Red Hat 9.0. We have also included the Ethereal RPMs on the accompanying CD-ROM. Remember, there might be newer versions that have been released since the writing of this book, and you can download the latest Ethereal RPM from the local archives at www.ethereal.com. Make sure that you are getting the proper RPM for your system, Red Hat Linux 9.0 in our case. Before you begin, you will need to have root privileges to install an RPM. Make sure you are logged in as root, or switch to root by typing **su root**, press **Enter**, and type the appropriate root password.

You will notice that there are quite a few different RPMs for Ethereal. We will not be using all of them for our installation, although they are all included on the accompanying CD-ROM in case you need them. The list below provides a short description of each RPM:

- **ethereal-base-0.10.0a-1.RH9.i386.rpm** This package is the base for Ethereal and contains the command-line utilities, plugins, and documentation for Ethereal. The graphical user interface is packaged separately in the GTK+ package.

- **ethereal-base-net-snmp-0.10.0a-1.RH9.i386.rpm** This package is also the base for Ethereal and contains the command-line utilities, plugins, and documentation for Ethereal. However it depends on the Net-SNMP libraries. The graphical user interface is packaged separately in the GTK+ package.

- **ethereal-base-no-snmp-0.10.0a-1.RH9.i386.rpm** This package is very similar to the ethereal-base-net-snmp-0.10.0a-1.RH9.i386.rpm. However, it does not depend on the Net-SNMP library.

- **ethereal–debuginfo–0.10.0a–1.RH9.i386.rpm** This package provides debug information for Ethereal. Debug information is useful when developing applications that use this package or when debugging this package.

- **ethereal–gnome–0.10.0a–1.RH9.i386.rpm** This package contains an Ethereal icon for Gnome 1.2 and desktop integration files.

- **ethereal–gtk+–0.10.0a–1.RH9.i386.rpm** This package contains the Ethereal GUI.

- **ethereal–gtk+–net–snmp–0.10.0a–1.RH9.i386.rpm** This package contains the Ethereal GUI and depends on the Net-SNMP libraries.

- **ethereal–gtk+–no–snmp–0.10.0a–1.RH9.i386.rpm** This package is very similar to the ethereal-gtk+-net-snmp-0.9.16-1.RH9.i386.rpm. However, it does not depend on the Net-SNMP library.

- **ethereal–kde–0.10.0a–1.RH9.i386.rpm** This package contains Ethereal icons for KDE2 and desktop integration files.

- **ethereal–usermode–0.10.0a–1.RH9.i386.rpm** This package contains Ethereal integration to the usermode execution package. It is required by the Gnome and KDE packages.

Let's begin the Ethereal installation process:

1. Open a terminal window by right clicking on the **desktop** and choosing **New Terminal**.

2. We will need to install two SNMP files for dependency reasons. Install the UCD-SNMP RPM by typing **rpm –ivh --nodeps /mnt/cdrom/snmp/ucd-snmp-4.2.3-1.i386.rpm** and pressing **Enter**. The *--nodeps* option indicates that we are installing this package regardless of the dependencies.

3. Next, install the Net–SNMP RPM by typing **rpm –ivh --nodeps --force /mnt/cdrom/snmp/net-snmp-5.0.9-3.i386.rh9.rpm** and pressing **Enter**. We are installing both packages because the Ethereal base packages complains about dependencies for each: *libnetsnmp.so.5*, which is in Net-SNMP, and *ucd-snmp*. We need to install Net SNMP with the *--force* option because it recognizes that UCD SNMP is already installed, and exits with errors.

4. Now that all dependencies have been met we can go ahead with the installation of the Ethereal base package. Type **rpm –ivh /mnt/ cdrom/ethereal/linux/ethereal-base-0.10.0a–1.RH9.i386.rpm** and press **Enter**.

5. Remember, the base package installs the supporting software, such as Tethereal, but not the actual Ethereal executable. We need to install the graphical environment package to get Ethereal. Type **rpm –ivh /mnt/ cdrom/ethereal/linux/ethereal-gtk+-0.10.0a–1.RH9.i386.rpm** and press **Enter**.

6. Technically, Ethereal is now installed in the /usr/sbin directory and can be run by typing **ethereal** at the command prompt. If you don't want to install the Gnome support you may stop here. We are going to continue with the Gnome support by installing one of its dependencies first. Type **rpm –ivh /mnt/cdrom/ethereal/linux/ethereal-user-mode-0.10.0a–1.RH9.i386.rpm** and press **Enter**.

7. Now we will install the final package for Gnome. Type **rpm –ivh /mnt/cdrom/ethereal/linux/ethereal-gnome-0.10.0a–1.RH9.i386.rpm** and press **Enter.**

Verify the installation by typing **ethereal** and pressing **Enter**. You should see the Ethereal GUI appear on your screen.

The following output shows how to install the Ethereal RPMs and their dependencies:

```
[root@localhost root]# rpm -ivh --nodeps /mnt/cdrom/snmp/ucd-snmp-4.2.3-
1.i386.rpm

Preparing...        ######################################## [100%]
   1:ucd-snmp        ######################################## [100%]
[root@localhost root]# rpm -ivh --nodeps --force /mnt/cdrom/snmp/net-snmp-
5.0.9-3.i386.rh9.rpm

Preparing...        ######################################## [100%]
   1:net-snmp        ######################################## [100%]
[root@localhost root]# rpm -ivh /mnt/cdrom/ethereal/linux/ethereal-base-
0.10.0a-1.RH9.i386.rpm

Preparing...        ######################################## [100%]
   1:ethereal-base   ######################################## [100%]
[root@localhost root]# rpm -ivh /mnt/cdrom/ethereal/linux/ethereal-gtk+-
0.10.0a-1.RH9.i386.rpm
```

```
Preparing...          ######################################### [100%]
   1:ethereal-gtk+    ######################################### [100%]
[root@localhost root]# rpm -ivh /mnt/cdrom/ethereal/linux/ethereal-
usermode-0.10.0a-1.RH9.i386.rpm
Preparing...          ######################################### [100%]
   1:ethereal-usermode  ####################################### [100%]
[root@localhost root]# rpm -ivh /mnt/cdrom/ethereal/linux/ethereal-gnome-
0.10.0a-1.RH9.i386.rpm
Preparing...          ######################################### [100%]
   1:ethereal-gnome ########################################### [100%]
```

The Gnome Ethereal package installs a nice icon for your desktop shortcut at /usr/share/pixmaps/ethereal.png. From the X Windows interface, use the Nautilus File Manager to browse to the */usr/sbin* directory. Right-click **ethereal** and choose **Make Link**. The link will appear on the screen and it will be highlighted. Right-click **link to ethereal** and choose **Properties**. Click the **Select Custom Icon** button. Browse down through the list of icons and choose the **ethereal.png** icon. Click **OK**. Click **Close** in the **link to ethereal properties** box. Now that you are back to the /usr/sbin folder, you can click the new **link to ethereal** icon and drag it to the desktop. You now have a desktop shortcut, with a very cool icon!

NOTE

When you need to find a particular dependency file and determine which package it belongs to, do a search on www.rpmfind.net for the filename. This will usually tell you what package, and what version contains that file.

Notes from the Underground...

Libcrypto Problems?

Several open source tools tend to fail to install because of various *libcrypto* errors. During our installation testing, this didn't happen on Red Hat 9.0, but it did happen on Red Hat 8.0. The base Ethereal package was complaining about a dependency on libcrypto.so.4. This library is part of the OpenSSL package and stored in the /lib directory. While, you technically don't need OpenSSL, you do need the libr-crypto.so.4 file. To solve this problem you can do one of three things: download and install the appropriate version of OpenSSL, create a symbolic link to a current libcrypto file that you already have, or extract the libcrypto file from OpenSSL and then create a symbolic link. Here is how to accomplish each of these:

1. Install the OpenSSL RPM using the following command: rpm –ivh openssl-0.9.7a-23.i386.rpm. This will place the libcrypto.so.0.9.7a file in the /lib directory. Follow the steps in #2 to create a symbolic link

2. If you already have a libcrypto file in your /lib directory, you can create a symbolic link to it for *libcrypto.so.4* (or whichever version the installation requires). Do this with the following command: **ln -s /lib/libcrypto.so.0.9.7a /lib/libcrypto.so.4**.

3. You also can extract the libcrypto file from the OpenSSL package with the following command: **rpm2cpio openssl-0.9.7a-2.i386.rpm | cpio -id ./lib/libssl.so.0.9.7a ./lib/libcrypto.so.0.9.7a**. It will create a *lib* subdirectory in your current directory. You will then need to copy it over to the real /lib directory with the following command: **cp lib/libcrypto.so.0.9.7a /lib**. Finally, follow the steps in #2 to create a symbolic link.

Sometimes the RPM installation will still complain about the dependency even after you have created the symbolic link. If this is the only thing preventing the installation, perform the installation with the --nodeps option.

Installing the Solaris Ethereal Package

Installing Ethereal from the Solaris packages is a very quick and easy process. We have included the Ethereal Solaris package, and supporting packages, on the accompanying CD-ROM. Remember, there might be newer versions that have been released since the writing of this book, and you can download the latest versions from the local archive at www.ethereal.com. Make sure that you are getting the proper package for your system, Solaris 9.0 for Sparc systems in our case. Before you begin, you will need to have root privileges to install the packages. Make sure you are logged in as root, or switch to root by typing **su root**, press **Enter**, and type the appropriate root password. We will now step through the process of installing the Ethereal package, but first we need to take care of some dependency issues.

1. Open a terminal window by right clicking the **desktop** and choosing **Tools | Terminal**.

2. Install the Glib package by typing **pkgadd –d /cdrom/syngress/gtk+_glib/glib-1.2.10-sol9-sparc-local** and pressing **Enter**. Confirm the installation of the **SMCglib** package by pressing **Enter**.

3. Install the GTK+ package by typing **pkgadd -d /cdrom/syngress/ gtk+_glib/gtk+-1.2.10-sol9-sparc-local** and pressing **Enter**. Confirm the installation of the **SMCgtk** package by pressing **Enter**.

4. Install the Ethereal package by typing **pkgadd –d /cdrom/syngress/ ethereal/solaris/ethereal-0.10.0-solaris2.9-sparc-local** and pressing **Enter**. Output will appear on the screen confirming the installation of the **ethereal** package. Press **Enter** to accept and proceed. You may get a message about installing conflicting files. These are attribute changes only, so you can accept the installation by typing **y** and pressing **Enter**. When the installation is complete, you should see a message stating that the installation was successful.

Ethereal is installed in the /usr/local/bin directory, which you may need to add to your path. You can verify the installation by typing **ethereal** and pressing **Enter**. You should see the Ethereal GUI appear on your screen.

NOTE

Most Solaris packages install in the /usr/local/bin directory. You will need to make sure this directory is part of your PATH environment variable. To see your current PATH setting, type **echo $PATH** and press **Enter**. To add the /usr/local/bin directory, type **PATH=$PATH:/usr/local/bin** and press **Enter**.

The following output shows the whole process of installing Ethereal and the supporting packages:

```
# pkgadd -d /cdrom/syngress/gtk+_glib/glib-1.2.10-sol9-sparc-local
The following packages are available:
   1  SMCglib      glib
                      (sparc) 1.2.10
Select package(s) you wish to process (or 'all' to process
all packages). (default: all) [?,??,q]: <enter>
Processing package instance <SMCglib> from </cdrom/syngress/gtk+_glib/glib-
1.2.10-sol9-sparc-local>
glib
(sparc) 1.2.10
The CLib Team
[output removed]
Installation of <SMCglib> was successful.
# pkgadd -d /cdrom/syngress/gtk+_glib/gtk+-1.2.10-sol9-sparc-local
The following packages are available:
   1  SMCgtk       gtk+
                      (sparc) 1.2.10
Select package(s) you wish to process (or 'all' to process
all packages). (default: all) [?,??,q]: <enter>
Processing package instance <SMCgtk> from </cdrom/syngress/gtk+_glib/gtk+-
1.2.10-sol9-sparc-local>
gtk+
(sparc) 1.2.10
The GTK Team
[output removed]
Installation of <SMCgtk> was successful.
```

www.syngress.com

```
# pkgadd -d /cdrom/syngress/ethereal/solaris/ethereal-0.10.0-solaris2.9
sparc-local
```

The following packages are available:

```
  1  ethereal        ethereal 0.10.0
                      (sparc) 0.10.0
```

Select package(s) you wish to process (or 'all' to process
all packages). (default: all) [?,??,q]: *<enter>*

Processing package instance <ethereal> from
</cdrom/syngress/ethereal/solaris/ethereal-0.10.0-solaris2.9-sparc-local>

ethereal 0.10.0

(sparc) 0.10.0

Ethereal Development Team

Executing checkinstall script.

Processing package information.

Processing system information.

Verifying disk space requirements.

Checking for conflicts with packages already installed.

The following files are already installed on the system and are being
used by another package:

```
* /usr/local <attribute change only>
  /usr/local/bin <attribute change only>
  /usr/local/lib <attribute change only>
  /usr/local/man <attribute change only>
  /usr/local/man/man1 <attribute change only>
  /usr/local/share <attribute change only>
```

* - conflict with a file which does not belong to any package.

Do you want to install these conflicting files [y,n,?,q] y

Checking for setuid/setgid programs.

Installing ethereal 0.10.0 as <ethereal>

Installing part 1 of 1.

```
/usr/local/bin/editcap
/usr/local/bin/ethereal
/usr/local/bin/idl2eth
/usr/local/bin/mergecap
/usr/local/bin/tethereal
/usr/local/bin/text2pcap
/usr/local/lib/ethereal/plugins/0.10.0/acn.la
```

```
/usr/local/lib/ethereal/plugins/0.10.0/acn.so
/usr/local/lib/ethereal/plugins/0.10.0/artnet.la
/usr/local/lib/ethereal/plugins/0.10.0/artnet.so
/usr/local/lib/ethereal/plugins/0.10.0/asn1.la
/usr/local/lib/ethereal/plugins/0.10.0/asn1.so
/usr/local/lib/ethereal/plugins/0.10.0/coseventcomm.la
/usr/local/lib/ethereal/plugins/0.10.0/coseventcomm.so
/usr/local/lib/ethereal/plugins/0.10.0/cosnaming.la
/usr/local/lib/ethereal/plugins/0.10.0/cosnaming.so
/usr/local/lib/ethereal/plugins/0.10.0/docsis.la
/usr/local/lib/ethereal/plugins/0.10.0/docsis.so
/usr/local/lib/ethereal/plugins/0.10.0/enttec.la
/usr/local/lib/ethereal/plugins/0.10.0/enttec.so
/usr/local/lib/ethereal/plugins/0.10.0/gryphon.la
/usr/local/lib/ethereal/plugins/0.10.0/gryphon.so
/usr/local/lib/ethereal/plugins/0.10.0/lwres.la
/usr/local/lib/ethereal/plugins/0.10.0/lwres.so
/usr/local/lib/ethereal/plugins/0.10.0/megaco.la
/usr/local/lib/ethereal/plugins/0.10.0/megaco.so
/usr/local/lib/ethereal/plugins/0.10.0/mgcp.la
/usr/local/lib/ethereal/plugins/0.10.0/mgcp.so
/usr/local/lib/ethereal/plugins/0.10.0/pcli.la
/usr/local/lib/ethereal/plugins/0.10.0/pcli.so
/usr/local/lib/ethereal/plugins/0.10.0/rdm.la
/usr/local/lib/ethereal/plugins/0.10.0/rdm.so
/usr/local/lib/ethereal/plugins/0.10.0/rtnet.la
/usr/local/lib/ethereal/plugins/0.10.0/rtnet.so
/usr/local/man/man1/editcap.1
/usr/local/man/man1/ethereal.1
/usr/local/man/man1/idl2eth.1
/usr/local/man/man1/mergecap.1
/usr/local/man/man1/tethereal.1
/usr/local/man/man1/text2pcap.1
/usr/local/man/man4/ethereal-filter.4
/usr/local/share/ethereal/diameter/dictionary.dtd
/usr/local/share/ethereal/diameter/dictionary.xml
```

```
/usr/local/share/ethereal/diameter/mobileipv4.xml
/usr/local/share/ethereal/diameter/nasreq.xml
/usr/local/share/ethereal/diameter/sunping.xml
/usr/local/share/ethereal/manuf
[ verifying class <none> ]
Installation of <ethereal> was successful.
```

NOTE

You have already seen the use of the pkgadd command on Solaris to install software. You can also type **pkginfo** to see a list of all installed packages. Sometimes this list is long, so it could take a while to scroll on the screen. If that is the case, *pipe* it to *more* by typing **pkginfo | more**. You can use the **pkgrm** command to remove a software package, for example **pkgrm ethereal**.

Building Ethereal from Source

Installing Ethereal from the source code is very beneficial in a number of ways. Not only will you have all of the source code, additional documentation, and miscellaneous files to peruse, you will also have the ability to control numerous aspects of the build process. Ethereal can be built from source on both the Windows and UNIX OS. We will only be focusing on the UNIX build, specifically Red Hat Linux 9.0, in this book. You can find documentation on building Ethereal from source on Windows in the README.win32 file that installed with the Ethereal software in C:\Program Files\Ethereal. Building software from source will give you a better feel for how the whole process works and what goes on behind the scenes. What you will take away is a wealth of knowledge about the software package, programming, and operating system management.

Installing Ethereal from Source on Red Hat Linux

Now we are ready to get into the essentials of building the Ethereal software from source code. The first thing we need to do is install all of the required dependencies. Remember previously we stated that we need certain files for Ethereal to operate smoothly and most effectively? By now we have already installed libpcap, so we are going to start by installing the rest of the prerequisites: GTK+, Glib, Net-SNMP, GNU adns, Zlib, and Perl. Remember, it is standard practice NOT to build software as root, but to change to root to do the *make install* step.

NOTE

As we stated previously, most installations follow the **configure | make | make install** format. However, in some instances, there may be other steps. Once the tar file has been extracted there is usually an INSTALL text file that is included in the software subdirectory. Take a look at this file by typing **more INSTALL** to verify the installation process.

Installing the Dependencies

Let's start with building the Glib and GTK+ programs. Remember these are needed to support the graphical interface capabilities of Ethereal. The version of Linux that we are using, Red Hat 9.0, has a version to Glib and GTK installed by default. We can see what versions we have of each by typing **glib-config –version** and **gtk-config --version,** respectively.

The following output shows the commands used and versions of each package:

```
[testuser@localhost testuser]$ glib-config --version
1.2.10
[testuser@localhost testuser]$ gtk-config --version
1.2.10
```

The versions displayed, 1.2.10, are new enough for Ethereal to support, but let's go ahead and install the most recent versions as well.

1. Open a terminal window by right-clicking the **desktop** and choosing **New Terminal**.

2. Change directories to **/tmp** by typing **cd /tmp** and pressing **Enter**.

3. Extract the Glib tarball by typing **tar –xvf /mnt/cdrom/gtk+_glib/glib-2.2.0.tar** and pressing **Enter**. This will

create a new directory in **/tmp** called **glib–2.2.0**. You will see the
extracted output displayed on the screen.

4. Change directories by typing **cd glib–2.2.0** and pressing **Enter**.

5. Run the configure script by typing **./configure** and pressing **Enter**.
    The configure script will analyze your system to make sure that depen-
    dencies, environment variables, and other parameters are acceptable. You
    will see a question-and-answer type of analysis displayed on the screen.

6. When the *configure* process is complete, and the command prompt is dis-
    played, make sure that there are no errors. If everything appears trouble-
    free, run the make utility simply by typing **make** and pressing **Enter**.
    This utility will compile the actual source code. You will see the output
    of the compiling on the screen.

7. The last step of the process is to distribute the executables and other
    files to their proper locations in the systems directories. We are going to
    switch to the root user to perform this step. If the *make utility* completes
    without errors type **su root** and press **Enter**. Enter the password for
    root and press **Enter**. Next, type **make install** and press **Enter**. Once
    again you will see the output of this process on the screen.

8. After the *make install* process is complete the command prompt will be
    displayed once again. If everything looks error free, you are done!

9. Next we will repeat the same process for GTK+. Log out from the root
    user mode by typing **exit** and pressing **Enter**. Next, go back to the
    /tmp directory by typing **cd /tmp** and pressing **Enter**.

10. Extract the Glib tarball by typing **tar –xvf
    /mnt/cdrom/gtk+_glib/gtk+-2.2.0.tar** and pressing **Enter**.

11. Change to the new directory by typing **cd gtk+-2.2.0** and pressing
    Enter.

12. Run the configure script by typing **./configure** and pressing **Enter**.

13. Run the make utility by typing **make** and pressing **Enter**.

14. Type **su root** and press **Enter**. Enter the password for root and press
    Enter.

15. Type **make install** and press **Enter**.

16. All done! Let's continue this process with the rest of the prerequisite
    software packages. Log out from the root user mode by typing **exit** and

pressing **Enter**. Next, go back to the/tmp directory by typing **cd /tmp** and pressing **Enter**.

17. Extract the Net-SNMP tarball by typing **tar −xvf /mnt/cdrom/snmp/net-snmp-5.0.9.tar** and pressing **Enter**.

18. Change to the new directory by typing **cd net-snmp-5.0.9** and pressing **Enter**.

19. Run the configure script by typing **./configure** and pressing **Enter**. You will be prompted with a series of questions for the configuration. Accept the defaults by pressing **Enter**.

20. Run the make utility by typing **make** and pressing **Enter**.

21. Type **su root** and press **Enter**. Enter the password for root and press **Enter**.

22. Type **make install** and press **Enter**.

23. Net-SNMP installation is complete. Log out from the root user mode by typing **exit** and pressing **Enter**. Next is GNU adns; return to the /tmp directory by typing **cd /tmp** and pressing **Enter**.

24. Extract the GNU adns tarball by typing **tar −xvf /mnt/cdrom/ adns/adns.tar** and pressing **Enter**.

25. Change to the new directory by typing **cd adns-1.1** and pressing **Enter**.

26. Run the configure script by typing **./configure** and pressing **Enter**.

27. Run the make utility by typing **make** and pressing **Enter**.

28. Type **su root** and press **Enter**. Enter the password for root and press **Enter**.

29. Type **make install** and press **Enter**.

30. GNU adns installation is complete. Log out from the root user mode by typing **exit** and pressing **Enter**. Next is Zlib, return to the /tmp directory by typing **cd /tmp** and pressing **Enter**.

31. Extract the Zlib tarball by typing **tar −xvf /mnt/cdrom/zlib/ zlib-1.1.4.tar** and pressing **Enter**.

32. Change to the new directory by typing **cd zlib-1.1.4** and press **Enter**.

33. Run the configure script by typing **./configure** and pressing **Enter**.

34. Run the make utility by typing **make** and pressing **Enter**.

35. Type **su root** and press **Enter**. Enter the password for root and press **Enter**.

36. Type **make install** and press **Enter**.

37. Zlib installation is complete. Log out from the root user mode by typing **exit** and pressing **Enter**. Next, we will perform the Perl installation. Return to the /tmp directory by typing **cd /tmp** and pressing **Enter**.

38. Extract the Perl tarball by typing **tar –xvf /mnt/cdrom/perl/ perl-5.8.1.tar** and pressing **Enter**.

39. Change to the new directory by typing **cd perl-5.8.1** and pressing **Enter**.

40. The INSTALL file in the /perl-5.8.1 directory gave some specific instructions for building Perl that differ from what we have been doing. The first thing it asks us to do is to remove two files. Do this by typing **rm –f config.sh Policy.sh** and pressing **Enter**.

41. The INSTALL file also gives us a different command for running the configure script. Type **sh Configure –de** and press **Enter**.

42. Next, run the make utility as usual by typing **make** and pressing **Enter**.

43. The INSTALL file gives us another make command to run next, so type **make test** and press **Enter**.

44. Type **su root** and press **Enter**. Enter the password for root and press **Enter**.

45. Finally, type **make install** and press **Enter**.

46. Log out from the root user mode by typing **exit** and press **Enter**. Finally, we will finish up with the PCRE installation. Return to the /tmp directory by typing **cd /tmp** and pressing **Enter**.

47. Extract the PCRE tarball by typing **tar –xvf /mnt/cdrom/ pcre/pcre-4.5.tar** and pressing **Enter**.

48. Change to the new directory by typing **cd pcre-4.5** and press **Enter**.

49. Run the configure script by typing **./configure** and pressing **Enter**.

50. Run the make utility by typing **make** and pressing **Enter**.

51. Type **su root** and press **Enter**. Enter the password for root and press **Enter**.

52. Type **make install** and press **Enter**. Log out from the root user mode by typing **exit** and press **Enter**.

Whew! That was a long process, but at least now we are up to date on all of our dependencies. Now we can get to the best part, building Ethereal!

The following output shows the whole process of extracting and installing the Ethereal source code dependencies. We have removed all of the output for brevity:

```
[testuser@localhost testuser]$ cd /tmp
[testuser@localhost tmp]$ tar -xvf /mnt/cdrom/gtk+_glib/glib-2.2.0.tar
[testuser@localhost tmp]$ cd glib-2.2.0
[testuser@localhost glib-2.2.0]$ ./configure
[testuser@localhost glib-2.2.0]$ make
[testuser@localhost glib-2.2.0]$ su root
Password: <password>
[root@localhost glib-2.2.0]# make install
[root@localhost glib-2.2.0]# exit
[testuser@localhost glib-2.2.0]$ cd /tmp
[testuser@localhost tmp]$ tar -xvf /mnt/cdrom/gtk+_glib/gtk+-2.2.0.tar
[testuser@localhost tmp]$ cd gtk+-2.2.0
[testuser@localhost gtk+-2.2.0]$ ./configure
[testuser@localhost gtk+-2.2.0]$ make
[testuser@localhost gtk+-2.2.0]$ su root
Password: <password>
[root@localhost gtk+-2.2.0]# make install
[root@localhost gtk+-2.2.0]# exit
[testuser@localhost gtk+-2.2.0]$ cd /tmp
[testuser@localhost tmp]$ tar -xvf /mnt/cdrom/snmp/net-snmp-5.0.9.tar
[testuser@localhost tmp]$ cd net-snmp-5.0.9
[testuser@localhost net-snmp-5.0.9]$ ./configure
[testuser@localhost net-snmp-5.0.9]$ make
[testuser@localhost net-snmp-5.0.9]$ su root
Password: <password>
[root@localhost net-snmp-5.0.9]# make install
[root@localhost net-snmp-5.0.9]# exit
[testuser@localhost net-snmp-5.0.9]$ cd /tmp
[testuser@localhost tmp]$ tar -xvf /mnt/cdrom/adns/adns.tar
[testuser@localhost tmp]$ cd adns-1.1
```

```
[testuser@localhost adns-1.1]$ ./configure
[testuser@localhost adns-1.1]$ make
[testuser@localhost adns-1.1]$ su root
Password: <password>
[root@localhost adns-1.1]# make install
[root@localhost adns-1.1]# exit
[testuser@localhost adns-1.1]$ cd /tmp
[testuser@localhost tmp]$ tar -xvf /mnt/cdrom/zlib/zlib-1.1.4.tar
[testuser@localhost tmp]$ cd zlib-1.1.4
[testuser@localhost zlib-1.1.4]$ ./configure
[testuser@localhost zlib-1.1.4]$ make
[testuser@localhost zlib-1.1.4]$ su root
Password: <password>
[root@localhost zlib-1.1.4]# make install
[root@localhost zlib-1.1.4]# exit
[testuser@localhost zlib-1.1.4]$ cd /tmp
[testuser@localhost tmp]$ tar -xvf /mnt/cdrom/perl/perl-5.8.1.tar
[testuser@localhost tmp]$ cd perl-5.8.1
[testuser@localhost perl-5.8.1]$ rm -f config.sh Policy.sh
[testuser@localhost perl-5.8.1]$ sh Configure -de
[testuser@localhost perl-5.8.1]$ make
[testuser@localhost perl-5.8.1]$ make test
[testuser@localhost perl-5.8.1]$ su root
Password: <password>
[root@localhost perl-5.8.1]# make install
[root@localhost perl-5.8.1]# exit
[testuser@localhost perl-5.8.1]$ cd /tmp
[testuser@localhost tmp]$ tar -xvf /mnt/cdrom/pcre/pcre-4.5.tar
[testuser@localhost tmp]$ cd pcre-4.5
[testuser@localhost pcre-4.5]$ ./configure
[testuser@localhost pcre-4.5]$ make
[testuser@localhost pcre-4.5]$ su root
Password: <password>
[root@localhost pcre-4.5]# make install
[root@localhost pcre-4.5]# exit
```

Building Ethereal

Now, onto the best part of all. Luckily, building Ethereal is a much shorter process than compiling all of those dependencies. However, installing the dependencies is what makes this process run much smoother. The Ethereal source code version of 0.10.0 was repackaged as version 0.10.0a due to some problems with the help files. We have included this version of Ethereal on the accompanying CD-ROM. Remember, there might be newer versions that have been released since the writing of this book, and you can download the latest versions from the local archive at www.ethereal.com.

1. Open a terminal window by right-clicking the **desktop** and choosing **New Terminal**.

2. Change directories to **/tmp** by typing **cd /tmp** and pressing **Enter**.

3. Extract the Ethereal tarball by typing **tar –xvf /mnt/cdrom/ethereal/source/ethereal-0.10.0a.tar** and pressing **Enter**. This will create a new directory in **/tmp** called **ethereal-0.10.0a**.

4. Change directories by typing **cd ethereal-0.10.0a** and pressing **Enter**.

5. Run the configure script by typing **./configure —enable-gtk2** and pressing **Enter**. By default, Ethereal does not compile with GTK+ version 2 library, which is why we needed to give it the optional parameter. At the end of the configure script output, you will see a summary of the options. These can be changed by using specific parameters with the configure script, and is discussed in section "Enabling and Disabling features via *configure*".

6. When the *configure* process is complete and the command prompt is displayed, make sure that there are no errors. If everything appears trouble-free, run the *make* utility simply by typing **make** and pressing **Enter**.

7. If the *make* utility completed without errors, type **su root** and press **Enter**. Enter the password for root and press **Enter**.

8. Next, type **make install** and press **Enter**.

9. After the *make install* process completes, the command prompt will be displayed once again. If everything looks error-free, you are done! Ethereal installs in /usr/local/bin, but this should be in your path already, so go ahead and type **ethereal** to run it.

The following output shows the whole process of extracting and installing the Ethereal source code. We have removed all of the output for brevity:

```
[testuser@localhost testuser]$ cd /tmp
[testuser@localhost tmp]$ tar -xvf /mnt/cdrom/ethereal/source/ethereal-
0.10.0a.tar
[testuser@localhost tmp]$ cd ethereal-0.10.0a
[testuser@localhost ethereal-0.10.0a]$ ./configure --enable-gtk2 The
Ethereal package has been configured with the following options.
                    Build ethereal : yes
                   Build tethereal : yes
                     Build editcap : yes
                    Build mergecap : yes
                   Build text2pcap : yes
                     Build idl2eth : yes
                     Build randpkt : no
                      Build dftest : no

                     Install setuid : no
                       Use plugins : yes
              Use GTK+ v2 library : yes
                       Use threads : no
             Build profile binaries : no
                  Use pcap library : yes
                  Use zlib library : yes
                  Use pcre library : yes
              Use GNU ADNS library : yes
          Use IPv6 name resolution : yes
      Use UCD SNMP/NET-SNMP library : yes (net-snmp)
[testuser@localhost ethereal-0.10.0a]$ make
[testuser@localhost ethereal-0.10.0a]$ su root
Password:
[root@localhost ethereal-0.10.0a]# make install
[root@localhost ethereal-0.10.0a]# exit
```

After running **./configure**, you will see a summary of some of the options you chose, indirectly or directly. Ensure that the summary reflects what you want. If it doesn't, re-run **./configure** with new options. The following section goes into more detail on the configure script's optional parameters.

NOTE

There are three programs listed in the configure output that you may not be familiar with, the first of which is configured by default. They are each very useful when you are developing for Ethereal, but you don't need to them just to use it. The idl2eth program is used by developers to convert a CORBA Interface Definition Language (IDL) file to C source code for an Ethereal plugin. The randpkt program is used to generate random packet capture files. It can generate 17 different types of packets with user specified maximum byte count and number of packets to create. Finally, the dftest program is a display filter compiler test program. It is used to show display filter byte-code for debugging dfilter routines.

Once the installation is complete the following programs are installed in /usr/local/bin: *ethereal, tethereal, editcap, mergecap, test2pcap,* and *idl2eth*. Plugins are installed in /usr/local/lib/ethereal/plugins/0.10.0a. Some important resources to note are the files in the /tmp/ethereal-0.10.0a/doc directory, they contain several good README files about the inner workings of Ethereal. There are also several helpful README files in the /tmp/ethereal-0.10.0a directory. Finally, the INSTALL and INSTALL.configure files located in /tmp/ethereal-0.10.0a are also a good resource.

NOTE

The *manuf* file is a text document, located in the /usr/local/share/ethereal directory, that contains a very large listing of well-known vendor MAC addresses. This can come in handy when troubleshooting network problems.

NOTE

The absolute latest version of Ethereal can be downloaded via the Concurrent Version System (CVS) daily snapshot. This is the version of Ethereal that the developers are currently working on, so you must be aware that this is a beta version that may contain bugs. The latest builds are available at www.ethereal.com/distribution/nightly-builds. To build the CVS version, you will also need the GNU autoconf, automake, libtool, and Perl. You may also need yacc or bison, python, and flex. You can find more information at www.ethereal.com/development.html.

Enabling and Disabling features via *configure*

During the *configure* script portion of the build process you can pass options to the installer to customize the application your specific needs. The following options were harvested from the INSTALL file in the Ethereal tarball. Since the tarball is included on your CD-ROM you can extract the archive at any time and have access to this file.

> **NOTE**
>
> Running *./configure —help* will give you information on the optional parameters, plus a whole lot more!

- *--sysconfdir=DIR* Ethereal installs a support file (manuf) in ${PREFIX}/etc by default, where ${PREFIX} comes from — prefix=DIR. If you do not specify any —prefix option, ${PREFIX} is "/usr/local". You can change the location of the manuf file with the **–sysconfdir** option.

- *--disable-usr-local* By default configure will look in /usr/local/{include,lib} for additional header files and libraries. Using this switch keeps configure from looking there.

- *--disable-ethereal* By default, if configure finds the GTK+ libraries, the Makefile builds Ethereal, the GUI packet analyzer. You can disable the build of the GUI version of Ethereal with this switch.

- *--enable-gtk2* Build Glib2/Gtk2+-based ethereal.

- *--disable-tethereal* By default the line-mode packet analyzer, Tethereal, is built. Use this switch to avoid building it.

- *--disable-editcap* By default the capture-file editing program is built. Use this switch to avoid building it.

- *--disable-mergecap* By default the capture-file merging program is built. Use this switch to avoid building it.

- *--disable-text2pcap* By default the hex-dump-to-capture file conversion program is built. Use this switch to avoid building it.

- *--disable-idl2eth* By default the IDL-to-ethereal-dissector-source-code converter is built. Use this switch to avoid building it.

- **--enable-dftest** By default the display-filter-compiler test program is not built. Use this switch to build it.

- **--enable-randpkt** By default the program that creates random packet-capture files is not built. Use this switch to build it.

- **--without-pcap** If you choose to build a packet analyzer that can analyze capture files but cannot capture packets on its own, but you *do* have libpcap installed, or if you are trying to build Ethereal on a system that doesn't have libpcap installed (in which case you have no choice but to build a version that can analyze capture files but cannot capture packets on its own), use this option to avoid using libpcap.

- **--with-pcap=DIR** Use this to tell Ethereal where you have libpcap installed, if it is installed in a non-standard location.

- **--without-zlib** By default, if configure finds zlib (a.k.a, libz), the wiretap library will be built so that it can read compressed capture files. If you have zlib but do not wish to build it into the wiretap library, used by Ethereal, Tethereal, and the capture-file utilities that come in this package, use this switch.

- **--with-zlib=DIR** Use this to tell Ethereal where you have zlib installed, if it is installed in a non-standard location.

- **--disable-ipv6** If configure finds support for IPv6 name resolution on your system, the packet analyzers will make use of it. To avoid using IPv6 name resolution if you have the support for it, use this switch.

- **--enable-setuid-install** Use this switch to install the packet analyzers as setuid. Installing Ethereal and Tethereal as setuid 'root' is dangerous. Repeat: IT'S DANGEROUS. Don't do it.

- **--with-ssl=DIR** If your SNMP library requires the SSL library, and your SSL library is installed in a non-standard location, you can specify where your SSL library is with this switch.

- **--without-net-snmp** If configure finds a supported version of the Net SNMP library on your system, the SNMP dissector will be enhanced to use routines from that SNMP library. Use this switch to avoid using the Net SNMP library even if you have it installed.

- ***--with-net-snmp=PATH*** Tell the configure script where your net-snmp-config shell script that comes with the Net-SNMP package is located, if not in a standard location.

- ***--without-ucd-snmp*** If configure finds a supported version of the UCD SNMP library on your system, the SNMP dissector will be enhanced to use routines from that SNMP library. Use this switch to avoid using the UCD SNMP library even if you have it installed.

- ***--with-ucd-snmp=DIR*** Tell the configure script where your UCD SNMP library is located, if not in a standard location.

- ***--without-plugins*** By default, if your system can support run-time loadable modules, the packet analyzers are build with support for plugins. Use this switch to build packet analyzers without plugin support.

- ***--with-plugins=DIR*** By default, plugins are installed in ${LIBDIR}/ethereal/plugins/${VERSION}. ${LIBDIR} can be set with --libdir, or defaults to ${EPREFIX/lib}. ${EPREFIX} can be set with --exec-prefix, or defaults to ${PREFIX}. ${VERSION} is the Ethereal version. Use this switch to change the location where plugins are installed.

Summary

In this chapter, we covered the basics of package management, including RPM, Solaris, and source code packages. We also covered complete installations of the libpcap and WinPcap libraries, and Ethereal for UNIX-based and Windows systems. We also learned how to install the necessary prerequisite software, and troubleshoot dependency issues. You are now armed with the knowledge and software necessary to continue with this book.

As stated previously in this chapter, it is important to keep your Ethereal installation up to date. This includes the packet capture libraries, the supporting prerequisite software, and the Ethereal software itself. You should also visit the Ethereal site frequently to keep up on the latest announcements, as well as subscribing to some of the mailing lists. Computer security is an ever-changing technology, and it is necessary to keep up with things to avoid system compromises.

We also strongly recommend that you keep your OS up to date as well, especially when it comes to security updates and patches. Windows makes this easy through the Windows Update interface. Red Hat Linux also has the option for Red Hat Network (RHN) updates. Solaris 9.0 contains a new feature called Patch Manager that provides automatic patch inventory and configuration-based analysis of systems.

All of these parts will come together to form a solid network analysis system that will assist your network troubleshooting and security efforts for years to come.

Solutions Fast Track

Getting Ethereal

☑ Ethereal can be downloaded as binaries or source code.

☑ There are Ethereal binaries available for more than twenty platforms.

☑ Ethereal source compiling prerequisites include libpcap, GTK+, Glib, Zlib, Perl, Net-SNMP, and GNU adns.

Packet Capture Drivers

☑ Packet capture drivers are responsible for capturing the raw network packets.

☑ Libpcap is a packet capture library for UNIX systems; Windows uses WinPcap.

☑ Sometimes RPMs are a version or two behind the current source code release.

☑ Ethereal must have libpcap (or WinPcap) installed to capture packets.

☑ Libpcap can be installed from a binary or source code.

☑ Uninstall older versions of WinPcap before installing newer ones.

Installing Ethereal on Windows

☑ Ethereal will install without WinPcap but can only be used to read saved capture files.

☑ Uninstall Ethereal by using the *uninstall.exe* program.

☑ Ethereal for Windows also installs tethereal, editcap, mergcap, and text2pcap.

Installing Ethereal on UNIX

☑ There are several different versions of Ethereal RPMs, each with a different purpose.

☑ The base Ethereal package does not install the Ethereal GUI program, you need to install the GTK+ RPM in addition to the base.

☑ The Solaris *pkgadd* process is much like the RPM process.

Building Ethereal from Source

☑ Source code installs are accomplished with the **configure | make | make install** process.

☑ Installing from source code gives you more control over the installation process.

☑ Installing from source gives you access to the source code and additional documentation.

☑ Ethereal installs by default in the /usr/local/bin directory.

☑ There are many options to the configure script to customize your install.

Frequently Asked Questions

The following Frequently Asked Questions, answered by the authors of this book, are designed to both measure your understanding of the concepts presented in this chapter and to assist you with real-life implementation of these concepts. To have your questions about this chapter answered by the author, browse to **www.syngress.com/solutions** and click on the **"Ask the Author"** form. You will also gain access to thousands of other FAQs at ITFAQnet.com.

Q: Can I mix methods of installation? For example, can I install libpcap with the RPM and then build Ethereal from source, or vice-versa?

A: Yes you can, as long as your OS supports the methods you are trying to use. For example, you can't use *pkgadd* on Linux.

Q: What if I installed Ethereal and then later upgraded to GTK+ v2?

A: No problem, just re-run the *configure* script for Ethereal with --**enable-gtk2** and then run **make** and **make install** again.

Q: A new version of Ethereal was released and I want to upgrade, how do I do that?

A: For Linux, you would use the **rpm –Uvh** command. For Solaris you would use the **pkgrm** command to remove the old version, then **pkgadd** to add to the new version. For Windows, simply run the new executable and it will upgrade your current version. If you have compiled the code from source you will need to perform the **configure | make | make install** process again for the new version.

Q: A new version of WinPcap was released, how do I upgrade to it?

A: First go to the directory with your current version of WinPcap (usually C:\Program Files\WinPcap) and run the *uninstall.exe* program. Reboot and proceed with installing the executable for the new version.

Q: I installed everything and it looks like it worked ok, but when I try to run Ethereal it says it can't find it?

A: Make sure the Ethereal directory is in the proper path, for example, */usr/local/bin*. Also, if you are installing the Linux RPMs, make sure you install the GTK+ version as well as the base version.

Q: Why do I have to install all this other stuff just to compile Ethereal?

A: Ethereal is a feature-rich, multi-faceted software program. It relies on the details of some previously written libraries to take care of the low level functions.

Q: I got really excited and installed Ethereal on my Windows system without installing WinPcap first. What should I do?

A: The Windows version of Ethereal can detect the presence of WinPcap at run time, so go ahead and install the current version of WinPcap and then run Ethereal.

Chapter 4

Using Ethereal

Solutions in this Chapter:

- Getting Started with Ethereal
- Exploring the Main Window
- Other Window Components
- Exploring the Menus
- Using Command Line Options

☑ Summary

☑ Solutions Fast Track

☑ Frequently Asked Questions

Introduction

Ethereal is an invaluable tool for providing insight into what is really happening on your network. This kind of insight is useful when implementing protocols, debugging network applications, testing networks, or trying to debug live networks. In almost any situation that involves interaction with the network at a technical level you can enhance your understanding of your problem by using Ethereal to see what is really going on.

Ethereal is also an excellent pedagogical aid. Being able to see and analyze actual network traffic is extremely instructive. It's one thing to read about the functioning of a protocol, it's quite another to be able to watch it in action and explore how it's really operating

This chapter covers the main components of the Ethereal Graphical User Interface (GUI). These parts are the Main Window and it's subcomponents the Menu Bar, Tool Bar, Summary Window, Protocol Tree Window, Data View Window, Filter Bar, and Information field. This chapter will also cover use of the context-sensitive pop-up windows available in the Summary Window, Protocol Tree Window, and Data View Window, and will also explain the various dialog boxes that are launched by the menus and toolbars.

You will learn how to perform basic tasks in Ethereal such as capturing network traffic, loading and saving capture files, performing basic filtering, printing packets, and using some of the more involved tools provided by Ethereal. Examples have been provided to show you step-by-step how some of the less obvious areas of Ethereal work.

All of the screenshots for this chapter were taken on Linux, and so they may look slightly different in terms of fonts or window decorations than the screenshots in some of the other chapters in this book, which were taken on Windows.

Getting Started with Ethereal

In order to use Ethereal you must first acquire Ethereal and install it. If you are running a Linux distribution it is likely that your distribution shipped with Ethereal. If you are running Windows or some version of UNIX (Solaris, HP-UX, AIX, etc) you will have to download Ethereal and install it.

You can download binary packages for Ethereal from the Ethereal website at www.ethereal.com. If there are no binary packets there for your platform, if they are not up to date, or compiled without options you need, you may download the source code from the Ethereal website and compile Ethereal yourself. Installing Ethereal is covered in detail in Chapter 3.

You may also wish to download the bgp.pcap.gz capture at www.ethereal.com/sample/bgp.pcap.gz, as it is used in many examples in this chapter. You can follow along through the examples with your own copy of Ethereal. Once you have installed Ethereal on the computer you wish to capture with, execute at the command line:

```
ethereal.
```

To launch Ethereal on Windows, select **Start | Programs | Ethereal | Ethereal**. The Main Window of the Ethereal application will now be displayed.

Exploring the Main Window

It is important for us to define a common set of labels for the different components of the Main Window so that we can speak clearly about them. Figure 4.1 shows the Main Window of Ethereal with its major components labeled.

Figure 4.1 Main Window

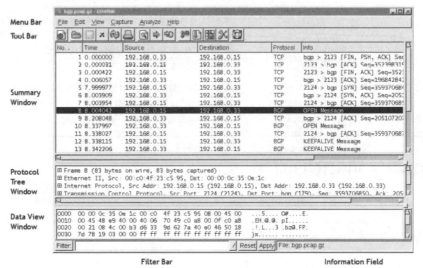

The Main Window components are described in Table 4.1:

Table 4.1 Main Window Components

Window Component	Description
Menu Bar	A typical application menu bar containing drop-down menu items.
Tool Bar	A toolbar containing buttons for some commonly used functions of Ethereal. The Tool Bar icons have tool tips that are displayed when you pause the mouse pointer over them.
Summary Window	A window providing a one-line summary for each packet in the capture.
Protocol Tree Window	A window providing a detailed decode of the packet selected in the Summary Window.
Data View Window	A window providing a view of the raw data in the packet selected in the Summary Window.
Filter Bar	A tool for applying filters to the Summary Window to restrict which packets in the capture are displayed, based upon their attributes.
Information Field	A small display area to provide information about the capture or field selected in the Protocol Tree Window.

Summary Window

The Summary Window displays a summary of each packet in the capture, one per line. One or more columns of summary data for each packet will be displayed. Typical columns are shown in Table 4.2.

Table 4.2 Summary Window Columns

Column Name	Description
No.	Frame number within the capture.
Time	The time from beginning of the capture to the time when the packet was captured (in seconds).
Source	Highest level source address. This will frequently be the IP (Internet Protocol) source address, but may also be the Media Access Control (MAC) address for layer 2 (L2) Ethernet protocols (see the Ethereal Name Resolution sidebar for a discussion of MAC addresses), or other address types for other protocols (IPX, AppleTalk, etc).
Destination	Highest level destination address. This will frequently be the IP destination address, but may also be the MAC address for L2 Ethernet protocols, or other address types for other protocols (IPX, AppleTalk, etc).
Protocol	Typically the highest level protocol decoded. Examples include user level protocols such as HyperText Transfer Protocol (HTTP), File Transfer Protocol (FTP), Simple Mail Transfer Protocol (SMTP).
Info	This field contains information that was determined by the highest level decode to be useful or informative as part of a summary for this packet.

You can use the Preferences feature to select which columns are displayed in the Summary Window (select **Edit | Preferences** from the Menu Bar).

The summary information for the packet selected in the Summary Window in Figure 4.1 is shown in Table 4.3.

Table 4.3 Summary Window Column Example

Column Name	Value
No.	8
Time	8.004042 seconds since the capture started
Source	IP number 192.168.0.15
Destination	IP number 192.168.0.33

Continued

Table 4.3 Summary Window Column Example

Column Name	Value
Protocol	BGP (Border Gateway Protocol)
Info	OPEN Message

We can immediately see that this is a packet carrying a message for opening a Border Gateway Protocol session between 192.168.0.15 and 192.168.0.33. More information on Border Gateway Protocol is available in RFC (Request for Comment) 1771 at www.ietf.org/rfc/rfc1771.txt?number=1771. RFCs are the documents that describe the protocols in use on the Internet. Many RFCs define protocol standards (although not all RFCs do).

You can select packets in the Summary Window by clicking on the row summarizing a given packet. The information for the selected packet will then be displayed in the Protocol Tree Window and the Data View Window. Once you have selected a packet in the Summary Window you can use the Protocol Tree Window to drill down into it in greater detail.

Protocol Tree Window

We can conceptualize a packet as a tree of fields and subtrees. For each protocol there is a tree node summarizing the protocol, which can be expanded to provide the values in that protocol's fields. Within some protocols there may be tree nodes summarizing more complicated data structures in the protocol. These tree nodes can be expanded to show those data structures. For any given node that has a subtree, we can expand it's subtree to reveal more information, or collapse it to only show the summary. The Protocol Tree Window allows you to examine the tree created by Ethereal from decoding a packet.

We'll take a moment now to drill down through the Protocol Tree Window into the packet we selected in the previous example (Figure 4.2).

Figure 4.2 Protocol Tree Window Collapsed

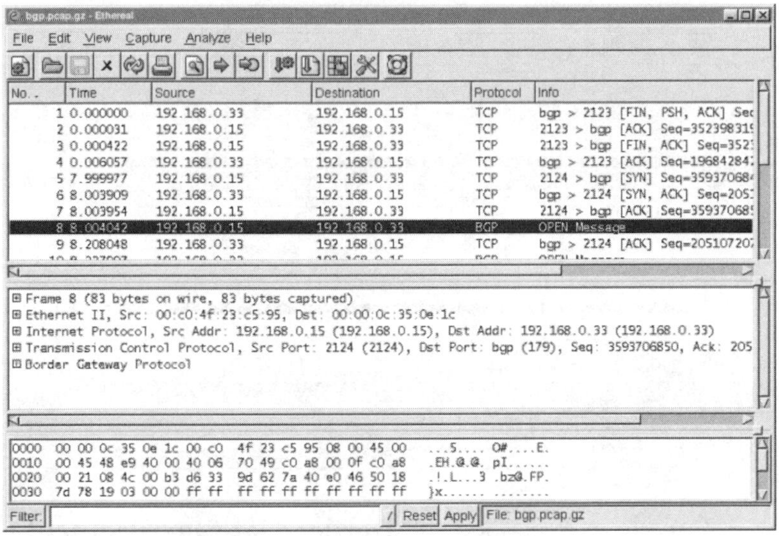

In the Protocol Tree Window, you can see that for each layer in the protocol stack for this packet we have a one-line summary of that layer (see Table 4.4).

Table 4.4 Protocol Layer Example

Layer	Protocol	Description
Packet Meta Data	Frame	83 bytes on wire, 83 bytes captured
Datalink (Layer 2/L2)	Ethernet II	Src Addr: 00:c0:4f:23:c5:95, Dst Addr: 00:00:0c:35:0e:1c
Network (Layer 3 / L3)	Internet Protocol (IP)	Src Addr: 192.168.0.15, Dst Addr: 192.168.0.33
Transport (Layer 4/ L4)	Transmission Control Protocol (TCP)	Src Port: 2124, Dst Port: bgp(179), Seq: 2593706850, Ack …
Application Layer (Layer 7 /L7)	Border Gateway Protocol (BGP)	

Each of these layers have little boxed plus (+) signs next to them indicating that they have a subtree that can be expanded to provide more information about that particular protocol.

Figure 4.3 Protocol Tree Window Expanded

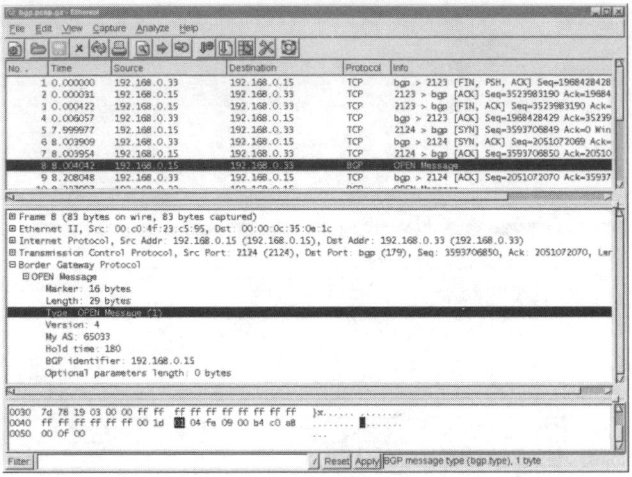

In Figure 4.3, we have expanded the **Border Gateway Protocol** tree to reveal that it contains one **OPEN Message**, and further expanded that **OPEN Message** to reveal the fields contained within it.

By selecting the **Type** field in the Protocol Tree Window, we've caused the **Information** field in the lower right corner to display the message *BGP message type (bgp.type), 1byte*. This indicates the long name of this field (*BGP message type*) and the display filter field name used to identify this field for filtering and colorization (*bgp.type*), as well as the size of this field in the packet (*1 byte*).

Data View Window

The Data View Window contains a series of rows, as show in Figure 4.4. Each row begins with a four-digit number representing the number of bytes the first octet (an octet is eight bits or one byte or two hexadecimal – also known as *hex* – digits) in that row is offset from the beginning of the packet. This offset is then followed by sixteen two-character hexadecimal bytes. The last item in each row is a series of sixteen ASCII (American Standard Code for Information Interchange, a common character encoding) characters representing the same 16 bytes from the packet. Not all bytes are conveniently displayable in ASCII. For those bytes a period (.) is substituted as a placeholder.

Figure 4.4 Data View Window

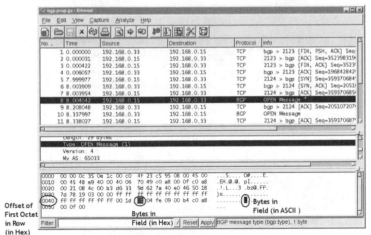

When a field in the Protocol Tree Window is selected, the bytes corresponding to that field are highlighted in the Data View Window. In our example we have selected the **BGP message type** field in the Protocol Tree Window. In the Data View Window we find that byte highlighted in the row with offset 0040 representing 0x40 hex or 64 bytes into the packet. The ninth byte in the row is highlighted, and has a value of 01 hex. In the ASCII representation we have a period (.) because the value 0x01 is not conveniently represented in ASCII.

When you click on a hex byte or ASCII character in the Data View Window, Ethereal will highlight the field in the Protocol Tree Window corresponding to the selected byte, and all bytes in the Data View Window associated with that **Protocol** field.

In Figure 4.5 we've clicked on the 7d at the beginning of row 0030. It just so happens that the 48th byte (0030 or hex 0x30) is the first byte of the two-byte Transmission Control Protocol (TCP) **Window Size** field. As a result, the TCP tree was automatically expanded and the **Window size** field was highlighted. Additionally the second byte, with value 78 hex, in the 0030 row, was also selected, since TCP Window Size is a two-byte field.

This feature of Ethereal makes it very easy to use the Protocol Tree Window and the Data View Window together to obtain a solid grasp of the relationships between the fields in a protocol and the actual bits on the wire.

Figure 4.5 Data View Window Byte Selection

Other Window Components

Filter Bar

The Filter Bar (Figure 4.6) allows you to enter a filter string restricting which packets are displayed in the Summary Window. Only packets that match the display filter string will be displayed in the Summary Window. A display filter string is a string defining some conditions on a packet that may or may not match a packet. For example, the display filter string *(ip.addr == 10.15.162.1 && bgp)* would match all packets with an IP address (source or destination) of 10.15.162.1 that are BGP protocol packets. Filtering will be explored in much greater depth in Chapter 5, but we will examine the basic functions of the Filter Bar briefly here.

Figure 4.6 Filter Bar

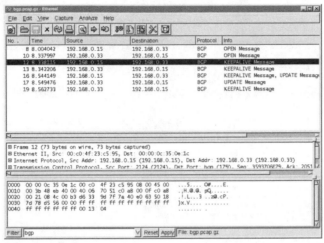

You can see in Figure 4.6 that we have applied a **bgp** filter. To apply a filter, enter the desired string into the **Filter:** text field and press **Enter** (or click the **Apply** button). Please note that your filter string will not be applied until you hit **Enter** or click the **Apply** button. In addition, note that filter strings are case-sensitive and the filter string **BGP** (uppercase) will not work. Traditionally, filter string labels like **bgp** are entirely in lowercase.

Once the display filter string **bgp** is applied, you will note that only BGP packets are displayed in the Summary Window. You should also note that the **No.** column displays jumps between the frame numbers of the displayed packets. This is because there are packets in the capture that are not being displayed, but are rather being suppressed by the **bgp** filter string. Previously used filters can be easily recalled, as shown in Figure 4.7.

Figure 4.7 Filter Bar Drop-down List

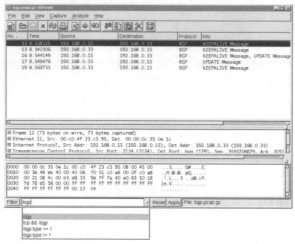

By clicking the drop-down arrow at the right end of the **Filter** field, you can access a list of previously applied filters. To use one of these filters, select it from the list and press **Enter** or click the **Apply** button.

To remove the currently displayed filter string and re-display all packets, click the **Reset** button.

If you click the **Filter:** button itself, the Display Filter dialog box will be displayed. This feature is described in the section entitled "Analyze".

Information Field

The **Information** field displays the name of the capture file or information about the protocol field selected in the Protocol Tree Window.

Exploring the Menus

All of the functionality available within Ethereal is accessible from the Menu Bar. In this section we will systematically explore that functionality and provide examples of its use.

File

The **File** menu provides access to loading, saving and printing capture files, as seen in Figure 4.8. **File** menu options are defined in Table 4.5.

Figure 4.8 File Menu

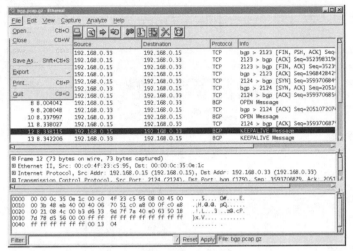

Table 4.5 File Menu Options

Menu Option	Description
Open…	Open a capture file.
Close	Close the current capture file.
Save	Save the current capture file.
Save As…	Save the current capture file with a different file-name/format.
Export	Display the **Export** submenu allowing the portion of the packet highlighted in the Data View Window to be exported as a hexadecimal dump.
Print…	Print the current capture file.
Quit	Quit the Ethereal application.

Open

To open a file (Figure 4.9), select **File | Open**.

Figure 4.9 Open Dialog Box

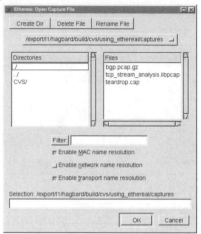

The Open dialog box provides normal mechanisms for navigation in selecting a file. Additionally, it provides a **Filter:** field where an Ethereal display filter string can be entered to filter which packets are read from the capture file. Clicking the **Filter:** button will open the Display Filter dialog box. The Display Filter dialog box is described in the section entitled "Analyze".

The Open dialog box also has checkboxes to enable name resolution for MAC addresses, network names, and transport names. To open a file, browse to the correct location and select the desired file, optionally provide a filter string, and enable or disable the name resolutions you wish to use. Finally, click the **OK** button.

Notes from the Underground...

Ethereal Name Resolution

Ethereal provides three kinds of name resolution to make some of the numbers found in network protocols more comprehensible. You can choose to enable or disable MAC name resolution, network name resolution, and transport name resolution, when opening a file, starting a capture, or while a capture is running. It is useful to understand what the different name resolutions mean.

Every host on a LAN is identified by a unique six-byte MAC address. These addresses are used in Ethernet frames to provide source and destination addresses at the Datalink Layer. MAC addresses are supposed to be globally unique. To achieve this end the IEEE (Institute of Electrical and Electronic Engineers), assigns blocks of MAC addresses to manufacturers. The first three bytes of every MAC address designate the manufacturer who produced the device. Ethereal is shipped with a list of the assigned prefixes and the manufacturers to whom they've been assigned. When you select the **Enable MAC name resolution** checkbox in the Open dialog box, Ethereal will resolve the first three bytes of the MAC address to a manufacturer and display that information for each MAC address. For example the prefix 00:00:0c has been assigned to Cisco Systems. When MAC address resolution is enabled Ethereal will display the MAC address *00:00:0c:35:0e 1c* as *00:00:0c:35:0e:1c (Cisco_35:0e:1c)*.

Every node on an IP network has an IP address. If you select the **Enable network name resolution** checkbox Ethereal will perform a reverse Domain Name System (DNS) lookup when it encounters an IP address to determine its associated domain name (like www.syngress.com). Ethereal will then display this domain name with the IP address. For example, the IP address *66.35.250.150* can be resolved via reverse DNS to the domain name slashdot.org. If network name resolution is enabled, Ethereal will display it as *slashdot.org (66.35.250.150)*.

Transport layer protocols like TCP and UDP (User Datagram Protocol, a connectionless transport protocol over IP defined in RFC 768 and viewable at www.ietf.org/rfc/rfc0768.txt?number=768) typically provide some form of multiplexing by allowing a source and destination

Continued

port to be specified. As a result, two hosts can have multiple clearly delineated conversations between them at the same time, as long as they have unique source port/destination port pairs for each conversation. Many protocols that use TCP or UDP for their transport layer have well-known ports that servers for those protocols traditionally listen on. When you select the **Enable transport name resolution** checkbox, Ethereal will display the name of the service that traditionally runs over each port. This behavior can be seen in many of our examples, where the port *179* has been labeled by the protocol that is well known to run over that port: *bgp*. It's important to note that most ports have no protocols associated with them.

Save As

The Save As dialog box, shown in Figure 4.10, is displayed by selecting **File | Save As**, or by selecting **File | Save** for a capture that has not previously been saved to file.

Figure 4.10 Save As Dialog Box

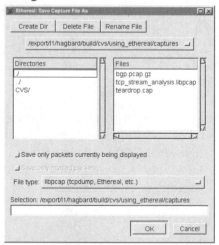

The Save As dialog box allows you to perform normal tasks for saving a capture file in the desired place and with the desired name. You can choose to save only the packets that pass the currently active display filter by enabling the **Save only packets currently being displayed** checkbox, or to save only marked packets by enabling the **Save only marked packets** checkbox. Marking packets will be explained later in the "Edit" section. Selecting both checkboxes will save only those marked packets that match the current display filter.

Finally, you can choose to save the file in one of a large number of supported capture file formats (Figure 4.11).

Figure 4.11 Save As Dialog: File Formats

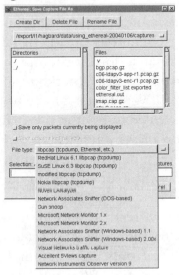

Print

The Print dialog box is displayed by selecting **File** | **Print** (Figure 4.12).

Figure 4.12 Print Dialog Box

The Print dialog box allows you to provide answers to the three questions relevant to printing in Ethereal:

1. How are you going to print?
2. Which packets are you going to print?
3. What information are you going to print for each packet?

The **Printer** section allows you to choose which packets you are going to print. You can choose as your output format either **Plain Text** or **Postscript**. Once you have selected your output format you may choose to print the output to a file by enabling the **Output to File:** checkbox and providing a filename in the **Output to File:** textbox. If you do not choose to print to file then you may provide a command to be executed to print in the **Print command:** textbox.

The **Print Range** section allows you to choose which packets you are going to print. You may choose to print only the packet currently selected in the Summary Window, only packets that are marked in the Summary Window (marked packets are discussed later in the "Edit" section), all packets displayed in the Summary Window by the currently applied filter, or all packets captured. You can choose to print only the packet currently selected in the Summary Window by selecting the **Selected packet only** radio button. To print only the packets that have been marked in the Summary Window, select the **Marked packets only** radio button. And, to print all packets displayed in the Summary Window by the currently applied display filter, selecting the **All packets displayed** radio button. Printing all packets displayed means that all packets that pass the currently applied filter will print, not just the packets that are currently visible in the Summary Window. If you are able to scroll up or down to a packet in the Summary Window, it is considered to be "displayed" for the purposes of this print range option. You can print all packets in the capture by selecting the **All packets captured** radio button.

The **Packet Format** section allows you to choose which information you are going to print for each packet. If you do not enable the **Print packet details** checkbox, then for each packet a one-line summary consisting of the columns currently being displayed in the Summary Window will be printed. Consider, for example, the state of Ethereal in Figure 4.3. Packet 8 is selected. If the **Print packet details** checkbox is unselected, the result of printing only the selected packet (packet 8) would be:

```
No. Time        Source        Destination    Protocol Info
  8 8.004042    192.168.0.15  192.168.0.33   BGP      OPEN Message
```

This output had some whitespace removed to contract it to fit the space. If you do enable the **Print packet details** checkbox, then more detailed information will be printed.

The **Details** section allows you to choose which details are printed for a packet when you have enabled the **Print packet details** checkbox. You may choose to print the protocol tree with all subtrees collapsed, the protocol tree with subtrees expanded (but only if those subtrees are expanded in the Protocol Tree Window), or with all subtrees in the protocol tree expanded. If you select the **All dissections collapsed** option, the protocol tree will be printed with all subtrees collapsed. For the situation shown in Figure 4.3, printing only the selected packet, the output would look like:

```
Frame 8 (83 bytes on wire, 83 bytes captured)

Ethernet II, Src: 00:c0:4f:23:c5:95, Dst: 00:00:0c:35:0e:1c

Internet Protocol, Src Addr: 192.168.0.15 (192.168.0.15), Dst Addr:
192.168.0.33 (192.168.0.33)

Transmission Control Protocol, Src Port: 2124 (2124), Dst Port: bgp (179),
Seq: 3593706850, Ack: 2051072070, Len: 29

Border Gateway Protocol
```

If you select the **Dissections as displayed** option, the protocol tree will be printed with those subtrees expanded that would be expanded in the Protocol Tree Window if that packet was selected in the Summary Window. Using this option to print only the selected packet from Figure 4.3 would produce output like:

```
Frame 8 (83 bytes on wire, 83 bytes captured)
Ethernet II, Src: 00:c0:4f:23:c5:95, Dst: 00:00:0c:35:0e:1c
Internet Protocol, Src Addr: 192.168.0.15 (192.168.0.15), Dst Addr:
192.168.0.33 (192.168.0.33)
Transmission Control Protocol, Src Port: 2124 (2124), Dst Port: bgp (179),
Seq: 3593706850, Ack: 2051072070, Len: 29
Border Gateway Protocol
    OPEN Message
        Marker: 16 bytes
        Length: 29 bytes
        Type: OPEN Message (1)
        Version: 4
        My AS: 65033
        Hold time: 180
```

```
    BGP identifier: 192.168.0.15

    Optional parameters length: 0 bytes
```

If you select the **All dissections expanded** option, the protocol tree will be printed with all subtrees expanded. Printing just the selected packet in Figure 4.8 with this option would produce the output:

```
Frame 8 (83 bytes on wire, 83 bytes captured)

    Arrival Time: Mar 29, 2000 23:56:56.957322000

    Time delta from previous packet: 0.000088000 seconds

    Time since reference or first frame: 8.004042000 seconds

    Frame Number: 8

    Packet Length: 83 bytes

    Capture Length: 83 bytes

Ethernet II, Src: 00:c0:4f:23:c5:95, Dst: 00:00:0c:35:0e:1c

    Destination: 00:00:0c:35:0e:1c (Cisco_35:0e:1c)

    Source: 00:c0:4f:23:c5:95 (DellComp_23:c5:95)

    Type: IP (0x0800)

Internet Protocol, Src Addr: 192.168.0.15 (192.168.0.15), Dst Addr:
192.168.0.33 (192.168.0.33)

    Version: 4

    Header length: 20 bytes

    Differentiated Services Field: 0x00 (DSCP 0x00: Default; ECN: 0x00)

        0000 00.. = Differentiated Services Codepoint: Default (0x00)

        .... ..0. = ECN-Capable Transport (ECT): 0

        .... ...0 = ECN-CE: 0

    Total Length: 69

    Identification: 0x48e9 (18665)

    Flags: 0x04

        .1.. = Don't fragment: Set

        ..0. = More fragments: Not set

    Fragment offset: 0

    Time to live: 64

    Protocol: TCP (0x06)

    Header checksum: 0x7049 (correct)

    Source: 192.168.0.15 (192.168.0.15)

    Destination: 192.168.0.33 (192.168.0.33)
```

```
Transmission Control Protocol, Src Port: 2124 (2124), Dst Port: bgp (179),
Seq: 3593706850, Ack: 2051072070, Len: 29
      Source port: 2124 (2124)
      Destination port: bgp (179)
      Sequence number: 3593706850
      Next sequence number: 3593706879
      Acknowledgement number: 2051072070
      Header length: 20 bytes
      Flags: 0x0018 (PSH, ACK)
            0... .... = Congestion Window Reduced (CWR): Not set
            .0.. .... = ECN-Echo: Not set
            ..0. .... = Urgent: Not set
            ...1 .... = Acknowledgment: Set
            .... 1... = Push: Set
            .... .0.. = Reset: Not set
            .... ..0. = Syn: Not set
            .... ...0 = Fin: Not set
      Window size: 32120
      Checksum: 0x1903 (correct)
Border Gateway Protocol
      OPEN Message
            Marker: 16 bytes
            Length: 29 bytes
            Type: OPEN Message (1)
            Version: 4
            My AS: 65033
            Hold time: 180
            BGP identifier: 192.168.0.15
            Optional parameters length: 0 bytes
```

Regardless of the option you choose for expanding protocol tree subtrees, if you enable the **Packet hex data** checkbox, following the protocol tree for each packet will be a hex dump of that packet. Printing only the packet selected in Figure 4.3, with the **All dissections collapsed** checkbox enabled and the **Packet hex data** checkbox enabled would produce this output:

```
Frame 8 (83 bytes on wire, 83 bytes captured)
Ethernet II, Src: 00:c0:4f:23:c5:95, Dst: 00:00:0c:35:0e:1c
```

```
Internet Protocol, Src Addr: 192.168.0.15 (192.168.0.15), Dst Addr:
192.168.0.33 (192.168.0.33)
Transmission Control Protocol, Src Port: 2124 (2124), Dst Port: bgp (179),
Seq: 3593706850, Ack: 2051072070, Len: 29
Border Gateway Protocol


0000   00 00 0c 35 0e 1c 00 c0 4f 23 c5 95 08 00 45 00    ...5....O#....E.
0010   00 45 48 e9 40 00 40 06 70 49 c0 a8 00 0f c0 a8    .EH.@.@.pI......
0020   00 21 08 4c 00 b3 d6 33 9d 62 7a 40 e0 46 50 18    .!.L...3.bz@.FP.
0030   7d 78 19 03 00 00 ff ff ff ff ff ff ff ff ff ff    }x.............
0040   ff ff ff ff ff ff 00 1d 01 04 fe 09 00 b4 c0 a8    ................
0050   00 0f 00                                           ...
```

Notes from the Underground…

Ghost of Ethereal Future: Print Dialog Improvements

Ethereal evolves very rapidly. It is not uncommon for there to be a new release of the software every four to six weeks. As a result, some things will change over time. An example of this is the Print dialog box, which has already been changed in CVS (Concurrent Version System, the source code control mechanism used by Ethereal) since the release of the 0.10.0a version of Ethereal (the latest release version as of the writing of this book). The new Print dialog box, which will likely be in Ethereal version 0.10.1, is shown in Figure 4.13

Continued

Figure 4.13 The New Print Dialog Box

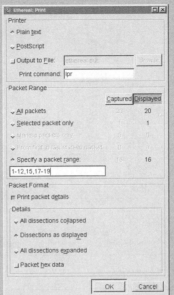

The **Packet Range** section has been rewritten to provide more options when selecting the range of packets to be printed. The **Captured** and **Displayed** buttons are used to determine whether the selection criteria apply to all packets captured or all packets displayed. There are also two new packet selection criteria, **From first to last marked packet**, which selects all packets between the first marked packet and the last marked packet, and **Specify a packet range**, which will allow you to specify a packet range like the one shown in Figure 4.13: *1-12,15,17,17-19*.

Edit

The Edit menu, shown in Figure 4.14, allows you to find and mark packets, as well as set user preferences. Descriptions of the Edit menu options are given in Table 4.6.

Figure 4.14 Edit Menu

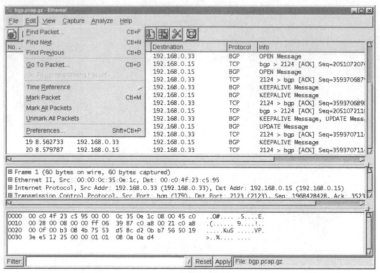

Table 4.6 Edit Menu Options

Menu Option	Description
Find Packet...	Search for a packet using a display filter or by searching for a matching hexadecimal string or character string.
Find Next	Find the next packet that matches the search defined in the Find Packet dialog box.
Find Previous	Find the previous packet that matches the search defined in the Find Packet dialog box.
Go To Packet...	Go to a packet by frame number.
Go To Corresponding Packet	When a field that refers to another frame is selected in the Protocol Tree Window, select the packet being referred to in the Summary Window.
Time Reference	A submenu for manipulating time references (for more details, see the section entitled "Time Reference Submenu".
Mark Packet	Mark the packet currently selected in the **Summary Window**. If the selected packet is already marked, then unmark it. Marking provides a mechanism for manually selecting a packet or group of packets to be subsequently printed or saved.

Continued

Table 4.6 Edit Menu Options

Menu Option	Description
Mark All Packets	Marks all packets that match the currently applied display filter.
Unmark All Packets	Unmark all packets that match the currently applied display filter.
Preferences...	Change user preferences, including preferences for packet decodes.

Find Packet

The Find Packet dialog box, show in Figure 4.15, is displayed when you select **Edit | Find Packet...**.

Figure 4.15 Find Packet Dialog Box

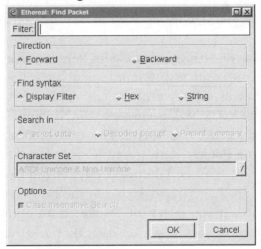

The Find Packet dialog box allows you to answer the three questions relevant to finding a packet in Ethereal:

1. What are we trying to find?
2. Which direction should we search in?
3. What type of thing are we trying to find?

The **Filter:** textbox allows you to define a search criteria by entering a string such as a display filter string, hex string, or ASCII string. If you need assistance constructing a filter string you can click the **Filter:** button to display the Display Filter dialog box. The Display Filter dialog box is described in more detail in the in the section entitled "Analyze".

The **Direction** section allows you to choose which direction you wish to search in–**Forward** from the packet currently selected in the Summary Window, or **Backward** from the packet currently selected in the Summary Window.

The **Find Syntax** section allows you define your search criteria. You may choose to search for packets that match a display filter string, packets that contain a hex string, or packets that contain a character string. If you select the **Display Filter** option, the string in the **Filter:** textbox will be interpreted as a display filter string and you will search for matches to that display filter string. If you select the **Hex** option, the string in the **Filter:** textbox will be interpreted as a hex string and you will search for packets that contain that hex string.

If you select the **String** option, the string in the **Filter:** will be interpreted as a character string and you will search for packets that contain that character string.

The search for character strings is handled differently than the search for hex strings. Hexadecimal string searches attempt to search for a packet containing a particular sequence of bytes anywhere in the raw data of that packet. The search for character strings will not look for a packet that contains a string anywhere in the packet. Instead, you can use the **Search In** section to specify whether to look for the string in the **Packet data** left over after decoding all possible fields, look for the character string in the **Decoded packet** displayed in the Protocol Tree Window, or look for the character string in the one-line **Packet summary** in the Summary Window. If you select the **Packet data** option, Ethereal will search for the character string in the packet data. By packet data, we mean the data in the packet that is left over after decoding the protocol fields. Selecting the **Find Decoded packet** will cause Ethereal to search for the character string in the protocol field strings that are displayed in the Protocol Tree Window. It does not matter if the subtree of the protocol tree containing the character string is collapsed or expanded. If you use the **Decoded packet** option, you must also use the **Character Set** drop-down list to select the character set for the character string you are trying to find. To make your character string search case-insensitive, enable the **Case Insensitive Search** checkbox.

Go To Packet

The Go To Packet dialog box, shown in Figure 4.16, can be displayed by selecting **Edit | Go To Packet Dialog**.

Figure 4.16 Go To Packet Dialog Box

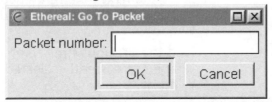

Enter a packet number in the **Packet Number** textbox and click **OK**. The packet with that packet number will be selected in the Summary Window.

Time Reference Submenu

The **Time Reference** submenu, shown in Figure 4.17, is displayed when you select **Edit | Time Reference**. The **Time Reference** submenu options are described in Table 4.7.

Figure 4.17 Time Reference Submenu

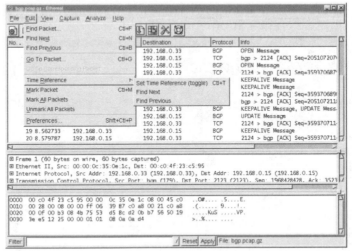

Table 4.7 Time Reference Submenu Options

Menu Option	Description
Set Time Reference (toggle)	Sets the packet currently selected in the Summary Window as a time reference packet.
Find Next	Finds the next time reference packet after the packet currently selected in the Summary Window.
Find Previous	Find the previous time reference packet before the packet currently selected in the Summary Window.

When the **Time** column in the Summary Window is configured to display the time that has elapsed since the beginning of the capture, then the time displayed is the number of seconds since the beginning of the capture or the last time reference packet.

In Figure 4.18 , we have set packets 5 and 10 as time reference packets. This is indicated by their **Time** column value (*REF*). Packets 1-4 are marked with the time since the beginning of the capture in which they were captured. Packets 6-9 are marked with the time since the time referencepacket 5. Packets 11 and greater are marked with the time since the time reference packet 10.

Figure 4.18 Time Reference Submenu Example

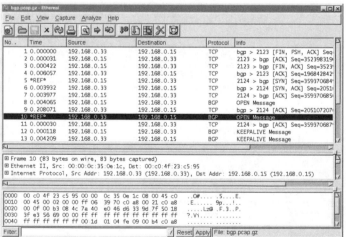

Preferences

The Preferences dialog box, shown in Figure 4.19, is displayed when you select **Edit | Preferences...**.

Figure 4.19 Preferences Dialog Box

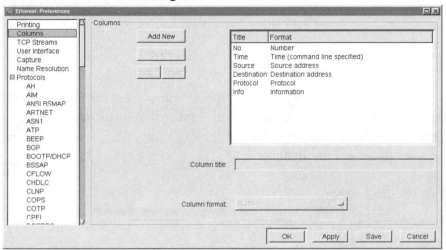

The Preferences dialog box allows you to set preferences for various subsystems of Ethereal, including setting preferences for decodes of various protocols. To edit preferences for an area of Ethereal, like **Columns** in Figure 4.19, select that area from the box on the left and change the settings displayed in the box on the right. It is strongly recommended that you browse through the protocol preferences for any protocol you use frequently, as protocol preferences can change the way a protocol is decoded or displayed.

When you have made your changes to Ethereal's preferences you can choose to apply them without closing the Preference dialog box by clicking the **Apply** button. To apply your settings and close the Preferences dialog box, click the **OK** button. To save your preferences for use in a different Ethereal session, click the **Save** button.

NOTE

The **Columns** preference, selected in Figure 4.19, is subtly broken in Ethereal. You can add, delete, or reorder columns in the Preferences dialog box, but your changes will not take effect unless you save them, then exit and restart Ethereal.

View

The **View** menu, shown in Figure 4.20, allows you to control how packets are displayed in the Summary Window, and the Protocol Tree Window. You can also set up color filters to color the packets in the Summary Window. The **View** menu options are described in Table 4.8.

Figure 4.20 View Menu

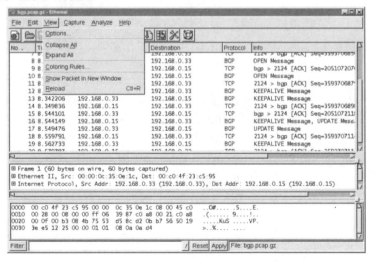

Table 4.8 View Menu Options

View Submenu Options

Menu Option	Description
Options...	Set the View options.
Collapse All	Collapse all subtrees in the Protocol Tree Window
Expand All	Expand all subtrees in the Protocol Tree Window

Continued

Table 4.8 View Menu Options

View Submenu Options	
Menu Option	**Description**
Coloring Rules…	Create and edit color filters to colorize the packets in the Summary Window that match a given display filter string.
Show Packet In New Window	For the packet currently selected in the Summary Window display it's Protocol Tree Window and Data View Window in a new window.
Reload	Reload the current capture file.

Display Options

The Display Options dialog box, shown in Figure 4.21, is displayed when you select **View | Options…**.

Figure 4.21 Display Options Dialog Box

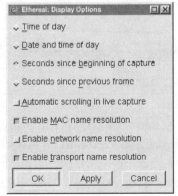

The Display Options dialog box allows you to choose which time value will be displayed in the **Time** column of the Summary Window, whether automatic scrolling will be enabled for live captures, and what type of name resolution will be enabled.

For a given packet, you may choose to have the **Time** column in the Summary Window display the **Time of day** when that packet was captured, **Date and time of day** when that packet was captured, **Seconds since beginning of capture** (or the last time reference packet) that packet was captured, or the **Seconds since the previous frame** that matched the current display filter.

In a live capture, you can choose to have old packets scroll up and out of view as new packets are captured and appended to the end of the Summary Window. To do so, enable the **Automatic scrolling in live capture** checkbox. You may choose your name resolution options in the Display Options dialog box as well. Refer back to the section entitled "Open" for more information about name resolution choices.

Apply Color Filters

The Apply Color Filters dialog box, shown in Figure 4.22, can be displayed by selecting **View | Coloring Rules…**.

Figure 4.22 Apply Color Filters Dialog Box

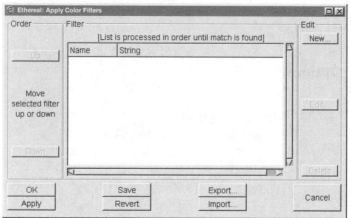

Ethereal has the ability to color packets in the Summary Window that match a given display filter string, making patterns in the capture data more visible. This can be immensely useful when trying to follow request response protocols where variations in the order of requests or responses may be interesting. You can color such traffic into as many categories as you'd like and will be able to see at a glance what is going on from the Summary Window instead of having to go through the Protocol Tree Window for each packet.

To create a color filter click the **New** button in the Apply Color Filters dialog box. The Edit Color Filter dialog box will be displayed (Figure 4.23).

Figure 4.23 Edit Color Filter Dialog Box

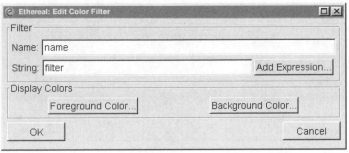

When the Edit Color Filter dialog box is first opened, the **Name** textbox will have the string *name* in it, and the **String** field will contain the string *filter*. To create a color filter you should first fill in a name for it in the **Name** textbox. Then, you should enter a filter string in the **String** textbox. You may use the **Add Expression** button to display the Filter Expression dialog box to assist you in constructing a filter string. The Filter Expression dialog box is described in the section entitled "Analyze". Once you have a name and filter string you are happy with, you need to select the foreground and background color to colorize the packets matching your filter string. Click the **Background Color…** button to set the foreground color, as shown in Figure 4.24.

Figure 4.24 Background Color Dialog Box

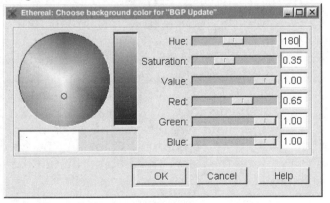

When you are happy with the color you have selected click the **OK** button. The Edit Color Filter dialog box (Figure 4.25) will be displayed.

Figure 4.25 Edit Color Filter

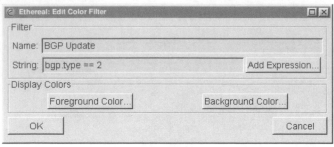

In Figure 4.25 we have created a filter named *BGP Update* with a filter string *bgp.type == 2*. The name and filter string will be colored to match our background color choice. Click the **Foreground Color...** button to set the foreground color and proceed as you did with the background color. When you are happy with your name, filter string, and text coloring click the **OK** to close the Edit Color Filter dialog box.

Notes from the Underground...

Ghost of Ethereal Future: GTK+2

Ethereal uses a widget set to provide its GUI elements (buttons, menus, radio buttons, file dialogs, color selection dialogs, etc.) called GTK+ (Gimp Tool Kit, www.gtk.org). By default, Ethereal builds with GTK+1, and so all of the screenshots you've seen in this book use GTK+1. There is already code in place in Ethereal for GTK+2, the next version of the GTK+ library. Many elements look very similar in GTK+2, just slightly cleaner, but a few things look very different. One of them is the color selection widget used in the Foreground Color and Background Color dialog boxes. You can see the new GTK+2 Foreground Color dialog box for Ethereal in Figure 4.26:

Continued

Figure 4.26 GTK+2 Foreground Color Dialog Box

Figure 4.27 shows the Apply Color Filters dialog box now populated with the new *BGP Update* entry and a *BGP* filter.

Figure 4.27 Apply Color Filters Dialog Box

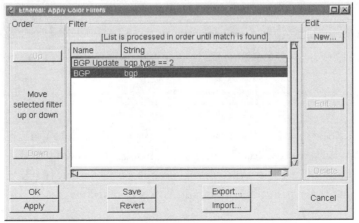

Click the **OK** button to apply the changes and close the dialog box. Click **Apply** to apply the changes and leave the dialog box open. If you wish to use your color filters with another Ethereal session, click **Save**.

If you click the **Revert** button, all coloring will be removed from the Summary Window, the color filters will be removed from the **Filter** list, and the saved color file will be deleted. Use the **Export** or **Import** buttons to export your color filters to another file or import the color filters from a file of your choice. This is very useful for sharing color filters with coworkers or between different machines on which you have Ethereal installed. Notice the order of the color filters in the **Filter** list in Figure 4.27. For every packet in the Summary View the color filters strings will be tried in order until one is matched. At that point, its associated color will be applied. The filters in the **Filter** list are applied from the top down, so the *BGP Update* color filter will be tried first. Only if the *BGP Update* color filter does not match a packet will Ethereal proceed to try the *BGP* color filter to that packet. An example of the application of these color filters can be seen in Figure 4.28.

Figure 4.28 Application of Color Filters

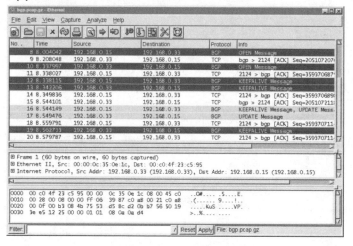

In Figure 4.28, the *BGP Update* messages (lines 16 and 17) are black text on light blue, not white text on dark blue, even though they would also match the white text on dark blue *BGP* color filter. This is because the black text on light blue *BGP Update* filter is applied first, and since it matches, no further color filter is tried.

Show Packet in New Window

You can display a packet's Protocol Tree Window and Data View Window in a new window by selecting a packet in the Summary Window and selecting **View | Show Packet in New Window** (see Figure 4.29). This is useful when you would like to be able to see detailed information about more than one packet at once. Note that the title bar shows the same information as the summary line for this packet in the Summary Window.

Figure 4.29 Show Packet in New Window

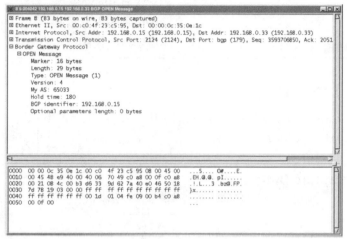

Capture

The **Capture** menu is shown in Figure 4.30, and the menu entries are explained in Table 4.9.

Figure 4.30 Capture Menu

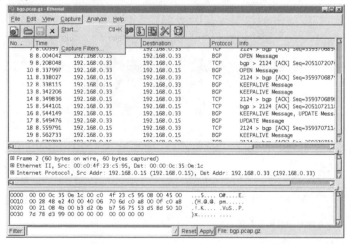

Table 4.9 Capture Menu Options

Menu Option	Description
Start…	Start a capture.
Stop	Stop a running packet capture.
Capture Filters…	Edit the capture filters.

Capture Options

The Capture Options dialog box, shown in Figure 4.31, can be displayed by selecting **Capture | Start…**.

Figure 4.31 Capture Options Dialog

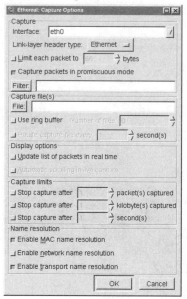

This dialog box allows us to answer the basic questions about capturing data:

1. What traffic are we capturing?

2. Where are we saving it?

3. How are we displaying it?

4. When do we stop capturing?

The **Capture** section allows us to choose which traffic we are capturing. When choosing what traffic to capture we can ask:

1.   Which interface are we capturing from?

2.   How much of each packet are we capturing?

3.   Which packets arriving at the interface are we capturing?

The **Interface** drop-down list allows us to choose which interface we are going to be capturing from. You can choose from the interfaces listed in the drop–down list, or if the interface you are seeking isn't listed there, you can enter it manually in the textbox. If both libpcap and the interface you select support multiple link layers for that interface, you can choose which link layer header type to capture using the **Link-layer header type:** selector.

The **Limit each packet to** field allows you to choose to capture less than the entire packet. If you enable the **Limit each packet to** checkbox and provide a number in the **Limit each packet to** textbox, then only the first number of bytes you indicate will be captured from each packet. Be aware that if you choose to capture less than the full packet Ethereal may mark many of your packets as fragments. This is because all of the data expected by the dissectors in Ethereal may not be present due to the packets having been truncated.

The **Capture packets in promiscuous mode** checkbox and the **Filter:** textbox allow you to choose which packets arriving at the interface will be captured. If you enable the **Capture packets in promiscuous mode** checkbox, Ethereal will put the interface into promiscuous mode before capturing data. Normally, an interface only passes onto the operating system packets that are addressed to the link layer address assigned to that interface. When an interface is in promiscuous mode it passes on all packets arriving at the interface to the operating system. So, if you choose not to capture in promiscuous mode, you will only capture packets addressed to or being sent by the interface on which you are capturing. If you choose to capture in promiscuous mode you will capture all packets arriving at the interface. Entering a tcpdump-style capture filter in the **Filter** textbox will cause Ethereal to only capture packets matching that capture filter. If you click on the **Filter** button then the Edit Capture Filter List dialog box will be displayed to allow you to choose among previously defined capture filters. See the section entitled "Edit Capture Filter List" for more details.

The **Capture File(s)** section allows you to choose where to save the capture. If you choose to leave this section blank, Ethereal will save the capture to a temporary file, and you can choose to save the capture at some later point by selecting

File | SaveAs. If you enter a filename in the **File** textbox, Ethereal will save the capture to that file. Clicking the **File** button will open the Save As dialog box. If you enable the **Use ring buffer** checkbox, you can save your capture to a ring buffer. Saving to a ring buffer will be dealt with in a separate section.

The **Display options** section allows you to choose how you are going to display packets as they are captured. By default, Ethereal does not update the list of packets in the Summary Window during capture, but only once the capture is stopped. If you enable the **Update list of packets in real time** checkbox, Ethereal will update the Summary Window as soon as a packet is captured and processed. By default, when Ethereal is updating the Summary Window during live capture, new packets are appended to the end of the Summary Window, and the Summary Window does not scroll up old packets to reveal new ones. To have the Summary Window scroll up to display the most recent packets, enable the **Automatic scrolling in live capture** checkbox. If you change your mind about whether you want automatic scrolling once a capture has started, you can select **View | Options** to enable or disable this feature.

The **Capture limits** section allows you to choose when to stop capturing. You can, of course, always manually stop a capture by selecting **Capture | Stop**, but it is sometimes convenient to set conditions under which the capture will automatically stop. There are three types of automatic limits to a capture supported by Ethereal:

1. Capture a specified number of packets.
2. Capture a specified number of kilobytes of traffic.
3. Capture for a specified number of seconds.

Ethereal will allow you to set up any combination of these three limits simultaneously—it is possible to limit the number of packets, the number of kilobytes, and the number of seconds at the same time. Whenever one of the limits is satisfied, the capture will stop.

If you enable the **Stop capture after... packet(s) captured** checkbox and enter a number of packets in the **Stop capture after... packet(s) captured** textbox, the capture will stop when it has reached the specified number of packets. If you enable the **Stop capture after... kilobyte(s) captured** checkbox and enter a number of kilobytes in the **Stop capture after... kilobytes(s) captured** textbox, the capture will stop once it has reached the specified number of kilobytes. If you enable the **Stop capture after... seconds(s)** checkbox and enter a number of packets in the **Stop capture after... sec-**

onds(s) textbox, the capture will stop when the specified number of seconds have elapsed since the beginning of the capture.

The **Name resolution** section allows you to choose the name resolution options for the capture. Name resolution options are described earlier in the chapter in the section entitled "Open".

When you have specified your capture choices via the Capture Options dialog box, you can start the capture by clicking the **OK** button. The **Capture Dialog** will then be displayed, as shown in Figure 4.32.

Figure 4.32 Capture Dialog Box

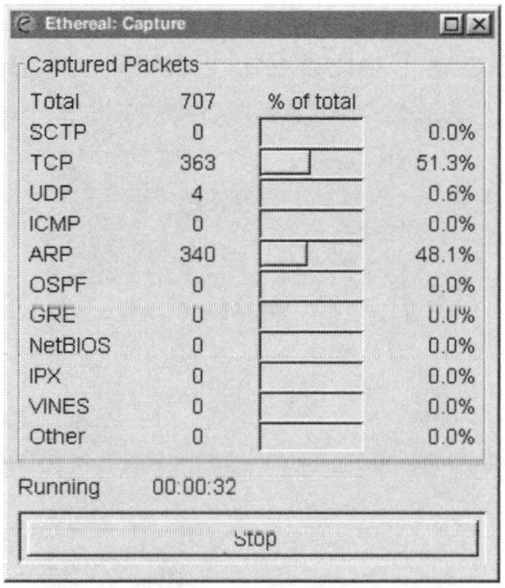

The Capture dialog box displays the number of packets of various protocols that have been captured, and the percentage of all captured traffic consisting of those protocols. In Figure 4.32 a total of 707 packets have been captured, of which 363 (51.3%) are TCP packets, 4 (0.6%) are UDP packets, and 340 (48.1%) are ARP (Address Resolution Protocol) packets. You can stop the capture at any time by clicking the **Stop** button.

Ring Buffer Captures

There are applications in which it makes sense to capture network traffic to a series of smaller files. Frequently, you may want to limit the number of such smaller files, and delete the oldest when starting a new one. Such a structure is called a ring buffer, because conceptually the data fills up a buffer and when it reaches the end it loops back to the beginning.

There are certain questions that need to be answered about using ring buffer files:

1. How many capture files in the ring buffer?

2. What are those capture files named?

3. When do we rotate to the next capture file?

To enable ring buffer captures, access the Capture Options dialog box and enable the **Use ring buffer** checkbox. The appearance of the Capture Options dialog box will change, as shown in figure 4.33.

Figure 4.33 Capture Options Dialog Box: Use Ring Buffer Selected

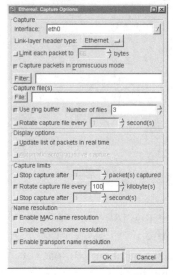

The **Rotate capture file every… second(s)** checkbox becomes available and the **Stop capture after… kilobytes captured** checkbox is renamed **Rotate capture file very… kilobyte(s)** and becomes unavailable.

The **Number of files** textbox allows you to choose how many files are in the ring buffer. If you choose zero, the number of ring buffer files is assumed to be infinite–no old files will be deleted to make room for new files.

The **File** textbox provides the base name for the filenames in the capture ring buffer. The base name is broken up into a prefix and a suffix. The filename of a ring buffer capture file is prefix_NNNNN_YYYYMMDDhhmmss.suffix. Where NNNNN is a five-digit zero-padded count indicating the sequence number of the ring buffer file, YYYY is a four-digit year, MM is the two-digit zero-padded month, DD is a two-digit zero-padded date, hh is a two-digit zero-padded hour, mm is a two-digit zero-padded minute, and ss is a two-digit zero-padded second. For example, if the file *foo.bar.libpcap* was the fifth capture file in the ring buffer created at 23:21:01 on January 8, 2004, it would be named *foo.bar_00005_20040108232101.libpcap*. It is important to note that the sequence numbers in the filenames increase monotonically. If a ring buffer has three files in it, when the fourth capture file is started it will have the sequence number 00004, and the file with the sequence number 00001 will be deleted. The sequence numbers are not recycled as we loop through the ring.

The **Rotate capture file every… kilobyte(s)** textbox and the optional **Rotate capture file every… second(s)** textbox allow you to choose when the capture files will be rotated. You must provide a kilobyte limit to the size of a capture file in the ring buffer by entering a number (or accepting the default value) in the **Rotate capture file every… kilobyte(s)** textbox. If a capture file reaches the number of kilobytes you have specified, a new capture file will be created to store any new packets captured, and the oldest capture file in the ring buffer may be deleted if the new capture file puts you over the limit specified in the **Number of files** textbox. If you enable the **Rotate capture file every… second(s)** checkbox and enter a number of seconds in the **Rotate capture file every… second(s)** textbox, if a capture file has been open for the number of seconds you specify, a new capture file will be created to store any new packets captured. The oldest capture file in the ring buffer may then be deleted if the new capture file puts you over the limit specified in the **Number of files** textbox.

NOTE

The **Use ring buffer** checkbox is incompatible with the **Update list of packets in real time** checkbox, and Ethereal will not allow you to enable **Use ring buffer** if you have already enabled **Update list of packets in real time**. Unfortunately, the reverse is not true–Ethereal will allow you to select **Update list of packets in real time** if **Use ring buffer** has already been selected. When this occurs, the **Use Ring buffer** checkbox will automatically (and without warning) be disabled. This, in turn, causes the **Rotate capture file every… kilobyte(s)** checkbox to revert to **Stop capture after… kilobyte(s)**, but it is left still selected, and with a value set (1 kilobyte by default). The net result is that not only do you not get a ring buffer capture in such a situation, but you also get your capture stopped after 1 byte.

Tools & Traps...

Handling Large Captures

Into everyone's life eventually falls a problem that involves enormous amounts of network data to analyze. Maybe it's an intermittent problem that happens only every couple of days where you need to see the message exchange that leads up to the problem. Maybe it's a problem on a fairly active network. Whatever the reason, the issue of capturing and analyzing large amounts of network traffic is a common one. As captures become larger, Ethereal consumes more memory, and filtering or finding packets begins to take a very long time.

In these situations it is best to use Tethereal, the console-based version of Ethereal, to do the actual capture and initial processing of the data. To capture to from an interface <interface> to a file <savefile> use this command:

```
tethereal -i <interface> -w <savefile>
```

If you have a limited amount of space and/or want to limit the size of your capture files, you can use the ring buffer functionality with Tethereal to capture from interface <interface> to <num_capture_files> capture files with maximum size each <filesize> and base filename <savefile> by executing the following at the command line:

```
tethereal -i <interface> -w <savefile> -b <num_capture_files> -a
filesize:<filesize>
```

Once you have captured the data you need, you can then use Tethereal to prune down the capture to a more manageable size. To use a display filter string <filter string> to filter a capture file <savefile> and save the results to a new capture file <newsavefile>, you would execute the following at the command line:

```
tethereal -r <savefile> -w <newsavefile> -R <filter string>
```

An example might be if you needed to extract all packets from the capture file that were captured between Jan 8, 2004 22:00 and Jan 8, 2004 23:00. To perform this feat you would execute the following at the command line:

Continued

```
tethereal -r <savefile> -w <newsavefile> -R '(frame.time >= "Jan 8,
2004 22:00:00.00" ) && (frame.time <= "Jan 8, 2004 23:00:00.00")'
```

Once you have pruned the data down to a size where Ethereal's performance is workable, open the capture file in Ethereal to perform more involved analysis.

Edit Capture Filter List

The Edit Capture Filter List dialog box is displayed by selecting **Capture | Capture Filters...** (Figure 4.34).

Figure 4.34 Edit Capture Filter List Dialog Box

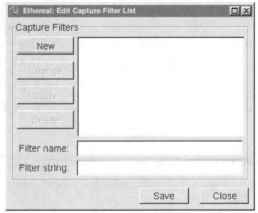

This dialog box allows you to create new tcpdump-style capture filters, described in Chapter 5, and to save them for later use. To create a new capture filter, provide a name for your filter in the **Filter name** textbox, provide a tcp-dump style capture filter string in the **Filter string** textbox, and click the **New** button. In Figure 4.35 we have created a capture filter named HTTP Traffic that provides filter string port 80.

Figure 4.35 Edit Capture Filter List Dialog Box Example

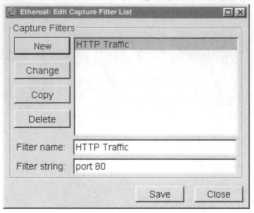

You can select an existing capture filter from the **Capture Filters** list and choose to change, delete, or copy it. To change an existing capture filter, select it from the **Capture Filters** list, change its name in the **Filter name** textbox and/or change its tcpdump style capture filter string in the **Filter string** textbox and then click the **Change** button. To copy an existing capture filter, select the capture filter from the **Capture Filters** list and click the **Copy**, as shown in Figure 4.36.

Figure 4.36 Edit Capture Filter List Dialog Box: Copy

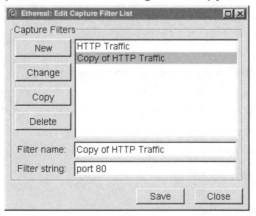

You can delete a capture filter by selecting it from the **Capture Filters** list and clicking the **Delete** button. If you wish to have your list of capture filters available in a subsequent Ethereal session, then you must click the **Save** button to save them to disk.

Analyze

The **Analyze Menu** is shown in Figure 4.37, and it's options are explained in Table 4.10.

Figure 4.37 Analyze Menu

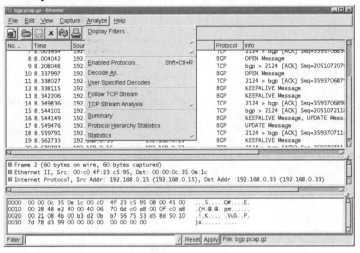

Table 4.10 Analyze Menu Options

Menu Option	Description
Display Filters...	Edit the display filters.
Match	Submenu for preparing and applying a display filter based upon the protocol field selected in the Protocol Tree Window.
Prepare	Submenu for preparing a display filter based upon the protocol field selected in the Protocol Tree Window.
Enabled Protocols...	Enable and disable the decoding of individual protocols.
Decode As...	Specify decoding certain packets as being part of a particular protocol.
User Specified Decodes	Report which user specified decodes are currently in force.
Follow TCP Stream	Display an entire TCP stream at once.
TCP Stream Analysis	Submenu for choosing a TCP Stream Analysis tool.

Continued

Table 4.10 Analyze Menu Options

Menu Option	Description
Summary	Display a summary of the capture file.
Protocol Hierarchy Statistics	Display statistics in a tree view for the protocols in the capture.
Statistics	Submenu for choosing a Statistics tool.

Edit Display Filter List

The Edit Display Filter List dialog box, shown in Figure 4.38, can be displayed by selecting **Analyze | Display Filter…**.

Figure 4.38 Edit Display Filter List Dialog Box

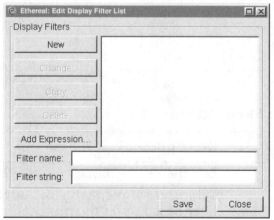

This dialog box is designed to help you construct a filter string. To create a new filter string, click the **Add Expression** button. The Filter Expression dialog box (Figure 4.39) will be displayed.

Figure 4.39 Filter Expression Dialog Box

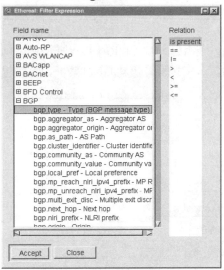

Select the protocol you are interested in for your filter expression and expand it to show which of its fields can be filtered. Select the desired filter field. When you pick a relation other than **is present**, the Filter Expression dialog box will change to show your options for that field, as shown in Figure 4.40.

Figure 4.40 Filter Expression Dialog: Equality

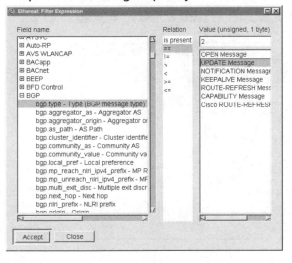

In this case, we have chosen the equality (==) relation. You can choose the value you wish to match and click the **Accept** button. The result will be to insert the filter expression you just constructed into the **Filter string:** textbox (Figure 4.41)

Figure 4.41 Edit Display Filter List Dialog Box: Filter String

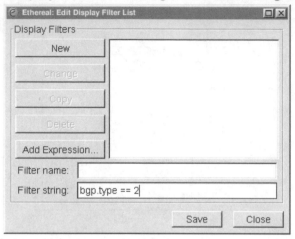

If you wish to save the filter string you have just created, type a name in the **Filter name** textbox and click the **New** button. The filter string will be added to the Display Filters List dialog box (Figure 4.42)

Figure 4.42 Edit Display Filter List Dialog Box: Filter Name

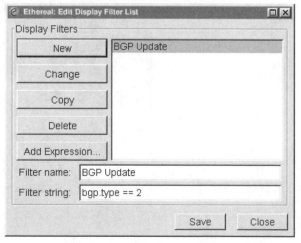

You can select an existing display filter from the list and choose to change, delete, or copy it. To change an existing display filter, select it from the list, change its name in the **Filter name** textbox and/or change its display filter string in the **Filter string** textbox and then click the **Change** button. To copy an existing display filter, select it from the list and click the **Copy** button.

You can save the list for use in later Ethereal sessions by clicking the **Save** Button.

If you have accessed the Edit Display Filter List dialog box from the filter bar or some other part of Ethereal from which you can apply a display filter, then an **OK** button will also be available. Use this button to apply the filter and close the dialog box. Use the **Apply** button to apply your filter and leave the dialog box open (see Figure 4.43).

Figure 4.43 Display Filter Dialog Box: OK/Apply Buttons

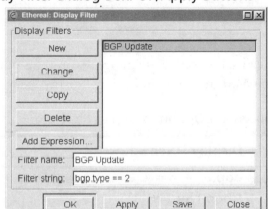

This has only been a very rudimentary introduction to display filtering; a more in-depth discussion can be found in the Chapter 5.

Match and Prepare Submenus

The **Match** and **Prepare** submenus have the same options and behave in the same way with one exception; the **Prepare** submenu items prepare a display filter string and place it in the **Filter** textbox. The **Match** submenu items prepare a display filter string, place it in the **Filter** textbox and apply it to the capture. Because of their close similarity we will only discuss the **Match** submenu.

The **Match** submenu becomes available when you have selected a field in the Protocol Tree Window with an associated filter name that can be used in a display filter string. An example is shown in Figure 4.44.

Figure 4.44 Match Submenu

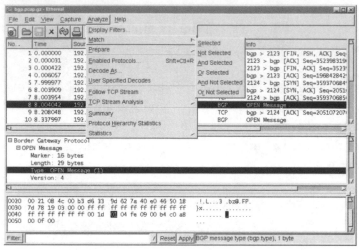

In Table 4.11, we can see the filter string that would be put in the **Filter:** textbox for each of the **Match** submenu options for the example in Figure 4.44.

Table 4.11 Match Submenu Option Examples

Menu Option	Display Filter String
Selected	bgp.type == 1
Not Selected	!(bgp.type == 1)
And Selected	(ip.addr == 192.168.0.15) && (bgp.type == 1)
Or Selected	(ip.addr == 192.168.0.15) || (bgp.type == 1)
And Not Selected	(ip.addr == 192.168.0.15) && !(bgp.type == 1)
Or Not Selected	(ip.addr == 192.168.0.15) || !(bgp.type == 1)

Enabled Protocols

The Enabled Protocols dialog box, shown in Figure 4.45, is displayed by selecting **Analyze | Enabled Protocols…**.

Figure 4.45 Enabled Protocols Dialog Box

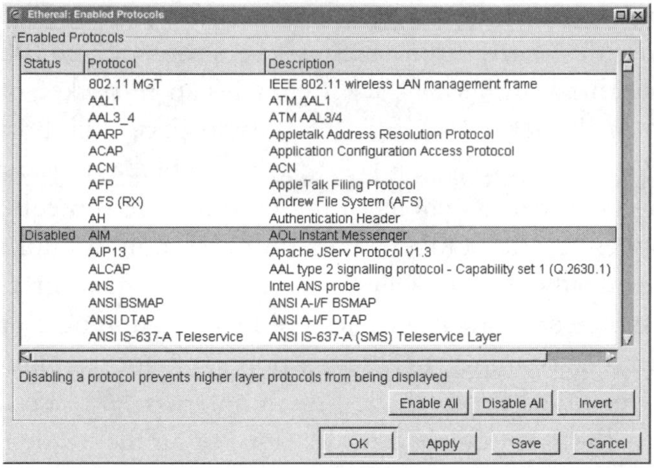

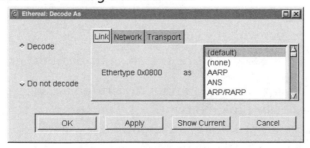

This dialog box allows you to enable or disable the decoding of one or more protocols. You can do this by clicking its Status column to toggle its status between *Enabled* and *Disabled*. Additionally, you can enable all protocols by clicking the **Enable All** button, disable all protocols by clicking the **Disable All** button, or enable all disabled protocols and disable all enabled protocols by clicking the **Invert** button. You can apply these settings to all Ethereal sessions by clicking the **Save** button.

Decode As

To force the decode of a packet, select it in the Summary Window and then select **Analyze | Decode As...**. The Decode As dialog box will be displayed, as shown in Figure 4.46.

Figure 4.46 Decode As Dialog Box: Link Tab

When Ethereal is decoding a packet it uses magic numbers in each protocol to decide which dissector to use to decode subsequent parts of the packet. Magic numbers are values that specify some higher-level protocol, like Ethertype 0x0800 specifying that an Ethernet packet contains an IP packet, or IP protocol 6 specifying that an IP packet contains a TCP payload, or TCP port 179 specifying that a TCP packet is carrying a BGP payload. There are occasions when you want to override Ethereal's choices in how to decode subsequent parts of the packet based on these magic numbers. The most common examples involve TCP ports. Ethereal frequently decides which dissector to call next for a TCP packet based upon the source or destination port. We may be running a protocol over a non-standard port, like running HTTP over port 7000 for example. The **Decode As** feature allows us to tell Ethereal about such non-standard cases.

Ethereal allows the user to force decodes based upon the magic numbers in the link layer, network layer, or transport layer. For the transport layer we have the option of decoding based on source, destination or both, as shown in Figure 4.47.

Figure 4.47 Decode As Dialog Box: Transport Tab

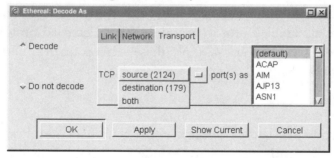

To force a particular decode you need to answer the questions:

1. After which layer do I want to start forcing my custom decode?

2. Which magic number do I want to key off of to determine whether to decode a packet with my custom decode?

3. Which protocol do I want the remaining traffic in the packet decoded as?

To choose the layer at which you want to start forcing your custom decode, select the appropriate tab (**Link**, **Network**, or **Transport**). You have a choice of which magic numbers to pick for the transport layer, where you can pick **source** port, **destination** port, or **both**. Then, you may select from the list of protocols as to how you want the remaining traffic in the packet decoded.

Click the **Show Current** button to open the Decode As: Show dialog box in order to see which decodes are currently being forced.

Decode As: Show

The Decode As: Show dialog box (Figure 4.48) can also be displayed by selecting **Analyze | User Specified Decodes** from the menu bar.

Figure 4.48 Decode As: Show

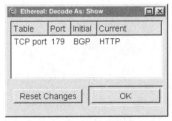

This dialog box displays the decodes you have specified through the Decode As Dialog box, one per line. The **Table** column shows the type of magic number for which we are showing the alternate decode, in this case the TCP port. The **Port** column shows the magic number for which we are providing an alternate decode, in this case 179. The **Initial** column shows the dissector that would normally be used to decode the payload of a packet with this magic number and magic number type, in this case BGP. And, finally, the **Current** column shows the dissector currently being used to decode the payload of packets having this magic number and magic number type, in this case HTTP.

Contents of TCP Stream

The Contents of TCP Stream window (Figure 4.49) can be displayed by selecting a TCP packet in the Summary Window and then selecting **Analyze | Follow TCP Stream** from the menu bar.

Figure 4.49 Contents of TCP Stream Window

In this example, a TCP packet that was part of an HTTP conversation with the web server for www.syngress.com is shown. By default, one side of the conversation is shown in red (the upper portion), the other in blue (the lower portion). For readability purposes the side of the conversation that is normally blue has been changed to white text on a dark blue background, using the **TCP Streams** color selector. By scrolling down in this window you are able to see all of the data exchanged during this TCP conversation. If you click the **Entire conversation** selector you can choose between displaying the entire conversation, or one of the directions (Figure 4.50).

Figure 4.50 Follow TCP Stream: Direction Selector

Clicking the **Save As** button will bring up a Save As dialog box for you to save the stream contents as a text file. Clicking the **Print** button will print the capture as text. Note there is no dialog box associated with the **Print** button. The **Filter out this stream** button will append the necessary filter string to the one in the filter bar and close the Contents of TCP Stream window. This can be very handy when going through a large capture. As you look at the possible TCP streams of interest one by one and exclude them from the Summary Window, you have finished considering them so only the unconsidered data remains.

You also have the option of choosing how the TCP stream is presented. In Figure 4.50 the **ASCII** option is selected. By choosing the **EBCDIC** option you could cause the stream to be presented with EBCDIC (Extended Binary Coded Decimal Interchange Code, a proprietary IBM character set). If you choose the **Hex Dump** option you will see a hexadecimal dump of the TCP stream. And, if you choose the **C Arrays** option, the TCP stream will be shown as a series of C arrays (arrays in the C programming language).

TCP Stream Analysis Submenu

The **TCP Stream Analysis** submenu, shown in Figure 4.51, can be displayed by selecting a TCP packet in the Summary Window and selecting **Analyze | TCP Stream Analysis** from the menu bar. **TCP Stream Analysis** submenu options are shown in Table 4.12.

Figure 4.51 TCP Analysis Submenu

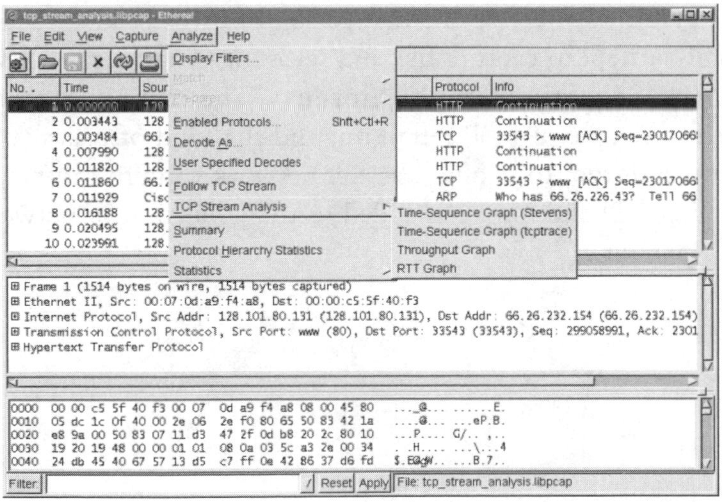

Table 4.12 TCP Stream Analysis Submenu Options

Menu Option	Description
Time-Sequence Graph (Stevens)	Displays a time-sequence graph in the style used by W. Richard Stevens' TCP/IP Illustrated book.
Time-Sequence Graph (tcptrace)	Displays a time-sequence graph in the style used by the tcptrace program, which can be found at www.tcptrace.org/.
Throughput Graph	Displays a graph of throughput versus time.
RTT Graph	Displays a graph of round trip time (RTT) versus sequence number.

Time-Sequence Graph (Stevens)

The time-sequence graph (Stevens) produces a simple graph of TCP sequence number versus time for the TCP stream containing the packet that was selected in the Summary window. The first derivative of this graph is the TCP traffic throughput. In an ideal situation where we have a constant throughput, the graph would be a straight rising line with its slope equaling the throughput. Unfortunately, things are seldom ideal, and you can learn a lot about where the source of throughput issues are coming from by looking at the time-sequence graph. In Figure 4.52, there is a graph showing a throughput problem. You can reproduce this graph by selecting the first packet of the tcp_stream_analysis.libpcap capture file, and selecting **Analysis | TCP Stream Analysis | Time-Sequence Graph (Stevens)**. The captured file used in this graph is a classic example of TCP retransmit and the kind of issues you use the TCP Stream Analysis tool to debug. The full network capture can be found on the accompanying CD, and has been added to the collection of network captures on the Ethereal website.

Figure 4.52 Time-Sequence Graph (Stevens)

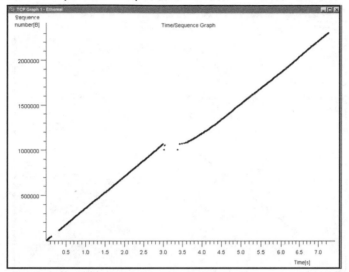

In Figure 4.52 (after about 0.3 seconds), the traffic has a nice even slope (constant throughput) until around 3 seconds, when there is a major disruption, as shown by the discontinuity in the graph. This gap suggests TCP retransmissions. The Steven's style time-sequence graph is simple, but you can see very clearly where your problems are.

Time-Sequence Graph (tcptrace)

The time-sequence graph (tcptrace) is also primarily a graph of TCP sequence numbers vs. time. Unlike the Stevens' style time-sequence graph, it conveys a lot more information about the TCP stream. In Figure 4.53 you can see that the tcptrace style time-sequence graph of this stream looks very similar to the Stevens' style time-sequence graph.

Figure 4.53 Time-Sequence Graph (tcptrace)

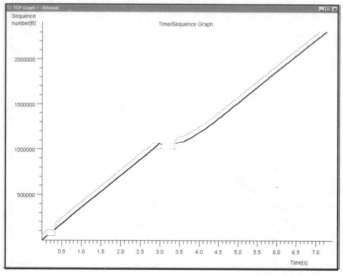

Explaining the elements shown in the tcptrace style time–sequence graph is made easier by using some of the graph manipulation tools that are available in all of the TCP stream analysis graphs. By performing a **Ctrl + right–click**, on the graph, you can magnify a portion of the graph, as shown in Figure 4.54.

Figure 4.54 Time-Sequence Graph (tcptrace): Magnify

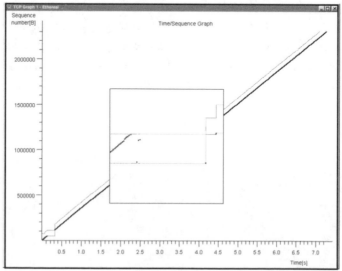

The box in the middle of the graph in Figure 4.54 is magnifying the region of discontinuity where packet loss has occurred. To get an even better view of it we can use the zoom feature. By clicking on the graph with the middle mouse button (if you have one) you can zoom in on the part of the graph you are clicking on. **Shift + middle-click** zooms out. When you have zoomed in/out, clicking and dragging with the right mouse button on the graph will allow you to move around in the zoomed graph. A zoom in on the region of discontinuity is shown in Figure 4.55.

Figure 4.55 Time-Sequence Graph (tcptrace): Zoom

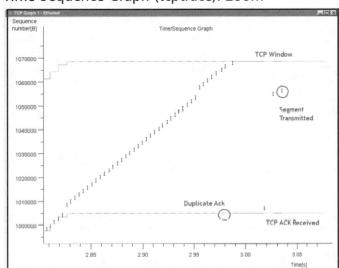

This is a zoom-in on the section of the graph just before the discontinuity. You can see the beginning of the discontinuity on the far right of the graph. Marked in bolded type are the different elements of the tcpgraph style time-sequence graph. The lower line represents the sequence number of the last ACK (TCP Acknowledgement) seen. The top line represents the TCP window. It consists of the sequence number of the last observed TCP ACK plus the last seen TCP window size advertised. The little hash marks on the lower line represent duplicate ACKs, and the little "I" bars represent transmitted segments.

Figure 4.56 is the same graph as Figure 4.55, but with different annotations to magnify what went wrong for this TCP stream. The capture behind this graph was taken from the receiver of a large transmission over TCP. Therefore, we generally only see the segments that we are receiving from the far end. What is seen in this graph is that early on the receiver missed two segments. The receiver continued to ACK the last segment received, and to receive subsequent segments until the segments received filled up the TCP window. A couple of other segments were lost along the way. Finally, we receive the second missed segment, the third missed segment, and then the fourth missed segment. But, because the first missed segment has not yet turned up, the receiver keeps sending the same duplicate ACK.

Figure 4.56 Time-Sequence Graph(tcptrace): Diagnosis

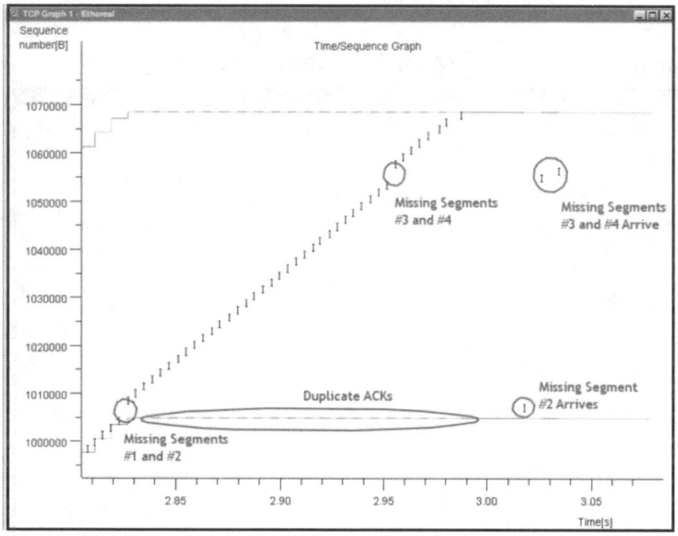

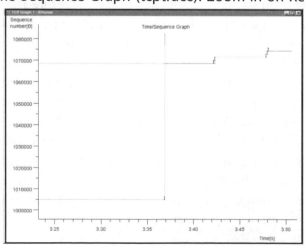

In Figure 4.57 we see how this logjam finally resolves:

Figure 4.57 Time-Sequence Graph (tcptrace): Zoom in on Retransmit

In Figure 4.57 you can see the missing segment, presumed to be a retransmit, arrive. At this point, an ACK is transmitted acknowledging the last received segment, the TCP window increases, and the receiver begins to receive segments again.

Throughput Graph

The throughput graph (Figure 4.58) shows the throughput of the TCP stream versus time.

Figure 4.58 Throughput Graph

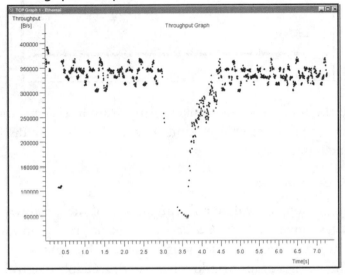

You can see in Figure 4.58 that the throughput fell off dramatically during the retransmit sequence seen in the time-sequence graphs.

RTT Graph

The RTT graph (Figure 4.59) shows the round trip time versus. sequence number.

Figure 4.59 RTT Graph

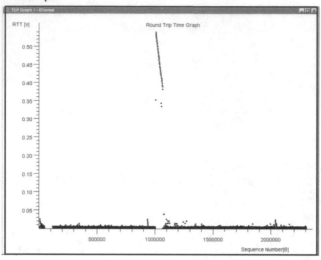

You can see the round trip time spike during around sequence number 1000000, roughly the same sequence number where we saw the discontinuity in the time-sequence graphs.

Graph Control

Throughout this section we will be referring to any of the windows containing a TCP stream analysis graph as a *graph window*. The term graph window may refer to a Stevens' or tcptrace style time-sequence graph, a throughput graph, or an RTT graph. Whenever a graph window is created, a Graph Control dialog box is also created, as shown in Figure 4.60.

Figure 4.60 Graph Control Dialog Box: Zoom Tab

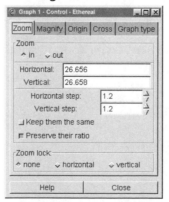

Notice that the number on the dialog box (1) matches the number on the graph window in Figure 4.56 (1). In the event that multiple graph windows are opened, you can use the index number to associate a Graph Control dialog box with its graph window.

The **Zoom** tab, shown in Figure 4.60, allows us to set the parameters related to the zoom functionality of the graph function. The **Horizontal** and **Vertical** textboxes are not for user entry of data, rather they show the amount of zoom currently employed in the graph window.

The **Horizontal step** and **Vertical step** textboxes allow you to set the horizontal and vertical zoom factors applied to the graph when you **Shift + middle-click** in the graph window. If you enable the **Keep them the same** checkbox, then whenever you change either the horizontal step or vertical step, the other will be changed to the same value. The **Preserve their ratio** checkbox causes the ratio between the horizontal step and the vertical step to be preserved. If the horizontal step was 1.2 and the vertical step was 2.4, when you changed the horizontal step to 1.3, then the vertical step would automatically change to 2.6.

The **Zoom lock** section allows you to lock either the horizontal or vertical so that zoom is not applied to them. If you enable the **horizontal** option, no matter what the value is for horizontal step, zooming will not change the horizontal scale at all. This is also true if you select the **vertical** option; no matter what the value is for vertical step, zooming will not change the vertical scale at all.

The **Magnify** tab, shown in Figure 4.61, allows you to control the parameters associated with the magnify functionality.

Figure 4.61 Graph Control Dialog Box: Magnify Tab

The **Width** and **Height** textboxes allow you to set the width and height of the magnification box that is displayed when you **Ctrl + right-click** in the graph window. The **X:** and **Y:** textboxes allow you to set the x and y offset of the magnification box from the location of the mouse pointer. This can be handy to offset the magnification box to somewhere where it won't occlude the graph. The **Horizontal:** and **Vertical:** textboxes allow you to set the zoom factor used to blow up the graph in the agnification box. The **Keep them the same** checkbox will cause the horizontal and vertical zoom factors to change in accordance with one another, and the **Preserve their ratio** checkbox will cause the ratio between the horizontal and vertical zoom factor to remain constant.

The **Origin** tab, shown in Figure 4.62, allows you to change the various origins of the graph.

Figure 4.62 Graph Control Dialog Box: Origin Tab

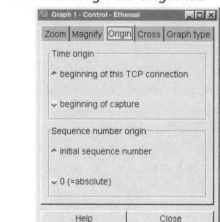

The **Time origin** section will allow you to choose the zero of time for your graph. If you select the **beginning of this TCP connection** option, you establish the beginning of the TCP connection as being graphed as your zero of time. If you select the **beginning of capture** option, you establish the beginning of the capture as your zero of time.

The **Sequence number origin** section will allow you to choose whether your actual TCP sequence numbers or the relative TCP sequence numbers (the TCP sequence numbers minus your initial TCP sequence number) are shown on the graph. It is frequently convenient to use the relative sequence number because it gives you some notion of how much data has been transmitted. If you select the **initial sequence number** option, the relative TCP sequence numbers will be used. If you select the **0 (=absolute)** option, the actual TCP sequence numbers will be used in the graph.

The **Cross** tab, shown in Figure 5.63, allows you to control whether crosshairs follow the mouse pointer in the graph window.

Figure 5.63 Graph Control Dialog Box: Cross Tab

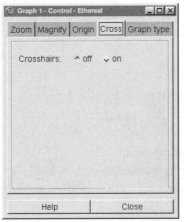

If you select the **off** radio button, there will be no crosshairs following the mouse pointer in the graph window. If you select the **on** option, there will be crosshairs following the mouse pointer in the graph window.

Once you have the graph window displayed, you can use the **Graph type** tab, shown in Figure 5.64, to change which type of graph is being displayed.

Figure 5.64 Graph Control Dialog Box: Graph Type Tab

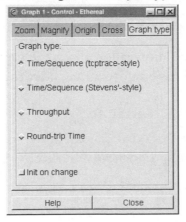

If you select the **Time/Sequence (tcptrace-style)** option, the time-sequence (tcpgraph) window will be displayed. If you select the **Time/Sequence (Stevens'-style)** option the time-sequence (Stevens'-style) window will be displayed. If you select the **Throughput** option, the throughput graph window will be displayed. If you select the **Round-trip Time** option, the RTT graph window will be displayed.

By default, if you have applied a zoom to the graph window for one graph type it will persist if you change graph types. If you enable the **Init on change** checkbox, each time you change graph types the zoom will be reset.

Summary

The Summary dialog box, shown in Figure 4.65, can be displayed by selecting **Analyze | Summary** from the menu bar.

Figure 4.65 Summary Dialog Box

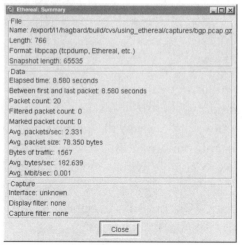

This dialog box provides information about the capture file, basic statistics about the capture data, and basic information about the capture.

Protocol Hierarchy Statistics

The Protocol Hierarchy Statistics dialog box, shown in Figure 4.66, can be displayed by selecting **Analyze | Protocol Hierarchy Statistics** from the menu bar.

Figure 4.66 Protocol Hierarchy Statistics Dialog Box

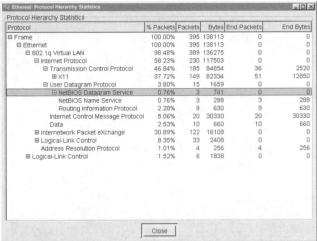

This dialog box provides a tree representation of protocols and statistics asso-ciated with them. Table 4.13 provides a description of what the columns mean:

Table 4.13 Protocol Hierarchy Statistics Columns

Column	Description
Protocol	The protocol on which statistics are being reported. The protocol may have sub-items on the tree repre-senting the protocols it contains. For example, IP con-tains TCP and UDP.
% Packets	Percentage of all packets in the capture that are of this protocol.
Packets	The number of packets in the capture that are of the protocol.
Bytes	The number of bytes in this capture containing this protocol.
End Packets	The number of packets for which this protocol is the last protocol in the decode. For example, a TCP SYN packet containing no data would be an end packet for TCP and counted in TCP's end packets count.
End Bytes	The number of bytes for which this protocol is the last protocol in the decode.

Statistics Submenu

The **Statistics** submenu, shown in Figure 4.67 provides a variety of specialized tools to analyze network traffic. These statistics are reported for certain protocol features.

Figure 4.67 Statistics Submenu

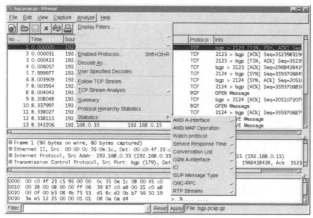

However, the tools in the **Statistics** submenu are quite specialized and beyond the scope of this book.

Help

The **Help** menu is shown in Figure 4.68, and the **Help** options are explained in Table 4.14.

Figure 4.68 Help Menu

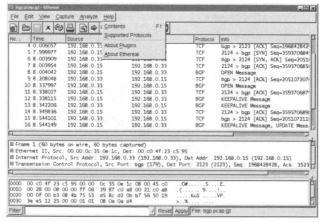

Table 4.14 Help Menu Options

Menu Option	Description
Contents	Displays the Contents for the Ethereal online help.
Supported Protocols	Displays a list of the supported protocols and the display filter fields they provide.
About Plugins	Displays a list of plugins being used and their versions.
About Ethereal	Displays information about Ethereal version and compile information.

Contents

The Contents dialog box, shown in Figure 4.69, can be displayed by selecting **Help | Contents** from the menu bar.

Figure 4.69 Help Contents Dialog Box

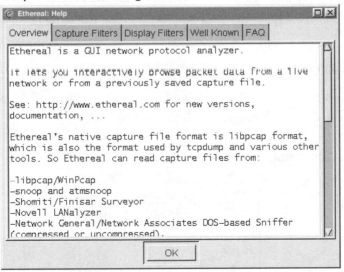

This dialog box provides tabs giving an overview of Ethereal, information about Capture Filters, information about Display Filters, some well-known information about networking, and answers to Frequently Asked Questions (FAQs).

Supported Protocols

The Supported Protocols dialog box, shown in Figure 4.70, can be displayed by selecting **Help | Supported Protocols** from the menu bar.

Figure 4.70 Supported Protocols Dialog Box

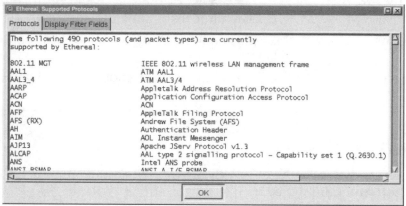

This dialog box provides a list of the protocols supported by the current version of Ethereal and a list of the display filter fields provided in the current version of Ethereal.

About Plugins

The About Plugins dialog box, shown in Figure 4.71, can be displayed by selecting **Help | About Plugins** from the menu bar.

Figure 4.71 About Plugins Dialog Box

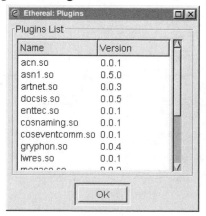

This dialog box provides a list of the plugins currently loaded into Ethereal and their versions. Ethereal will load all plugins available to it at start time, but there is no GUI that allows you to load or unload a plugin.

About Ethereal

The About Ethereal dialog box, as shown in Figure 4.72, can be displayed by selecting **Help | About Plugins** from the menu bar.

Figure 4.72 About Ethereal Dialog Box

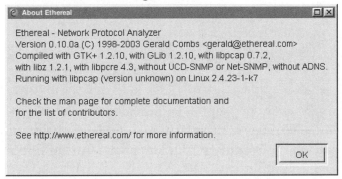

This dialog box contains information about the version of Ethereal you are running and which options it was compiled with. This information is important to know if you are ever reporting a bug to the Ethereal developers.

Pop-up Menus

Ethereal has context-sensitive pop-up menus to assist you in performing tasks. None of these menus actually provide any additional functionality beyond what is available through the menu bar, but they are easier and quicker to use in some circumstances.

Summary Window Pop-up Menu

The Summary Window pop-up menu, shown in Figure 4.73, can be displayed by right-clicking on the Summary Window.

Figure 4.73 Summary Window Pop-up Menu

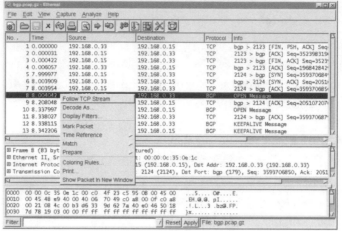

The Summary Window pop-up menu provides functionality that has been covered earlier in the chapter. Table 4.15 indicates where to find more information in this chapter on the Summary Window pop-up menu options.

Table 4.15 Summary Window Pop-up Menu References

Menu Option	Reference
Follow TCP Stream	See "Analyze: Contents of TCP Stream
Decode As...	See "Analyze: Decode As"
Displayer Filters...	See "Analyze: Display Filters
Mark Packet	See "Edit: Mark Packet"
Time Reference	See "Edit: Time Reference"
Match	See "Analyze: Match"
Prepare	See "Analyze: Prepare"
Coloring Rules...	See "Analyze: Coloring Rules"
Print...	See "File: Print"
Show Packet in New Window	See "View: Show Packet in New Window"

Protocol Tree Window Pop-up Menu

The Protocol Tree pop-up menu, shown in Figure 4.74, can be displayed by right-clicking on the Protocol Tree Window.

Figure 4.74 Protocol Tree Window Pop-up Menu

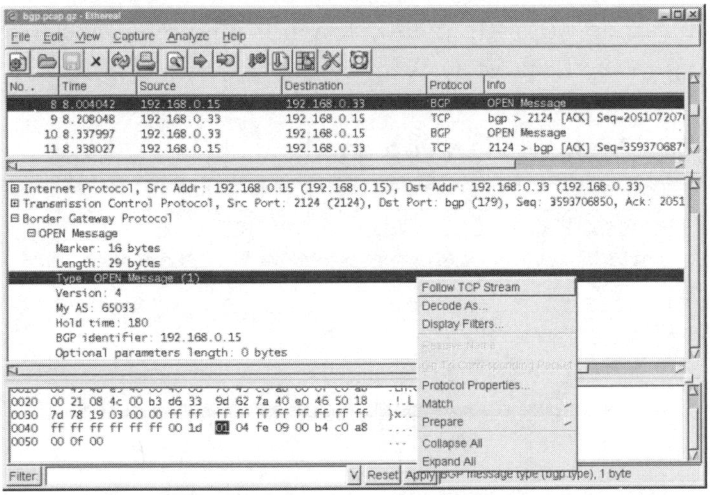

The Protocol Tree Window pop-up menu provides functionality that has been covered earlier in the chapter. Table 4.16 includes descriptions for some items and indicates where to find more information in this chapter for other items.

Table 4.16 Protocol Tree Window Pop-up Menu References/Descriptions

Menu Option	Reference/Description
Follow TCP Stream	See "Analyze: Follow TCP Stream"
Decode As...	See "Analyze: Decode As"
Displayer Filters...	See "Analyze: Display Filters"
Resolve Name	Forces resolution of all names for this packet. See the Ethereal Name Resolution sidebar for more information about Ethereal name resolution. Note that this option is only available if all name resolution is disabled.
Go To Corresponding Packet	See "Edit: Go To Corresponding Packet"
Protocol Properties...	See "Edit: Preferences"
Match	See "Analyze: Match"
Prepare	See "Analyze: Prepare"
Collapse All	See "View: Collapse All"
Expand All	See "View: Expand All"

Data View Window Pop-up Menu

The Data View Window pop-up menu, shown in Figure 4.75, can be displayed by right-clicking in the Data View Window.

Figure 4.75 Data View Window Pop-up Menu

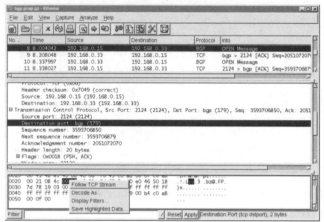

The Data View Window pop-up menu provides functionality that has been covered earlier in this chapter. Table 4.17 indicates where to find more information in this chapter on the Data View Window pop-up menu options.

Table 4.17 Data View Window Pop-up Menu References

Menu Option	Reference
Follow TCP Stream	See "Analyze: Follow TCP Stream"
Decode As…	See "Analyze: Decode As"
Displayer Filters…	See "Analyze: Display Filters"
Save Highlighted Data…	See "File: Export"

Using Command Line Options

Ethereal supports a large number of command line options to control its behavior when first run. This section will document some of the most commonly used options. Several of the other options are used to manipulate certain aspects of the GUI (font, height of Summary Window, Protocol Tree Window, Data Window, etc.) or set elements like link type or automatic scrolling. However, these options are not as common and will not be covered in this section.

Capture and File Options

The most commonly used Ethereal options are those related to captures and files. Table 4.18 lists some of the most common command line options related to these tasks.

Table 4.18 Capture and File Command Line Options

Command Line Option	Description
-i <interface>	Set the name of the interface used for live captures to <inteface>.
-k –i option.	Start capture immediately. This requires the
-a <test>:<value>	Sets an autostop condition for the capture. <test> may be one of duration or filesize. If the <test> is duration then <value> must be the number of seconds the capture should run before it stops. If <test> is file-size then <value> is the number of kilo-bytes that should be captured before the capture stops.
-c <count>	Sets the number of packets to read before stopping the capture. After <count> packets have been read the capture will stop.
-r <filename>	Read the capture saved in <filename>.
-w <filename>	Write the capture to <filename>.
-b <count>	Enable the use of <count> files in a ring buffer for captures. A maximum capture size must be specified with the –a file-size:<value> option.

To start capturing immediately on interface **eth0** and write the results to a ring buffer with **3** files of maximum size **100** kilobytes with base filename **foo.bar.libpcap** you would execute the following at the command line:

```
ethereal –i eth0 –k –w foo.bar.libpcap –b 3 –a filesize:100
```

Filter Options

Ethereal will allow you to specify filter information from the command line as well. Table 4.19 lists some of the most commonly used filter related command line options.

Table 4.19 Filter Command Line Options

Command Line Option	Description
-f <capture filter >	Set the tcpdump style capture filter string to <filter string>.
-R <display filter>	Only applicable when reading a capture from a file with the –r option. Applies the display filter <display filter> to all packets in the capture file and discard those that do not match.

To extract all packets from a capture file bgp.pcap.gz with **bgp.type == 2**, you would execute the following at the command line:

```
ethereal -r bgp.pcap.gz -R "bgp.type == 2"
```

Other Options

Other commonly used options are shown in Table 4.20.

Table 4.20 Other Command Line Options

Command Line Option	Description
-N <flags>	Turns on name resolution. Depending on which letters follow –N, various names will be resolved by Ethereal. **n** will cause network name resolution to be turned on, **t** will enable transport name resolution, **m** will enable MAC address resolution, and **C** will enable asynchronous DNS lookups for network name resolution.
-v	Print the Ethereal version information.
-h	Print Ethereal's help information.

Summary

In this chapter you have learned the major components of the Ethereal GUI. You have also learned the major functionality of the Ethereal application and how to access it.

You should now be able to perform network captures, open saved network captures, and print captures. You are also equipped to use display filters to filter the packets displayed in the Summary Window, color the packets in the Summary Window for easier readability, or find a packet in the capture with particular characteristics.

We've shown how to navigate the protocol tree in the Protocol Tree Window to drill down into the contents of a packet, and use the protocol tree fields to prepare new display filter strings.

Finally, you now know how to force a packet or group of packets to be decoded by a particular dissector. You have learned how to enable and disable decoding of particular protocols, and should have some understanding of how to use some of the more commonly used tools in Ethereal to gain better visibility into TCP Streams.

Solutions Fast Track

Getting started with Ethereal

☑ Binary Ethereal packages for Windows, Linux, and various UNIX flavors can be downloaded from www.ethereal.com.

☑ Source code can be downloaded and compiled from www.ethereal.com if the binary packages available don't meet your needs.

☑ Ethereal can be launched by typing **ethereal** at the command line.

Exploring the Main Windows

☑ The Summary Window provides a one-line summary for each packet.

☑ The Protocol Tree Window provides a detailed decode of the packet selected in the Summary Window.

☑ The Data View Window provides the hexadecimal (or hex) dump of the packets' actual bytes.

Other Window Components

☑ The filter bar provides a quick mechanism for filtering the packets displayed in the Summary Window.

☑ Clicking the filter bar's **Filter:** button will display the Display Filter dialog box to help you construct a display filter string.

☑ The **Information** field will show the display filter field name of the field selected in the Protocol Tree Window.

Exploring the Menus

☑ Most preferences can be set in the Preferences dialog box.

☑ There are context-sensitive pop-up menus available by right-clicking on the Summary Window, Protocol Tree Window, or Data View Window.

☑ Packets in the Summary Window can be color-coded for easy reading by using the Apply Color Filters dialog box.

Using Command Line Options

☑ Ethereal can apply display filters to packets read from a file with the **–R** flag, discarding packets that don't match the filter.

☑ Ethereal uses **–r** to indicate a file to read from and **–w** to indicate a file to write to.

☑ Ethereal can be made to start capturing from an interface immediately on startup by using the **–i** and **-k** options.

Frequently Asked Questions

The following Frequently Asked Questions, answered by the authors of this book, are designed to both measure your understanding of the concepts presented in this chapter and to assist you with real-life implementation of these concepts. To have your questions about this chapter answered by the author, browse to **www.syngress.com/solutions** and click on the **"Ask the Author"** form. You will also gain access to thousands of other FAQs at ITFAQnet.com.

Q: Why is Ethereal so slow displaying data during capture? It seems to lock up.

A: Your version of Ethereal may have been compiled without the ADNS (Asynchronous DNS) library. If so, Ethereal is stopping to do a DNS lookup for the source and destination IP address in each packet it decodes. It can take a long time for DNS queries to time out if they fail, and during this time Ethereal may lock up while waiting for those failures. To solve this problem, get a version of Ethereal with ADNS compiled in. To work around this problem unselect **Enable Network Name Resolution** in the Capture Options dialog box when starting a capture or in the File dialog box when opening a capture file.

Q: Why is it when I select some fields in the Protocol Tree Window I don't see the field name in the Information field? How can I filter on the field if I can't find out its name?

A: Ethereal has been developed over many years by a team of volunteer programmers. Many different people have written the dissectors, which decode the protocols in Ethereal, at many different times. Not all dissector authors associated a filterable field with each field they display in the Protocol Tree. You will not be able to filter on such fields. If such filtering is important to you for a particular protocol, you are encouraged to alter the source code for that dissector to include the capacity and submit it to the Ethereal team for inclusion.

Q: Why do I sometimes see an IP address or a TCP/UDP port number or a MAC address twice, once in parenthesis and once not?

A: When name resolution is turned off for an address type, or when no name is found for a given address, Ethereal will insert the actual address into the place where the name would have gone. As a result, a place where you would have seen the name with the address in parentheses (or vice versa) will just show two copies of the address. Don't worry about it ☺

Q: I need more complicated capture filtering than tcpdump-style capture filters provide; can I use Ethereal's display filters to restrict what I capture?

A: The short answer is no. Ethereal will not allow you to use display filters to filter on capture. However, there is a sort of workaround to achieve this. While Ethereal will not allow you to use display filters on capture, Tethereal will. To capture from an interface <interface> to a file <savefile> filtering with a display filter string <filter string> you would execute at the command line:

```
tethereal –i <interface> -w <savefile> -R <filter string>
```

Tethereal will capture from <interface> and only save to <savefile> those packets that match <filter string>. In many cases display filter strings will not be nearly as fast as the tcpdump-style capture filters, but if only display filters will do, this hack will let you use them.

Q: Does Ethereal really capture all the traffic arriving at an interface when capturing in promiscuous mode?

A: That depends. Ethereal gets whatever is captured by libpcap. Sometimes due to high load on the system you are capturing from, or just due to trying to capture from too high bandwidth an interface, packets may be lost for a number of reasons, including being dropped by the kernel. Keep this in mind as you work.

Q: Why am I seeing packets that aren't addressed to or being sent by my local interface even though I've turned off capturing in promiscuous mode?

A: There may be other applications running, like Snort, on the system you are capturing from that have put the interface into promiscuous mode. Whether Ethereal puts the interface in promiscuous mode, or some other application does, if the interface is in promiscuous mode you will see all traffic that arrives at it, not just the traffic addressed to or sent from the interface.

Chapter 5

Filters

Solutions in this Chapter:

- Writing Capture Filters
- Writing Display Filters

☑ Summary

☑ Solutions Fast Track

☑ Frequently Asked Questions

Introduction

When capturing packets from a network interface, Ethereal's default behavior is to capture all packets that the operating system's device driver provides. On a lightly loaded home network this is not a problem, but on a busy network at a large enterprise, the deluge of packets would prove too much for the user to handle. Ethereal provides *capture filters*, which allow you to capture only the packets which you are interested in. By using capture filters, the operating system (OS) sends only selected packets to Ethereal for processing.

Once your packets are loaded into Ethereal, there still may be too many packets for you to easily focus on the problem you're trying to solve. For this situation Ethereal provides *display filters,* which allow you to specify which packets are shown in Ethereal's Graphical User Interface (GUI). As all of the packets are still in memory, they will once again become visible when you reset your display filter.

The reason that there is a distinction between *capture filters* and *display filters* is not due to their different uses, but instead to how they are implemented in Ethereal. The Ethereal program does not know how to capture packets from network interfaces by itself. Instead, it relies on a program library to do the packet capturing. On UNIX this library is *pcap* (also known as *libpcap*), maintained by the same group that develops *tcpdump*, the venerable UNIX command-line sniffer available at www.tcpdump.org. On Windows, this library is *WinPcap*, a device driver and dynamic link library (DLL) that provides a *pcap* interface for Windows programs. For convenience, we'll refer to *pcap* and *WinPcap* simply as *pcap*, since for our purposes they are operationally equivalent.

It is the pcap library that provides the capture-filtering mechanism to Ethereal. The pcap library provides a very fast filtering engine, which is important because running a filter on a packet uses processing power from your computer. The packet data has to be analyzed to determine if it passes the filter condition. Inasmuch, if the analysis takes a long time, your operating system might not have time to address the next incoming packet resulting in a dropped packet.

The speed of capture filters is great for live captures, but pcap's filter language is not powerful or expressive enough for many sniffing or analysis needs. The language itself allows you to test only a few fields from a few protocols. To overcome this deficiency, display filters were introduced to Ethereal. These display filters are a packet filter language completely distinct from pcap's packet filter language. Almost every protocol and field that Ethereal knows how to retrieve from a packet has a name. Ethereal enables you to use the protocol names and field names to filter packets for display. Display filters rely on a complete dissection of the packet by Ethereal, and thus are much slower than capture filters, which operate differently. Each type of filter has its place; capture filters are good for quickly discarding packets from a live network interface, while display filters are good for fine-tuning which packets you see after the packets have been loaded into Ethereal.

Writing Capture Filters

Ethereal's capture filters use the pcap library's filter mechanism. These filters are often called tcpdump filters, as tcpdump is the most famous program that uses the pcap library, and the filter syntax itself is documented in the tcpdump man-page, or manual page. Any program that uses pcap, like tcpdump or Ethereal, can use this filter syntax.

While tcpdump can decode many protocols, its filter language cannot directly address other protocols. The keywords defined in the tcpdump filter language are oriented mostly toward layer 2 and TCP/IP filtering, with few exceptions.

NOTE

A *manpage*, *man page*, or *manual page*, is the documentation that comes with a UNIX program. Man pages can be read with the UNIX **man** command. For example, to read the tcpdump man page, you would type **man tcpdump**. The Ethereal man page can be read with **man ethereal**. Many man pages are available as HyperText Markup Language (HTML) on the web. The tcpdump man page is at www.tcpdump.org/tcpdump_man.html and Ethereal man pages can be viewed at www.ethereal.com by clicking on the links under **Information | Documentation** on the left-hand side of the web page.

Tcpdump Syntax Explained

The tcpdump filter language gives you many ways to look at data inside a packet. The language is designed to give you easy access to the most commonly used fields from the layer 2 and TCP/IP (Transmission Control Protocol/Internet Protocol) group of protocols by providing keywords that are used to match values of host addresses, hardware addresses, and ports. But, the filter language can handle more than just layer 2 and TCP/IP protocols. It also allows you to look for a number of specific protocols, look at arbitrary bytes in the packet data, and look at meta-data bout the packet.

Host Names and Addresses

Probably the most common use of a tcpdump filter is to capture network traffic originating from or destined for a particular Internet Protocol (IP) address. You can identify an IPv4 (Internet Protocol version 4), IPv6 (Internet Protocol version 6) address, or a hostname by using the **host** keyword. For example, to captures all IPv4 packets that have a source or destination address of 192.168.1.1, you would use:

```
host 192.168.1.1
```

Or, you can use an IPv6 address to capture IPv6 packets:

```
host 2::8100:2:30a:c392:fc5a
```

You can also use a hostname or a DNS (Domain Name Service), either which resolves to either an IPv4 or IPv6 address:

```
host wizard

host www.ethereal.com
```

These three examples will return any IP packet, including Transmission Control Protocol (TCP), User Datagram Protocol (UDP), and any other protocol riding on top of IP, as long as it has an IP source address or IP destination address matching the given IP address or hostname. Furthermore, if the hostname resolves to more than one IP address, as Domain Name System (DNS) entries can, then all of those resolved IP addresses are used in the match.

If you would like to narrow the filter to capture packets that only originate from an IP address, then you use the **src** (short for source) keyword modifier:

```
src host 192.168.1.1
```

Similarly, to match a destination IP address, you use the **dst** (short for destination) keyword modifier:

```
dst host 192.168.255.255
```

You can also use a shorthand notation which takes advantage of the fact that **host** is understood from **src** and **dst**, so that you can check host addresses without using **host**:

```
src 192.168.1.1
dst 192.168.255.255
```

The **host** keyword lets you check for an IP address. Similarly, you can use the **net** keyword to check for an IP network. Use the **net** keyword in combination with an address formatted in classless interdomain routing (CIDR) notation. CIDR notation is made up of an IPv4 address and a number, separated by a slash. The number after the slash specifies the number of bits, out of the thirty-two bits in the IPv4 address, that make up the network portion of the address. If you want to look at packets coming from any host on the 192.168.100.0 network, which uses 24 bits for the network number (a 255.255.255.0 netmask), then you would use this capture filter:

```
src net 192.168.100.0/24
```

Hardware Addresses (MAC Addresses)

If, instead of using IP addresses, you wish to capture packets based on the hardware address of the network card, you use the **ether** (short for Ethernet) modifier. For example, to find all broadcast packets, which are packets destined for the hardware address ff:ff:ff:ff:ff:ff, use:

```
ether host ff:ff:ff:ff:ff:ff
```

There are also **fddi** (fiber distributed data interface) and **tr** (token-ring) keywords that match the hardware addresses of NICs (Network Interface Cards). However, since Ethernet, FDDI, and token-ring all contain 6-byte hardware addresses in their protocol headers, the tcpdump filter language treats **ether**, **fddi**, and **tr** as synonyms. It doesn't matter which of the three topologies your interface card has, you can use any of the three keywords. In practice, **ether** is most commonly used.

The **ether** modifier is placed before the **dst** and **src** modifiers; to capture packets destined for a particular hardware address, you enter:

```
ether dst host ff:ff:ff:ff:ff:ff
```

Again, you can use short hand, because **dst** implies **host**, and instead enter:

```
ether dst ff:ff:ff:ff:ff:ff
```

To filter packets based on the source hardware address, the **src** modifier is again used:

```
ether src host 00:f9:06:aa:01:03
ether src 00:f9:06:aa:01:03
```

Ports

The **port** keyword can be used to capture packets that are destined for certain applications, because some applications communicate on well-known TCP and UDP ports. For example, to capture only Hypertext Transfer Protocol (HTTP) packets, which are commonly sent on TCP port 80, you can use:

```
port 80
```

However, this checks for packets on both UDP port 80 and TCP port 80. To narrow it to TCP, **tcp** can be used as a qualifier:

```
tcp port 80
```

Or, if you have **http** defined for a port number in the /etc/services file on UNIX, you can use:

```
tcp port http
```

The **udp** keyword is also available in case you want to capture UDP packets on a certain port. In either instance, the directional qualifiers **src** and **dst** can be used. If you are sniffing for UDP requests being sent to a DNS server, you would want to capture UDP packets destined for port 53, as that's the port for DNS.

```
udp dst port 53
```

If you want the replies, you would look for UDP packets with a source of port 53:

```
udp src port 53
```

Logical Operations

The tcpdump filter language allows you to combine several statements with logical operators to create complicated filters. The logic operator **not** reverses the value of a test, while **and** and **or** let you join multiple tests. These three logic keywords have alternate representations, which are used in the C programming language:

- **not** is equivalent to **!**
- **and** is equivalent to **&&**
- **or** is equivalent to **||**

You can also use parentheses when you need to group multiple statements with logical operations. Parentheses are not always needed, but can be used to make the filter easier to understand.

As an example of negation, to capture everything except DNS lookups, use:

```
not port 53
```

Normally, **port 53** would capture any TCP or UDP packets with a source or destination port of 53. The logical keyword **not** reverses the sense of the filter, so that everything is captured except for TCP or UDP packets with a source or destination port of 53.

The logical operator **and** is used to require that multiple conditions in a test be true. For example, to look at telnet packets to or from the host www.ethereal.com, this filter would be used:

```
host www.ethereal.com and port telnet
```

If you wanted either telnet packets or ssh packets, you would use **or**:

```
port telnet or port ssh
```

To combine the **port telnet or port ssh** test with a test for the www.ethereal.com host, you use **and,** but you also need to use parentheses:

```
host www.ethereal.com and ( port telnet or port ssh )
```

The logical operators **and** and **or** have the same precedence, which means that they are analyzed in the order that they are listed in the capture filter. If the parentheses are not used, the capture filter would test for telnet packets to or from the host www.ethereal.com, or ssh packets to or from any IP:

```
host www.ethereal.com and port telnet or port ssh
```

Protocols

The tcpdump filter syntax provides some protocol names as keywords, allowing you to test for the existence of these protocols. These protocol keywords are:

- **aarp** AppleTalk Address Resolution Protocol
- **ah** Authentication Header
- **arp** Address Resolution Protocol
- **atalk** AppleTalk

- **clnp** Connectionless Network Protocol
- **decnet** Digital Equipment Corporation Network protocol suite
- **esis** (or "es–is") End System-to-Intermediate System
- **esp** Encapsulating Security Payload
- **icmp** Internet Control Message Protocol
- **icmp6** Internet Control Message Protocol, for IPv6
- **igmp** Internet Group Management Protocol
- **igrp** Interior Gateway Routing Protocol
- **ip** Internet Protocol
- **ip6** Internet Protocol version 6
- **ipx** Internetwork Packet Exchange
- **isis** (or "is–is") Intermediate System-to-Intermediate System
- **iso** International Organization for Standardization
- **lat** Local Area Transport
- **mopdl** Maintenance Operation Protocol
- **moprc** Maintenance Operation Protocol
- **netbeui** NetBIOS Extended User Interface
- **pim** Protocol Independent Multicast
- **rarp** Reverse Address Resolution Protocol
- **sca** Systems Communication Architecture
- **sctp** Stream Control Transmission Protocol
- **stp** Spanning Tree Protocol
- **tcp** Transmission Control Protocol
- **udp** User Datagram Protocol
- **vrrp** Virtual Router Redundancy Protocol

For example, to capture all ICMP packets the capture filter is one word:

```
icmp
```

To capture everything that is not an IPX packet, use negation and the protocol keyword:

```
not ipx
```

We've talked about ports in TCP and UDP packets, but some protocols use
the concept of *protocol* to indicate what type of payload it is carrying. For
example, the IP header contains a *protocol* field whose numeric value indicates the
type of payload it is carrying. Possible values for this protocol field are 1 for
ICMP, 6 for TCP, and 17 for UDP. On a UNIX system, you can find a list of IP
protocol numbers in the /etc/protocols file.

The tcpdump filter syntax allows you to test the **proto** field (short for protocol) for the protocols that have it. You can use the **proto** keyword with the
ether, **fddi**, **tr**, **ppp**, **ip**, **ip6**, and **iso** protocol keywords. For example, while you
can test for the presence of the TCP protocol via the **tcp** keyword, you could
also check for 6 as the value of the IP protocol field, as "6" designates TCP.

```
ip proto 6
```

Protocol Fields

While tcpdump can decode many protocols, the tcpdump filter syntax does not
let you easily test for the values of all fields that tcpdump knows how to parse.
You've seen that many protocol names are provided as keywords, but very few
fields within these protocols have names in the tcpdump filter syntax.

Tcpdump filters do allow you to grab and compare values out of the packet,
so that if the offset of a field within a protocol is known, its value can be
checked. This method is not as elegant as using a field name, but it works.

To retrieve a single byte from a packet, you use square brackets to indicate
the offset of that byte from the beginning of a particular protocol. Offsets start at
zero, so that **tcp[0]** would give the first byte in the TCP header, while **tcp[1]**
would give the second byte. Table 5.1 shows the bit layout of the TCP header, as
defined by RFC (Request For Comments) 793, available at www.ibiblio.org/
pub/docs/rfc/rfc793.txt.

Table 5.1 TCP Header Layout

0	1	2	3	4	5	6	7	8	9	10	11	12	13	14	15	16	17	18	19	20	21	22	23	24	25	26	27	28	29	30	31
Source Port																Destination Port															
Sequence Number																															
Acknowledgment Number																															
Data Offset				Reserved						URG	ACK	PSH	RST	SYN	FIN	Window															
Checksum																Urgent Pointer															
Options																								Padding							
Data																															

Instead of a one-byte integer, you can also retrieve either a two-byte integer or a four-byte integer, using a colon inside the square brackets: **tcp[0:2]** and **tcp[0:4]**. Multi-byte integers are always extracted in network order, also known as big-endian order. To compute the value of multi-byte network-order integers, use these formulas:

- **2-byte** value = byte0 $\star$ 0x100 + byte1
- **4-byte** value = byte0 $\star$ 0x1000000 + byte1 $\star$ 0x10000 + byte2 $\star$ 0x100 + byte3

The numbers preceded by "0x" in the formulas are hexadecimal numbers.

Unfortunately, only some protocols allow you to retrieve bytes from their data. Interestingly, some protocols whose names could not be used as keywords allow you to retrieve their data by using square brackets. Square brackets can be used to retrieve bytes from these protocols:

- **arp** Address Resolution Protocol
- **atalk** Appletalk
- **decnet** Digital Equipment Corporation Network protocol suite
- **ether** Ethernet
- **fddi** Fiber Distributed Data Interface
- **icmp** Internet Control Message Protocol
- **igmp** Internet Group Management Protocol
- **igrp** Interior Gateway Routing Protocol
- **ip** Internet Protocol
- **lat** Local Area Transport
- **link** Link layer
- **mopdl** Maintenance Operation Protocol
- **moprc** Maintenance Operation Protocol
- **pim** Protocol Independent Multicast
- **ppp** Point-to-Point Protocol
- **rarp** Reverse Address Resolution Protocol
- **sca** Systems Communication Architecture

- **sctp** Stream Control Transmission Protocol
- **tcp** Transmission Control Protocol
- **tr** Token-Ring
- **udp** User Datagram Protocol
- **vrrp** Virtual Router Redundancy Protocol

The value that is retrieved from the packet data is an integer, which can be compared with any of the numeric relations shown in Table 5.2.

Table 5.2 Numeric Relations

Numeric Relation	Meaning
>	Greater Than
>=	Greater Than or Equal To
<	Less Than
<=	Less Than or Equal To
= or ==	Equal To
!=	Not Equal To

Additionally, the arithmetic operators **+**, **-**, *****, and **/** are provided, as are the bit-wise operators **&** and **|**. The bitwise operator **&** allows you to logically AND the bits of integers, while **|** allows you to logically OR the bits.

For example, the **icmp** keyword will let you filter for any ICMP packet. But there are different types of ICMP packets, depending on their function. What if you wanted to look only for ICMP *ping* packets? The ICMP ping, or echo request/reply, packet layout is shown in Table 5.3. It comes from RFC 792, available at www.ibiblio.org/pub/docs/rfc/rfc792.txt.

Table 5.3 ICMP Echo Request/Reply Header Layout

0 1 2 3 4 5 6 7	8 9 10 11 12 13 14 15	16 17 18 19 20 21 22 23 24 25 26 27 28 29 30 31
Type	Code	Checksum
Identifier		Sequence Number
Data….		

The ICMP protocol has a field called *type*, which indicates what type the ICMP packet is. If the *type* field is 8, then the packet is an ICMP *echo (ping) request*, while if the *type* field is 0, then the packet is an ICMP *echo (ping) reply*. That type field is a one-byte field at the very beginning of the ICMP protocol header. This capture filter tests for packets that are either ICMP *ping requests* or ICMP *ping replies* by retrieving that first byte:

```
icmp[0] == 8 or icmp[0] == 0
```

As a convenience, the libpcap authors have made available some constant value keywords that are named after ICMP fields. Their values give the offset and the possible values of those fields. The value keywords can be used so that the numbers they stand for need not be remembered. For example, the *icmptype* is equal to the offset of the ICMP *type* field (which is 0), the *icmp-echo* variable is equal to 8, which means that the ICMP packet is an echo request, and *icmp-echoreply* is equal to 0, which means that the ICMP packet is an echo reply. The test for ICMP ping requests and replies can be written as:

```
icmp[icmptype] == icmp-echo or icmp[icmptype] == icmp-echoreply
```

The keywords that define constant values for field offsets are listed in Table 5.4.

Table 5.4 Constant Value Keywords

Keyword	Value	Used in Protocol
icmptype	0	icmp
icmpcode	1	icmp
tcpflags	13	tcp

Table 5.5 lists the keywords that provide names for the ICMP *type* values.

Table 5.5 ICMP type Constant Value Keywords

Keyword	Value
icmp-echoreply	0
icmp-unreach	3
icmp-sourcequench	4
icmp-redirect	5
icmp-echo	8
icmp-routeradvert	9

Continued

Table 5.5 ICMP type Constant Value Keywords

Keyword	Value
icmp-routersolicit	10
icmp-timxceed	11
icmp-paramprob	12
icmp-tstamp	13
icmp-tstampreply	14
icmp-ireq	15
icmp-ireqreply	16
icmp-maskreq	17
icmp-maskreply	18

Bitwise Operators

The TCP *flags* field is a bit-field. Bit-fields are integers in which the individual bits are used as separate fields. For example, the TCP *flags* field is an 8-bit integer field, but the bits in that integer represent independent fields that are either true or false, or 1 or 0. In the tcpdump filter language, the fields for TCP *flags* have keywords with constant values, as shown in Table 5.6.

Table 5.6 TCP Flags Constant Value Keywords

Keyword	Value
tcp-fin	0x01
tcp-syn	0x02
tcp-rst	0x04
tcp-push	0x08
tcp-ack	0x10
tcp-urg	0x20

The tcpdump filter language defines keywords with constant values for the TCP flags field because it is very common to test for values of this field when looking at TCP problems, especially when related to firewalls or Network Address Translation (NAT). It is important to know how to use bit-field operators properly because complications arise when multiple bits can be set in the bit-field. The TCP flags field can have multiple bits set. Table 5.7 shows the flags field of a TCP packet with its SYN bit (**tcp-syn**) set.

Table 5.7 TCP SYN Packet Flags Bit-field

URG	ACK	PUSH	RST	SYN	FIN
0	0	0	0	1	0

In this case, only the **tcp-syn** bit is set, so the value 0x02 can be tested, which is the value of **tcp-syn**:

```
tcp[tcpflag] == 0x02
```

or

```
tcp[tcpflag] == tcp-syn
```

However, in the case of the second packet in a TCP handshake, a SYN/ACK packet, both the **tcp-syn** and **tcp-ack** bits are set, as shown in Table 5.8.

Table 5.8 TCP SYN/ACK Packet Flags Bit-field

URG	ACK	PUSH	RST	SYN	FIN
0	1	0	0	1	0

When SYN and ACK are both set, the TCP flags field will equal 0x02 + 0x10, or 0x12. Thus the filter **tcp[tcpflag] == tcp-syn** will fail to show the packets that have SYN plus any other field set; the filter will give you packets that have only SYN set. To write a filter to test for the SYN bit being set, you need to use the bitwise-AND operator to mask out all the bits except for the SYN bit.

```
tcp[tcpflag] & tcp-syn == 0x02
```

or:

```
tcp[tcpflag] & tcp-syn == tcp-syn
```

The bitwise arithmetic using **&** (bitwise AND) when comparing a TCP flags field that has SYN and ACK set is shown in Table 5.9.

Table 5.9 TCP SYN/ACK Packet Bitwise AND Against tcp-syn

	URG	ACK	PUSH	RST	SYN	FIN	Value	Meaning
	0	1	0	0	1	0	0x12	SYN/ACK
AND	0	0	0	0	1	0	0x02	tcp-syn
	0	0	0	0	1	0	0x02	tcp-syn

In this case, the bitwise AND produces a result of 0x02, which is equal to **tcp-syn**, so we have determined that the SYN bit is indeed set. By using the bitwise AND, you can tell if any particular bit in the bit-field is set, even if other bits in the bit-field are set. Table 5.10 shows the bitwise arithmetic when the TCP packet is an ACK packet, and the TCP flags field has only ACK set.

Table 5.10 TCP ACK Packet Bitwise-AND Against tcp-syn

	URG	ACK	PUSH	RST	SYN	FIN	Value	Meaning
	0	1	0	0	0	0	0x10	ACK
AND	0	0	0	0	1	0	0x02	tcp-syn
	0	0	0	0	0	0	0x00	0

The result is 0x00, which does not equal **tcp-syn**, so a TCP ACK packet does not pass the **tcp[tcpflag] & tcp-syn == tcp-syn** test.

Packet Size

The tcpdump filter language allows you to test metadata about the packet instead of data from the packet itself. The packet size is available in a variable named *len*. It can be tested with the standard arithmetic operators. To test for packets smaller than 100 bytes, use this filter:

```
len < 100
```

The **less** and **greater** operators are built-in shorthand keywords for testing the **len** variable against a number. **less 100** is the same as **len <= 100**, while **greater 1500** is the same as **len >= 1500**.

Tools & Traps…

Testing Capture Filters

Would you like to test your capture filter without actually loading Ethereal? Capture filters are the same filters that tcpdump uses, so you can supply the capture filter on tcpdump's command line to see if tcpdump can understand your capture filter:

```
$ tcpdump less 100
```

If your capture filter makes use of punctuation that is normally special to the UNIX shell, you need to enclose your capture filter in single quotes:

```
$ tcpdump 'len > 1500'
```

Tcpdump has a **–d** option, which shows you the Berkeley Packet Filter (BPF) code used to operate the capture filter. BPF is the mechanism that many operating systems provide for packet capture filters. You can read about BPF "The BSD Packet Filter: A New Architecture for User-Level Packet Capture", by Steven McCanne and Van Jacobson, at www.tcpdump.org/papers/bpf-usenix93.pdf. Here's an example of BPF code:

```
$ tcpdump -d  'len > 0xff'
(000) ld        #pktlen
(001) jgt       #0xff               jt 2    jf 3
(002) ret       #96
(003) ret       #0
```

Examples

The following list includes a few examples of capture filters.

- All HTTP packets: **tcp port 80**

- Non-HTTP packets: **not tcp port 80** or **!tcp port 80** or **tcp port not 80** or **tcp port !80**

- HTTP browsing to www.ethereal.com: **tcp port 80 and dst www.ethereal.com**

- HTTP browsing to hosts other than www.ethereal.com: **tcp port 80 and not dst www.ethereal.com**

- IPX packets: **ipx**

- IPX packets destined for IPX network 00:01:F0:EE: not possible, because you cannot retrieve bytes using the **ipx** keyword

- TCP packets: **tcp** or **ip proto 5**

- TCP SYN packets: **tcp[tcpflag] & tcp-syn == tcp-syn**

- IP packets with total length > 255: **ip[2:2] > 0xff**

- IP or IPX packets: **ip or ipx**

Using Capture Filters

Tethereal accepts capture filters on the command-line with the **–f** option, as shown in this example.

```
# tethereal -i eth1 -f icmp
Capturing on eth1
  0.000000    10.0.0.5 > 10.0.0.1      ICMP Echo (ping) request
  0.000062    10.0.0.1 -> 10.0.0.5     ICMP Echo (ping) reply
  1.010753    10.0.0.5 -> 10.0.0.1     ICMP Echo (ping) request
  1.010814    10.0.0.1 -> 10.0.0.5     ICMP Echo (ping) reply
```

Remember that the argument to **–f** is a single argument. If your capture filter has spaces in it, you need to surround the capture filter in quotes so that it is passed as the single argument of the **–f** option:

```
# tethereal -i eth1 -f 'icmp[0] == 0 or icmp[0] == 8'
```

Conveniently, Tethereal, like tcpdump, will also accept any leftover arguments on the commandline and use them as a capture filter.

```
# tethereal -i eth1 icmp[0] == 8
```

When making use of this facility, you cannot use the **–f** option.

```
# tethereal -f icmp -i eth1 icmp[0] == 8
tethereal: Capture filters were specified both with "-f" and with additional
command-line arguments
```

Be aware of characters that are special to the UNIX shell when using capture filters on the command line. This filter should be picking up echo requests and echo replies, but only echo replies are seen.

```
# tethereal  -i eth1 icmp[0] == 0 || icmp[0] == 8
Capturing on eth1
  0.000000     10.0.0.1 -> 10.0.0.5      ICMP Echo (ping) reply
  1.009672     10.0.0.1 -> 10.0.0.5      ICMP Echo (ping) reply
  2.016646     10.0.0.1 -> 10.0.0.5      ICMP Echo (ping) reply
```

The problem is that the two vertical bars (||) are interpreted by the UNIX shell. The two vertical bars and the rest of the command line are never seen by tethereal. To avoid this behavior, use quotes around the capture filter:

```
# tethereal  -i eth1  'icmp[0] == 0 || icmp[0] == 8'
Capturing on eth1
  0.000000     10.0.0.5 -> 10.0.0.1      ICMP Echo (ping) request
  0.000057     10.0.0.1 -> 10.0.0.5      ICMP Echo (ping) reply
  1.010248     10.0.0.5 -> 10.0.0.1      ICMP Echo (ping) request
  1.010299     10.0.0.1 -> 10.0.0.5      ICMP Echo (ping) reply
```

Ethereal, like Tethereal, accepts capture filters with the **–f** option. If you use Ethereal's **–k** option, Ethereal will immediately start capturing packets. You can use the **–k** option to start a capture and use the **–f** option to supply a capture filter. Besides **–k** and **–f**, Ethereal and Tethereal share many of the same capture-related command line options. However, Ethereal will not accept leftover arguments on the command line and treat them as part of a capture filter.

```
ethereal [ -vh ] [ -klLnpQS ] [ -a <capture autostop condition> ] ...
        [ -b <number of ringbuffer files>[:<duration>] ]
        [ -B <byte view height> ] [ -c <count> ] [ -f <capture filter> ]
        [ -i <interface> ] [ -m <medium font> ] [ -N <resolving> ]
        [ -o <preference setting> ] ... [ -P <packet list height> ]
        [ -r <infile> ] [ -R <read filter> ] [ -s <snaplen> ]
        [ -t <time stamp format> ] [ -T <tree view height> ]
        [ -w <savefile> ] [ -y <link type> ] [ -z <statistics string> ]
        [ <infile> ]
tethereal [ -vh ] [ -DlLnpqSVx ] [ -a <capture autostop condition> ] ...
        [ -b <number of ring buffer files>[:<duration>] ] [ -c <count> ]
        [ -d <layer_type>==<selector>,<decode_as_protocol> ] ...
```

```
[ -f <capture filter> ] [ -F <output file type> ] [ -i <interface> ]
[ -N <resolving> ] [ -o <preference setting> ] ... [ -r <infile> ]
[ -R <read filter> ] [ -s <snaplen> ] [ -t <time stamp format> ]
[ -T pdml|ps|text ] [ -w <savefile> ] [ -y <link type> ]
[ -z <statistics string> ]
```

Being a graphical application, Ethereal also accepts capture filters in its graphical user interface. Before starting to capture packets, the **Capture Options** dialog box, as shown in Figure 5.1, provides a **Filter** text entry box where you can type a capture filter.

Figure 5.1 Capture Options Dialog Box

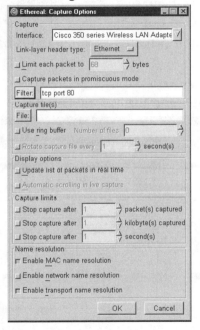

Writing Display Filters

Ethereal's display filter mechanism is designed differently than tcpdump's filters. Tcpdump is a packet analyzer that knows how to decode many protocols, but it relies on libpcap's filtering engine. Libpcap is a separate library that does not know how to parse many protocols, so libpcap's filter language is poor in relation to tcpdump's ability in this respect.

In Ethereal, the protocol-dissection mechanism is intertwined with the display filter mechanism. For almost every item you see in the protocol tree in the middle pane of Ethereal's GUI, Ethereal has a field name that you can use in a display filter. The Appendix of this book has a list of some commonly used display-filter field names that Ethereal defines, while the CD-ROM that accompanies this book provides HTML pages that show all the display-filter field names for Ethereal version 0.10.0a. These HTML pages are in the /filters directory on the CD-ROM. You can also use the **Help | Supported Protocols | Display Filter Fields** option in Ethereal to see a similar list. Perhaps the easiest way to find the display-filter name of a field that you're interested in is to highlight that field in the Ethereal GUI. When highlighted, Ethereal will provide the display-filter field name in the right-hand side of the status bar at the bottom of the GUI. Figure 5.2 shows that **ip.len** is the name of the IP Total Length field. The **ip.len** field name is shown in parentheses in the status bar on the bottom right of the Ethereal window.

Figure 5.2 Display Filter Name for IP Total Length

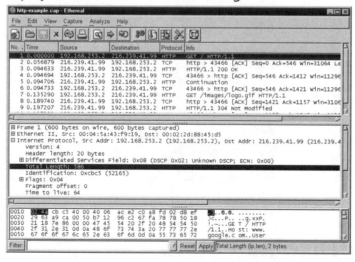

Even the protocol names themselves have display-filter names. Figure 5.3 shows that the **ip** field name represents the IP protocol.

Figure 5.3 Display Filter Name for IP

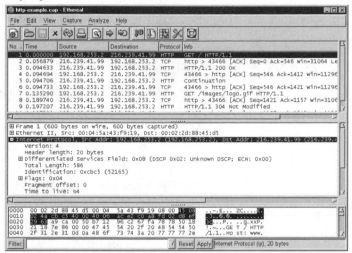

Writing Expressions

To test for the existence of a protocol or a field, the display filter is simply the display-filter field name of that protocol or field. To show all IP packets, use:

```
ip
```

This shows all packets where the IP protocol is present. You could also show all packets where a field is present:

```
ip.len
```

Because IP packets always have a *total length* (**ip.len**) field, this is functionally equivalent to testing merely for **ip**. But some protocols, like TCP, can vary the fields that are present in a protocol header. TCP has optional fields, one of which is *MSS option*, represented by the **tcp.options.mss_val** field name. To find all packets that have the **tcp.options.mss_val** field, just name the field in the display filter:

```
tcp.options.mss_val
```

Display-filter fields in Ethereal are typed. This means that depending on its type, a field can hold only certain values. The types in the display filter language are shown in Table 5.11.

Table 5.11 Display Filter Field Types

Display Filter Field Types	Possible Values
Unsigned Integer	Non-negative integers. Can be 8-, 16-, 24-, 32, or 64-bits wide
Signed Integer	Integers. Can be 8-, 16-, 24-, 32-, or 64-bits wide
Boolean	True or False
Frame Number	Like a 32-bit Unsigned Integer, but with special behaviors
Floating Point	Decimal number, i.e., real numbers
Double-precision Floating Point	Floating point number that can store more digits
String	Sequence of characters
Byte String	A sequence of hexadecimal digits
Hardware Address	A six-byte long Byte String with name-lookup capabilities
IPv4 Address	IPv4 address with name-lookup capabilities
IPv6 Address	IPv6 address with name-lookup capabilities
IPX Network	4-byte IPX network number with name-lookup capabilities
Absolute Time	Date/time stamp
Relative Time	Number of seconds between two absolute times
None	A field that holds no value and is used only as a label or placeholder
Protocol	Protocol keywords

The operators that can be used to compare values are shown in Table 5.12.

Table 5.12 Operators Used to Compare Values

Operators	Meanings
> or gt	Greater Than
>= or ge	Greater Than or Equal To
< or lt	Less Than
<= or le	Less Than or Equal To

Continued

Table 5.12 Operators Used to Compare Values

Operators	Meanings
== or eq	Equal To
!= or ne	Not Equal To
contains	A string or byte string is found within another
matches	A regular expression matches a string

Multiple relations can be combined with the logical operators **and** and **or**. You can negate the logical meanings with **not**. Parenthesis can be used to group logical operations correctly.

NOTE

The **matches** operator only works if your copy of Ethereal was compiled with support for the Perl Compatible Regular Expressions (PCRE) library. Perl is a very popular scripting language which has regular expression built into its syntax, giving programmers a powerful way to search for strings. The PCRE library, available at www.pcre.org, enables other programs, like Ethereal, to use regular expressions that are in the same syntax as those provided by Perl. Furthermore, the **matches** operator was introduced to Ethereal in version 0.10.0, and only works with string fields. During the development of this book, the **matches** operator has been extended to work on byte sequences and protocols, just like the **contains** operator. When Ethereal 0.10.1 is released, the **matches** operator will work on all the same fields that the **contains** operator currently supports.

Integers

Integer fields hold numeric values. The numeric values are integers, or whole numbers without fractional parts. Integers can be expressed in decimal, octal, or hexadecimal notation. The octal notation requires an initial "0" (zero), while hexadecimal notation requires an initial "0x" (zero x). Table 5.13 shows examples of how to write the same integer in decimal, octal, and hexadecimal representations.

Table 5.13 Different Representations for the Same Integer

Display Filter	Integer Notation
eth.len > 1500	Decimal
eth.len > 02734	Octal
eth.len > 0x5dc	Hexadecimal

Integer fields are categorized as signed or unsigned, and as 8-bit, 16-bit, 24-bit, 32-bit, or 64-bit in width. These two categories describe how the integers are stored in a computer's memory. The categories determine the range of values that the integer can be (see Table 5.14).

Table 5.14 Range of Values According to Integer

Bit Width	Signed Range	Unsigned Range
8-bit	-2^7 to 2^7-1 -128 to 127	0 to 2^8-1 0 to 255
16-bit	-2^{15} to $2^{15}-1$ -32,768 to 32,767	0 to $2^{16}-1$ 0 to 65,535
24-bit	-2^{23} to $2^{23}-1$ -8,388,608 to 8,388,607	0 to $2^{24}-1$ 0 to 16,777,215
32-bit	-2^{31} to $2^{31}-1$ -2,147,483,648 to 2,147,483,647	0 to $2^{32}-1$ to 4,294,967,295
64-bit	-2^{63} to $-2^{63}-1$	0 to $2^{64}-1$

Some integer fields also have labels representing specific values that the field can be. For example, the Systems Network Architecture (SNA) Transmission Group Segmenting Field, or **sna.th.tgsf**, can have four distinct values, as shown in Table 5.15.

Table 5.15 SNA Transmission Group Segmenting Field

Integer Field/Value	Label
0	Not Segmented
1	Last segment
2	First segment
3	Middle segment

In these cases, either the integer value or the label can be used when testing for values of **sna.th.tgsf**. These display filters are equivalent:

```
sna.th.tgsf == 2
sna.th.tgsf == "First segment"
```

This example also shows one instance of how text (or, in programmer jargon, *strings*) can be represented in a display filter. Note that the label is enclosed by double quotes. More ways of representing strings will be discussed in the section about string fields.

You can use the **Filter Expression** dialog box, described later in this chapter, to look at the possible values for fields that have label values. You can also use the tables in the Appendix of this book, or the HTML pages in the /filters directory on the accompanying CD-ROM to find the same information.

Some integer fields are of a type called *frame number*. This is a special integer type within Ethereal that acts like a 32-bit unsigned integer type, but if you right-click on such a field in the GUI, the pop-up menu will have an option called **Go to Corresponding Frame** which brings you to the frame mentioned by the field. This is used for protocols that make use of request/response packet pairs. For example, the Server Message Block (SMB) and NetWare Core Protocol (NCP) protocols make use of frame-number fields. Figure 5.4 shows an SMB response packet with a field **smb.response_to**, which gives the frame number of the request packet. Being able to jump to the request packet by clicking on a field in the reply packet can be handy when debugging network problems.

Figure 5.4 SMB Response

Booleans

Boolean fields are fields that have a true or false value. They can be compared against the strings *True* and *False*, in lower-case, upper-case, or any combination of case, or against the values 1 and 0, which are Ethereal's internal representation of True and False, respectively. In some cases, boolean fields, like integer fields, have labels that better describe the 1 or 0 value. For example, the **sna.rh.sdi** field, the SNA Sense Data Included field, is a boolean field that has the labels *Included* and *Not Included*, which describe its values more accurately than *True* or *False*. These display filters are equivalent:

```
sna.rh.sdi == 0
sna.rh.sdi == "Not Included"
sna.rh.sdi == false
```

Floating Point Numbers

Floating point numbers are different from integer numbers in that they contain fractional parts. Even if the number to the right of the decimal point is 0 (or decimal comma, if your locale uses commas instead of periods), it's still a fractional part of the number. Floating point numbers can be positive or negative. Ethereal provides two types of floating point numbers: regular floating point numbers, and double-precision floating point numbers. The difference between the two is that double-precision floating point numbers can more accurately represent numbers than regular floating point numbers because more digits can be stored. In practice, all of Ethereal's floating point numbers are of the double-precision type.

Floating point numbers, either regular or double-precision, are not frequently found in protocols, but they do exist. For example, the **who** protocol, which is the format of the messages sent by the *rwhod* program on UNIX systems announcing load averages and current logins, has floating point numbers. Some example display filters are:

```
who.loadav_5 > 3.5
who.loadav_10 <= 10
who.loadav_10 <= 10.0
```

Strings

Some fields hold text values. Sequences of characters are called *strings* in programming jargon and in Ethereal. If the string you want to represent has no spaces and is not the same as the name of a field, you can use the string directly in your display filter:

```
sna.rh.csi == ASCII
```

However, if the string has a space in it, or is the same as the name as a field, the string will have to be enclosed in double quotes:

```
sna.rh.sdi == "Not included"
```

If the string you're providing has a double quote in it, you need to use a backslash followed by a double-quote to embed that double quote in the string. The following display filter looks for a double-quote, followed by **Y, E, S,** followed by another double-quote.

```
http contains "\"Yes\""
```

The backslash also allows you to embed 8-bit unsigned integers, that is, single bytes, inside the string by using either hexadecimal or octal notation:

```
frame contains "\0777"
frame contains "\xff"
```

And if you're really looking for a backslash, then you use a backslash followed by another backslash. To look for **\begin,** the display filter would look like:

```
http contains "\\begin"
```

Ethereal's display filter syntax currently only allows you to look for ASCII (American Standard Code for Information Interchange) strings. While the **Edit | Find Packet** GUI option allows you to search for ASCII and Unicode strings, the display filter language doesn't allow you to search any other string-encoding, including Unicode or EBCDIC (Extended Binary Coded Decimal Interchange Code) strings. Hopefully, a future version of Ethereal will provide an extension to the display filter language to allow you to denote the character encoding you want when looking for a string. Similarly, be aware that all string comparisons are case-sensitive. In the display filter language, searching for *GOOD* will not uncover *good,* as the former is in uppercase, while the latter is in lowercase. Once again, perhaps a future modification to Ethereal will add the ability to perform case-insensitive comparisons.

The **matches** operator lets you search for text in string fields using a regular expression. The operator is named after the Perl match operator (**m//**), and in fact, the regular expressions supported by Ethereal are the same regular expressions that Perl uses. Ethereal manages this by using the Perl Compatible Regular Expressions

(PCRE) library, which other popular applications also use. This is helpful because you don't need to learn an Ethereal-specific regular expression syntax if you already happen to know regular expressions from Perl, Python, PHP (a recursive acronym which stands for "PHP: Hypertext Preprocessor"), Apache, Exim, or many other applications.

The best documentation for Perl regular expressions comes from the Perl regular expression manual page, available on-line at www.perldoc.com/perl5.8.0/pod/perlre.html. The Python documentation at www.python.org/doc/current/lib/re-syntax.html also provides a useful summary of regular expression syntax. An entire book could be written on regular expressions, but in short, by using a special syntax, you can search for patterns of strings, instead of just simple strings, in a string field. For example, if you want to look for a directory name with a numeric digit in NetWare Core Protocol's **ncp.directory_name** field, you would use:

```
ncp.directory_name matches "\d"
```

If you wanted directory names that start with an "f" or an "F", and have numeric digits, the display filter would be:

```
ncp.directory_name matches "^[Ff].*\d"
```

As you can see, regular expression syntax is cryptic if you haven't practiced it. But once you learn it, regular expressions are powerful tools that can help you find just about anything.

Byte Sequences

Sequences of bytes, including Ethernet addresses, are represented by a sequence of hexadecimal digits, in upper-case or lower-case, separated by colons, periods, or dashes. For example, the broadcast Ethernet address ff:ff:ff:ff:ff:ff can be also be represented as ff.ff.ff.ff.ff.ff or as ff-ff-ff-ff-ff-ff.

Ethernet addresses are byte sequences, but are special because names can be assigned to them via an *ethers* file that you create. On UNIX, the global file is /etc/ethers, and the personal file is $HOME/.ethereal/ethers. On Windows, the global *ethers* file would be placed in the Ethereal installation directory, and the personal file would be created as %APPDATA%\Ethereal\ethers, or if %APP-DATA% doesn't exist, then %USERPROFILE%\Application Data\Ethereal\ethers. The *ethers* file has the format of one hardware address and one name per line, separated by any amount of spaces or tabs:

```
00:09:f6:01:cc:b3    picard
01:1a:e3:01:fe:37    worf
```

When a name exists for an Ethernet address, the name can be used in the display filter:

```
eth.src == 00:09:f6:01:cc:b3
eth.src == picard
```

Internally, Ethereal treats protocols as a special field type, but in one aspect, protocols act like byte sequence fields. The **contains** operator can be used to search through the bytes that belong to each protocol in the packet. The bytes in a packet that are specific to a protocol are treated as belonging to that protocol in the display filter language. The exception is the special **frame** pseudo-protocol. At the top of every protocol tree, Ethereal places a pseudo-protocol that contains metadata about the packet, including the arrival time and the length of packet. These fields don't actually appear in the packet data, but are relevant to the packet. Ethereal regards all the bytes in the packet as belonging to the **frame** pseudo-protocol. Therefore, you can use the **contains** operator to search for any bytes or ASCII text within the entire packet by checking if the **frame** protocol contains the bytes or text.

```
frame contains "POST"
frame contains 50:4f:53:54
```

You can, of course, limit your search to a more specific protocol if you know that the text should appear there. For example, to search for *GET* in the **http** protocol, use:

```
http contains "GET"
```

Addresses

You've already seen an example of an address field in the discussion about hardware address fields in the Byte Sequences section. Address fields have the distinction of being represented by either a numeric value or a name. The Ethernet address field is both an address field and a byte-sequence field. The other address fields are the IPv4 address, IPv6 address, and IPX network fields.

IPv4 address fields can be compared against the dotted-quad format of IPv4 addresses, or hostnames and DNS names. The *dotted-quad* notation is four numbers separated by periods, or *dots*. In this example, the source IP address field name is **ip.src**, while the destination IP address field name is **ip.dst**:

```
ip.src == 192.168.1.1
```

```
ip.dst == wizard
ip.dst == www.ethereal.com
```

If you want to test if either the source IP address or the destination IP address is *wizard*, you can use the logic **or** operator to combine two tests:

```
ip.src == wizard or ip.dst == wizard
```

But Ethereal provides another field, **ip.addr**, which stands for either **ip.src** or **ip.dst**:

```
ip.addr == wizard
```

You will find that most of the fields that have a concept of source and destination will provide a third field that tests for either source or destination, to help you write succinct display filters.

To test if an IPv4 address is within a certain subnet, the **==** operator and classless interdomain routing (CIDR) notation can be used, which works with dotted-quad notation, hostnames, or DNS names. In CIDR notation, the IPv4 address or hostname is followed by a slash and the number of bits that make up the network portion of the IPv4 address.

```
ip.addr == 192.168.1.0/24
ip.addr == wizard/24
```

IPv6 address fields are similar in name to their IPv4 counterparts: **ipv6.src** for the source address, **ipv6.dst** for the destination address, and **ipv6.addr** to test either source or destination address. For example,

```
ipv6.dst == 2::8100:2:30a:c392:fc5a or ipv6.dst == 2::8100:2:30a:c392:fc5a
ipv6.addr == 2::8100:2:30a:c392:fc5a
```

IPX addresses are comprised of two parts, the network address and the node address. This is comparable to an IPv4 address, where part of the 32-bit IPv4 address is the network portion, and the other part refers to a specific host on that IPv4 network. In IPX, however, the network and node (that is, the host) are separate fields instead of being combined into a single value.

The IPX node fields are hardware-address type fields, but the IPX network fields are unsigned 32-bit integer fields. Ethereal treats IPX network fields differently than normal integer fields in that Ethereal allows you to give names to IPX network numbers. This is useful if you need to analyze IPX packets in an environment where there are many different IPX networks; names are easier to remember than numbers. To define the IPX network names, you create a file called *ipxnets*. On UNIX, you can create a global *ipxnets* file in /etc/ipxnets, and a personal file, whose values override the global values, in $HOME/.ethereal/ipxnets. On Windows, the global file is the *ipxnets* file in the Ethereal installation directory, while the personal file is %APPDATA%\Ethereal\ipxnets, or if %APPDATA% doesn't exist, then %USERPROFILE%\Application Data\Ethereal\ipxnets. The format of the *ipxnets* file is the same as the *ethers* file, except that the hexadecimal bytes representing the IPX network number can be separated by periods, dashes, colons, or nothing. Here is an example from the Ethereal man page:

```
C0.A8.2C.00            HR
c0-a8-1c-00            CEO
00:00:BE:EF            IT_Server1
110f                    FileServer3
```

Given this *ipxnets* file, these two display filters are equivalent:

```
ipx.src.net == 0xc0a82c00
ipx.src.net == HR
```

> **NOTE**
>
> Storing hardware addresses in an /etc/ethers file used to be common practice on UNIX systems, but many UNIX systems these days no longer come with an /etc/ethers file. However, the /etc/ipxnets file has no such history. It is a file unique to Ethereal. Don't expect to find an intalled /etc/ipxnets file on a UNIX system, even if that system comes with an /etc/ethers file.

Time Fields

There are two types of time fields in Ethereal. While they are related to each other, they are represented very differently. An absolute time is a timestamp that combines a date and a time in order to specify a specific moment in time. A relative time is just a floating point number; it's the number of seconds (including fractional seconds) between two absolute times.

Absolute times are represented as strings of the format

```
Month Day, Year Hour:Minute:Seconds
```

They can include fractions of a second, with nanosecond resolution

```
Month Day, Year Hour:Minute:Seconds.Nsecs
```

To look at packets that arrived before December 31st, 2003, at 5:03AM, the display filter would be:

```
frame.time < "Dec 31, 2003 05:03:00"
```

Ethereal provides the **frame.time_delta** field to record the difference in arrival times between a packet and its immediate predecessor. Currently, the only way to represent this relative time is with a floating point number that indicates seconds with nanosecond resolution:

```
frame.time_delta > 0.02
```

Maybe in the future Ethereal will allow the use of units, such as "1 min 5.3 secs".

Other Field Types

Some fields have no values associated with them. They don't have an integer value, string value, or any other value. You can test for the existence of these fields, but they don't have a value that you can check with ==, <, >, or any other relation. These no-value fields are generally used by the protocol dissector to place text or a branch in a protocol tree.

If you inspect the protocol trees in your packet captures, you'll eventually discover that some of the items in the protocol tree don't have any display-filter field associated with them. In some cases, protocol dissectors merely add text to the protocol tree, without labeling the text as belonging to a field. Figure 5.5 shows how the HTTP protocol dissector does this for the HTTP headers. It places the *User-Agent* field in the protocol tree without giving it a display-filter field name.

Figure 5.5 HTTP Headers as Text

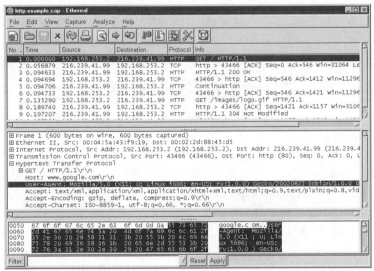

Unfortunately, you cannot create a display filter to search for these types of text labels. However, if the text is found in the packet data, the **contains** operator can be used to search for the text in a protocol, or even the entire packet by using the frame pseudo-protocol. To find HTTP packets where the *User-Agent* is "Mozilla", as in Figure 5.5, use **contains**:

```
http contains "User-Agent: Mozilla"
```

Ranges

The string, byte sequence, and protocol field types have something in common besides being searchable by the **contains** operator - they are all sequences of bytes. Strings are sequences of characters, but characters are really just bytes. The other field types - integers, floating points, times, etc., - can be thought of as single values rather than sequences of anything. Sometimes it is useful to take a portion of a string, byte sequence, or protocol, that is, slice the data into a smaller section, and compare it against a value. You can slice a sequence by using the *ranges* functionality of Ethereal's display filter language. The *ranges* syntax uses square brackets: [and].

To obtain a single byte from a sequence, use the offset of that byte in square brackets. The offset is the position of the byte starting at the beginning of the named field. As typical for computer languages, Ethereal's display filter language offsets begin at 0. To compare the very first byte in an Ethernet address to the hexadecimal value 0xaa, use:

```
eth.addr[0] == aa
```

The hexadecimal byte value **aa** is not interpreted as the string **"aa"**, nor can you provide a integer value by typing **0xaa**.

Since 0 is the offset of the first byte, 1 is the offset of the second byte. To compare the second byte of the bytes in the **telnet** portion of the packet to the hexadecimal value 0xff, use:

```
telnet[1] == ff
```

A sample of a full hexadecimal table can be found at: www.cookwood.com/cookwood/html4_examples/4files/colorhex/hexchart.html

Ranges can do more for you than extracting single bytes. You can extract actual ranges of bytes from the fields. Use a colon to separate the offset from the number of bytes in the brackets. To compare the first three bytes of a token-ring address to 00:06:29, type the length of the slice after the colon. The length is 3 because we are comparing three bytes:

```
tr.addr[0:3] == 00:06:29
```

If you would rather provide ranges of offsets rather than offset/length pairs, then a hyphen in the brackets can be used. This display filter also compares the first three bytes of a token-ring address to 00:06:29, but by slicing the **tr.addr** field from offset 0 up to, and including, byte 2.

```
tr.addr[0-2] == 00:06:29
```

When using the colon notation to give byte offset and range length, you can choose not to provide either the offset or the length, yet keep the colon.

```
eth[:2] == ff:ff
http[10:] contains 00:01:02
```

When the offset is not provided, as in the **eth[:2]** case, then the offset is assumed to be zero. When the length is not provided, as in the **http[10:]** case, then the range includes all the bytes until the end of the field or protocol mentioned.

Within the brackets, you can use commas to concatenate, or combine, multiple ranges of the same field. For example, if you wish to look at the first byte (offset = 0) and third byte (offset = 2) of the token-ring protocol, then you can either create two ranges, combining them with the **and** logical operator, or simply combine the ranges into one range using a comma inside the square brackets:

```
tr[0] == ff and tr[2] == ee
tr[0,2] == ff:ee
```

The comma operator can combine any number of ranges, so the following monstrosity is entirely legal:

```
tr[0-2,4:3,7,9] == 01:02:03:04:05:06:07:08
```

Table 5.16 is a summary of the range syntax options.

Table 5.16 Range Syntax

Range Syntax	Meaning
[offset]	Slice a single byte at "offset"
[offset : length]	Slice "length" bytes starting at "offset"
[$offset_1$ – $offset_2$]	Slice bytes from "$offset_1$" to "$offset_2$", inclusive
[: length]	Slice "length" bytes starting at offset 0
[offset :]	Slice bytes from "offset" to end of field
[range , range]	Combine any range syntax with another

NOTE

The Ethereal documentation states that you are supposed to be able to use negative numbers as offsets. Negative offsets indicate the offset counting *backwards* from the end of the field. But, in our testing this doesn't work as advertised. It is extremely likely that this will be fixed in a future version of Ethereal.

Logical Operations

You've already seen many examples of combining multiple relations in the same display filter with the **and** operator. The **and** logical operator tests that the two relations it combines are true. To filter for a specific source IP address and a specific destination IP address, use **and**.

```
ip.src == 192.168.1.1 and ip.dst == 192.168.2.2
```

The **or** logical operator tests if either, or both, of the two relations that it joins is true. If you wanted to test an IP address to see if it was one of two values, you use **or**.

```
ip.addr == 192.168.3.3 or ip.addr == 192.168.4.4
```

The **not** logical operator reverses the sense of the relation. To find NetWare Core Protocol packets that have an **ncp.directory_name** field which does not contain the string "System", you would use this display filter:

```
not ncp.directory_name contains "System"
```

Parentheses are used to group relations according to how **not**, **and**, and **or**, should combine them. These two display filters are not the same, due to the presence of parenthesis.

```
not eth.dst eq ff:ff:ff:ff:ff:ff and ip.len gt 1000
not (eth.dst eq ff:ff:ff:ff:ff:ff and ip.len gt 1000)
```

In the first example, **not** negates the meaning of the **eq**. In the second example, **not** negates the meaning of the grouped expression, which is an **and** expression.

Multiple Occurrences of Fields

Some protocols occur more than once per packet. This can happen when you're looking at encapsulated or tunneled protocols. For example, Protocol Independent Multicast (PIM) can run on top of IPv6 and at the same time send other IPv6 data. Thus, you can have two instances of IPv6 in a single packet by using PIM. More commonly, the same field can occur more than once in a single protocol. Some protocols have repeated fields, like the ring/bridge pairs in source-routed token-ring packets.

In other cases where the protocol does not normally have multiple occurrences of fields, Ethereal will create multiple occurrences of fields to enhance the filtering. As mentioned in the discussion about address fields, there are many fields that have a source version and a destination version. In those cases, the protocol dissector adds two generic (non-source, non-destination) versions of the field so that a display filter can test both the source and destination fields in one statement. Table 5.17 shows some examples of those fields.

Table 5.17 Generic Versions of Source and Destination Fields

Source Field	Destination Field	Generic Version
eth.src	eth.dst	eth.addr
fddi.src	fddi.dst	fddi.addr
ip.src	ip.dst	ip.addr
ipx.src.net	ipx.dst.net	ipx.net
ipx.src.node	ipx.dst.node	ipx.node
tcp.srcport	tcp.dstport	tcp.port
tr.src	tr.dst	tr.addr
udp.srcport	udp.dstport	udp.port

Care must be given when testing fields that occur more than once in a packet. For example, if you have a packet capture that has a lot of HTTP traffic in it, as does the example in Figure 5.6, and want to use a display filter to hide the HTTP traffic because you're not interested in it, you might be tempted to use this display filter, where 80 is the TCP port for HTTP:

```
tcp.port != 80
```

Figure 5.6 TCP Ports for HTTP Traffic

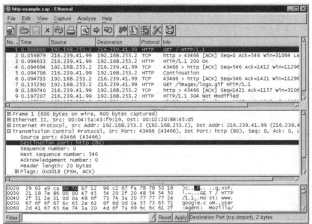

Unfortunately, this doesn't work. Why? This display filter is saying "show me all the packets which have a **tcp.port** that does not equal 80." Take a look at Figure 5.6; one **tcp.port**, the destination port, is 80, while the other **tcp.port**, the source port, is 43,466. This packet does pass the **tcp.port != 80** filter, because it has one **tcp.port** which is not equal to 80.

What you want to say instead is "show me all the packets where none of the **tcp.port** values are equal to 80." Or equivalently, "show me the packets which do not have at least one **tcp.port** equal to 80." In the correct display filter language, this is:

```
not tcp.port == 80
```

It takes some getting used to, but once you understand what the display filter language is doing, you will become more comfortable with it.

Tools & Traps…

Other Uses of Display Filters

Display filters are used for other reasons in Ethereal besides limiting which packets are shown to you in Ethereal's main window. Ethereal allows you to use them any time it would like you to select packets. The **View | Coloring Rules** facility for colorizing packet summaries lets you use display filters to select which packets to colorize. The **Analyze | Statistics | IO** reports allow you to select packets with display filters. And the **File | Open** dialog box allows you to supply a display filter for use when reading a capture file from disk. This facility is unique among the various uses of display filters. While reading a capture file, if a packet does not match the display filter, the packet is skipped and is not loaded into Ethereal's memory. In this way, this *read* display filter acts like a capture filter, in that it limits the packets that are loaded into Ethereal's memory. But of course, it uses the display filter syntax, not the capture filter syntax.

Hidden Fields

If you look closely at some protocols in the protocol dissection tree, you might start to notice that some fields that should be present simply are not visible. For example, if you look at the Ethernet portion of a protocol tree in Figure 5.7, you'll find the Ethernet *Source* address (**eth.src**) and the Ethernet *Destination* address (**eth.dst**), but you'll never find a field labeled "Source or Destination Address", which is the description for the **eth.addr** field. This is because **eth.addr** was placed in the protocol tree as a hidden field to aid in writing display filters. You can use the hidden fields in display filters, but you never see them in the protocol tree. Ethereal does this for convenience, and to keep the protocol tree from having duplicate information. Unfortunately, there is no option to make Ethereal display hidden fields. Maybe in the future there will be.

Figure 5.7 Ethernet Source and Destination Address Fields

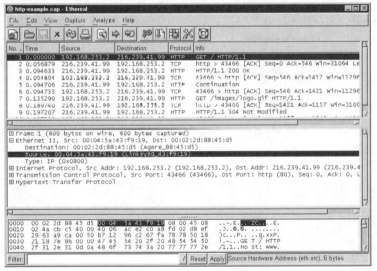

Notes from the Underground...

Undocumented Glossary Option

Ethereal and Tethereal have an undocumented command line switch that produces a glossary of protocol and field names. The **-G** switch causes both programs to output the glossary, then quit. Even the format of the output is undocumented, but you can look at the epan/proto.c file in the Ethereal source code. Search for *proto_registrar_dump_fields*. This comment is the function that documents the format.

```
/* Dumps the contents of the registration database
 * to stdout. An indepedent
 * program can take this output and format it into
 * nice tables or HTML or
 * whatever.
 *
 * There is one record per line. Each is either a
 * protocol or a header
 * field, differentiated by the first field.
 * The fields are tab-delimited.
 *
 * Protocols
 * ---------
 * Field 1 = 'P'
 * Field 2 = protocol name
 * Field 3 = protocol abbreviation
 *
 * Header Fields
 * -------------
 * Field 1 = 'F'
 * Field 2 = field name
 * Field 3 = field abbreviation
 * Field 4 = type ( text representation of the ftenum type )
```

Continued

```
    * Field 5 = parent protocol abbreviation
    */
```

You can see this glossary by running **ethereal –G** or **tethereal** **–G**. The **–G** option can also take a parameter. The **–G protocols** option makes ethereal or tethereal show the glossary only for protocols. The **–G fields** option shows both protocols and non-protocol fields, just like the **–G** option with no additional parameter. You can also look at doc/Makefile.am (or doc/Makefile.nmake, for Windows) and doc/dfilter2pod.pl in the Ethereal source distribution to see how the Ethereal build system uses the **-G** switch to produce the *ethereal-filter* manual page.

Filter List Dialog Boxes

Ethereal allows you to save both capture filters and display filters, and use them again in the future by selecting from a menu. This is nice when you have complicated filters or many filters that you use often. Ethereal maintains two distinct lists of filters, one for capture filters and another for display filters. The user interfaces for both lists of filters are almost identical, so they will be explained together.

The **Capture | Start** menu item presents the **Capture Options** user interface, shown in Figure 5.8. Next to the text entry box where you can type in a capture filter, there is a button labeled **Filter:**. Clicking this button brings up the **Capture Filter** user interface. Another way to open the Capture Filter dialog box is to select the **Capture | Capture Filters** menu item.

Figure 5.8 Capture Options Dialog Box

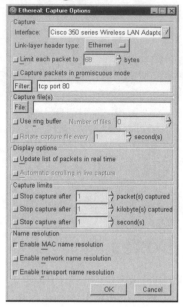

As shown in Figure 5.9, at the bottom of the main Ethereal window is the text entry box where you can type in a display filter. Next to this box is a button labeled **Filter:**. Clicking this button brings up the **Display Filter** user interface. The **Display Filter** user interface can also be opened from the **Analyze | Display Filters** menu option.

Figure 5.9 Ethereal Main Window and Filter Button

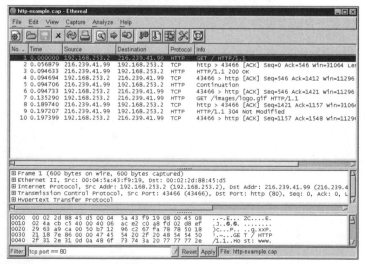

You'll notice that the **Capture Filter** window in Figure 5.10 and the **Display Filter** window in Figure 5.11 are nearly identical. The only functional differences are the existence of an **Add Expression** button and an **Apply** button in the **Display Filter** window, unless the **Display Filter** window was opened via **Analyzer | Display** Filters. The **Add Expression** button brings up a user interface to create display filters by pointing and clicking. The **Apply** button applies the display filter to a currently loaded capture file, thereby possibly changing the packets that are displayed in the main Ethereal GUI. The **Capture Filter** window does not have an **Apply** button because capture filters do not affect the currently-loaded capture file.

Figure 5.10 Capture Filter Dialog Box

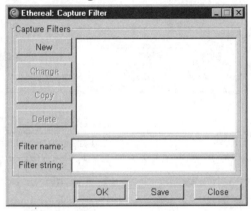

Figure 5.11 Display Filter Dialog Box

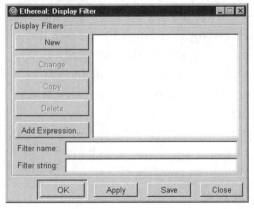

To add a new filter to the list, enter a meaningful name in the **Filter name** text entry box and enter the filter itself in the **Filter string** text entry box. Then click the **New** button. This adds the named filter to the list, as shown in Figure 5.12.

Figure 5.12 Display Filter Dialog After Clicking New

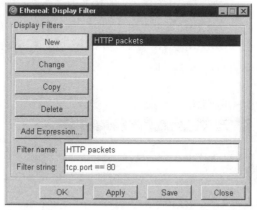

To change either the name or the contents of a filter, highlight the name of the filter in the list of filters by clicking on it. The name of the filter you just clicked on and its contents should now appear in the **Filter name** and **Filter string** text-entry boxes. Clicking on the text in either or both of these will allow you to modify the filter name and contents. When you are ready to save the modification, click the **Change** button.

To create a new filter based on a currently saved filter, highlight the name of the filter you wish to copy. The filter's name and contents should appear in the **Filter name** and **Filter string** text entry boxes. Click the **Copy** button and a new filter will be created and put into the list of filters. The new filter will be named "Copy of …", where "…" is the name of the filter you highlighted. The contents will be an exact replica of the contents of the original filter, as shown in Figure 5.13. At this point, you can modify the name or contents of the new filter as you would any other filter. Of course, be sure to click the **Change** button after changing your new copy, otherwise the changes won't be saved.

Figure 5.13 Display Filter Dialog After Clicking Copy

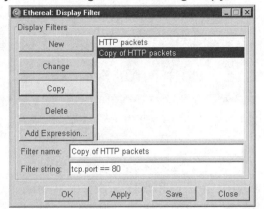

To delete a filter from the filter list, highlight the name of the filter, and ensure that its name and contents appear in the **Filter name** and **Filter string** text entry boxes. Click the **Delete** button and it will disappear.

Clicking the **OK** button in the **Display Filter** or **Capture Filter** window will do two things: it will save your filter modifications in memory, but not to disk, and if you have a filter currently highlighted, it will place that filter in the text entry box from which the **Display Filter** or **Capture Filter** window was opened. For **Capture Filters**, the filter is placed in the **Capture Options** window, the **Capture Filter** window is closed, and you can continue to modify your options for capturing packets. For **Display Filters**, the filter is placed in the text entry box at the bottom of the main Ethereal window and is applied to the currently loaded capture file. At this point, if you quit the Ethereal program, your modifications to the display or capture filter list will be lost.

If you want to save your modifications to the filter lists, you must press the **Save** button in the **Display Filter** and **Capture Filter** windows.

The **Close** button in the **Display Filter** and **Capture Filter** windows also saves your modifications in memory only, and closes the filter window, but unlike the **OK** button, does not apply your filter to the **Capture Options** window or the main Ethereal window.

Notes from the Underground…

Exchanging Filters With Your Friends

Do you need an easy way to exchange your extensive collection of capture filters or display filters with your friends? Ethereal saves your capture filters in a file names *cfilters*, and your display filters in a file name *dfilters*. On a UNIX system, those files are in your $HOME/.ethereal directory, while on a Windows system those files are in %APPDATA%\Ethereal, or if %APPDATA% isn't defined, in %USERPROFILE%\Application Data\Ethereal. These two files, *cfilter* and *dfilter*, are simple text files, with one record per line. You can paste new entries into these files and the next time you start Ethereal, the new filters will be available in Ethereal.

Filter Expression Dialog Box

It's impossible to remember all the field names that are available in Ethereal's display filter language because there are over 15,000 of them. Ethereal comes with a manual page named *ethereal-filter*, which lists all the fields. This book comes with a CD-ROM with HTML pages, in the /filters directory, that provide a searchable index of all the fields, and the Appendix has the same tables from some of the more commonly used protocols. The Ethereal program itself, however, provides a user interface which lets you peruse the protocols and fields they contain and construct a display filter.

From the **Display Filter** window, click the **Add Expression** button. The **Filter Expression** window, shown in Figure 5.14, appears.

Figure 5.14 Filter Expression Dialog Box

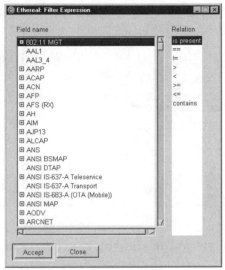

On the left is a list of all protocols. Each protocol that has fields, which is most of them, can be opened by clicking on the square next to the protocol's name, thereby presenting a list of the protocol's fields. When a field name is selected in the list, the relations that apply to that field are shown in the **Relation** list. The relations are: **is present**, **==**, **!=**, **>**, **<**, **>=**, **<=**, and **contains.** The **matches** keyword does not appear in this list; this is an oversight that surely will be fixed in a future version of Ethereal. Not all the relations apply to all field types, so only the applicable relations for the selected field are shown.

The default relation is **is present**, which does not require any other value to compare against. But if you select another relation, one that does require a comparison value, then a **Value** text entry box appears to the right of the relation list. This is shown in Figure 5.15. If the field can be sliced into ranges, then a **Range** text entry box appears under the **Relation** list.

Figure 5.15 Filter Expression Dialog With Operation That Accepts Values

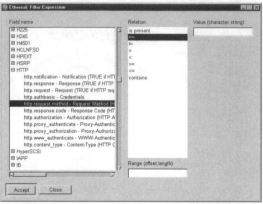

If the selected field has labels that represent its possible values, the list possible values will appear under the **Value** text entry box. An example is shown in Figure 5.16.

Figure 5.16 Filter Expression With Field That Has Labeled Values

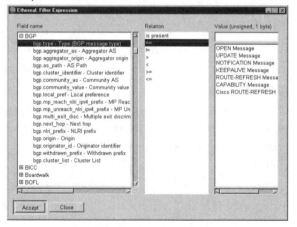

The text you type into the **Value** and **Range** text entry boxes are the same that you would type into a normal display filter. If you're happy with the selections you have made, click the **Accept** button. Ethereal will put the display filter in the **Filter string** text entry box of the **Display Filter** dialog box at the current location of your cursor. In this way, after creating one display filter, you could manually type a logical operator (**and** or **or**) into the **Filter string** text entry box and click **Add Expression** again. When you accept the second display filter, it is appended to your display filter in the **Filter string** text entry box, as that's where your cursor is.

Summary

If you're trying to pinpoint a network problem, or understand how a particular network operation works, the amount of extraneous traffic on the network can overwhelm you. Filters are the way to manage this huge amount of information. Capture filters allow you to limit the amount of packets that Ethereal receives from the operating system. Display filters allow you to limit the packets that are shown in Ethereal's main window, giving you the opportunity to concentrate on the problem at hand.

Ethereal's capture filter syntax is the same as tcpdump's filter syntax. This is because both Ethereal and tcpdump use a library called libpcap; it is this library that provides the filter engine. The filter engine provided by libpcap, while fast, does not provide many protocol or field names in its language. To find data for fields whose names are not provided in the filter language, the user must extract bytes from the packet by using offsets from the beginning of the protocol fields.

Ethereal's display filter syntax is unique to Ethereal. It is part of Ethereal's protocol dissection engine, and provides names for almost all protocols and fields that Ethereal can dissect. Display filters are slower to process packets than capture filters, but the trade-off is ease of use.

You can maintain a collection of capture filters and display filters through Ethereal's graphical user interface. You can also create display filters through a point-and-click interface. To find the names of all the available fields and protocols in the display filter language, Ethereal provides some information in its GUI and manual pages. Additionally, this book provides that information on the included CD-ROM.

Solutions Fast Track

Writing Capture Filters

- ☑ Capture filters operate quickly and are good for limiting the number of packets captured by Ethereal.

- ☑ The capture filter language has keywords for comparing host names and addresses, hardware addresses, ports, and protocols.

☑ Tcpdump can dissect many protocols and fields, but only a handful of those protocols and fields are available in the tcpdump filter (or "capture filter") language.

☑ To test individual fields in a bit-field correctly, you must use the bitwise AND operator: **&**.

Writing Display Filters

☑ Display filters are slower than capture filters, but allow you to test almost any field or protocol that Ethereal knows how to dissect.

☑ Display filter fields are typed; each type of field can hold only certain types of values.

☑ The **contains** operator searches for text; the **matches** operator searches using regular expressions.

☑ Take care when testing fields that occur multiple times in a packet; the way you might think to test these fields may be the wrong way.

☑ The **Capture Filter** and **Display Filter** dialog boxes let you save your filters.

☑ The **Filter Expression** dialog box lets you create display filters by pointing and clicking.

Frequently Asked Questions

The following Frequently Asked Questions, answered by the authors of this book, are designed to both measure your understanding of the concepts presented in this chapter and to assist you with real-life implementation of these concepts. To have your questions about this chapter answered by the author, browse to **www.syngress.com/solutions** and click on the **"Ask the Author"** form. You will also gain access to thousands of other FAQs at ITFAQnet.com.

Q: My capture filter or display filter that uses multiple **and**s or **or**s doesn't work the way I intended it to work.

A: The precedence of the operations may not be what you're expecting it to be. This means that the parts of your filter are being run in an order that you didn't expect. Use parentheses to group the parts properly.

Q: I'm using **contains** to look for a certain string that I know should be there, but Ethereal can't find it.

A: Look closely at the hex-dump when you have the field that you're interested in selected; the encoding of the string may be Unicode or EBCDIC, which won't work with the **contains** operator. Only ASCII strings are currently compatible with **contains**.

Q: I want to find all packets that do not have an IP address of 1.2.3.4. Why does **ip.addr != 1.2.3.4** show all packets instead of limiting the packets to what I want?

A: The **ip.addr** field occurs more than once in a packet. Your display filter is running correctly; it shows you all packets that have at least one **ip.addr** that is not equal to **1.2.3.4**. You want **not ip.addr == 1.2.3.4**.

Q: The filters that I enter in the **Capture Filter** or **Display Filter** windows aren't there when I quit Ethereal and start Ethereal again.

A: Don't forget to click the **Save** button in those windows. The **OK** button merely saves the changes to the filters in memory; the **Save** button saves them to disk.

Q: My filter can be expressed very easily in both the capture filter and display filter languages. Which should I choose?

A: If your network has very little traffic on it, then it's easier not to supply a capture filter and use only display filters. But if you have a lot of traffic on the network, especially extraneous traffic, and you're sure that your filter will provide all the packets that you need to look at to solve your problem, then use a capture filter. If you're not sure where to find the clues that will help you solve your problem, capture everything and use a display filter to look for packets that might help you.

Q: Ethereal comes with a manual for its display filter language. Where's the manual for the capture filter language?

A: It's provided by the tcpdump manual page. It's also on-line at www.tcpdump.org/tcpdump_man.html.

## Chapter 6

Other Programs Packaged with Ethereal

Solutions in this Chapter:

- Tethereal
- Editcap
- Mergecap
- Text2pcap

- ☑ Summary
- ☑ Solutions Fast Track
- ☑ Frequently Asked Questions

Introduction

Most people who are familiar with Ethereal tend to use the Ethereal Graphical User Interface (GUI). However, when Ethereal is installed it also comes with several other supporting programs: the command line version of Ethereal, called *Tethereal*, and three other programs to assist you in manipulating capture files; editcap, mergecap, and text2pcap. These supporting programs can be used together to provide very powerful capture file manipulation. For example, files can be captured with Tethereal, edited with editcap, and merged into a single packet capture file with mergecap. They can then be viewed with Tethereal or Ethereal. As you read this chapter you will see the vast capabilities and the granular control these supporting programs give you when manipulating capture files.

Tethereal

Tethereal is the command line version of Ethereal. It can be used to capture, decode, and print to screen live packets from the wire or to read saved capture files. Some of the same features apply to both Tethereal and Ethereal as they use the same capture library, libpcap, and most of the same code. Tethereal can read all of the same packet capture formats as Ethereal, and will automatically determine the type. If Tethereal is compiled with the zlib library, it can automatically uncompress and read files that have been compressed with gzip. The advantage to using Tethereal is that it is highly scriptable.

The following information is the usage output for the Tethereal program, also notice the various types of formats in which Tethereal can save files by using the **–F** option:

```
[root@localhost ethereal-0.10.0a]# tethereal -h
This is GNU tethereal 0.10.0a
Compiled with GLib 2.2.1, with libpcap 0.7.2, with libz 1.1.4, with libpcre
4.5,with Net-SNMP 5.0.9, with ADNS.
Running with libpcap (version unknown) on Linux 2.4.20-6
tethereal [ -vh ] [ -DlLnpqSVx ] [ -a <capture autostop condition> ] ...
        [ -b <number of ring buffer files>[:<duration>] ] [ -c <count> ]
        [ -d <layer_type>==<selector>,<decode_as_protocol> ] ...
        [ -f <capture filter> ] [ -F <output file type> ] [ -i <interface> ]
        [ -N <resolving> ] [ -o <preference setting> ] ... [ -r <infile> ]
        [ -R <read filter> ] [ -s <snaplen> ] [ -t <time stamp format> ]
```

```
[ -T pdml|ps|text ] [ -w <savefile> ] [ -y <link type> ]
[ -z <statistics string> ]
```
Valid file type arguments to the "-F" flag:

```
libpcap - libpcap (tcpdump, Ethereal, etc.)
rh6_1libpcap - RedHat Linux 6.1 libpcap (tcpdump)
suse6_3libpcap - SuSE Linux 6.3 libpcap (tcpdump)
modlibpcap - modified libpcap (tcpdump)
nokialibpcap - Nokia libpcap (tcpdump)
lanalyzer - Novell LANalyzer
ngsniffer - Network Associates Sniffer (DOS-based)
snoop - Sun snoop
netmon1 - Microsoft Network Monitor 1.x
netmon2 - Microsoft Network Monitor 2.x
ngwsniffer_1_1 - Network Associates Sniffer (Windows-based) 1.1
ngwsniffer_2_0 - Network Associates Sniffer (Windows-based) 2.00x
visual - Visual Networks traffic capture
5views - Accellent 5Views capture
niobserverv9 - Network Instruments Observer version 9
default is libpcap
```

The following command line options are used to control Tethereal's data capture and output:

- **–a** *test:value* This option is used when capturing to a file. It specifies to Tethereal when to stop writing to the file. The criterion is in the form of *test:value*, where test is either *duration* or *file size*. Duration will stop writing to a file when the specified number of seconds have elapsed, and file size will stop writing to a file after a size of value kilobytes have been reached.

- **–b** *number of ring buffer files [:duration]* This option is used with the **–a** option, and causes Tethereal to continue capturing data to successive files. This is known as *ring buffer* mode and it will keep saving files up to the number specified within the option. When the first file reaches the maximum size, as specified with the **–a** option, Tethereal will begin writing to the next file. When all files are full, it will continue to write new files as it removes the older ones. However, if the *number of files* is specified as 0, the number of files that Tethereal writes to will be unlimited, and will only be restricted to the size of the partition. An optional duration parameter can also be specified so that Tethereal will switch to the next file when the instructed number of seconds has elapsed. This will happen even if the current file is not yet full. The file names that are created are based on the number of the file and the creation date and time. You can only save files in the libpcap format when this option is used.

- **–c** *count* This option sets the default number of packets to read when capturing data. For example, if you only want to capture 100 packets you would specify **–c 100**.

- **–d** *layer type==selector, decode-as protocol* This option allows you to specify the way in which traffic is decoded. The parameters denote that if the layer type has a specified value then packets should be decoded as the specified protocol. For example **–d tcp.port==8080, http** would decode all traffic to and from Transmission Control Protocol (TCP) port 8080 as HyperText Transfer Protocol (HTTP) traffic. This is valuable for applications that allow you to run services on non-standard ports.

- **–D** This option instructs Tethereal to print a list of available interfaces on the system. It will print the interface number, name, and description and then return to the command prompt. You can then supply the number or the name to the **–i** flag to specify an interface on which to capture data. Specifying this option causes Tethereal to actually open and attempt to capture on each interface that it finds. It will only display the interfaces on which this was successful. Also, if you need to be logged in as root to run Tethereal but are not, this option will not display any available interfaces.

- **–f** *capture filter expression* This option allows you to set the filter expression to use when capturing data. For example **tethereal -f tcp port 80** will only capture incoming and outgoing HTTP packets.

- **–F** *type* This option is used to set the format of the output of the capture file. For example, if you want to save a file in the Sun snoop format so that snoop can read the capture file, you would use the **–F snoop** option.

- **–h** This option prints the version of Tethereal in use and the help options, then exits.

- **–i** *interface* This option specifies the interface that you want to use to capture data. The **–D** option can be used to find out the names of your network interfaces. You can use the number or the name as a parameter to the **–i** option. If you run Tethereal without the **–i** option it will search the list of interfaces and choose the first non-loopback interface that it finds. If it doesn't find any non-loopback interfaces, it will use the first loopback interface. If this doesn't exist ether, Tethereal will exit with an error.

- **–l** This option flushes the standard output after each packet is printed instead of waiting until it fills up. It is normally used when piping a capture to a script so that the output for each packet is sent as soon as it is read and dissected.

- **–L** This option lists the data link types that are supported by an interface and then exits. You can specify an interface to use or Tethereal will choose the first one it finds as stated in the **–i** option information.

- **–n** This option is used to disable network object name resolution, such as host names and port names.

- **–N** *resolving flags* This option is used to enable name resolving for specified address types and port numbers. The **m** flag enables MAC address resolution, the **n** flag enables network address resolution, and the **t** flag enables transport-layer port number resolution. The **C** flag enables concurrent (asynchronous) Domain Name System (DNS) lookups if Tethereal is compiled with Asynchronous DNS (ADNS). The **–N** option overrides the **–n** option.

- **–o** *prefname:value* This option allows you to set a preference value that will override any default value or value read from a preference file. The parameter to this option is in the format of *prefname:value*, where *prefname* is the name of the preference as it would appear in the preference file and *value* is the value to which it should be set.

- **–p** This option tells Tethereal to not put the interface in promiscuous mode. This will cause Tethereal to only read traffic sent to and from the system on which Tethereal is running, broadcast traffic, and multicast traffic.

- **–q** This option allows you to turn off the packet count when capturing network packets to a file. The count will still be displayed at the end of the capture. On some systems, such as various BSD systems, that support the SIGINFO signal, typing **control–T** will cause the current count status to be displayed.

- **–r** *file* This option reads and processes a saved capture file.

- **–R** *filter* This option causes a read filter to be applied before displaying or writing the packets to a file. Packets that do not match the filter will be discarded.

- **–s** *snaplen* This option allows you to set the default snapshot length to use when capturing data. The parameter *snaplen* specifies the length, in bytes, of each network packet that will be read or saved to disk.

- **–S** This option decodes and displays the packets even when writing to a file.

- **–t format** This option allows you to set the format of the packet timestamp that is displayed on the summary line. The format parameter will specify the method used to display the data. Relative time is specified by the **r** parameter and displays the time elapsed between the first packet and the current packet. Absolute time is specified by the **a** parameter and is the actual time the packet was captured. The absolute date and time is specified by the **ad** parameter and is the actual time and date the packet was captured. The delta time is specified by the **d** parameter and displays the time since the previous packet was captured. By default, the time is specified as relative.

- **–T pdml|ps|text** This option allows you to set the display format to use when viewing packet data. When using the Packet Details Markup Language (PDML) option, the protocol data tree is always displayed.

- **–v** This option prints the Tethereal version information and then exits.

- **–V** This option displays the capture in protocol tree form instead of the default summary packet form.

- **–w** *file* This option writes the packets to the file name specified following the option. If the option specified is – then standard output is used.

- **–x** This option displays the capture in a hexadecimal and ASCII dump format along with the summary or protocol tree view.

- **−y** *type* This option allows you to set the data link type to use while capturing packets. You can use the **−L** option to lists the data link types that are supported by an interface.

- **−z** *statistics* This option will enable Tethereal to collect various types of statistics about the data that is being captured. The results will be displayed after reading the capture file.

By default, Tethereal will display packets to the screen in summary line form. These are the same lines that are displayed in the Ethereal summary pane. However, it does not print the *frame number* field when capturing and displaying real time. The **−V** option can be used to print detailed information about the packets instead of just a summary. Tethereal can also read saved data capture files, and print the information in either summary (default) or detailed form (**−V**). This method will display the frame numbers with the saved packets. Finally, the **−x** command will cause Tethereal to print a hexadecimal and ASCII dump of the packet data with either the summary line or detailed protocol tree. Tethereal has a very strong display filter language and can also use the TCPDump filter syntax as well. These can be used to narrow down the type of traffic that you want to capture.

When using Tethereal to write a capture to a file, the file will be written in libpcap format by default. It will write all of the packets and all of the detail about the packets to the output file, thus the **−V** and the **−x** options aren't necessary. Since Tethereal and Ethereal are compatible with many other sniffers, you can also write the output in several different formats. The **−F** option can be used to specify a format in which to write the file.

The following is a basic example of using Tethereal to perform a capture and display the output in a protocol tree view along with the associated hexadecimal and ASCII output:

```
C:\Program Files\Ethereal>tethereal -V -x
Capturing on \Device\NPF_{A302C81E-256D-4C92-8A72-866F2E1ED55F}
Frame 1 (114 bytes on wire, 114 bytes captured)
    Arrival Time: Nov 28, 2003 22:14:16.221349000
    Time delta from previous packet: 0.000000000 seconds
    Time since reference or first frame: 0.000000000 seconds
    Frame Number: 1
    Packet Length: 114 bytes
    Capture Length: 114 bytes
```

```
IEEE 802.3 Ethernet
    Destination: ff:ff:ff:ff:ff:ff (Broadcast)
    Source: 00:05:5d:ee:7e:53 (D-Link_ee:7e:53)
    Length: 100
Logical-Link Control
    DSAP: NetWare (0xe0)
    IG Bit: Individual
    SSAP: NetWare (0xe0)
    CR Bit: Command
    Control field: U, func = UI (0x03)
        000. 00.. = Unnumbered Information
        .... ..11 = Unnumbered frame
Internetwork Packet eXchange
    Checksum: 0xffff
    Length: 96 bytes
    Transport Control: 0 hops
    Packet Type: PEP (0x04)
    Destination Network: 0x00000000 (00000000)
    Destination Node: ff:ff:ff:ff:ff:ff (Broadcast)
    Destination Socket: SAP (0x0452)
    Source Network: 0x00000000 (00000000)
    Source Node: 00:05:5d:ee:7e:53 (D-Link_ee:7e:53)
    Source Socket: Unknown (0x4008)
Service Advertisement Protocol
    General Response
    Server Name: TARGET1!!!!!!!!!A5569B20ABE511CE9CA400004C762832
        Server Type: Microsoft Internet Information Server (0x064E)
        Network: 00 00 00 00
        Node: 00:05:5d:ee:7e:53
        Socket: Unknown (0x4000)
        Intermediate Networks: 1
0000  ff ff ff ff ff ff 00 05 5d ee 7e 53 00 64 e0 e0   ........].~S.d..
0010  03 ff ff 00 60 00 04 00 00 00 00 ff ff ff ff ff   ....`...........
0020  ff 04 52 00 00 00 00 00 05 5d ee 7e 53 40 08 00   ..R......].~S@..
0030  02 06 4e 54 41 52 47 45 54 31 21 21 21 21 21 21   ..NTARGET1!!!!!!
0040  21 21 41 35 35 36 39 42 32 30 41 42 45 35 31 31   !!A5569B20ABE511
```

```
0050   43 45 39 43 41 34 30 30 30 30 34 43 37 36 32 38    CE9CA400004C7628
0060   33 32 00 00 00 00 00 00 05 5d ee 7e 53 40 00 00    32.......].~S@..
0070   01 01
```

The following is an example of using Tethereal to capture traffic on interface 4 and output the data to a file called *output*. The output files will have a maximum file size of 5 kilobytes each and when they are full a new output file will be created. This will continue up to a maximum of 10 output files. The following example is the command used to perform this capture:

```
C:\Program Files\Ethereal>tethereal -i4 -a filesize:5 -b 10 -w output
```

The output files generated are appended with the file number, date, and timestamp. You will see the following 10 output files start at number 43 because they have begun to drop the oldest file as they create new files, so that a maximum of 10 files exist at all times:

```
output_00043_20031128212900
output_00044_20031128212900
output_00045_20031128212900
output_00046_20031128212900
output_00047_20031128212901
output_00048_20031128212903
output_00049_20031128212958
output_00050_20031128213045
output_00051_20031128213211
output_00052_20031128213316
```

The following is an example of using a Tethereal capture filter to capture all traffic except packets to and from HTTP port 80:

```
C:\Program Files\Ethereal>tethereal -f "tcp port !80"
Capturing on \Device\NPF_{A302C81E-256D-4C92-8A72-866F2E1ED55F}
  0.000000 D-Link_ed:3b:c6 -> Broadcast    ARP Who has 192.168.100.40?
Tell 192.168.100.5
  0.000026 D-Link_ee:7e:53 -> D-Link_ed:3b:c6 ARP 192.168.100.40 is at
00:05:5d:ee:7e:53
  0.000066 D-Link_ee:7e:53 -> D-Link_ed:3b:c6 ARP 192.168.100.40 is at
00:05:5d:ee:7e:53
 10.089720 00000000.00055dee7e53 -> 00000000.ffffffffffff IPX SAP General
Response
```

```
10.089763 00000000.00055dee7e53 -> 00000000.ffffffffffff IPX SAP General
Response
```

The following is an example of using a Tethereal read filter to output the Telnet data packets from a file called *capture*:

```
C:\Program Files\Ethereal>tethereal -r capture -R "telnet"
   7   10.071157 192.168.100.122 -> 192.168.100.132 TELNET Telnet Data ...
   8   10.071464 192.168.100.132 -> 192.168.100.122 TELNET Telnet Data ...
   9   10.071515 192.168.100.132 -> 192.168.100.122 TELNET Telnet Data ...
  11   10.076114 192.168.100.132 -> 192.168.100.122 TELNET Telnet Data ...
  12   10.076155 192.168.100.132 -> 192.168.100.122 TELNET Telnet Data ...
  14   10.089546 192.168.100.122 -> 192.168.100.132 TELNET Telnet Data ...
  15   10.089672 192.168.100.132 -> 192.168.100.122 TELNET Telnet Data ...
```

The following is an example of using Tethereal to read a libpcap capture file called *capture2* and output it to a file called *netmon_output* in the Microsoft Network Monitor 2.x format; editcap can also be used to perform this function:

```
C:\Program Files\Ethereal>tethereal -r capture2 -w netmon_output -F netmon2
```

The following is an example of using the Tethereal statistics function to display a report of all bytes and frames for each protocol detected during the capture, the statistics will display after you end the capture by typing **Ctrl + C**:

```
C:\Program Files\Ethereal>tethereal -z io,phs
<cntrl-c>

==================================================================
Protocol Hierarchy Statistics
Filter: frame
frame                                   frames:560 bytes:115233
  eth                                   frames:560 bytes:115233
    ip                                  frames:558 bytes:115005
      udp                               frames:53 bytes:10383
        dns                             frames:21 bytes:3215
        data                            frames:8 bytes:496
        isakmp                          frames:24 bytes:6672
      tcp                               frames:505 bytes:104622
        http                            frames:107 bytes:81798
    llc                                 frames:2 bytes:228
```

```
       ipx                                    frames:2 bytes:228
         ipxsap                               frames:2 bytes:228
===================================================================
```

The following is an example of using the Tethereal statistics function to display a report of all TCP conversations that take place during the capture, the statistics will display after you end the capture by typing **Ctrl + C**:

```
C:\Program Files\Ethereal>tethereal -z conv,tcp
```

<cntrl-c>

```
=========================================================================
TCP Conversations
Filter:<No Filter>
                                               |          <-       | |
->
 | |      Total        |
                                            | Frames  Bytes | | Frames
Bytes
 | | Frames   Bytes |
192.168.100.40:2077  <-> 64.12.26.97:http       18       1934       36
368
4       54       5618
192.168.100.40:2078  <-> 205.188.1.95:http      4        216        8
48
0       12       696
=========================================================================
```

Tethereal Statistics

Included are some additional examples and supplementary information to the following Tethereal man (short for *manual*) page statistics information:

COMMAND -z *dcerpc,rtt,uuid,major.minor[filter]*

DESCRIPTION Collect call and reply Response Time Test (RTT) data for Distributed Computing Environment Remote Procedure Call (DCE RPC) interface *uuid*, version *major.minor*. Data collected is the number of calls for each procedure, MinRTT, MaxRTT and AvgRTT. If the optional filterstring is provided, the statistics will only be calculated on those calls that match that filter. Current supported DCE RPC programs are:

ATSVC, BOSSVR, BUTC, CDS_CLERK, CONV, DEC_DFS, DFS, DNSSERVER, DRSUAPI, DTSPROVIDER, DTSSTIME_REQ, EPM, FLDB, FTSERVER, INITSHUTDOWN, KRB5RPC, LSA, LSA_DS, MAPI, MGMT, Messenger, NSPI, OXID, REMACT, REP_PROC, RPC_Browser, RPC_NETLOGON, RS_ACCT, RS_ATTR_RS_BIND, RS_PGO, RS_REPADM, RS_REPLIST, RS_UNIX, SAMR, SECIDMAP, SPOOLSS, SRVSVC, SVCCTL, TAPI, TKN4lnt, UBIKDISK, UBIKVOTE, WINREG, WKSSVC, cds_solicit, cprpc_server, dce_update, roverride, rpriv, re_misc, rsec_login.

EXAMPLE 1   -z dcerpc,rtt,12345778-1234-abcd-ef00-0123456789ac,1.0 will collect data for the Microsoft Security Account Manager (SAMR) interface.

EXAMPLE 2
-z dcerpc,rtt,12345778-1234-abcd-ef00-0123456789ac, 1.0ip.addr==192.168.100.40 will collect SAMR RTT statistics for the host 192.168.100.40. Notice that there is no comma between the *major.minor* and *filter*. The Tethereal man page example shows that a comma is placed between these parameters, however this will cause Tethereal to report an error and exit.

NOTES   This option can be used multiple times on the command line.

COMMAND   **-z io,ph**s**[,***filter***]**

DESCRIPTION   Creates protocol hierarchy statistics listing both number of frames and bytes. If no *filter* is specified the statistics will be calculated for all frames. If a filter is specified, statistics will be only calculated for those packets that match the filter.

EXAMPLE 1   **-z io,phs** will generate statistics for all traffic.

EXAMPLE 2   **-z io,phs,ip.addr==192.168.100.40** will generate statistics for all traffic to and from the host 192.168.100.40.

NOTES   This option can be used multiple times on the command line.

COMMAND   **-z io,***stat*,*interval***[,***filter***][,***filter***][,***filter***]…**

DESCRIPTION   Collects frame and bytes statistics for the capture in intervals of *interval* seconds. *Intervals* can be specified either as whole or fractional seconds. Interval can be specified in microsecond (ms) resolution. If no *filter* is specified the statistics will be calculated for all frames. If one or more filters are specified, statistics will be calculated for all filters and presented with one column of statistics for each filter. io,stat can also calculate COUNT() SUM() MIN() MAX() and AVG() using a slightly different filter syntax:

[COUNT|SUM|MIN|MAX|AVG](<field>)<filter>. One important thing to note here is that the field that the calculation is based on *must* also be part of the filter string or else the calculation will fail. Also, be aware that a field can exist multiple times inside the same packet and will then be counted multiple times in those packets. COUNT(<field>) can be used on any type which has a display filter name. It will count how many times this particular field is encountered in the filtered packet list. SUM(<field>) can only be used on named fields of integer type. This will sum together every occurrence of this field's value for each interval. MIN/MAX/AVG(<field>) can only be used on named fields that are either integers or relative time fields. This will calculate the maximum, minimum or average that is seen in each interval. If the field is a relative time field the output will be presented in seconds and three digits after the decimal point. The resolution for time calculations is 1ms; anything smaller will be truncated.

EXAMPLE 1   -z io,stat,1,ip.addr==192.168.100.40 will generate 1 second statistics for all traffic to and from host 192.168.100.40.

EXAMPLE 2   -z io,stat,0.001,"http&&ip.addr==192.168.100.40" will generate 1ms statistics for all HTTP frames to and from host 192.168.100.40.

EXAMPLE 3   -z io,stat,0.010,AVG(smb.time)smb.time will calculate the average time for Server Message Block (SMB) frames during each 10ms interval.

EXAMPLE 4   -z io,stat,0.010,COUNT(http.request)http.request will count the total number of HTTP requests seen in each 10ms interval.

EXAMPLE 5   -z io,stat,0.010,SUM(frame.pkt_len)frame.pkt_len will report the total number of bytes seen in all the frames within a 10ms interval.

EXAMPLE 6   –z io,stat,0.010,"smb.time&&ip.addr ==192.168.100.40",MIN(smb.time) "smb.time&&ip.addr== 192.168.100.40",MAX(smb.time)"smb.time&&ip.addr==192.168 .100.40",AVG(smb.time)"smb.time&&ip.addr==192.168.100.40" will calculate statistics for all SMB response times we see to and from host 192.168.100.40 in 10ms intervals. The output will be displayed in 4 columns; number of frames/bytes, minimum response time, maximum response time, and average response time.

NOTES   This option can be used multiple times on the command line.

COMMAND   –z conv,*type*[,*filter*]

DESCRIPTION   Creates a table that lists all conversations that could be seen in the capture. *type* specifies which type of conversation we want to generate the statistics for, currently the supported ones are "eth" Ethernet, "fc" Fibre Channel, "fddi" FDDI, "ip" IP addresses, "ipx" IPX addresses, "tcp" TCP/IP socketpairs, "tr" TokenRing, and "udp" UDP/IP socketpairs. Both IPv4 and IPv6 are supported. If the optional filter string is specified, only those packets that match the filter will be used in the calculations. The table is presented with one line for each conversation and displays number of frames/bytes in each direction as well as total number of frames/bytes. The table is sorted according to total number of bytes.

EXAMPLE   –z conv,ip,ip.addr==192.168.100.40 will list IP conversations for host 192.168.100.40.

NOTES   None.

COMMAND   –z proto,colinfo,*filter*,*field*

DESCRIPTION   Appends all *field* values for the packet to the COL_INFO information line. This feature can be used to append arbitrary fields to the COL_INFO line in addition to the normal content of the COL_INFO line. *field* is the display filter name of a field which value should be placed on the COL_INFO line. *filter* is a filter string that controls for which packets the field value will be presented on COL_INFO line. *field* will only be presented on the COL_INFO line for the packets which match *filter*. In order for Tethereal to be able to extract the *field* value from the packet, *field* MUST be part of the *filter* string. If not, Tethereal will be unable to extract its value.

EXAMPLE 1   -z proto,colinfo,tcp.len,tcp.len will add the TCP segment length, "tcp.len", field to COL_INFO for all packets containing the "tcp.len" field.

EXAMPLE 2
-z proto,colinfo,"tcp.len&&ip.src==192.168.100.40",tcp.len will put "tcp.len" on COL_INFO but only for packets coming from host 192.168.100.40.

NOTES   This option can be used multiple times on the command line.

COMMAND   -z rpc,rtt,*program*,*version*[,*filter*]

DESCRIPTION   Collects call and reply RTT data for *program/version*. The data collected is the number of calls for each procedure, MinRTT, MaxRTT and AvgRTT. If the optional filter string is provided, the statistics will only be calculated on those calls that match that filter.

EXAMPLE 1   -z rpc,rtt,100003,3 will collect data for Network File System (NFS) v3.

EXAMPLE 2   -z rpc,rtt,100003,3,nfs.fh.hash==0x12345678 will collect NFS v3 RTT statistics for a specific file.

NOTES   This option can be used multiple times on the command line.

COMMAND   -z rpc,programs

DESCRIPTION   Collects call and reply RTT data for all known ONC-RPC programs/versions. Data collected is the number of calls for each protocol/version, MinRTT, MaxRTT and AvgRTT.

EXAMPLE   -z rpc,programs will collect data for all known ONC-RPC programs/versions.

NOTES   This option can only be used once on the command line.

COMMAND -z smb,rtt[,*filter*]

DESCRIPTION Collects call and reply RTT data for SMB. The data collected is the number of calls for each SMB command, MinRTT, MaxRTT and AvgRTT. The data will be presented as separate tables for all normal SMB commands, all Transaction2 commands and all NT Transaction commands. Only those commands that are seen in the capture will have its statistics displayed. Only the first command in a "xAndX" command chain will be used in the calculation. So for common "SessionSetupAndX + TreeConnectAndX" chains, only the "SessionSetupAndX" call will be used in the statistics. This is a flaw that might be fixed in the future. If the optional filter string is provided, the stats will only be calculated on those calls that match that filter.

EXAMPLE 1 **-z smb,rtt** will collect all SMB statistics.

EXAMPLE 2 **-z smb,rtt,ip.addr==192.168.100.40** will only collect statistics for SMB packets exchanged by the host at IP address 192.168.100.40.

NOTES This option can be used multiple times on the command line.

COMMAND **-z smb,sids**

DESCRIPTION When this feature is used Tethereal will print a report with all the discovered Security Identifiers (SIDs) and account name mappings. Only those SIDs where the account name is known will be presented in the table. For this feature to work you will need to either to enable "**Edit|Preferences|Protocols|SMB|Snoop SID to** name mappings" in the preferences or you can override the preferences by specifying **–o smb.sid_name_snooping:TRUE** on the Tethereal command line.

EXAMPLE **–o smb.sid_name_snooping:TRUE -z** smb,sids will enable the mapping preference and report all discovered SMB SIDs.

NOTES The current methods used by Tethereal to find the SID. Name mapping is relatively restricted but is hoped to be expanded in the future.

COMMAND **-z mgcp,rtd[,**_filter_**]**

DESCRIPTION Collects requests and response Response Time Delay (RTD) data for Media Gateway Control Protocol (MGCP). This is similar to **-z smb,rtt**. The data collected is the number of calls for each known MGCP Type, MinRTD, MaxRTD and AvgRTD. Additionally you get the number of duplicate requests/responses, unresponded requests, responses that don't match with any request. If the optional filter string is provided, the stats will only be calculated on those calls that match that filter.

EXAMPLE 1 **-z mgcp,rtd** will collect all statistics for all MGCP traffic.

EXAMPLE 2 **-z mgcp,rtd,ip.addr==192.168.100.40** will collect statistics for MGCP packets exchanged by the host at IP address 192.168.100.40.

NOTES This option can be used multiple times on the command line.

COMMAND **-z h225,counter[,**_filter_**]**

DESCRIPTION Count ITU-T H.225 messages and their reasons. The first column provides a list of H.225 messages and H.225 message reasons, which occur in the current capture file. The second column displays the number of occurrences of each message or reason.

EXAMPLE 1 **-z h225,counter** will collect all H.225 messages and their reasons.

EXAMPLE 2 **-z h225,counter,ip.addr==192.168.100.40** will collect statistics for H.225 packets exchanged by the host at IP address 192.168.100.40.

NOTES This option can be used multiple times on the command line.

COMMAND **-z h225,srt[,**_filter_**]**

DESCRIPTION Collect request and response SRT (Service Response Time) data for ITU-T H.225 RAS. The data collected is number of calls of each ITU-T H.225 RAS Message Type, Minimum SRT, Maximum SRT, Average SRT, Minimum in Frame, and Maximum in Frame. Additionally it displays the number of Open Requests (Unresponded Requests), Discarded Responses (responses without matching requests), and Duplicate Messages.

EXAMPLE 1   **–z h225,srt** will collect all SRT data for all ITU-T H.225 RAS traffic.

EXAMPLE 2   **–z h225,srt,ip.addr==192.168.100.40** will collect SRT statistics for ITU-T H.225 RAS packets exchanged by the host at IP address 192.168.100.40.

NOTES   This option can be used multiple times on the command line.

Notes from the Underground…

XML Compatible Protocol Dissection

A new feature to Tethereal in version 0.10.0 is the ability to display output in PDML format by using the **–T pdml** option. The Politecnico Di Torino group, known for Analyzer and WinPcap, created the PDML specification. PDML is a simple language to format information related to packet decodes. The PDML data that Tethereal produces differs slightly from the specification and is not readable by Analyzer. The Tethereal PDML output contains the following flags:

- **<pdml>** This PDML file is delimited by the <pdml> and </pdml> tags. This tag does not have any attributes.
  Example: <pdml version="0" creator="ethereal/0.10.0">

- **<packet>** A PDML file can contain multiple packets by using the <packet> element. This tag does not have any attributes.

- **<proto>** A packet can contain multiple protocols, designated by the <proto> element. The <proto> tag can have the following attributes:

  name The display filter name for the protocol.

  showname The label used to describe this protocol in the protocol tree.

Continued

pos The starting offset within the packet data where this protocol starts

size The number of octets in the packet data that this protocol covers.

Example: <proto name="ip" showname="Internet Protocol, Src Addr: 192.168.100.132

(192.168.100.132), Dst Addr: 192.168.129.201 (192.168.129.201)" size="20" pos="14">

■ **<field>** A protocol can contain multiple fields, designated by the <field> element. The <field> tag can have the following attributes:

name The display filter name for the field.

showname The label used to describe this field in the protocol tree.

pos The starting offset within the packet data where this field starts.

size The number of octets in the packet data that this field covers.

value The actual packet data, in hex, that this field covers.

show The representation of the packet data as it appears in a display filter.

Example: <field name="ip.version" showname="Version: 4" size="1"

pos="14" show="4" value="45"/>

Two tools are provided in the ethereal-0.10.0a/tools directory to assist with PDML output parsing. EtherealXML.py is a Python module used to read a PDML file and call a specified callback function. Msnchat is a sample program that uses EtherealXML to parse PDML output for MSN chat conversations. It takes one or more capture files as input, invokes Tethereal with a specified read filter, and produces HTML output of the conversations. The usage output for msnchat is as follows:

```
[root@localhost tools]# ./msnchat -h
msnchat [OPTIONS] CAPTURE_FILE [...]
```

Continued

```
 -o FILE        name of output file

 -t TETHEREAL   location of tethereal binary

 -u USER        name for unknown user
```

The following command can be used to read and parse a saved capture file called msn_test1:

```
[root@localhost tools]# ./msnchat -o outfile msn_test1
```

When viewed with a web browser, the HTML outfile looks like the following:

```
---- New Conversation @ Dec 30, 2003 14:21:08 ----

(14:21:08) Luke: hello

(14:21:22) Unknown: how are you?

(14:21:53) Luke: are we meeting at noon?

(14:22:03) Unknown: yes, at the secret location.

(14:22:11) Luke: great, see you then

(14:22:17) Unknown: ok

(14:22:18) Unknown: bye
```

You can add a name for the Unknown user by typing the following command:

```
[root@localhost tools]# ./msnchat -o outfile -u Leia msn_test1
```

The HTML output would then look like the following:

```
---- New Conversation @ Dec 30, 2003 14:21:08 ----

(14:21:08) Luke: hello

(14:21:22) Leia: how are you?

(14:21:53) Luke: are we meeting at noon?

(14:22:03) Leia: yes, at the secret location.

(14:22:11) Luke: great, see you then

(14:22:17) Leia: ok

(14:22:18) Leia: bye
```

The msnchat code will give you a good idea of how to write your own scripts to parse capture files, manipulate the PDML data, and print the output in HTML format.

Editcap

Editcap is a program used to remove or select packets from a file and to translate the format of captured files. It doesn't capture live traffic; it only reads data from a saved capture file and then saves some or all of the packets to a new capture file. Editcap can read all of the same types of files that Ethereal can, and by default writes to libpcap format. Editcap can also write captures to standard and modified versions of libpcap, Sun snoop, Novell LANalyzer, Networks Associate's Sniffer, Microsoft Network Monitor, Visual Network traffic capture, Accellent 5Views capture, and Network Instruments Observer version 9 captures. Editcap can determine the file type that it is reading, and is also capable of reading files that are compressed with gzip.

By default editcap writes all of the packets in the capture file to the output file. If you specify a list of packet numbers on the command line, those packets will *not* be written to the output capture file. If the **–r** option is specified, it will reverse the default configuration and write only the specified packets to the output capture file. You can also specify a range of packets to include or exclude in the output capture file.

The following information is the usage output for the editcap program:

```
C:\Program Files\Ethereal>editcap -h
Usage: editcap [-r] [-h] [-v] [-T <encap type>] [-F <capture type>]
               [-s <snaplen>] [-t <time adjustment>
               <infile> <outfile> [ <record#>[-<record#>] ... ]
   where -r specifies that the records specified should be kept, not deleted,
                          default is to delete
         -v specifies verbose operation, default is silent
         -h produces this help listing.
         -T <encap type> specifies the encapsulation type to use:
             ether - Ethernet
             tr - Token Ring
```

```
slip - SLIP
ppp - PPP
fddi - FDDI
fddi-swapped - FDDI with bit-swapped MAC addresses
rawip - Raw IP
arcnet - ARCNET
arcnet_linux - Linux ARCNET
atm-rfc1483 - RFC 1483 ATM
linux-atm-clip - Linux ATM CLIP
lapb - LAPB
atm-pdus - ATM PDUs
atm-pdus-untruncated - ATM PDUs - untruncated
null - NULL
ascend - Lucent/Ascend access equipment
isdn - ISDN
ip-over-fc - RFC 2625 IP-over-Fibre Channel
ppp-with-direction - PPP with Directional Info
ieee-802-11 - IEEE 802.11 Wireless LAN
ieee-802-11-radio - IEEE 802.11 Wireless LAN with radio
 information
linux-sll - Linux cooked-mode capture
frelay - Frame Relay
frelay-with-direction - Frame Relay with Directional Info
chdlc - Cisco HDLC
ios - Cisco IOS internal
ltalk - Localtalk
prism - IEEE 802.11 plus Prism II monitor mode header
pflog-old - OpenBSD PF Firewall logs, pre-3.4
hhdlc - HiPath HDLC
docsis - Data Over Cable Service Interface Specification
cosine - CoSine L2 debug log
wlan - IEEE 802.11 plus AVS WLAN monitor header
whdlc - Wellfleet HDLC
sdlc - SDLC
tzsp - Tazmen sniffer protocol
enc - OpenBSD enc(4) encapsulating interface
```

```
       pflog - OpenBSD PF Firewall logs
       chdlc-with-direction - Cisco HDLC with Directional Info
       bluetooth-h4 - Bluetooth H4
       mtp2 - SS7 MTP2
       mtp3 - SS7 MTP3
       default is the same as the input file
 -F <capture type> specifies the capture file type to write:
       libpcap - libpcap (tcpdump, Ethereal, etc.)
       rh6_1libpcap - RedHat Linux 6.1 libpcap (tcpdump)
       suse6_3libpcap - SuSE Linux 6.3 libpcap (tcpdump)
       modlibpcap - modified libpcap (tcpdump)
       nokialibpcap - Nokia libpcap (tcpdump)
       lanalyzer - Novell LANalyzer
       ngsniffer - Network Associates Sniffer (DOS-based)
       snoop - Sun snoop
       netmon1 - Microsoft Network Monitor 1.x
       netmon2 - Microsoft Network Monitor 2.x
       ngwsniffer_1_1 - Network Associates Sniffer (Windows-based)
        1.1
       ngwsniffer_2_0  Network Associates Sniffer (Windows-based)
        2.00x
       visual - Visual Networks traffic capture
       5views - Accellent 5Views capture
       niobserverv9 - Network Instruments Observer version 9
       default is libpcap
 -s <snaplen> specifies that packets should be truncated to
    <snaplen> bytes of data
 -t <time adjustment> specifies the time adjustment
    to be applied to selected packets
    A range of records can be specified as well
```

The following command line options are used to control Editcap's data translation and output:

- **–F** *type* This option is used to set the format of the output capture file. For example, if you want to save a file in the Sun snoop format so that snoop can read the capture file, you would use the **–F snoop** option.

- **–h** This option prints the help options of editcap, then exits.

- **–r** This option will cause the packets whose numbers are specified on the command line to be written to the output capture file. This is opposite of the default action, which is to remove the packets that are specified on the command line. Packets can only be specified as a consecutive range in the *start-end* format, or individually; they cannot be comma delimited.

- **–s** *snaplen* This option will set the snapshot length to use when writing the data to the output capture file. Packets that are larger than the *snaplen* will be truncated. This option is helpful if you only want to save the packet headers, or if the program you will be importing the capture file into can only read packets of a certain size.

- **–t** [-]*seconds*[.*fractional seconds*] This option will allow you to specify a time adjustment to apply to selected frames in the output capture file. The time adjustment is specified in seconds and fractions of seconds. An option of **–t 3600** will advance the timestamp on the selected frames by one hour, while the option of **–t –3600** will reduce the timestamp on the selected frames by one hour. This option is useful when you need to synchronize packet traces with other logs from different devices.

- **–T** *type* This option sets the packet encapsulation type of the output capture file. The default type is the same encapsulation type as the input file. This option forces the encapsulation type of the output capture file to be a specified type, however the packet headers will remain the same encapsulation type as the input capture file. This is because the encapsulation type is stored as meta-data, outside of the packet data. The encapsulation type is a single variable that is changed, thus allowing the packet data and headers of the original packet to remain unchanged.

- **–v** This option will cause editcap to print various messages to the screen while it is processing files.

The following is an example of using editcap to translate the first five packets, plus packets 10, 15, and 17 from a tethereal libpcap capture file called *capture* to a Sun snoop output file called *capture_snoop*:

```
C:\Program Files\Ethereal>editcap -r -v -F snoop capture capture_snoop 1-5
10 15 17

File capture is a libpcap (tcpdump, Ethereal, etc.) capture file.
```

```
Add_Selected: 1-5
Inclusive ... 1, 5
Add_Selected: 10
Not inclusive ... 10
Add_Selected: 15
Not inclusive ... 15
Add_Selected: 17
Not inclusive ... 17
Record: 1
Record: 2
Record: 3
Record: 4
Record: 5
Record: 10
Record: 15
Record: 17
```

The next example uses editcap to translate all packets, except packets 5 through 120, from a libpcap capture file called *capture* to a libpcap output file called *capture_out*:

```
C:\Program Files\Ethereal>editcap -v capture capture_out 5-120
File capture is a libpcap (tcpdump, Ethereal, etc.) capture file.
Add_Selected: 5-120
Inclusive ... 5, 120
Record: 1
Record: 2
Record: 3
Record: 4
Record: 121
Record: 122
```

The next example uses editcap to adjust the timestamp forward by five and a half seconds on all packets. It uses an NAI Sniffer Pro capture file called *capture.dump* as input and saves the output to a Novell LANalyzer file called *capture_out*:

```
C:\Program Files\Ethereal>editcap -v -F lanalyzer -t 5.5 capture.dump
capture_out
```

```
File capture is a libpcap (tcpdump, Ethereal, etc.) capture file.
Record: 1
Record: 2
Record: 3
Record: 4
Record: 5
Record: 6
Record: 7
Record: 8
Record: 9
Record: 10
output removed
```

The next example uses editcap to save the first 35 bytes of the input capture file called *capture* to the output capture file called *capture_out*. This will include the full Ethernet and IP headers in the output file:

```
C:\Program Files\Ethereal>editcap -v -s 35 capture capture_out
File capture is a libpcap (tcpdump, Ethereal, etc.) capture file.
Record: 1
Record: 2
Record: 3
Record: 4
Record: 5
Record: 6
Record: 7
Record: 8
Record: 9
Record: 10
output removed
```

The next example uses editcap to translate input capture file called *capture* to the output capture file called *capture_out* with an encapsulation type of IEEE 802.11 Wireless LAN:

```
C:\Program Files\Ethereal>editcap -v -T ieee-802-11 capture capture_out
File capture is a libpcap (tcpdump, Ethereal, etc.) capture file.
Record: 1
Record: 2
```

```
Record:  3

Record:  4

Record:  5

Record:  6

Record:  7

Record:  8

Record:  9

Record:  10

output removed
```

Mergecap

Mergecap is used to combine multiple saved capture files into a single output
file. Mergecap can read all of the same types of files that Ethereal can, and by
default writes to libpcap format. Mergecap can also write the output capture file
to standard and modified versions of libpcap, Sun snoop, Novel LANalyzer, NAI
Sniffer, Microsoft Network Monitor, Visual Network traffic capture, Accellent
5Views capture, and Network Instruments Observer version 9 captures.
Mergecap can determine the file type that it is reading, and is also capable of
reading files that are compressed with gzip. By default, the packets from the input
files are merged in chronological order based on each packet's timestamp. If the
–a option is specified, packets will be copied directly from each input file to the
output file regardless of timestamp.

The following information is the usage output for the mergecap program:

```
C:\Program Files\Ethereal>mergecap -h

mergecap version 0.10.0

Usage: mergecap [-hva] [-s <snaplen>] [-T <encap type>]

        [-F <capture type>] -w <outfile> <infile> [...]

  where -h produces this help listing.

        -v verbose operation, default is silent

        -a files should be concatenated, not merged

            Default merges based on frame timestamps

        -s <snaplen>: truncate packets to <snaplen> bytes of data

        -w <outfile>: sets output filename to <outfile>

        -T <encap type> encapsulation type to use:

            ether - Ethernet
```

```
tr - Token Ring
slip - SLIP
ppp - PPP
fddi - FDDI
fddi-swapped - FDDI with bit-swapped MAC addresses
rawip - Raw IP
arcnet - ARCNET
arcnet_linux - Linux ARCNET
atm-rfc1483 - RFC 1483 ATM
linux-atm-clip - Linux ATM CLIP
lapb - LAPB
atm-pdus - ATM PDUs
atm-pdus-untruncated - ATM PDUs - untruncated
null - NULL
ascend - Lucent/Ascend access equipment
isdn - ISDN
ip-over-fc - RFC 2625 IP-over-Fibre Channel
ppp-with-direction - PPP with Directional Info
ieee-802-11 - IEEE 802.11 Wireless LAN
ieee-802-11-radio - IEEE 802.11 Wireless LAN with radio
   information
linux-sll - Linux cooked-mode capture
frelay - Frame Relay
frelay-with-direction - Frame Relay with Directional Info
chdlc - Cisco HDLC
ios - Cisco IOS internal
ltalk - Localtalk
prism - IEEE 802.11 plus Prism II monitor mode header
pflog-old - OpenBSD PF Firewall logs, pre-3.4
hhdlc - HiPath HDLC
docsis - Data Over Cable Service Interface Specification
cosine - CoSine L2 debug log
wlan - IEEE 802.11 plus AVS WLAN monitor header
whdlc - Wellfleet HDLC
sdlc - SDLC
tzsp - Tazmen sniffer protocol
```

```
        enc - OpenBSD enc(4) encapsulating interface
        pflog - OpenBSD PF Firewall logs
        chdlc-with-direction - Cisco HDLC with Directional Info
        bluetooth-h4 - Bluetooth H4
        mtp2 - SS7 MTP2
        mtp3 - SS7 MTP3
        default is the same as the first input file
-F <capture type> capture file type to write:
        libpcap - libpcap (tcpdump, Ethereal, etc.)
        rh6_1libpcap - RedHat Linux 6.1 libpcap (tcpdump)
        suse6_3libpcap - SuSE Linux 6.3 libpcap (tcpdump)
        modlibpcap - modified libpcap (tcpdump)
        nokialibpcap - Nokia libpcap (tcpdump)
        lanalyzer - Novell LANalyzer
        ngsniffer - Network Associates Sniffer (DOS-based)
        snoop - Sun snoop
        netmon1 - Microsoft Network Monitor 1.x
        netmon2 - Microsoft Network Monitor 2.x
        ngwsniffer_1_1 - Network Associates Sniffer (Windows-based)
          1.1
        ngwsniffer_2_0 - Network Associates Sniffer (Windows-based)
          2.00x
        visual - Visual Networks traffic capture
        5views - Accellent 5Views capture
        niobserverv9 - Network Instruments Observer version 9
        default is libpcap
```

The following command line options are used to control Editcap's data translation and output:

- **–a** This option will ignore the timestamps in the input capture files and merge the capture files one after the other. When this option is omitted the packets in the input files are merged in chronological order based on the packet timestamps.

- **–F** *type* This option is used to set the format of the output capture file. For example, if you want to merge capture files and save them in the Sun snoop format so that snoop can read the output file, you would use the **–F snoop** option.

- **–h** This option prints the help options of mergecap, then exits.

- **–s** *snaplen* This option will set the snapshot length to use when writing the data to the output capture file. Packets that are larger than the *snaplen* will be truncated. This option is helpful if you only want to save the packet headers, or if the program you will be importing the capture file into can only read packets of a certain size.

- **–T** *type* This option sets the packet encapsulation type of the output capture file. The default type is the same encapsulation type as the input files, if they are all the same. If the input files do not all have the same encapsulation type, the encapsulation type of the output file will be set to WTAP_ENCAP_PER_PACKET. However, libpcap and other capture formats do not support this type of encapsulation. The **–T** option forces the encapsulation type of the output capture file to be a specified type, however the packet headers will remain the same encapsulation type as the input capture file.

- **–v** This option will cause mergecap to print various messages to the screen while it is processing files.

- **–w** *file* This option writes the packets to the file name specified following the option. This option is required for mergecap to merge files.

The following is an example of using mergecap to merge the first 35 bytes of each of the four capture files (*capture1, capture2, capture3, and capture4*) into a single Sun snoop output file called *merge_snoop* in chronological order by packet timestamp, it will keep reading packets until the end of the last file is reached:

```
C:\Program Files\Ethereal>mergecap -s 35 -v -F snoop -w merge_snoop
capture1 capture2 capture3 capture4

mergecap: capture1 is type libpcap (tcpdump, Ethereal, etc.).

mergecap: capture2 is type libpcap (tcpdump, Ethereal, etc.).

mergecap: capture3 is type libpcap (tcpdump, Ethereal, etc.).

mergecap: capture4 is type libpcap (tcpdump, Ethereal, etc.).

mergecap: opened 4 of 4 input files

mergecap: selected frame_type Ethernet (ether)

Record: 1

Record: 2

Record: 3

Record: 4
```

```
Record: 5
Record: 6
Record: 7
Record: 8
Record: 9
Record: 10
output removed
```

The following is an example of using mergecap to merge four capture files (*capture1, capture2, capture3, and capture4*) into a single output file called *merge_file* regardless of packet timestamp, it will write all of the packets of capture1, followed by capture 2, and so on:

```
C:\Program Files\Ethereal>mergecap -v -a -w merge_file capture1 capture2
capture3 capture4
mergecap: capture1 is type libpcap (tcpdump, Ethereal, etc.).
mergecap: capture2 is type libpcap (tcpdump, Ethereal, etc.).
mergecap: capture3 is type libpcap (tcpdump, Ethereal, etc.).
mergecap: capture4 is type libpcap (tcpdump, Ethereal, etc.).
mergecap: opened 4 of 4 input files
mergecap: selected frame_type Ethernet (ether)
Record: 1
Record: 2
Record: 3
Record: 4
Record: 5
Record: 6
Record: 7
Record: 8
Record: 9
Record: 10
output removed
```

The following is an example of an attempt to use mergecap to merge three capture files with different encapsulation types (*capture1, capture2, and capture3*) into a single output file called *merge_encap* The merge will attempt to set the default encapsulation type and then report an error because libpcap does not understand that type of encapsulation:

```
C:\Program Files\Ethereal>mergecap -v -w merge_encap capture1 capture2
capture3
mergecap: capture1 is type libpcap (tcpdump, Ethereal, etc.).
mergecap: capture2 is type libpcap (tcpdump, Ethereal, etc.).
mergecap: capture3 is type libpcap (tcpdump, Ethereal, etc.).
mergecap: opened 3 of 3 input files
mergecap: multiple frame encapsulation types detected
         defaulting to WTAP_ENCAP_PER_PACKET
         capture1 had type (null) ((null))
         capture2 had type Ethernet (ether)
mergecap: selected frame_type (null) ((null))
mergecap: Can't open/create merge_encap:
         That file format doesn't support per-packet encapsulations
```

The following is an example of an attempt to use mergecap to merge three capture files with different encapsulation types (*capture1, capture2, and capture3*) into a single output file called *merge_encap*, the –T option is used to force an Ethernet encapsulation type for the output file:

```
C:\Program Files\Ethereal>mergecap -v -T ether -w merge_encap capture1
capture2 capture3
mergecap: capture1 is type libpcap (tcpdump, Ethereal, etc.).
mergecap: capture2 is type libpcap (tcpdump, Ethereal, etc.).
mergecap: capture3 is type libpcap (tcpdump, Ethereal, etc.).
mergecap: opened 3 of 3 input files
Record: 1
Record: 2
Record: 3
Record: 4
Record: 5
Record: 6
Record: 7
Record: 8
Record: 9
Record: 10
output removed
```

Text2pcap

Text2pcap generates capture files by reading ASCII hexadecimal dump captures and writing the data to a libpcap output file. It is capable of reading a hexdump of single or multiple packets, and building capture files from it. Text2pcap can also read hexdumps of application level data only, by creating dummy Ethernet, IP, and User Datagram Protocol (UDP) or TCP headers so Ethereal and other sniffers can read the full data. The user can specify which of these headers to add.

Text2pcap uses the octal dump (od) format of hexadecimal output. Octal dump is a UNIX command that is used to output a file or standard input to a specified form, such as octal, decimal, or hexadecimal format. The format is specified by the parameters given to the **–t** option. The command **od –t x1** will generate output that text2pcap can understand (the **x1** describes the format of hexadecimal). The following is an example of the type of hexadecimal dump that text2pcap can read:

```
0000   00 05 5d ee 7e 53 08 00 20 cf 5b 39 08 00 45 00    ..].~S.. .[9..E.
0010   00 9a 13 9e 40 00 3c 06 e0 70 c0 a8 64 7a c0 a8    ....@.<..p..dz..
0020   64 84 00 17 05 49 0e a9 91 43 8e d8 e3 6a 50 18    d....I...C...jP.
0030   c1 e8 ba 7b 00 00 4c 61 73 74 20 6c 6f 67 69 6e    ...{..Last login
0040   3a 20 53 75 6c 20 4c 6f 76 20 20 32 20 31 37 3a    : Sun Nov  2 17:
0050   30 36 3a 35 33 20 66 72 6f 6d 20 31 39 32 2e 31    06:53 from 192.1
0060   36 38 2e 31 30 30 2e 31 33 32 0d 0a 53 75 6e 20    68.100.132..Sun
0070   4d 69 63 72 6f 73 79 73 74 65 6d 73 20 49 6e 63    Microsystems Inc
0080   2e 20 20 20 53 75 6e 4f 53 20 35 2e 39 20 20 20    .   SunOS 5.9
0090   20 20 20 20 47 65 6e 65 72 69 63 20 4d 61 79 20       Generic May
00a0   32 30 30 32 0d 0a 23 20                            2002..#
```

The beginning of each line has an offset of more than two hexadecimal, or octal, digits that is used to track the bytes in the output. If the offset is 0, this indicates the beginning of a new packet. If there are multiple packets in a file they will be output to the packet capture file with one second between each packet. If a line doesn't have this offset it is ignored. The text output at the end of the line is also ignored. Text files can also contain comments that begin with the # character. Text2pcap has the ability to support commands and options by using the **#TEXT2PCAP** command at the beginning of the line. Text2pcap currently doesn't have any commands and options supported, but future development could incorporate methods to control the way the hexadecimal dump is processed.

The following is the usage output for the text2pcap program:

```
Usage: text2pcap [-h] [-d] [-q] [-o h|o] [-l typenum] [-e l3pid] [-i proto]
        [-m max-packet] [-u srcp,destp] [-T srcp,destp] [-s
srcp,destp,tag]
        [-S srcp,destp,tag] [-t timefmt] <input-filename> <output-filename>
where <input-filename> specifies input filename (use - for standard input)
      <output-filename> specifies output filename (use - for standard
      output)

[options] are one or more of the following
 -h                 : Display this help message
 -d                 : Generate detailed debug of parser states
 -o hex|oct         : Parse offsets as (h)ex or (o)ctal. Default is hex
 -l typenum         : Specify link-layer type number. Default is 1
                        (Ethernet).
                      See net/bpf.h for list of numbers.
 -q                 : Generate no output at all (automatically turns off -d)
 -e l3pid           : Prepend dummy Ethernet II header with specified L3PID
                        (in HEX)
                      Example: -e 0x800
 -i proto           : Prepend dummy IP header with specified IP protocol (in
                        DECIMAL).
                      Automatically prepends Ethernet header as well.
                      Example: -i 46
 -m max-packet    : Max packet length in output, default is 64000
 -u srcp,destp    : Prepend dummy UDP header with specified dest and source
                        ports (in DECIMAL).
                      Automatically prepends Ethernet and IP headers as well
                      Example: -u 30,40
 -T srcp,destp    : Prepend dummy TCP header with specified dest and source
                        ports (in DECIMAL).
                      Automatically prepends Ethernet and IP headers as well
                      Example: -T 50,60
 -s srcp,dstp,tag: Prepend dummy SCTP header with specified dest/source
                        ports and verification tag (in DECIMAL).
                      Automatically prepends Ethernet and IP headers as well
                      Example: -s 30,40,34
```

```
-S srcp,dstp,ppi: Prepend dummy SCTP header with specified dest/source
                  ports and verification tag 0. It also prepends a dummy
                  SCTP DATA chunk header with payload protocol identifier
                  ppi.
                  Example: -S 30,40,34
-t timefmt       : Treats the text before the packet as a date/time code;
                   the specified argument is a format string of the sort
                   supported by strptime.
                   Example: The time "10:15:14.5476" has the format code
                   "%H:%M:%S."
                   NOTE:    The subsecond component delimiter must be
                            specified (.) but no pattern is required; the
                            remaining number is assumed to be fractions
                            of a second.
```

The following command line options are used to control text2pcap's data processing and output:

- **–h** This option prints the help options of text2pcap, then exits.

- **–d** This option displays debugging information during the processing. Like verbose options it can be used several times for more information.

- **–q** This option causes text2pcap to be quiet while processing.

- **–o h|o** This option specifies either hexadecimal or octal formats for the offset of the output. The default is hexadecimal.

- **–l** *typenum* This option lets you specify the data link layer type of encapsulation for the packet. This option is used when your hexdump is a complete, encapsulated packet. The encapsulation type is specified as a number using the *typenum* parameter. A complete list of encapsulation types and their associated numbers can be found in the /libpcap-0.7.2/bpf/net/bpf.h file included in the libpcap source distribution. For example Point-to-Point Protocol (PPP) is encapsulation type 9. The default is Ethernet, encapsulation type 1.

- **–e l3pid** This option allows you to include a dummy Ethernet header for each packet. You would use this option when your dump file has any type of layer 3 header, such as IP, but no layer 2 information.

- **−i** *proto* This option allows you to include a dummy IP header for each packet. The *proto* parameter allows you to specify the IP protocol in decimal format. You would use this option when your dump file has complete layer 4 information, but no layer 3 IP information. This option will also include the necessary Ethernet information. For example, **−i 88** will set the set the protocol to Enhanced Interior Gateway Routing Protocol (EIGRP).

- **−m** *max-packet* This option will allow you to set the maximum packet length with the *max-packet* parameter. The default is 64000.

- **−u** *srcport, destport* This option allows you to include a dummy UDP header for each packet. The *srcport* and *destport* parameters allow you to specify the source and destination UDP ports in decimal format. You would use this option when your dump file has does not contain any UDP layer 4 or below information. This option will also include the necessary IP and Ethernet information.

- **−T** *srcport, destport* This option allows you to include a dummy TCP header for each packet. The *srcport* and *destport* parameters allow you to specify the source and destination TCP ports in decimal format. You would use this option when your dump file has does not contain any TCP layer 4 or below information. This option will also include the necessary IP and Ethernet information.

- **−s** *srcport, destport, tag* This option allows you to include a dummy Stream Control Transmission Protocol (SCTP) header for each packet. The *srcport* and *destport* parameters allow you to specify the source and destination SCTP ports in decimal format. The *tag* parameter allows you to specify a verification tag. You would use this option when your dump file has does not contain any SCTP layer 4 or below information. This option will also include the necessary IP, Ethernet, and CRC32C checksum information.

- **−S** *srcport, destport, ppi* This option allows you to include a dummy SCTP header for each packet. The *srcport* and *destport* parameters allow you to specify the source and destination SCTP ports in decimal format. The *ppi* parameter allows you to specify a payload protocol identifier for a dummy SCTP DATA chunk header. The verification tag will automatically be set to 0. You would use this option when your dump file has does not contain any SCTP layer 4 or below information. This option will also include the necessary IP, Ethernet, and CRC32C checksum information.

■ **–t** *timefmt* This option allows you to specify a time format for the text before the packet. The *timefmt* parameter follows the format of strptime(3), such as "%H:%M:%S.", which converts a character string to a time value.

The following is an example of using text2pcap to read a hexadecimal dump, *hex_sample.txt*, and output it to the *libpcap_output* file:

```
C:\Program Files\Ethereal>text2pcap hex_sample.txt libpcap_output
Input from: hex_sample.txt
Output to: libpcap_output
Wrote packet of 168 bytes at 0
Read 1 potential packets, wrote 1 packets
```

The next example uses text2pcap to read a file with multiple hexadecimal packets, *hex_sample2.txt*, and output the format as Telnet/TCP packets to the *libpcap_output2* file:

```
C:\Program Files\Ethereal>text2pcap -T 1297,23 hex_sample2.txt
libpcap_output2
Input from: hex_sample2.txt
Output to: libpcap_output2
Generate dummy Ethernet header: Protocol: 0x800
Generate dummy IP header: Protocol: 6
Generate dummy TCP header: Source port: 1297. Dest port: 23
Wrote packet of 62 bytes at 0
Wrote packet of 62 bytes at 62
Wrote packet of 60 bytes at 124
Wrote packet of 69 bytes at 184
output removed
Read 76 potential packets, wrote 76 packets
```

The od command can also be piped into the text2pcap program. Text2pcap will then read the output of the od command as standard input. The next example uses text2pcap to read a data stream as input and output the format as HTTP/TCP packets to the output.pcap file. The –Ax parameter to the od command prints the offsets as hexadecimal. The –m1460 parameter to text2pcap specifies a maximum packet size of 1460 bytes. The maximum Ethernet packet size is 1500 bytes, minus the 20 bytes for each the IP and TCP header, leaves 1460 bytes for the data. By default the −T parameter will create TCP, IP, and Ethernet dummy headers. The following shows the command and associated output:

```
[root@localhost root]# od -Ax -tx1 input | text2pcap -m1460 -T1234,80 -
output.pcap
Input from: Standard input
Output to: output.pcap
Generate dummy Ethernet header: Protocol: 0x800
Generate dummy IP header: Protocol: 6
Generate dummy TCP header: Source port: 1234. Dest port: 80
Wrote packet of 1460 bytes at 0
Wrote packet of 1460 bytes at 1460
Wrote packet of 1460 bytes at 2920
Wrote packet of 788 bytes at 4380
Read 4 potential packets, wrote 4 packets
```

Summary

As we have shown in this chapter, Ethereal is more than the GUI; it is a suite of programs that provide command line capturing, formatting, and manipulating capabilities. The programs can be used together to provide even more processing capabilities, while output from one program can be piped as input to another. Since these programs are command line, they also provide powerful scripting capabilities.

Tethereal provides just about all of the same processing capabilities as Ethereal, without the GUI functionality. Editcap, although used primarily for removing packets from a capture file, can also be used to translate capture files into various formats. Mergecap provides the ability to merge various capture files together, even from different network analyzers. This is a great resource when you're performing audits or incident response and you need to combine captures from various source such as sniffers, IDS, and logs. Text2pcap allows you to translate hexadecimal data streams to sniffer readable packet captures. You can even add dummy Layer 2-4 data when you only have an application output stream.

Solutions Fast Track

Tethereal

- ☑ Tethereal can read packets from the network or from a packet capture file.

- ☑ Tethereal can decode and print the captured packets to screen or save them to a file.

- ☑ One of the best advantages to using Tethereal is that it is highly scriptable.

- ☑ Tethereal can apply both capture filters and display filters to the packet captures.

- ☑ Tethereal can collect various types of statistic about the data that is being captured.

- ☑ Like editcap, Tethereal can be used to translate capture file formats.

Editcap

☑ Editcap can be used to remove packets from a capture file or to translate the format of capture files.

☑ The **–t** option in editcap is used to apply a time adjustment to the timestamps of the packets.

☑ The snapshot length can be specified with the **–s** option to decrease the size of each packet.

☑ Editcap can specify an encapsulation type for the packets in the output file with the **–T** option.

Mergecap

☑ Mergecap can merge several packet capture files into a single output file.

☑ Mergecap can read capture files of various formats and output them to a single format.

☑ By default, the packets from the input files are merged in chronological order based on each packets timestamp, however if the **–a** option is specified, packets will be copied directly from each input file to the output file regardless of timestamp.

☑ Mergecap can merge capture files with different encapsulation types into a single output file by using the **–T** option to force the output encapsulation type.

Text2pcap

☑ Text2pcap reads ASCII hexadecimal dump captures and writes the data to a libpcap output file.

☑ Text2pcap can insert dummy Ethernet, IP, and UDP or TCP headers.

☑ The command **od –t x1** will generate output that text2pcap can understand.

☑ An offset of 0 indicates the beginning of a new packet.

☑ Text2pcap options give you a lot of control over the dummy headers, timestamps, and encapsulation type for each packet.

Frequently Asked Questions

The following Frequently Asked Questions, answered by the authors of this book, are designed to both measure your understanding of the concepts presented in this chapter and to assist you with real-life implementation of these concepts. To have your questions about this chapter answered by the author, browse to **www.syngress.com/solutions** and click on the **"Ask the Author"** form. You will also gain access to thousands of other FAQs at ITFAQnet.com.

Q: What is the difference between using Tethereal and editcap to translate the format of capture files?

A: Nothing – they both perform the same function. However, editcap would be a more efficient method of converting files because Tethereal contains a lot of code for protocol dissection, whereas editcap is a smaller program with only a few functions. You can also use the Ethereal GUI to do the same thing by choosing **Save As** from the **File** menu.

Q: Can mergecap combine gzipped files?

A: Yes, mergecap can automatically uncompress, read, and merge gzip files.

Q: What types of things can I do to make scripting with Tethereal faster?

A: One way to make scripting faster with Tethereal is to use the **–l** option to flushes the standard output after each packet is printed instead of waiting until it fills up. This way each packet is sent as soon as it is read and dissected. You can also use the **–n** option to disable network object name resolution to make the process faster.

Q: Can I use filters to specify what packets to remove with editcap?

A: No, editcap does not have the capability to use filters. You must know the packet numbers that you want to include or exclude from the output capture file. You can use Tethereal to read a capture file, apply filters, and output the results to a new capture file.

## Chapter 7

Integrating Ethereal with Other Sniffers

Solutions in this Chapter:

- **Reading Capture Files with Ethereal**
- **Saving Capture Files with Ethereal**
- **Ethereal Integration**

☑ **Summary**

☑ **Solutions Fast Track**

☑ **Frequently Asked Questions**

Introduction

We have spent quite a lot of time discussing Ethereal and its features and benefits. However, there may come a time when you need to use other packet capturing programs or utilities. Maybe your company has already purchased a commercial product, or you may have various systems with preinstalled monitoring utilities. Either way, these products may be useful for troubleshooting or for grabbing remote captures. In addition, you may still be able to benefit from Ethereal's numerous features because of its compatibility with several popular products and utilities.

Ethereal's expansive compatibility is due to the wiretap library that it uses. When you compile Ethereal from source, the files for this feature are installed in the ethereal-0.10.0a/wiretap directory. Ethereal developers began writing the wiretap library as a future replacement for libpcap. The wiretap library, once further developed, will offer many benefits over libpcap. For now, wiretap is still under development. If you want to contribute, you can find more information in the README.developer file in the wiretap subdirectory. In this chapter we are going to look at the current benefits that the wiretap library adds to Ethereal by importing and exporting files from various packet capture utilities.

Reading Capture Files with Ethereal

Ethereal can read and process previously saved capture files from a variety of packet capture programs and utilities. Because Ethereal uses the popular libpcap-based capture format, it interfaces easily with other products that use libpcap. As mentioned earlier, the wiretap library enables Ethereal to read a variety of other capture files as well. Ethereal can automatically determine what type of file it is reading and can also uncompress gzip files. It really is as easy as opening the file! The following is a list of capture formats that Ethereal can read:

- Tcpdump
- Sun snoop and atmsnoop
- Microsoft Network Monitor
- Network Associates Sniffer (compressed or uncompressed)
- Shomiti/Finisar Surveyor
- Novell LANalyzer

- Cinco Networks NetXRay

- AG Group/WildPackets EtherPeek/TokenPeek/AiroPeek

- RADCOM's WAN/LAN analyzer

- Visual Networks' Visual UpTime

- Lucent/Ascend router debug output

- Toshiba's Integrated Services Digital Network (ISDN) routers dump output

- Cisco Secure Intrusion Detection System (IDS) iplog

- Advanced IBM Unix (AIX) iptrace

- HP-UX nettl

- ISDN4BSD project's i4btrace output

- Point-To-Point Protocol Daemon (pppd) logs (pppdump-format)

- VMS's TCPIPtrace utility

- DBS Etherwatch VMS utility

- CoSine L2 debug

- Accellent's 5Views LAN agent output

- Endace Measurement Systems' ERF capture format

- Linux Bluez Bluetooth stack "hcidump –w" traces

- Network Instruments Observer version 9

To open a saved capture file, select **File | Open**. The Open Capture File dialog box will appear, as shown in Figure 7.1. This dialog box allows you to search for the capture file that you would like to open. There are many other features of this dialog box that are covered in detail in Chapter 4. Once you have browsed through the directories in the left-hand pane and clicked on the file you want to open in the right-hand pane, click **OK** to open the file. If Ethereal can interpret the capture file, it will display it in the main window; otherwise, you will see an error message like the one in Figure 7.2.

Figure 7.1 Open Capture File Dialog Box

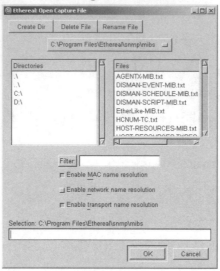

Figure 7.2 File Open Error

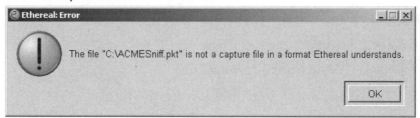

Saving Capture Files with Ethereal

Ethereal can also save captured packets to a file in several different formats. You can even choose to save all packets or a subset of the packets. These capture files can then be opened by the associated products or utilities. The following is a list of formats that Ethereal can save as:

- libpcap (tcpdump, Ethereal, etc.)
- Red Hat Linux 6.1 libpcap (tcpdump)
- SuSE Linux 6.3 libpcap (tcpdump)
- modified libpcap (tcpdump)
- Nokia libpcap (tcpdump)

- Novell LANalyzer

- Network Associate's Sniffer (DOS-based)

- Sun snoop

- Microsoft Network Monitor 1.x

- Microsoft Network Monitor 2.x

- Network Associates Sniffer (Windows-based) 1.1

- Network Associates Sniffer (Windows-based) 2.00x

- Visual Networks traffic capture

- Accellent 5Views capture

- Network Instruments Observer version 9

To save a packet capture to a file, select **File | Save As**. The Save Capture File As dialog box will appear, as shown in Figure 7.3. This dialog box allows you to choose the file format and the location where you would like to save the file. There are many other features of this dialog box that are covered in detail in Chapter 4. Browse through the directories in the left-hand pane to the desired location where you would like to save your capture file. Next, choose the correct output type from the **File Type** pull-down menu. Type in a file name under **Selection** and click **OK**.

Figure 7.3 Save Capture File As Dialog Box

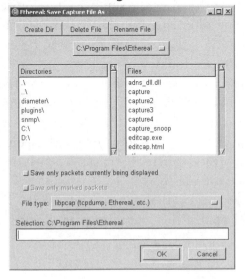

Ethereal Integration

The rest of this chapter outlines the procedures that you use to import and export files between Ethereal and various compatible products. We have included a variety of examples from open source programs, a few operating systems utilities, and two commercial packages. Specifically, this section covers Tethereal, TCPDump, WinDump, Snort, Snoop, Microsoft Network Monitor, EtherPeek, NAI's Netasyst, and HP-UX's nettl.

Tethereal

Tethereal (also discussed in chapters 5 and 6) is the command line version of Ethereal. It can be used to capture live packets from the wire or to read saved capture files. Tethereal and Ethereal both use the same capture library, libpcap, as well as most of the same code, and so exchanging files between the two is the simplest method of integration.

Tethereal will display packets on the screen in summary line form by default. These are the same lines that are displayed in the Ethereal summary pane. However, it does not print the frame number field when capturing and displaying in real time. The **–V** option can be used to print detailed information about the packets instead of just a summary. Tethereal can also read saved data capture files, and print the information in either summary (default) or detailed form (**–V**). This method will display the frame numbers with the saved packets. Finally, the **–x** command will cause Tethereal to print a hexadecimal and ASCII dump of the packet data with either the summary line or detailed protocol tree. Tethereal has a very strong filter language, called a *display* filter, and can also use the TCPDump capture filter syntax as well. These can be used to narrow down the type of traffic that you are looking to capture.

When using Tethereal to write a capture to a file, the file will be written in libpcap format by default. It will write all of the packets and all of the detail about the packets to the output file, thus the **–V** and the **–x** options aren't necessary. Since Tethereal and Ethereal are compatible with many other sniffers, you can write the output in several different formats. The **–F** option can be used to specify a format to write the file to.

The following information is the usage output for the Tethereal application. Notice the various formats that the capture can be saved as with the **–F** option:

```
[root@localhost ethereal-0.10.0a]# tethereal -h
This is GNU tethereal 0.10.0a
```

```
Compiled with GLib 2.2.1, with libpcap 0.7.2, with libz 1.1.4, with libpcre
4.5,with Net-SNMP 5.0.9, with ADNS.
Running with libpcap (version unknown) on Linux 2.4.20-6
tethereal [ -vh ] [ -DlLnpqSVx ] [ -a <capture autostop condition> ] ...
        [ -b <number of ring buffer files>[:<duration>] ] [ -c <count> ]
        [ -d <layer_type>==<selector>,<decode_as_protocol> ] ...
        [ -f <capture filter> ] [ -F <output file type> ] [ -i <interface> ]
        [ -N <resolving> ] [ -o <preference setting> ] ... [ -r <infile> ]
        [ -R <read filter> ] [ -s <snaplen> ] [ -t <time stamp format> ]
        [ -T pdml|ps|text ] [ -w <savefile> ] [ -y <link type> ]
        [ -z <statistics string> ]
Valid file type arguments to the "-F" flag:
        libpcap - libpcap (tcpdump, Ethereal, etc.)
        rh6_1libpcap - RedHat Linux 6.1 libpcap (tcpdump)
        suse6_3libpcap - SuSE Linux 6.3 libpcap (tcpdump)
        modlibpcap - modified libpcap (tcpdump)
        nokialibpcap - Nokia libpcap (tcpdump)
        lanalyzer - Novell LANalyzer
        ngsniffer - Network Associates Sniffer (DOS-based)
        snoop - Sun snoop
        netmon1 - Microsoft Network Monitor 1.x
        netmon2 - Microsoft Network Monitor 2.x
        ngwsniffer_1_1 - Network Associates Sniffer (Windows-based) 1.1
        ngwsniffer_2_0 - Network Associates Sniffer (Windows-based) 2.00x
        visual - Visual Networks traffic capture
        5views - Accellent 5Views capture
        niobserverv9 - Network Instruments Observer version 9
        default is libpcap
```

Tethereal is covered in more detail in Chapter 6; however, the following command line options are used in our examples:

- **–a** *test:value* This option is used when capturing to a file, to specify to Tethereal when to stop writing to the file. The criterion is in the form of *test:value*, where test is either duration or filesize. Duration will stop writing to a file when the value of seconds have elapsed, and filesize will stop writing to a file after a size of value kilobytes have been reached.

- **–F** *type* This option is used to set the format of the output of the capture file.

- **–i** *interface* This option will specify the interface that you want to use to capture data. The **–D** option can be used to find out what your network interfaces are.

- **–q** This option allows you to turn off the packet count when capturing network packets to a file. The count will still be displayed at the end of the capture.

- **–r** *file* This option will read and process a saved capture file.

- **–R** *filter* This option causes a read filter to be applied before displaying or writing the packets to a file.

- **–S** This option will still decode and display the packets even when writing to a file.

- **–w** *file* This option will write the packet to the file name specified following the option.

Capturing and Saving Data With Tethereal

The following examples show you how to capture and save traffic with Tethereal using various options and filter. The output can then be opened and analyzed with Ethereal.

This example captures packets on interface 1 and logs all HyperText Transfer Protocol (HTTP) packets to a file called *capture_http*. Notice the counter counts 46 packets before exiting with **Ctrl + C**.

```
[root@localhost root]# tethereal -i 1 -w capture_http -R http
Capturing on eth0
46
```

This example captures packets and logs all packets except those going to Internet Protocol (IP) destination address 192.168.129.201 to a file called *capture_filter*.

```
[root@localhost root]# tethereal -w capture_filter -R "ip.dst ne
192.168.129.201"
Capturing on eth0
14
```

The next example captures all packets for a duration of 60 seconds and logs the output to a file called *capture_duration*. It also uses the **–q** option to keep the packet count from displaying on the screen while the capture is taking place, however, the total count is displayed once the capture is complete.

```
[root@localhost root]# tethereal -q -w capture_duration -a duration:60
Capturing on eth0
17 packets captured
```

Finally, we wanted to show an example of how Tethereal can capture packets and output them to a file of a different format. We used the **–F** option to output the capture to Snoop format. The Snoop capture utility will be described in detail later in this chapter. We also used the **–S** option to display the packets on the screen while the capture is also being written to a file.

```
[root@localhost root]# tethereal -S -w capture_snoop -F snoop
Capturing on eth0
  0.000000  192.168.1.1 -> 192.168.1.2   ICMP Echo (ping) request
  0.000246  192.168.1.2 -> 192.168.1.1   ICMP Echo (ping) reply
  0.994147  192.168.1.1 -> 192.168.1.2   ICMP Echo (ping) request
  1.003309  192.168.1.2 -> 192.168.1.1   ICMP Echo (ping) reply
  2.004822  192.168.1.1 -> 192.168.1.2   ICMP Echo (ping) request
  2.005064  192.168.1.2 -> 192.168.1.1   ICMP Echo (ping) reply
  3.003506  192.168.1.1 -> 192.168.1.2   ICMP Echo (ping) request
  3.003758  192.168.1.2 -> 192.168.1.1   ICMP Echo (ping) reply
  4.993195  192.168.1.2 -> Intel_8b:c6:c2 ARP Who has 192.168.1.1?   Tell
192.168.1.2
  4.993688  192.168.1.1 -> 192.168.1.2   ARP 192.168.1.1 is at
00:03:47:8b:e6:e2
```

Now that we have the output saved to capture files, all we need to do is open it with Ethereal. Once you have opened Ethereal, select **File | Open**. Browse to the location of the capture file and select it, then click **OK**. Ethereal will open it and automatically read the Snoop format file that we saved! Figure 7.4 shows the Ethereal output of the *tethereal capture_snoop* file.

Figure 7.4 Ethereal Display of Tethereal Capture

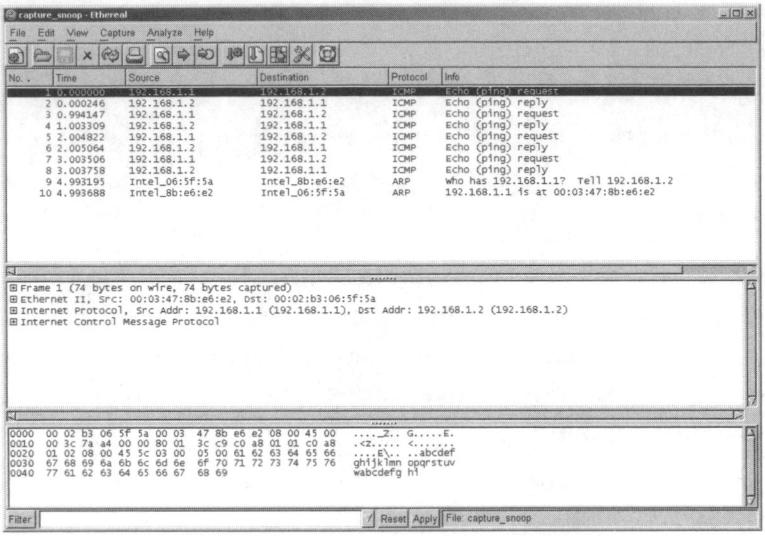

Reading Ethereal Files With Tethereal

Tethereal can read and process all of the same types of files that Ethereal reads. This means you can capture files with Ethereal or another supported network analyzers, and then read them with Tethereal. Let's provide an example of saving captured data with Ethereal and reading it with Tethereal. Once you have captured your data with Ethereal, access the **File | Save As** menu item. Browse to the location where you would like to save your capture. Next, choose the correct output type from the **File Type** pull-down menu. In our case we are saving to **libpcap (tcpdump, Ethereal, etc**.*).* Type in a file name under **Selection** and click **OK**. If preferred, you could choose any of the file types listed, as Tethereal will automatically read and process them all!

The following example uses Tethereal to read a file that we saved with Ethereal, called ethereal_capture. The file will be processed and the output will be displayed on the screen in summary line form. You can also use the **–V** option for more detailed information.

```
C:\Program Files\Ethereal>tethereal -r ethereal_capture
   1    0.000000 192.168.100.132 -> 192.168.129.201 TCP 1673 > 4243 [SYN]
Seq=3548821018 Ack=0 Win=16384 Len=0
   2    0.000261 192.168.100.132 -> 192.168.129.201 TCP 1673 > 4243 [SYN]
Seq=3548821018 Ack=0 Win=16384 Len=0
```

```
  3    2.058006 192.168.100.132 -> 192.168.129.201 TCP 1674 > 4243 [SYN]
Seq=3551633783 Ack=0 Win=16384 Len=0
  4    2.058269 192.168.100.132 -> 192.168.129.201 TCP 1674 > 4243 [SYN]
Seq=3551633783 Ack=0 Win=16384 Len=0
```

TCPDump

TCPDump is the oldest and most commonly used network sniffer. It is command line-based and runs on UNIX-based systems. It was developed by the Network Research Group (NRG) of the Information and Computing Sciences Division (ICSD) at Lawrence Berkeley National Laboratory (LBNL) and is now being actively developed and maintained at www.tcpdump.org.

TCPDump can be used to read live packets from the wire, or to read previously saved packet captures. Ethereal uses the same packet capture library as TCPDump, libpcap. It also uses a very extensive filter language. Ethereal uses this same filter language for its capture filters. When it is finished capturing data it will display the packets received and packets dropped. The detail and length of the TCPDump output can be controlled by various options including **–q**, **–v**, **–vv**, **–vvv**, and **–X**. When capturing to a file, however, all of the packet detail is logged.

NOTE

To run TCPDump you must have root privileges or it must be installed **setuid** to root.

The following information is the usage output for the TCPDump program:

```
[root@localhost root]# tcpdump -h
tcpdump version 3.7.2
libpcap version 0.7.2
Usage: tcpdump [-adeflnNOpqRStuvxX] [ -c count ] [ -C file_size ]
                [ -F file ] [ -i interface ] [ -r file ] [ -s snaplen ]
                [ -T type ] [ -U user ] [ -w file ] [ -E algo:secret ]
                [ expression ]
```

Particularly interesting command line options include the following:

- **–C** *file_size* This option is used when writing output to a file. It will create a new file when the associated parameter *file_size* (in MB) is reached.

- **–i** *interface* This option lets you choose which interface to use to capture packets.

- **–n** This option stops Domain Name System (DNS) lookups. This can make the sniffer more efficient and stealthy.

- **–q** This option makes the output shorter by printing less protocol information.

- **–r** *file* This option will allow you to process a previously saved libpcap capture file.

- **–s** *snaplen* This option is the *snaplen*, the number of bytes of data from each packet that will be captured. The default is 68, so you will want to set this to something larger to get the whole packet, either 65535 or 0, which means capture the whole packet.

- **–v** This option prints more verbose output.

- **–vv** This option prints even more verbose output.

- **–vvv** This option prints the most verbose output.

- **–w** *file* This option writes packets to a file instead of the displaying them on the screen.

- **–X** This option will print the packet hexadecimal and ASCII data.

Capturing and Saving Data With TCPDump

The following examples show you how to capture and save traffic with TCPDump using various options and filters; the output can then be opened and analyzed with Ethereal.

This example captures all packets in their entirety by using the **snaplen=0** option and logs the output to a file called *capture_all*.

```
[root@localhost root]# tcpdump -s 0 -w capture_all
tcpdump: listening on eth0
16 packets received by filter
0 packets dropped by kernel
```

This example captures all Internet Control Message Protocol (ICMP) packets in their entirety and logs the output to a file called *icmp_capture*. Notice that the *icmp* parameter has to be *escaped* with either the "\" or the "\\" because it is also considered a reserved keyword. In the capture filter language, if you use *icmp* as a value for "proto", it must be escaped with a slash. If you are typing such a filter on the UNIX command line, the backslash is special for UNIX shells, so the backslash must be escaped with another backslash.

```
[root@localhost root]# tcpdump -s 0 -w icmp_capture ip proto \\icmp
tcpdump: listening on eth0
8 packets received by filter
0 packets dropped by kernel
```

This example captures all packets in their entirety for destination IP 192.168.1.1 going to and from Transmission Control Protocol (TCP) port 21 and logs the output to a file called *ftp_capture*. When you are using more than one parameter for comparison they need to be enclosed in single or double quotes. This is because the **&&** and **||** parameters also have meaning in the UNIX shell. If you just type **tcpdump –s 0 –w ftp_capture dst host 192.168.1.1 && tcp port 21** the UNIX shell will interpret the && for its own purposes and run only *tcpdump –s 0 –w ftp_capture dst host 192.168.1.1*. Then if the tcpdump process exits with a zero return value (successful), the UNIX shell will attempt to run *tcp port 21*, but there is no "tcp" program, so it will fail. Using quotes keeps the UNIX shell from interpreting the && and || for its own purposes.

```
[root@localhost root]# tcpdump -s 0 -w ftp_capture 'dst host 192.168.1.1 &&
tcp port 21'
tcpdump: listening on eth0
15 packets received by filter
0 packets dropped by kernel
```

This example specifies the capture filter via a different type of format. It is using the *byte-offset* method and compares the byte to a value. This example is capturing all packets in their entirety where the 9th-byte offset is equal to 6 and logging the output to a file called *tcp_capture*. This means it is capturing all TCP packets, because the 9th-byte offset represents the protocol and 6 is the decimal value for TCP.

```
[root@localhost root]# tcpdump -vvv -X -s 0 -w tcp_capture ip[9]=6
tcpdump: listening on eth0
```

```
3207 packets received by filter
284 packets dropped by kernel
```

Now that we have our output saved to capture files, all we need to do is open it with Ethereal. Once you have opened Ethereal, select **File | Open**. Browse to the location of the capture file and select it, then click **OK**. Ethereal will open it and automatically read it! Figure 7.5 shows the Ethereal output of the TCPDump *tcp_capture* file. This is a port scanning attempt; notice the scanner is using a static source port of 58173.

Figure 7.5 Ethereal Display of TCPDump Capture

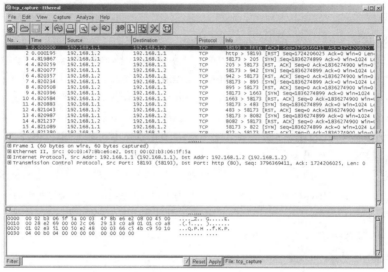

Reading Ethereal Files With TCPDump

TCPDump can also read and process libpcap-formatted capture files. This means you can capture files with Ethereal and then read them with TCPDump. Let's provide an example of saving captured data with Ethereal and reading it with TCPDump. Once you have captured your data with Ethereal, select **File | Save As**. Browse to the location where you would like to save your capture. Next, choose the correct output type from the **File Type** pull-down menu. In our case we are saving to **libpcap (tcpdump, Ethereal, etc**.*)*. Type in a file name under **Selection** and click **OK**.

The following example uses TCPDump to read a file that we saved with Ethereal, called *ethereal_capture*. The file will be processed and the output will be displayed on screen. You can use the other options discussed earlier to make the output more verbose.

```
[root@localhost root]# tcpdump -r ethereal_capture
20:49:45.461642 192.168.1.1 > 192.168.1.2: icmp: echo request
20:49:45.461833 192.168.1.2 > 192.168.1.1: icmp: echo reply
20:49:46.461055 192.168.1.1 > 192.168.1.2: icmp: echo request
20:49:46.461289 192.168.1.2 > 192.168.1.1: icmp: echo reply
20:49:47.461110 192.168.1.1 > 192.168.1.2: icmp: echo request
20:49:47.461346 192.168.1.2 > 192.168.1.1: icmp: echo reply
20:49:48.461224 192.168.1.1 > 192.168.1.2: icmp: echo request
20:49:48.461455 192.168.1.2 > 192.168.1.1: icmp: echo reply
```

WinDump

WinDump is the Windows version of TCPDump. It uses the WinPcap library, which is the Windows version of libpcap. It is actively maintained at http://windump.polito.it. WinDump can be used to read live packets from the wire, or to read previously saved packet captures. It has all of the same features and capabilities as TCPDump. It also uses the same extensive filter language as TCPDump. For the examples in this section we are using WinDump version 3.8 Alpha, which is the most recent version at the time of this writing. We are also using WinPcap version 3.0 alpha.

The following information is the usage output for the WinDump program:

```
C:\>windump -h
windump version current-cvs.tcpdump.org, based on tcpdump version current-
cvs.tcpdump.org
WinPcap version 3.0 alpha, based on libpcap version current-cvs.tcpdump.org
Usage: windump [-aAdDeflnNOpqRStuvxX] [-B size] [-c count] [ -C file_size ]
               [ -F file ] [ -i interface ] [ -r file ] [ -s snaplen ]
               [ -T type ] [ -w file ] [ -E algo:secret ] [ expression ]
```

The only options that are different from the TCPDump options are the following two additions:

- **–B** *size* This option sets the driver's buffer *size* in Kilobytes. This will help reduce packet loss and increase performance.

- **–D** This option will display a list of available interface cards on the system.

Capturing and Saving Data With WinDump

The examples provided in the TCPDump section can also be applied here. The following examples show you how to capture and save traffic with WinDump using various options and filters. The output can then be opened and analyzed with Ethereal.

This example shows the use and output of the **–D** option for you to see the different network cards available on your computer:

```
C:\>windump -D
1.\Device\NPF_NdisWanIp (NDISWANIP NdisWan Adapter)
2.\Device\NPF_NdisWanIpx (NdisWan Adapter)
3.\Device\NPF_NdisWanBh (NdisWan Adapter)
4.\Device\NPF_{A302C81E-256D-4C92-8A72-866F2E1ED55F} (PRISM10 D-LINK Air
WIRELESS ADAPTER)
5.\Device\NPF_{13698EE2-3DC8-45B1-A300-1B70CEADBE62} (Intel(R) PRO Adapter)
```

This example captures all packets in their entirety by using the **snaplen=0** option and logs the output to a file called *capture1*.

```
C:\>windump -i 4 -s 0 -w capture1
windump: listening on \Device\NPF_{A302C81E-256D-4C92-8A72-866F2E1ED55F}
28 packets received by filter
0 packets dropped by kernel
```

This example captures all packets that have only the **TCP SYN** flag set and logs the output to a file called *capture2*. It uses the *byte-offset* method and compares it to a value. The value of 2 in the 13th-byte offset means that the SYN flag is set. If you want to capture packets that have their SYN flag and another flag set, you would need to use **tcp[13] & 2 == 2**.

```
C:\>windump -i 4 -s 0 -w capture2 tcp[13]==2
windump: listening on \Device\NPF_{A302C81E-256D-4C92-8A72-866F2E1ED55F}
58 packets received by filter
0 packets dropped by kernel
```

Now that we have our output saved to a capture file, all we need to do is open it with Ethereal. Once you have opened Ethereal, select **File | Open**.

Browse to the location of the capture file and select it, then click **OK**. Figure 7.6 displays the Ethereal output of the WinDump *capture2* file. Notice that the source port is steadily increasing, but the destination port stays the same. This is actually personal digital assistant (PDA) software searching for a PDA device.

Figure 7.6 Ethereal Display of WinDump Capture

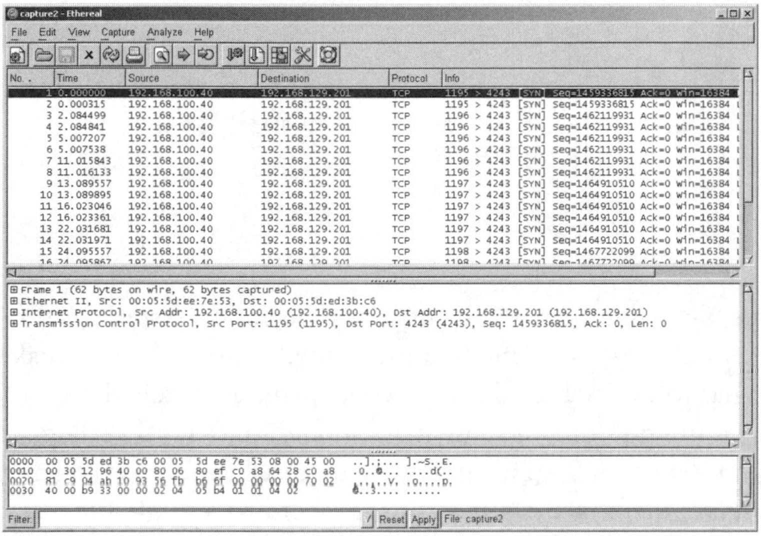

Reading Ethereal Files With WinDump

WinDump can also read and process libpcap formatted capture files. This means you can capture files with Ethereal and then read them with WinDump. Let's provide an example of saving captured data with Ethereal and reading it with WinDump. Once you have captured your data with Ethereal, select **File | Save As**. Browse to the location where you would like to save your capture. Next, choose the correct output type from the **File Type** pull-down menu. In our case we are saving to **libpcap (tcpdump, Ethereal, etc**.*)*. Type in a file name under **Selection** and click **OK**.

The following example uses WinDump to read a file that we saved with Ethereal, called *ethereal_capture*. The file will be processed and the output will be displayed on the screen. You can use the other options discussed earlier to make the output more verbose.

```
C:\>windump -r ethereal_capture
10:31:50.084831 arp who-has 192.168.1.2 tell 192.168.1.1
10:31:50.085184 arp reply 192.168.1.2 is-at 0:2:b3:6:5f:5a
```

```
10:31:50.085195 IP 192.168.1.1 > 192.168.1.2: icmp 40: echo request seq 256
10:31:50.087034 IP 192.168.1.2 > 192.168.1.1: icmp 40: echo reply seq 256
10:31:51.077790 IP 192.168.1.1 > 192.168.1.2: icmp 40: echo request seq 512
10:31:51.078193 IP 192.168.1.2 > 192.168.1.1: icmp 40: echo reply seq 512
10:31:52.079235 IP 192.168.1.1 > 192.168.1.2: icmp 40: echo request seq 768
10:31:52.079438 IP 192.168.1.2 > 192.168.1.1: icmp 40: echo reply seq 768
10:31:53.080678 IP 192.168.1.1 > 192.168.1.2: icmp 40: echo request seq
1024
10:31:53.080841 IP 192.168.1.2 > 192.168.1.1: icmp 40: echo reply seq 1024
10:31:55.085369 arp who-has 192.168.1.1 tell 192.168.1.2
10:31:55.085397 arp reply 192.168.1.1 is-at 0:3:47:8b:e6:e2
```

Snort

Snort is a free, open-source network intrusion detection system (NIDS). It will
compare observed network traffic to a predefined set of rules and make a decision about what to do, such as alerting, when a rule is matched. Snort has the
capability of running in one of three main modes: sniffer, packet logger, and network intrusion detection engine. Sniffer mode reads the packets from the network and displays them to the screen or logs them to a single file. Packet logger
mode logs the packets in a categorized system to the disk. The NIDS mode
matches traffic against the rule set and performs an action based upon what it
sees. When Snort operates in sniffer mode and logs the capture data to a single
file, this file is in binary format. It uses the same libpcap format as TCPDump.
This makes packet collection much faster because Snort doesn't need to translate
the data to human-readable format.

We will be looking at some of the packet sniffer options of Snort; however,
only two options are needed to log capture data to a file: the log file option **–L**
and the binary option **–b**. You will specify the name of the log file to create, and
Snort appends a timestamp to the end of the specified filename. Since Snort uses
libpcap, it can also use all of the filtering syntax of TCPDump. Therefore the
filter examples we gave for TCPDump and WinDump can be applied here as
well.

The following information is the usage output for the Snort program:

```
C:\Snort\bin>snort

-*> Snort! <*-

Version 2.0.2-ODBC-MySQL-WIN32 (Build 92)
```

By Martin Roesch (roesch@sourcefire.com, www.snort.org)

1.7-WIN32 Port By Michael Davis (mike@datanerds.net, www.datanerds.net/~mike)

1.8 - 2.0 WIN32 Port By Chris Reid (chris.reid@codecraftconsultants.com)

USAGE: snort [-options] <filter options>

       snort /SERVICE /INSTALL [-options] <filter options>

       snort /SERVICE /UNINSTALL

       snort /SERVICE /SHOW

Options:

-A	Set alert mode: fast, full, console, or none (alert file alerts only)
-b	Log packets in tcpdump format (much faster!)
-c <rules>	Use Rules File <rules>
-C	Print out payloads with character data only (no hex)
-d	Dump the Application Layer
-e	Display the second layer header info
-E	Log alert messages to NT Eventlog. (Win32 only)
-f	Turn off fflush() calls after binary log writes
-F <bpf>	Read BPF filters from file <bpf>
-h <hn>	Home network = <hn>
-i <if>	Listen on interface <if>
-I	Add Interface name to alert output
-k <mode>	Checksum mode (all,noip,notcp,noudp,noicmp,none)
-l <ld>	Log to directory <ld>
-L <file>	Log to this tcpdump file
-n <cnt>	Exit after receiving <cnt> packets
-N	Turn off logging (alerts still work)
-o	Change the rule testing order to Pass|Alert|Log
-O	Obfuscate the logged IP addresses
-p	Disable promiscuous mode sniffing
-P <snap>	Set explicit snaplen of packet (default: 1514)
-q	Quiet. Don't show banner and status report
-r <tf>	Read and process tcpdump file <tf>
-R <id>	Include 'id' in snort_intf<id>.pid file name
-s	Log alert messages to syslog
-S <n=v>	Set rules file variable n equal to value v
-T	Test and report on the current Snort configuration

```
        -U              Use UTC for timestamps

        -v              Be verbose

        -V              Show version number

        -W              Lists available interfaces. (Win32 only)

        -w              Dump 802.11 management and control frames

        -X              Dump the raw packet data starting at the link layer

        -y              Include year in timestamp in the alert and log files

        -z              Set assurance mode, match on established sesions (for
                        TCP)

        -?              Show this information
<Filter Options> are standard BPF options, as seen in TCPDump
```

Particularly interesting command line options include the following:

- **–b**   This option will allow you to log the packets in TCPDump binary format.

- **–d**   This option will dump the application layer traffic.

- **–e**   This option will display the data link header information.

- **–i** *interface*   This option allows you to specify which interface to use to capture data.

- **–L** *file*   This option allows you to specify a name to call the output TCPDump log file.

- **–r** *file*   This option allows you to read and process a TCPDump formatted capture file.

- **–v**   This option specifies verbose output. It is a required option for the packet-sniffing mode.

Capturing and Saving Data With Snort

The following examples show how to capture and save traffic with Snort using various options and filters. Once captured and saved, the output can then be opened and analyzed with Ethereal.

This example demonstrates how to use Snort as a simple real-time network analyzer. This will display the packets along with all of the application and data link layer information. Packets will continue to scroll on the screen until you press **Ctrl + C**. When the capture is complete it will display some capture statistics as shown:

```
C:\Snort\bin>snort -dve -i 4
Running in packet dump mode
Log directory = log
Initializing Network Interface \Device\NPF_{A302C81E-256D-4C92-8A72-
866F2E1ED55F
}
        --== Initializing Snort ==--
Initializing Output Plugins!
Decoding Ethernet on interface \Device\NPF_{A302C81E-256D-4C92-8A72-
866F2E1ED55F
}
        --== Initialization Complete ==--
-*> Snort! <*-
Version 2.0.2-ODBC-MySQL-WIN32 (Build 92)
By Martin Roesch (roesch@sourcefire.com, www.snort.org)
1.7 WIN32 Port By Michael Davis (miko@datanerds.net,
www.datanerds.net/~mike)
1.8 - 2.0 WIN32 Port By Chris Reid (chris.reid@codecraftconsultants.com)
11/03-23:37:10.146209 0:5:5D:EE:7E:53 -> 0:5:5D:ED:3B:C6 type:0x800
len:0x4A
192.168.100.132 -> 192.168.100.5 ICMP TTL:128 TOS:0x0 ID:35224 IpLen:20
DgmLen:6
0
Type:8  Code:0  ID:1024   Seq:3328  ECHO
61 62 63 64 65 66 67 68 69 6A 6B 6C 6D 6E 6F 70   abcdefghijklmnop
71 72 73 74 75 76 77 61 62 63 64 65 66 67 68 69   qrstuvwabcdefghi


=+=+=+=+=+=+=+=+=+=+=+=+=+=+=+=+=+=+=+=+=+=+=+=+=+=+=+=+=+=+=+=+=+=+=+=+
[output removed]
========================================================================
Snort analyzed 19 out of 19 packets, dropping 0(0.000%) packets
Breakdown by protocol:              Action Stats:
     TCP: 0          (0.000%)        ALERTS: 0
     UDP: 6          (31.579%)       LOGGED: 0
    ICMP: 12         (63.158%)       PASSED: 0
     ARP: 1          (5.263%)
   EAPOL: 0          (0.000%)
```

```
    IPv6: 0                (0.000%)
     IPX: 0                (0.000%)
   OTHER: 0                (0.000%)
 DISCARD: 0                (0.000%)

========================================================================
Wireless Stats:
Breakdown by type:
    Management Packets: 0              (0.000%)
    Control Packets:    0              (0.000%)
    Data Packets:       0              (0.000%)

========================================================================
Fragmentation Stats:
Fragmented IP Packets: 0              (0.000%)
    Fragment Trackers: 0
   Rebuilt IP Packets: 0
   Frag elements used: 0
Discarded(incomplete): 0
   Discarded(timeout): 0
  Frag2 memory faults: 0

========================================================================
TCP Stream Reassembly Stats:
        TCP Packets Used: 0              (0.000%)
        Stream Trackers: 0
         Stream flushes: 0
          Segments used: 0
    Stream4 Memory Faults: 0

========================================================================
pcap_loop: read error: PacketReceivePacket failed
Run time for packet processing was 10.315000 seconds
```

This example captures raw packets and logs the output to a binary file called *test.log*. Don't forget that Snort will append a timestamp to the end of that filename. It will continue capturing until you press **Ctrl + C**, at which time it will display the statistics information.

```
C:\Snort\bin>snort -i 4 -b -L test.log
```

If you want to see what is going on while also logging to a file, you can combine the options as follows:

```
C:\Snort\bin>snort -dve -i 4 -b -L test.log
```

This example captures raw packets and logs them to a binary file called *http.log*, but also uses a filter syntax. It is capturing all traffic on port 80.

```
C:\Snort\bin>snort -i 4 -b -L http.log port 80
```

Now that we have our output saved to capture files, all we need to do is open it with Ethereal. Once you have opened Ethereal, select **File | Open**. Browse to the location of the capture file and select it, then click **OK**. Figure 7.7 shows the Ethereal output of the Snort *http.log* file.

Figure 7.7 Ethereal Display of Snort Capture

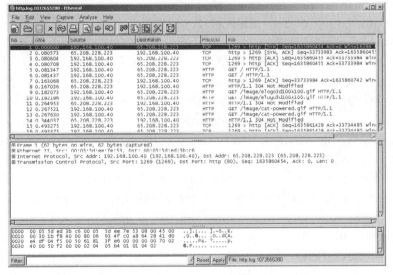

Reading Ethereal Files With Snort

Snort can also read and process TCPDump libpcap formatted capture files. This means you can capture files with Ethereal and then read them with Snort. This would be great to use in running captured data through some rules files! Once you have captured your data with Ethereal, select **File | Save As** menu item. Browse to the location where you would like to save your capture. Next, choose the correct output type from the **File Type** pull-down menu. In our case we are saving to **libpcap (tcpdump, Ethereal, etc.)**. Type in a file name under **Selection** and click **OK**.

The following example uses Snort to read a file that we saved with Ethereal, called *libpcap_capture*. The file will be processed and the output will be displayed on the screen.

```
C:\Snort\bin>snort -r libpcap_capture
No run mode specified, defaulting to verbose mode
Running in packet dump mode
Log directory = log
TCPDUMP file reading mode.
Reading network traffic from "libpcap_capture" file.
snaplen = 65535
[output removed]
```

Snoop

Snoop is a command line network analyzer that is built into the Solaris operating system. Captured packets can be displayed on the screen or saved to a file for later inspection. Snoop uses a different format for storing captures to a file, as documented in Request for Comment (RFC) 1761. However, Ethereal has the ability to interpret this format and open the saved capture file for inspection.

Snoop can display packets in the default single-line summary form, a verbose multiple summary line form, or a very detailed form. When it displays packets in summary form, only the highest protocol layer data is displayed. For example, a File Transfer Protocol (FTP) packet will have the FTP information displayed, but not the underlying IP, TCP, and Ethernet frame information. Verbose options can be used to display summary lines for each protocol in the packet or all of the packet information.

Snoop also has efficient filtering capabilities for capturing a subset of packets from the network. Some are implemented at the kernel level, and others at the snoop packet filter level. The snoop *man* (or *manual*) page provides detail for using the filtering syntax. The man page for snoop also warns that snoop may drop packets when processing real-time packets due to higher overhead. Using the **–D** option will display the number of dropped packets during the capture. Using the **–o** option to output raw packets to a file for later offline analysis, offers a more reliable capture. When using the **–o** option the **–V**, **–v**, and **–x** options won't make any difference because all of the packet information is logged in detail.

WARNING

Snoop does not reassemble IP fragments. When an IP packet is fragmented, interpretation of higher level protocols stop at the end of the first fragment.

The following information is the usage output for the snoop program:

```
Usage:   snoop
         [ -a ]                       # Listen to packets on audio
         [ -d device ]                # settable to le?, ie?, bf?, tr?
         [ -s snaplen ]               # Truncate packets
         [ -c count ]                 # Quit after count packets
         [ -P ]                       # Turn OFF promiscuous mode
         [ -D ]                       # Report dropped packets
         [ -S ]                       # Report packet size
         [ -i file ]                 # Read previously captured packets
         [ -o file ]                 # Capture packets in file
         [ -n file ]                 # Load addr-to-name table from file
         [ -N ]                      # Create addr-to-name table
         [ -t  r|a|d ]               # Time: Relative, Absolute or Delta
         [ -v ]                       # Verbose packet display
         [ -V ]                       # Show all summary lines
         [ -p first[,last] ]        # Select packet(s) to display
         [ -x offset[,length] ]     # Hex dump from offset for length
         [ -C ]                       # Print packet filter code
         [ -q ]                       # Suppress printing packet count
         [ -r ]                       # Do not resolve address to name
         [ filter expression ]
Example:
         snoop -o saved  host fred
         snoop -i saved -tr -v -p19
```

Particularly interesting command line options include the following:

- **–d** *device* This option allows you to specify which network interface device to use to capture packets, for example *lo0* or *hme0*. To see what interfaces you currently have you can use **ifconfig –a** or **netstat –i**.

- **–i** *file* This option allows you to read in a previously captured snoop file.

- **–o** *filename* This is the option that you would use to output the captured packets to a file specified by *filename*. During the capture, a number count of packets saved in the file is displayed on the screen.

- **–q** This option allows you to turn off the packet count when capturing network packets to a file. This may improve the performance of your capture by lessening the processing while capturing packets.

- **–r** This option disables the resolving of IP addresses to names. This will prevent snoop from generating network traffic when capturing packets, and may improve the performance of your capture by lessening the processing while capturing packets.

- **–s** *snaplen* By default the whole packet is captured with snoop. This option allows you to truncate each packet to a desired length. This will also help with performance because snoop won't be capturing and interpreting as much information.

- **–V** Using the upper-case *V* option will display output in verbose summary mode. This mode displays a summary line for each protocol layer in the packet. This is a little more information than the default summary line mode. Instead of just printing the FTP summary information, it will also include the IP, TCP, and Ethernet summary information.

- **–v** Using the lower-case *v* option will display output with the most detail.

- **–x** *offset* **[,** *length***]** This option will allow you to display the data in hexadecimal and ASCII format. The *offset* and *length* values select a portion of the packet to display, however using an *offset* of 0 will display the whole packet. If a *length* value is not provided, the rest of the packet will be displayed.

> **NOTE**
>
> Snoop can only be run by the root user. A regular non-root user will receive the following:
>
> $ snoop
>   snoop: /dev/hme: Permission denied

Capturing and Saving Data With Snoop

The following examples show you how to capture and save traffic with Snoop using various options and filters. The output can then be opened and analyzed with Ethereal.

This example captures all packets to and from 192.168.100.122 and logs the output to a file called *capture_snoop*. Notice the counter counts ten packets before exiting with **Ctrl + C**.

```
# snoop -o capture_snoop host 192.168.100.122
Using device /dev/hme (promiscuous mode)
10 ^C
```

This example captures all packets to or from port 23 and logs the output to a file called *telnet_capture_snoop*.

```
# snoop -o telnet_capture_snoop port 23
Using device /dev/hme (promiscuous mode)
76 ^C
```

This example captures all packets between 192.168.100.122 and 192.168.100.132 that are TCP packets on port 21 and logs the output to a file called *ftp_capture_snoop*. Notice that the **–q** option suppresses the packet count.

```
# snoop -q -o ftp_capture_snoop 192.168.100.122 192.168.100.132 and port 21
and tcp
Using device /dev/hme (promiscuous mode)
^C
```

Now that we have our output saved to capture files, all we need to do is open it with Ethereal. Once you have opened Ethereal, select **File | Open**. Browse to the location of the capture file and select it, then click **OK**. Ethereal will open it and automatically read it! Figure 7.8 shows the Ethereal output of the snoop *telnet_capture_snoop* file. Notice that all 76 of the packets that the snoop counter listed are there. Tethereal can also read the data saved in the snoop capture by using the command **tethereal -r telnet_capture_snoop**. You may have to use the full path name to the *telnet_capture_snoop* file. The **-V** option can be used to display the output in detail format.

Figure 7.8 Ethereal Display of Snoop Capture

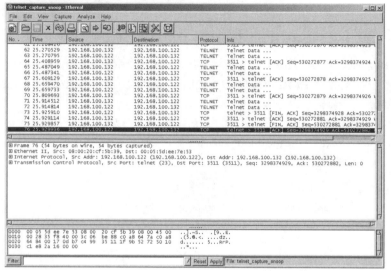

Reading Ethereal Files With Snoop

Snoop can also read and process properly formatted capture files. This means you can capture files with Ethereal and then read them with Snoop, as long as you save them in the Snoop format. Once you have captured your data with Ethereal, select **File | Save As**. Browse to the location where you would like to save your capture. Next, choose the correct output type from the **File Type** pull-down menu. In our case we are saving to **Sun snoop**. Type in a file name under **Selection** and click **OK**.

The following example uses Snoop to read a file that we saved with Ethereal, called *ethereal_capture*. The file will be processed and the output will be displayed on the screen in summary line mode. You can use the other options discussed to create more detailed output. Look how easy it is to read this Telnet user name and password!

```
# snoop -i ethereal_capture
   1   0.00000 192.168.100.132 -> unknown       TELNET C port=1948
```

```
 2  0.00009         unknown -> 192.168.100.132 TELNET R port=1948
 3  0.00268 192.168.100.132 -> unknown      TELNET C port=1948
 4  0.04485         unknown -> 192.168.100.5 DNS C 132.100.168.192.in-
                    addr.arpa.Internet PTR ?
 5  1.31293 192.168.100.5 -> BROADCAST    DHCP/BOOTP DHCPACK
 6  3.69467         unknown -> 192.168.100.5 DNS C 132.100.168.192.in-
                    addr.arpa.Internet PTR ?
 7  3.98945         ? -> (broadcast)  ETHER Type=6000 (DEC unass,
                    experimental), size = 114 bytes
 8  1.02158         unknown -> 192.168.100.132 TELNET R port=1948
 9  0.00383 192.168.100.132 -> unknown      TELNET C port=1948
10  0.00006         unknown -> 192.168.100.132 TELNET R port=1948
11  0.00285 192.168.100.132 -> unknown      TELNET C port=1948
12  0.00006         unknown -> 192.168.100.132 TELNET R port=1948
13  0.00042         unknown -> 192.168.100.132 TELNET R port=1948
14  0.00365 192.168.100.132 -> unknown      TELNET C port=1948
15  0.04792         unknown -> 192.168.100.132 TELNET R port=1948
16  0.00300 192.168.100.132 -> unknown      TELNET C port=1948
17  0.00174         unknown -> 192.168.100.132 TELNET R port=1948
18  0.12602 192.168.100.132 -> unknown      TELNET C port=1948
19  0.00011         unknown -> 192.168.100.132 TELNET R port=1948
20  0.00313 192.168.100.132 -> unknown      TELNET C port=1948
21  0.04600         unknown -> 192.168.100.132 TELNET R port=1948
22  0.00306 192.168.100.132 -> unknown      TELNET C port=1948
23  0.00056         unknown -> 192.168.100.132 TELNET R port=1948
24  0.00323 192.168.100.132 -> unknown      TELNET C port=1948
25  0.04312         unknown -> 192.168.100.132 TELNET R port=1948
26  1.12780 192.168.100.132 -> unknown      TELNET C port=1948 r
27  0.00033         unknown -> 192.168.100.132 TELNET R port=1948 r
28  0.17501 192.168.100.132 -> unknown      TELNET C port=1948
29  0.11204 192.168.100.132 -> unknown      TELNET C port=1948 o
30  0.00032         unknown -> 192.168.100.132 TELNET R port=1948 o
31  0.10154 192.168.100.132 -> unknown      TELNET C port=1948 o
32  0.00026         unknown -> 192.168.100.132 TELNET R port=1948 o
```

```
33   0.09330 192.168.100.132 -> unknown      TELNET C port=1948 t
34   0.00024       unknown -> 192.168.100.132 TELNET R port=1948 t
35   0.16460 192.168.100.132 -> unknown      TELNET C port=1948
36   0.00029       unknown -> 192.168.100.132 TELNET R port=1948
37   0.12786 192.168.100.132 -> unknown      TELNET C port=1948
38   0.00007       unknown -> 192.168.100.132 TELNET R port=1948 Password:
39   0.20041 192.168.100.132 -> unknown      TELNET C port=1948
40   0.29647       unknown -> 192.168.100.5 DHCP/BOOTP DHCPREQUEST
41   0.00320 192.168.100.5 -> BROADCAST    DHCP/BOOTP DHCPACK
42   0.10855 192.168.100.132 -> unknown      TELNET C port=1948 p
43   0.04762       unknown -> 192.168.100.132 TELNET R port=1948
44   0.18569 192.168.100.132 -> unknown      TELNET C port=1948 a
45   0.04430       unknown -> 192.168.100.132 TELNET R port=1948
46   0.19398 192.168.100.132 -> unknown      TELNET C port=1948 s
47   0.04604       unknown -> 192.168.100.132 TELNET R port=1948
48   0.11211 192.168.100.132 -> unknown      TELNET C port=1948 s
49   0.03763 192.168.100.5 -> BROADCAST    DHCP/BOOTP DHCPACK
50   0.01023       unknown -> 192.168.100.132 TELNET R port=1948
51   0.15034 192.168.100.132 -> unknown      TELNET C port=1948 w
52   0.04966       unknown -> 192.168.100.132 TELNET R port=1948
53   0.13519 192.168.100.132 -> unknown      TELNET C port=1948 o
54   0.04491       unknown -> 192.168.100.132 TELNET R port=1948
55   0.03270 192.168.100.132 -> unknown      TELNET C port=1948 r
56   0.04717       unknown -> 192.168.100.132 TELNET R port=1948
57   0.14906 192.168.100.132 -> unknown      TELNET C port=1948 d
58   0.04094       unknown -> 192.168.100.132 TELNET R port=1948
59   0.13336 192.168.100.132 -> unknown      TELNET C port=1948
60   0.00081       unknown -> 192.168.100.132 TELNET R port=1948
61   0.13279 192.168.100.132 -> unknown      TELNET C port=1948
62   0.00011       unknown -> 192.168.100.132 TELNET R port=1948 Last
                        login: Tue Nov
63   0.20013 192.168.100.132 -> unknown      TELNET C port=1948
64   1.64003 192.168.100.132 -> unknown      TELNET C port=1948 e
65   0.00033       unknown -> 192.168.100.132 TELNET R port=1948 e
66   0.16253 192.168.100.132 -> unknown      TELNET C port=1948
67   0.09867 192.168.100.132 -> unknown      TELNET C port=1948 x
```

```
68   0.00028        unknown -> 192.168.100.132  TELNET R port=1948 x
69   0.20159 192.168.100.132 -> unknown        TELNET C port=1948
70   0.15897 192.168.100.132 -> unknown        TELNET C port=1948 i
71   0.00039        unknown -> 192.168.100.132  TELNET R port=1948 i
72   0.07751 192.168.100.132 -> unknown        TELNET C port=1948 t
73   0.00025        unknown -> 192.168.100.132  TELNET R port=1948 t
74   0.16339 192.168.100.132 -> unknown        TELNET C port=1948
```

Microsoft Network Monitor

Microsoft Network Monitor is a tool that comes with Windows 2000 Server . It is used to detect and troubleshoot network problems, including identifying network traffic patterns and statistics. It is not installed by default, but it can be added by selecting **Management and Monitoring Tools | Network Monitor Tools** during installation or later using **Add/Remove Programs**. Network Monitor can capture packets directly from the network and display, filter, save and print captured packets. It can also open previously saved capture files that are in the proper format. For our example we are using the Network Monitor 2.0 Lite version that is included with Windows 2000Server .

The Network Monitor main window includes four window panes, as shown in Figure 7.9. The top left pane is the Graph pane, and is a graphical representation of current network activity. The middle left pane is the Session Statistics pane, and displays statistics about current individual network data. The bottom pane is the Station Statistics pane, and it displays statistics about session sent to and from the computer that is running Network Monitor. Finally, the top right pane is the Total Statistics pane, and it displays summary statistics about network activity detected since the capture process began.

Figure 7.9 Microsoft Network Monitor Window

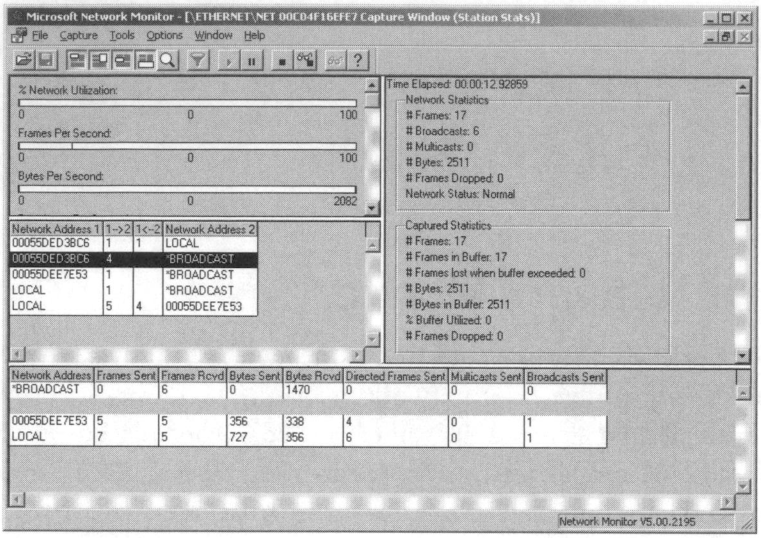

NOTE

The Windows 2000 Network Monitor does not capture packets in promiscuous mode. To do that you need to use the version of Network Monitor included with Systems Management Server version 2.0.

Capturing and Saving Data With Network Monitor

To begin a capture, select **Capture | Start**. You will notice the statistics begin changing, connections appear, and the time elapsed increasing. Once you have captured data, you can display it by selecting **Capture | Stop and View**. The Frame View window will open a listing of the captured data in a summary line view. If you double-click on one of the lines, the window will change to a three-pane view. This view has a summary top pane, a detailed protocol tree middle pane, and a hexadecimal data dump bottom pane. Figure 7.10 shows the Frame View window.

Figure 7.10 Microsoft Network Monitor Frame View Window

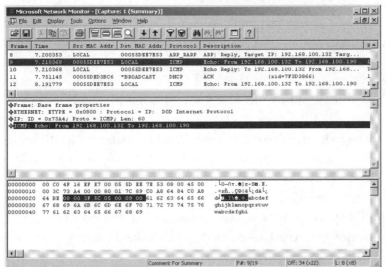

Once you have captured and viewed your data, you can save the capture to a file by selecting **File | Save As**. You can choose the location that you would like to save the file, give it a filename, and click **Save**. Now that we have our output saved to a capture file, all we need to do is open it with Ethereal. Once you have opened Ethereal, select **File | Open**. Browse to the location of the capture file and select it, then click **OK**. Ethereal will open it and automatically read it! Figure 7.11 shows the Ethereal output of the Network Monitor *netmon_capture.cap* file.

Figure 7.11 Ethereal Display of Network Monitor Capture

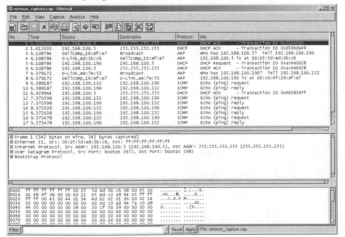

Reading Ethereal Files With Network Monitor

Network Monitor can also read and process properly formatted capture files. This means you can capture files with Ethereal and then read them with Network Monitor, as long as you save them in the Network Monitor format. Once you have captured your data with Ethereal, select **File | Save As**. Browse to the location where you would like to save your capture. Next, choose the correct output type from the **File Type** pull-down menu. In our case we are saving to **Microsoft Network Monitor 2.x**. Type in a file name under **Selection,** make sure to give it a .cap extension, and click **OK**. Network Monitor will open the file even without the extension, but this makes finding it easier.

You can now open up the Ethereal capture file in Network Monitor by selecting **File | Open**. Browse to the location of the saved file, select it and click **Open**. You will now see the packets displayed in the Frame View window.

WildPackets EtherPeek

EtherPeek by WildPackets, is a commercial graphical network analyzer that works on 10/100/1000 Mbps Ethernet networks. It runs on Windows XP and 2000, and there is even a version for Macs! Other network analyzers by WildPackets include TokenPeek, AiroPeek, and GigaPeek.

EtherPeek can capture traffic from more than one network adapter at a time so that you can correlate various network occurrences. EtherPeek offers two distinct ways of looking at the network: the monitor statistics view and the packet capture view. The monitor statistics view lets you looks at various data including network, protocol, and node statistics. It's important to note that you will not be able to save packets with this function—you will only be able to view them. The packet capture view allows you to view packet decodes of a capture, view saved captures, or save your current capture to a file. For our example we will be focusing on the packet capture view. We are using EtherPeek version 5.1, and a demo version can be downloaded from www.wildpackets.com. However, the demo version doesn't include the ability to save capture files. You will need to speak to a sale representative if you would like to try additional features.

Capturing and Saving Data With EtherPeek

To begin a capture with EtherPeek, click on the **Capture** menu and select **Start Capture** to open a new capture window. The first time you do this you will see the Capture Options dialog box. This dialog box allows you to choose parameters such as which network adapter to use, the name of the capture, size of the capture buffer, and much more. If you do not want this dialog box to appear each time you start a capture you can uncheck the **Show this dialog when creating a new capture window** option. Once you have selected the appropriate settings, click **OK**. Next, you will see the main capture window. Click the **Start Capture** button in the upper right-hand corner to start the capture. The button will change to **Stop Capture**, and the status bar in the bottom left will change from *Idle* to *Capturing*. You will also see packets start appearing in the packet list. Once you have captured enough data, you can stop the capture by clicking on the **Stop Capture** button in the upper right-hand corner. You can click on any one of the packets in the packet list to display the protocol tree view and hex view. You can also do this while you are still capturing packets. Figure 7.12 shows an example of the Packet Decode view of the Capture Window.

Figure 7.12 The Packet Decode of the Capture Window

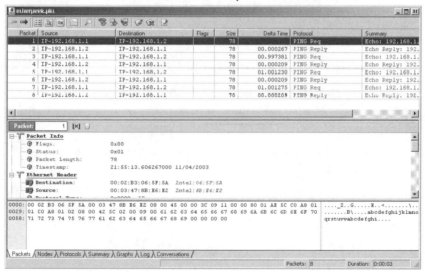

NOTE

To see all three panes in the Capture Window, make sure you have enabled the toggle buttons on the menu bar for **Show Packet List**, **Show Decode View**, and **Show Hex View**.

Once you have captured and viewed your data, you can save the capture to a file by selecting **File | Save All Packets**. You can choose the location that you would like to save the file and select the file type. If you want Ethereal to read the capture file you will need to save it as either *EtherPeek Classic Packet File* or *Networks Associate's Sniffer DOS* file. Next, enter a filename and click **Save**. Now that we have our output saved to a capture file, all we need to do it open it with Ethereal. Once you have opened Ethereal, select **File | Open**. Browse to the location of the capture file and select it, then click **OK**. Ethereal will open it and automatically read it. Figure 7.13 shows the Ethereal output of the EtherPeek *etherpeek.pkt* file.

Figure 7.13 Ethereal Display of EtherPeek Capture

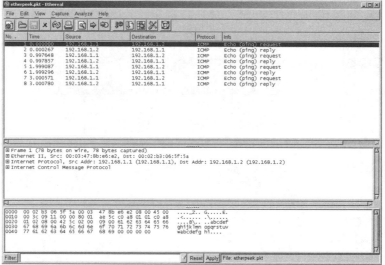

Reading Ethereal Files With EtherPeek

EtherPeek can also read and process properly formatted capture files. This means you can capture files with Ethereal and then read them with EtherPeek, as long as you save them in the proper format. Ethereal doesn't offer EtherPeek as a format to save files, unless you are already reading an Etherpeek file; however, there are still methods that you can use to transfer files from Ethereal to EtherPeek. Once you have captured your data with Ethereal, select **File | Save As**. Browse to the location where you would like to save your capture. Next, choose the correct output type from the **File Type** pull-down menu. In our case we are saving to **libpcap (tcpdump, Ethereal, etc.)**. Type in a filename under **Selection,** make sure to give it a .dmp extension, and click **OK**.

You can now open up the Ethereal capture file in EtherPeek by selecting **File | Open**. Browse to the location of the saved file, select it and click **Open**. You will now see the packets displayed in the Capture Window!

We also tested several other methods of transferring files between Ethereal and EtherPeek and these are some that worked:

- Save as file type **Novell LANalyzer** and give the file name a .tr1 extension.

- Save as file type **Network Associates Sniffer (DOS-based)** and give the file name a .enc extension.

- Save as file type **Network Associates Sniffer (Windows-based) 1.1** and give the file name a .cap extension.

- Save as file type **Network Associates Sniffer (Windows-based) 2.00x** and give the file name a .cap extension.

Network Associates' Sniffer Technologies Netasyst

The Netasyst Network Analyzer is a commercial graphical network analyzer for 10/100 Mbps Ethernet networks that runs on Windows XP and 2000. There are several different versions of the Netasyst product offering support for one or more of the following: LAN support, wireless support, the Expert analysis engine, and some offer combinations of the three.

Netasyst can monitor network traffic in real time and display various statistics through its monitor applications such as the Dashboard. The monitor applications display data on network load and errors, protocol usage, node usage, and many other useful statistics. Netasyst also has a capture function that stores and decodes network packets. You can view current network packets, view saved packet captures, or save your capture to a file. For our example we will be focusing on the packet capture feature; however Netasyst has many other features and enhancements. We are using Netasyst WLX version 1.0.003 for our example. You can download a time-limited free trial at www.nai.com.

Capturing and Saving Data With Netasyst

To begin a capture with Netasyst, click on the **Capture** menu and select **Start**. This will open up the real-time Expert window and a capture gauge that shows the number of packets captured and the percentage of used buffer space. Once you have captured enough data, you can stop the capture by clicking on the **Capture** menu and selecting **Stop and Display.** This will open the Packet Display window. You can click on the **Decode** tab at the bottom of the window to bring up a three-pane view of the packets, as shown in Figure 7.14.

Figure 7.14 The Packet Display Window

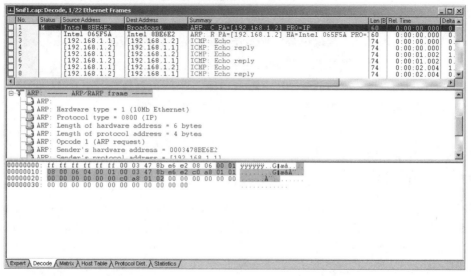

Once you have captured and viewed your data, you can save the capture to a file by selecting **File | Save As**. You can choose the location that you would like to save the file and the file type. We will be using the default **Sniffer Files** file type. Next, enter a filename and click **Save**. Now that we have our output saved to a capture file, all we need to do is open it with Ethereal. Once you have opened Ethereal, select **File | Open**. Browse to the location of the capture file and select it, then click **OK**. Ethereal will open it and automatically read it. Figure 7.15 shows the Ethereal output of the Netasyst *Snif1.cap* file.

Figure 7.15 Ethereal Display of Netasyst Capture

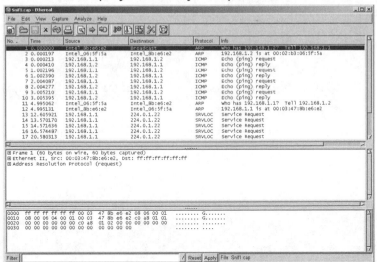

> **NOTE**
>
> Ethereal can also open Netasyst files that are saved in a compressed format.

Reading Ethereal Files With Netasyst

Netasyst can also read and process properly formatted capture files. This means you can capture files with Ethereal and then read them with Netasyst, as long as you save them in the proper format. Ethereal doesn't offer Netasyst as a format to save files, but, there are still methods that you can use to transfer files from Ethereal to Netasyst. Once you have captured your data with Ethereal, select **File | Save As**. Browse to the location where you would like to save your capture. Next, choose the correct output type from the **File Type** pull-down menu. In our case we are saving to **Network Associates Sniffer (Windows-based) 2.00x**. Type in a file name under **Selection,** make sure to give it a .cap extension, and click **OK**.

You can now open up the Ethereal capture file in Netasyst by selecting **File | Open**. Browse to the location of the saved file, select it and click **Open**. You will now see the packets displayed in the Packet Display Window.

We also tested several other methods of transferring files between Ethereal and Netasyst and these are some that worked:

- Save as file type **Novell LANalyzer** and give the filename a .tr1 extension.

- Save as file type **Network Associates Sniffer (DOS-based)** and give the filename a .enc extension.

- Save as file type **Network Associates Sniffer (Windows-based) 1.1** and give the filename a .cap extension.

Notes from the Underground…

What happened to Sniffer Pro?

You have probably noticed that a lot of the Ethereal documentation, as well as this book, make reference to Network Associate's Sniffer and Sniffer Pro products when talking about interoperability. If you don't already own a copy of Sniffer Pro, you probably visited the NAI website to get more information. However, there isn't any product listed called Sniffer Pro.

Network Associates launched a new product line called Netasyst Network Analyzer, which replaces some of the older Sniffer products, specifically Sniffer Basic, Sniffer Pro, and Sniffer Investigator. This new product line is targeted to small to medium sized customers and businesses. You will notice that the Netasyst products are "Powered by Sniffer Technologies". This is the division of Network Associates that also made Sniffer Pro. Netasyst is compatible with Ethereal using the same capture file format as the previous NAI Sniffer versions.

HP-UX's nettl

The HP-UX operating system has a built-in command, **nettl**, to perform packet capturing and network monitoring. Nettl stands for NETwork Tracing and Logging and is used to control the network tracing and logging facility. Tracing is used to capture incoming and outgoing network packets. Logging is used to capture network activities such as state changes, errors, and connection establishment.

The **netfmt** command can be used to format binary trace and log data gathered from the tracing and logging facility. It is used to read binary trace information from previously saved capture files. Netfmt filters are out of the scope of this book, so we won't be covering them here, however they are documented in the netfmt man page.

> **NOTE**
>
> To run **nettl** you must have a user ID of 0, meaning root privileges. The only exception to this is the nettl –**status** option.

The following information is the usage output for the nettl program:

```
/etc/nettl -start
/etc/nettl -stop
/etc/nettl -status [info]
/etc/nettl -traceon kind [kind...] -entity subsystem [subsystem...]
[-
file name] [-card dev_name] [-size limit] [-tracemax maxsize] [-m
bytes]
/etc/nettl -traceoff -entity subsystem [subsystem...]
/etc/nettl -log class -entity subsystem [subsystem...]
/etc/nettl -firmlog 0|1|2 -card dev_name
```

Particularly interesting command line options include the following:

- **–start (-st)** This option is used to initialize the tracing and logging facility. It is used alone with no other options.

- **–stop (-sp)** This option is used to terminate the tracing and logging facility. It is used alone with no other options.

- **–status (-ss)** This option is used to report the status of the tracing and logging facility. It is used alone with no other options.

- **–traceon (-tn)** *kind* This option is used to start tracing on a specified subsystem. It must be used after the **–start** option. *Kind* specifies the trace masks to be used for capturing, for example: pduin 0x20000000, pduout 0x10000000, and loopback 0x00800000. Multiple kinds can be specified separately or combined into a single number. For example, both pduin and pduout can be specified with 0x30000000.

- **–entity (-e)** *subsystem* This option is used to specify the protocol layers or software modules. The keyword *all* can be used to specify all subsystems. The **nettl –ss** command can be used to get a listing of all supported subsystems. Examples include network, transport, ns_ls_nfs, ns_ls_ip, ns_ls_tcp, and ns_ls_udp.

- **–file (-f)** *name* This option is used to save the captured data to a file. It is used with the first use of the **–traceon** command. It automatically appends the .TRC0 extension to the filename. If you would like to start saving to a file with a different name, you will have to turn tracing off and turn it back on with the new name. If tracing is started and the trace file with name.TRC0 already exists, the new data will be appended to the end of the file. If a trace file fills up, nettl will automatically create a new file of name.TRC1. Currently only two generations of trace files can exist with the same filename.

- **–tracemax (-tm)** *maxsize* This option is used to specify the maximum size for both trace files, .TRC0 and .TRC1, combined. The default is 1 MB.

- **–size (-s)** *limit* This option is used to set the trace buffer size, up to 512 Kilobytes, that is used to hold trace file messages until they are written to the file. The default is 32 KB. This value may need to be increased if nettl is dropping packets.

- **–traceoff (-tf)** This option is used to stop tracing on a specified subsystem. It can be specified with the *all* keyword to stop all traces. The trace file can then be viewed with the **netfmt** command.

NOTE

When saving your trace to a file, the filename must not exceed 8 characters in length. Longer names will be truncated and you will have to use the **nettl –status** command to view the actual name of the trace file.

Capturing and Saving Data with nettl

The following examples show you how to capture and save traffic with nettl to be opened and analyzed with Ethereal.

This example shows how to capture all incoming and out going IP traffic and log it to the file *nettl.TRC0*.

```
# nettl -tn pduin pudout -e ns_ls_ip -f nettl
```
or
```
# nettl -tn 0x30000000 -e ns_ls_ip -f nettl
```

If you would like to verify the capture before sending it to Ethereal, you can use the **netfmt** command. The following example shows the use and the output of the **netfmt** command:

```
# netfmt -f nettl.TRC0
^^^^^^^^^^^^^^^^^^^^^^^^^^^^^^^ARPA/9000
NETWORKING^^^^^^^^^^^^^^^^^^^^^^^^^@#%
  Timestamp               : Sun Nov 09 MST 2003 10:42:30.708797
  Process ID              : [ICS]          Subsystem          : NS_LS_IP
  User ID ( UID )         : -1             Trace Kind         : PDU IN
TRACE
  Device ID               . -1             Path ID            : 0
  Connection ID           : 0
  Location                : 00123

~~~~~~~~~~~~~~~~~~~~~~~~~~~~~~~~~~~~~~~~~~~~~~~~~~~~~~~~~~~~~~~~~~~~~~~~~~~
Received 48 bytes via IP  Sun Nov 09 10:42:30.070879 MST 2003    pid=[ICS]
   0: 45 00 00 30 8c 96 40 00 80 06 ea a9 c0 a8 01 0b  E..0..@.........
  16: c0 a8 01 2c 08 82 00 17 1a 7d fb 7e 00 00 00 00  ...,.....}.~....
  32: 70 02 40 00 a1 02 00 00 02 04 05 b4 01 01 04 02  p.@.............
vvvvvvvvvvvvvvvvvvvvvvvvvvvvvvvARPA/9000
NETWORKINGvvvvvvvvvvvvvvvvvvvvvvvvvvv@#%
  Timestamp               : Sun Nov 09 MST 2003 10:42:30.708878
  Process ID              : [ICS]          Subsystem          : NS_LS_IP
  User ID ( UID )         : -1             Trace Kind         : PDU OUT
TRACE
  Device ID               : -1             Path ID            : 0
  Connection ID           : 0
  Location                : 00123

~~~~~~~~~~~~~~~~~~~~~~~~~~~~~~~~~~~~~~~~~~~~~~~~~~~~~~~~~~~~~~~~~~~~~~~~~~~
```

```
Transmitted 44 bytes via IP  Sun Nov 09 10:42:30.070887 MST 2003
pid=[ICS]
    0: 45 00 00 2c 84 06 00 00 40 06 73 3e c0 a8 01 2c   E..,....@.s>...,
   16: c0 a8 01 0b 00 17 08 82 09 cd a2 d6 1a 7d fb 7f   .............}..
   32: 60 12 80 00 c9 54 00 00 02 04 05 b4 -- -- -- --   `....T..........
^^^^^^^^^^^^^^^^^^^^^^^^^^^^^^ARPA/9000
NETWORKING^^^^^^^^^^^^^^^^^^^^^^^^^^^^@#%
   Timestamp               : Sun Nov 09 MST 2003 10:42:30.709065
   Process ID              : [ICS]          Subsystem        : NS_LS_IP
   User ID ( UID )         : -1             Trace Kind       : PDU IN
TRACE
   Device ID               : -1             Path ID          : 0
   Connection ID           : 0
   Location                : 00123

~~~~~~~~~~~~~~~~~~~~~~~~~~~~~~~~~~~~~~~~~~~~~~~~~~~~~~~~~~~~~~~~~~~~~~~~~
Received 46 bytes via IP  Sun Nov 09 10:42:30.070906 MST 2003   pid=[ICS]
    0: 45 00 00 28 8c 97 40 00 80 06 ea b0 c0 a8 01 0b   E..(..@.........
   16: c0 a8 01 2c 08 82 00 17 1a 7d fb 7f 09 cd a2 d7   ...,.....}......
   32: 50 10 44 70 1c a2 00 00 20 20 20 20 20 20 -- --   P.Dp....      ..
vvvvvvvvvvvvvvvvvvvvvvvvvvvvvvARPA/9000
NETWORKINGvvvvvvvvvvvvvvvvvvvvvvvvvvvvv@#%
   Timestamp               : Sun Nov 09 MST 2003 10:42:30.724471
   Process ID              : 1227           Subsystem        : NS_LS_IP
   User ID ( UID )         : 0              Trace Kind       : PDU OUT
TRACE
   Device ID               : -1             Path ID          : 0
   Connection ID           : 0
   Location                : 00123

~~~~~~~~~~~~~~~~~~~~~~~~~~~~~~~~~~~~~~~~~~~~~~~~~~~~~~~~~~~~~~~~~~~~~~~~~
Transmitted 71 bytes via IP  Sun Nov 09 10:42:30.072447 MST 2003
pid=1227
    0: 45 00 00 47 97 ca 00 00 40 11 00 00 7f 00 00 01   E..G....@.......
   16: 7f 00 00 01 d1 00 00 35 00 33 00 33 00 01 01 00   .......5.3.3....
   32: 00 01 00 00 00 00 00 00 02 31 31 01 31 03 31 36   .........11.1.16
   48: 38 03 31 39 32 07 69 6e 2d 61 64 64 72 04 61 72   8.192.in-addr.ar
   64: 70 61 00 00 0c 00 01 -- -- -- -- -- -- -- -- --   pa..............
[output removed]
```

Now that we have our output saved to capture files, all we need to do is open it with Ethereal. Once you have opened Ethereal, select **File | Open**. Browse to the location of the capture file and select it, then click **OK**. Ethereal will open it and automatically read it. Figure 7.16 shows the Ethereal output of the *nettl.TRC0* capture file.

Figure 7.16 Ethereal Display of nettl Capture

Reading Ethereal Files with nettl

Currently Ethereal does not have the ability to save capture files into the HP-UX nettl format. If you are reading a nettl formatted file, you can re-save into that format, but you can't convert a native Ethereal capture, or any of the other supported formats, into the HP-UX nettl format. Future wiretap enhancements could someday add this ability.

Notes from the Underground...

Zethereal

Zethereal is a free GNU General Public licensed version of Ethereal written by Philippe Biondi for the Sharp Zaurus. It is a Qt-embedded interface for the Ethereal program. Zethereal is currently at version 1.0.0 and can be downloaded in both binary and source code format from www.cartel-info.fr/pbiondi/zaurus. You may need to install the provided libraries, libpcap and libglib for binary installation. The following installation notes are from the Zethereal README file:

- you must first download ethereal sources (works with 0.9.5, maybe with others)
- compile it (./configure [—disable-ethereal] && make)
- untar zethereal tarball into the ethereal sources root directory
- cd qtopia
- ./mklibzethereal
- have your qpe developing environment set up ok (http://docs.zaurus.com/index.php?id=linux_compiler_setup_howto)
- tmake zethereal.pro -o Makefile
- make

Figure 7.17 shows the interface for Zethereal. It differs from the regular version of Ethereal due to the limited screen space for a hand-held device.

Continued

Figure 7.17 Zethereal User Interface

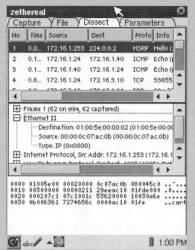

The Zethereal website also contains extensive notes for cross-compiling source code on the Sharp Zaurus. Since Zethereal uses libpcap and is based on the original Ethereal source code, Zethereal capture files are easily readable by Ethereal.

Summary

Ethereal's compatibility with other sniffers is by far one of its greatest strengths. The use of the libpcap packet driver makes it extremely compatible with other products that are also libpcap-based. There may even be some compatible products that we don't know about! The development of the wiretap library shows great promise. It has already given Ethereal its significant ability to read and process capture files from a number of non-libpcap sources. Future wiretap development will continue to have a big influence on Ethereal and its features.

In this chapter we gave several examples of products and utilities that are compatible with Ethereal. That number will continue to grow as Ethereal matures and new products are developed. Ethereal's compatibility encourages the use of many different means of collecting and analyzing data. You should make use of the tools and utilities that you have to make troubleshooting easier and most efficient. Most importantly, if you come across a new tool that you find is compatible with Ethereal, or one that should be, let the development team know about it!

Solutions Fast Track

Reading Capture Files with Ethereal

☑ Wiretap enables Ethereal to read a variety of capture formats.

☑ Ethereal can automatically determine what type of file it is reading when it opens it.

☑ Ethereal can read capture files from over twenty different products.

☑ Ethereal can open compressed files.

Saving Capture Files with Ethereal

☑ Ethereal can save capture files in over ten different formats.

☑ When saving a capture file, you can save all of the packets or just the ones you want.

Ethereal Integration

☑ Tethereal's default format for saving capture files is libpcap.

☑ TCPDump will only capture the first 68 bytes of a file unless you increase the *snaplen*.

☑ WinDump's **–D** option displays a list of available interface cards on the system.

☑ Snort can run in three modes: sniffer, packet logger, and network intrusion detection system.

☑ Snoop uses the **–o** option to capture packets to a file.

☑ Microsoft Network Monitor comes with Windows 2000 Server, but it isn't installed by default.

☑ EtherPeek can capture traffic from more than one network adapter at a time.

☑ You can use several different methods to transfer files between Ethereal and Netasyst.

☑ The HP-UX tracing and logging facility needs to be started with the **nettl –start** command before tracing can occur.

Frequently Asked Questions

The following Frequently Asked Questions, answered by the authors of this book, are designed to both measure your understanding of the concepts presented in this chapter and to assist you with real-life implementation of these concepts. To have your questions about this chapter answered by the author, browse to **www.syngress.com/solutions** and click on the **"Ask the Author"** form. You will also gain access to thousands of other FAQs at ITFAQnet.com.

Q: When I am saving a file to a specified format in Ethereal, do I have to give it the proper filename extension?

A: No, Ethereal will still save it to the right format regardless of the extension, however some other programs will only look for certain extensions when opening a file. So it is safer to give it the appropriate extensions.

Q: Can I capture from multiple network interfaces with Ethereal?

A: No, not at the current time. The wiretap functionality will hopefully someday have that feature built into it. However, we have opened multiple instances of Ethereal before and captured from two different interfaces that way. Libpcap cannot capture on multiple interfaces at once. However, Linux provides a pseudo–interface called *any*, which, when read, will provide packets coming from any network interface that is currently up. You can use **–i any**, or select **any** in the Capture dialog box in Ethereal.

Q: I have tcpdump and snoop running on all of my servers. Can I view their capture files at the same time for correlation with Ethereal?

A: Yes, but you will have to use **mergecap** first to merge all of the files together. Frames are merged in chronological order by default, so if your time clocks are all synchronized you should be able to see what was going on throughout your network when you open the merged capture file with Ethereal.

Q: I have a packet capture file that I saved with Ethereal. Can I use an IDS to see if there are any intrusion attempts in it?

A: Yes, you can save your capture as a binary file (libpcap) and then read it into Snort with a command like **snort –r ethereal.log –l ./logs –c snort.conf**. This will run the packet capture through the rules files that you have created. A lot of honeynets use this process to analyze data, and the Honeynet Project has a customized snort.conf file for this purpose at http://project.honeynet.org/paper/honeynet/tools.

## Chapter 8

Real World Packet Captures

Solutions in this Chapter:

- Scanning
- Remote Access Trojans
- Dissecting Worms

☑ Summary

☑ Solutions Fast Track

☑ Frequently Asked Questions

Introduction

Now that you have learned about Ethereal, how it works, and how to use it, you are armed and ready to read real network packet captures. In this chapter we discuss real world packet captures and traffic that you could be seeing on your network. You will learn how to read the captures, what to look for, and how to identify various types of network traffic. The Honeynet Project at http://project.honeynet.org provided some of the packet capture data in this chapter, which we have included on the accompanying CD-ROM in the /captures directory. They have a great challenge called Scan of the Month that will exercise your capture analysis abilities.

Scanning

Network scanning is used to identify available network resources. Also known as *discovery* or *enumeration*, network scanning can be used to discover available hosts, ports, or resources on the network. Once a vulnerable resource is detected it can be exploited and the device compromised. Sometimes there is an actual intruder behind the scanning and sometimes it is a result of worm activity. We will be focusing on active intruder scanning in this section, while worm activity will be covered in a later section. Security professionals also use network scanning to assist in securing and auditing the network. In this section we will be using Scan1.log, which contains several different types of scans and was provided by the Honeynet Research Alliance as part of the Honeynet Project Scan of the Month challenge. Scan1.log is located on the accompanying CD-ROM in the /captures directory.

NOTE
_____

The Transmission Control Protocol (TCP) protocol is connection-oriented and is initialized by completing a 3-way handshake. The TCP 3-way handshake consists of an initial packet sent with the SYN flag, a return packet with both the SYN and ACK flags, and completed with a packet with an ACK flag.

TCP Connect Scan

The first scan that we will be analyzing is the TCP Connect scan. It is used to determine which ports are open and listening on a target device. This is the most basic form of scanning because it completes the TCP 3-way handshake with open ports, and immediately closes them. An intruder sends a SYN packet and analyzes the response. A response packet with the Reset (RST) and Acknowledgment (ACK) flags set indicates the port is closed. If a SYN/ACK is received it indicates that the port is open and listening. The intruder will then respond with an ACK to complete the connection followed by a RST/ACK to immediately close the connection. This aspect of the scan makes it easily detectable because the connection attempts error messages will be logged.

Figure 8.1 shows the attacker, 192.168.0.9, sending SYN packets to the target, 192.168.0.99. Most ports respond with a RST/ACK packet, however the highlighted packets show the SYN/ACK response, and subsequent ACK followed by the RST/ACK, exchanged on the domain name system (DNS) port. You will also notice that the intruder's source port increases by one for each attempted connection.

Figure 8.1 TCP Connect Scan

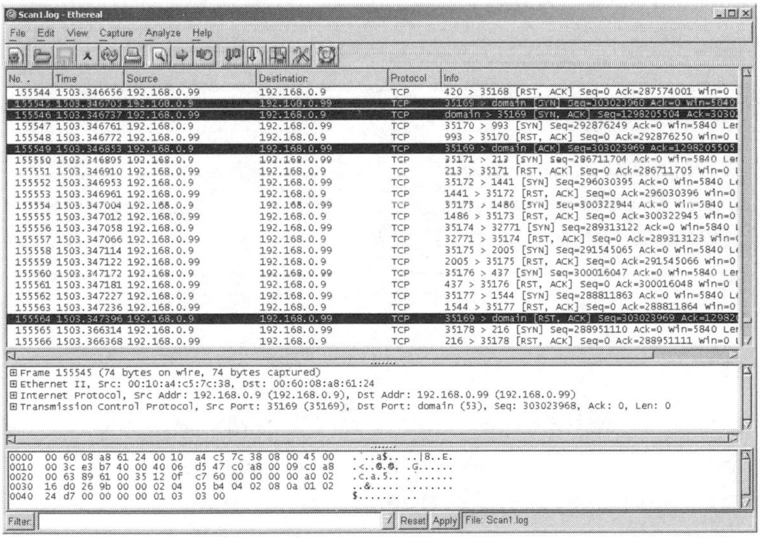

Figure 8.2 shows the active ports on the target device. You can find these by using a filter such as **tcp.flags.syn==1&&tcp.flags.ack==1** or **tcp.flags==18**,

to view packets with the SYN and ACK flags set. The filter will show multiple responses for each port, as several scanning methods were used. We removed the duplicates by saving the marked packets to a file.

> **NOTE**
>
> The filter **tcp.flags==18** will display packets with the SYN and ACK flags set because the binary value of the TCP flags field of a SYN/ACK packet is 00010010, which equals 18 in decimal format.

Figure 8.2 SYN/ACK Responses

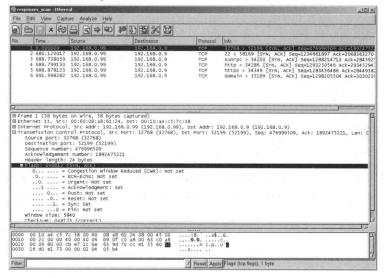

SYN Scan

The next scan that we will be analyzing is a TCP SYN scan, also known as a *half-open scan* because a full TCP connection is never completed. It is used to determine which ports are open and listening on a target device. An intruder sends a SYN packet and analyzes the response. If an RST/ACK is received it indicates the port is closed. If a SYN/ACK is received it indicates that the port is open and listening. The intruder will then follow with an RST to close the connection. SYN scans are known as stealth scans because not as many devices will notice or log them, as they never create a full connection. However, many current firewalls and Intrusion Detection Systems (IDSs) will notice this type of activity.

In Figure 8.3, the attacker, 192.168.0.9, is sending SYN packets to the target, 192.168.0.99. Most ports respond with an RST/ACK packet, however the highlighted packets show the SYN/ACK response, and subsequent RST exchange on the https port. You will also notice that the intruder is using a somewhat static pair of source ports, 52198 and 52199.

Figure 8.3 SYN Scan

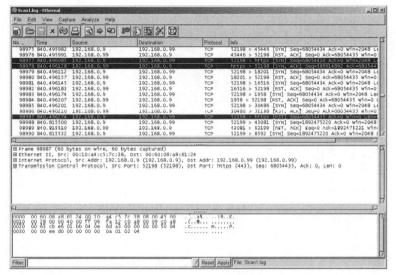

Xmas Scan

The Xmas scan determines which ports are open by sending packets with invalid flag settings to a target device. It is considered a stealth scan because it may be able to bypass some firewalls and IDSs more easily than the SYN scans. This Xmas scan sends packets with the Finish (FIN), Push (PSH), and Urgent (URG) flags set. Closed ports will respond with an RST/ACK and open ports will drop the packet and not respond. However, this type of scan will not work against systems running Microsoft Windows, Cisco, BSDI, HP/UX, MVS, and IRIX. They will all respond with RST packets, even from open ports.

Notice in Figure 8.4 that the attacker, 192.168.0.9, is sending packets to the target 192.168.0.99 with the FIN, PSH, and URG flags set. Most ports respond with an RST/ACK packet, however the highlighted packet for the sunrpc port never receives a response. This is an indication that the port is open and has dropped the packet. You will also notice that the intruder is using decoy addresses of 192.168.0.1, 192.168.0.199, and 192.168.0.254. Decoy addresses are often used to obscure the real intruder's Internet Protocol (IP) address making it harder to track down the real source of the scan. Looking closely at those packets reveals the same Media Access Control (MAC) address for all IP addresses. You will also notice that the intruder is using a somewhat static pair of source ports, 35964 and 35965.

Figure 8.4 Xmas Scan

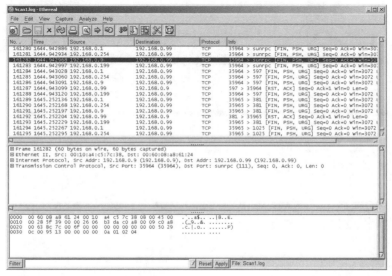

Null Scan

The Null scan determines which ports are open by sending packets with invalid flag settings to a target device. It is considered a stealth scan because it may be able to bypass some firewalls and IDSs easier than the SYN scans. This Null scan sends packets with all flags turned off. Closed ports will respond with an RST/ACK and open ports will drop the packet and not respond. However, this type of scan will not work against systems running Microsoft Windows, Cisco, BSDI, HP/UX, MVS, and IRIX. They will all respond with RST/ACK packets, even from open ports.

In Figure 8.5, the attacker, 192.168.0.9, is sending packets to the target 192.168.0.99 with all flags turned off, as indicated by the empty brackets []. Most ports respond with an RST/ACK packet, however the highlighted packet for the https port never receives a response. This is an indication that the port is open and has dropped the packet. Notice that the intruder is using a somewhat static pair of source ports, 42294 and 42295.

Figure 8.5 Null Scan

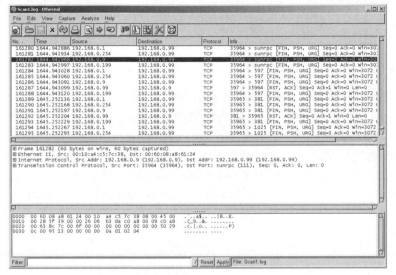

Remote Access Trojans

The term *trojan horse* originally came from the Greek epic poem the Iliad, by Homer. In the story of the Trojan war, the Greeks left a large wooden horse as an apparent peace offering to the Trojans. Once the horse was brought inside the city walls of Troy, the Greek soldiers that were hiding inside of the hollow horse emerged and assisted in capturing the city. In the information security field, trojans are malicious programs that are often disguised as other programs such as jokes, games, network utilities, and sometimes even the trojan removal program itself! Trojans are often used to distribute backdoor programs without the victim being aware that they are being installed. Backdoors operate in a client–server architecture and allow the intruder to have complete control of a victim's computer, remotely over the network. They give an intruder access to just about every function of the computer including logging keystrokes, activating the webcam, logging passwords, uploading and downloading files, and much, much more. They even have password protection and encryption features for intruders to protect the computers they own! There are hundreds, maybe even thousands, of trojan programs circulating the Internet, usually with many variations of the code. This makes them very difficult to detect with antivirus software.

In this section we will be using Scan2.log that was provided by the Honeynet Research Alliance as part of the Honeynet Project Scan of the Month challenge. Scan2.log is located on the accompanying CD-ROM in the /captures directory. We will also be using our own, lab-created backdoor packet captures called subseven_log and netbus_log, also located on the accompanying CD-ROM in the /captures directory.

SubSeven Legend

SubSeven Legend (also referred to as SubSeven) is one of the most common Windows backdoor trojans. It is an older program and most virus software can detect it, but there are many variations of it floating around the Internet. SubSeven is smart enough to notify the intruder, via Internet Relay Chat (IRC), e-mail, or some other method, that the victim computer is online. It runs over a TCP connection with a default port of 27374, although this port is configurable. SubSeven has numerous features that allow the intruder to completely control the victim computer.

Figure 8.6 shows a packet capture of a SubSeven Legend client-server interaction. SubSeven Legend is the anniversary edition of SubSeven. The intruder is running the client on 192.168.1.1, which is connected to the server on the victim computer at 192.168.1.200. You will notice that the server is running on the default port 27374 and data is being pushed between the client and server.

Figure 8.6 SubSeven Legend Backdoor Trojan

Using the Follow TCP Stream feature of Ethereal will show what is going on between the SubSeven server and client. Figure 8.7 shows the connection day and time and the version of the SubSeven server. Next, it shows that the intruder performed a directory listing of C:\, and downloaded the file secret.txt. However, the data for this file is obscured.

Figure 8.7 SubSeven Client-Server Interaction

NetBus

The NetBus backdoor trojan is also one of the older and more common Windows backdoor trojans. It is easily detectable using antivirus software, but like SubSeven, many variations exist. It runs over a TCP connection with default ports of 12345 and 12346, but is configurable. Like SubSeven it has numerous features that allow the intruder to completely control the victim computer.

Figure 8.8 shows a packet capture of a NetBus client-server interaction. The intruder is running the client on 192.168.1.1, which is connected to the server on the victim computer at 192.168.1.200. You will notice that the server is running on the default ports 12345 and 12346 and data is being pushed between the client and server. The two separate source ports indicate two distinct TCP connections.

Figure 8.8 NetBus Backdoor Trojan

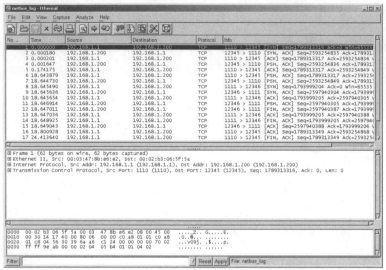

Using the Follow TCP Stream feature of Ethereal will show what is going on between the NetBus server with the port 12345 and the client. Figure 8.9 shows the version of the NetBus server and also shows that the intruder downloaded the file C:\temp\secret.txt. Figure 8.10 shows the client revealing the contents of the downloaded file! This means that not only the intruder, but anyone else on the line with a sniffer, can read the contents of the file as it is transmitted.

Figure 8.9 NetBus Client-Server Interaction

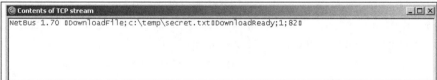

Figure 8.10 NetBus Client-Server Content

```
Contents of TCP stream                                              _ □ ×
this is a confidential document.
□
meet me at the tower at 2pm.
□
see you then
```

RST.b

RST.b is a newer, less widely used, backdoor access trojan that affects various Linux platforms. The backdoor listens in promiscuous mode for User Datagram Protocol (UDP) packets to any port. To access the backdoor, the intruder sends a UDP packet containing the payload "DOM". There is more information on this backdoor at www.qualys.com/alert/remoteshellb.html.

Figure 8.11 shows a packet capture of an intruder scanning for systems infected with the RST.b trojan. We filtered on UDP to focus in on the last nine UDP packets. The intruder uses different source IP addresses and random destination ports to prevent IDSs from detecting the scan. Because the RST.b trojan listens in promiscuous mode, it will respond to UDP packets, containing the "DOM" payload, on any port.

Figure 8.11 RST.b Backdoor Scan

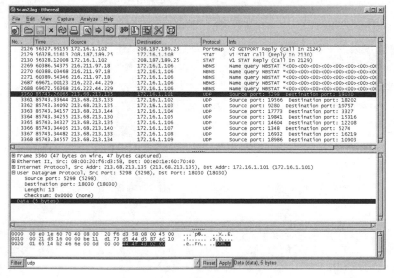

Notes from the Underground…

Trojans, Viruses, and Worms: What is the difference?

Many people get confused over the difference between a virus, a worm, and a trojan. The terms tend to be used interchangeably, but they are really three very distinct entities. They each use different ways to infect computers, and each has different motivations behind its use.

A virus is a program that can infect files by attaching to them, or replacing them, without the knowledge of the user. A virus can execute itself, and replicate itself to other files within the system. To do this, it often attaches to executable files, known as host files. Viruses travel from computer to computer when users transmit infected files or share storage media, such as a floppy disk. Viruses may be benign or malicious. A benign virus does not have any destructive behavior; it presents more of an annoying or inconvenient behavior, such as displaying messages on the computer at certain times. A benign virus still consumes valuable memory, CPU time, and disk space. Malignant viruses are the most dangerous because they can cause widespread damage, such as altering software and data, removing files or erasing the entire system. However, there are no viruses that can physically damage your computer hardware. There are several types of viruses, including the following:

- **File infector** A virus that attaches to an executable file.
- **Boot sector** A virus that places code in the boot sector of a computer so that it is executed every time the computer is booted.
- **Master boot record** A virus that infects the first physical sector of all disks.
- **Multi-partite** A virus that will use a number of infection methods.
- **Macro** A virus that attaches itself to documents in the form of macros.

A trojan is a program that is covertly hiding another, potentially malicious, program. The trojan is often created to appear as something fun or beneficial, such as a game or helpful utility. However, when a user executes the program, the hidden malicious program is also executed

Continued

without the user's knowledge. The malicious program is then running in memory and could be controlling backdoor access for the intruder, or destroying system files or data. A trojan could also contain a virus or a worm. Trojans do not replicate or propagate themselves; they are often spread by unknowing users who open an e-mail attachment to execute a file downloaded from the Internet.

A worm is a program much like a virus that has the added functionality of being able to replicate itself without the use of a host file. With a worm, you don't have to receive an infected file, or use an infected floppy to become infected; the worm does this all on its own. A worm actively replicates itself and propagates itself throughout computer networks. Not only will a worm consume valuable system resources, it can also consume network bandwidth while it is propagating or attempting to propagate.

Dissecting Worms

Throughout the past few years we have seen not only an increase in worm activity, but also an increase in the severity of worm attacks on systems and networks. Internet worms are becoming faster, smarter, and stealthier. Most worms attack vulnerabilities in software for which patches have been readily available for quite some time before the exploit appeared. Complex worms are beginning to emerge that have the ability to exploit several vulnerabilities and propagate in a number of different ways. This makes reverse engineering and defending against the worm more difficult. This section will explore three well-known worms: SQL Slammer, Code Red, and Ramen.

SQL Slammer Worm

The SQL Slammer worm began propagating on the Internet on January 25, 2003. It exploits a vulnerability in the Resolution Service of Microsoft SQL Server 2000 and Microsoft Desktop Engine (MSDE) 2000. It is also known as the W32.Slammer worm, Sapphire worm, and W32.SQLExp.Worm. It is known as the fastest spreading worm, and infected most vulnerable systems within 10 minutes. As the worm propagated and compromised more systems, the Internet showed significant signs of degradation.

The SQL Slammer worm exploits a stack buffer overflow vulnerability that allows for the execution of arbitrary code. Once a system is compromised, the worm will attempt to propagate itself by sending 376-byte packets to randomly chosen IP addresses on UDP port 1434. All vulnerable systems that are discovered will become infected and also begin to scan for more vulnerable systems. With this type of exponential growth, no wonder it spread so fast! This type of propagation leads to a lot of other problems including performance issues, crashed systems, and denial of service. Details on the SQL Slammer worm including the patch, instructions on applying ingress and egress filtering, and recovery from a compromised system can be found in the CERT Advisory at www.cert.org/advisories/CA-2003-04.html.

The Scan3.log file, provided by the Honeynet Research Alliance as part of the Honeynet Project Scan of the Month challenge, shows evidence of the SQL Slammer worm attempting propagation. Scan3.log is located on the accompanying CD-ROM in the /captures directory. After you open the packet capture in Ethereal, apply the UDP filter with destination port 1434, and you will see the Slammer scan traffic, as shown in Figure 8.12. You will notice that there are 55 packets from random source addresses that are sending a UDP packet to port 1434. The UDP packet also has a length of 384 bytes, which is the 376 bytes of data plus the 8-byte header. All of the packets are incoming to the target 172.16.134.191, and none are going out, which lets us know the system is not compromised; it is just the target of the randomly generated IP addresses on other compromised systems. You will also notice that each of the packets contains data, and although it is a bit scrambled you can make out the various parts of the exploit code such as: ws2_32.dll, kerne32.dll, GetTickCount, socket, and send to.

Figure 8.12 SQL Slammer Propagation Attempt

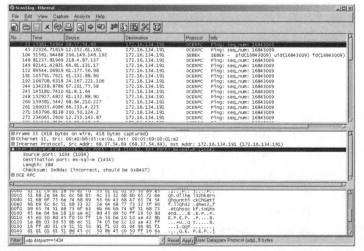

Notes from the Underground…

Why did Slammer spread so fast?

SQL Slammer has been the fastest spreading worm to date. A detailed analysis of the spread of the SQL Slammer worm can be found at www.caida.org/analysis/security/sapphire. There are several key attributes of the worm that allowed it to spread at such an alarming rate. These are outlined as follows:

- **Random scanning** The random scanning of the worm allowed for initial exponential growth.

- **Simple and fast scanner** The worm could scan as fast as the compromised computer could transmit packets or the network could deliver them.

- **Small size** The SQL Slammer worm was only 376 bytes.

- **UDP** The use of a single UDP packet allowed for efficient propagation because the connection does not have to wait for a response.

The propagation of the Slammer worm caused worldwide disruption in approximately 10 minutes. Fast spreading Internet worms are a significant milestone in computer security, and a reality that should be met with all available countermeasures.

Code Red Worm

The Code Red worm was originally discovered on July 16, 2001, and since then there have been many variants including Code Red II and III. The worm infects Microsoft Windows NT, 2000, and beta versions of XP that are running IIS 4.0 and 5.0 Web servers. Code Red exploits a known buffer overflow vulnerability in the IIS Indexing services IDQ.DLL file. Details on the Code Red worm including the patches, workarounds, and recovery from a compromised system can be found in the CERT Advisory at www.cert.org/advisories/CA-2001-19.html.

The Code Red worm operates in 3 stages, which are time sensitive: propagation, denial of service, and sleep. Although there are many variations, the general pattern of behavior is as follows:

- **Propagation mode** This stage takes place from the 1st to the 19th of the month. An infected system will randomly generate IP addresses and attempt to connect to them on HyperText Transfer Protocol (HTTP) port 80. If a system is discovered and is vulnerable, the exploit code will be sent via an HTTP GET request and the web page of the server will be defaced. The original worm defaced web pages by displaying "Welcome to www.worm.com! Hacked By Chinese!" However, some new variations will not deface the web page. The worm places a file, C:\notworm, on the system to signal that it has been infected. This way, if the system gets infected again, the worm will go into an infinite sleep state. If the c:\notworm file does not exist, then this is the first time this system has been infected, and it will create new threads to continue the propagation scanning. This propagation activity will continue until the 20th of the month.

- **Denial of Service mode** This stage begins on the 20th and lasts until the 27th. In this stage, the worm will attempt to packet-flood a specific IP address that is designated in the code by sending large amounts of data to HTTP port 80 of the target. The first target was originally the Whitehouse website at 198.137.240.91. By directing the flood to the IP address instead of the DNS host name, it was easy for Whitehouse.gov system administrators to change the IP, thus making the flood ineffective.

- **Sleep** This stage causes the worm to enter a sleep state from the 28th until the end of the month. It will remain in memory, but will not be active, until the cycle repeats on the 1st

 The CodeRed_Stage1 capture, Figure 8.13, shows the Code Red exploit and propagation in action. The CodeRed_Stage1 file is located on the accompanying CD-ROM in the /captures directory. The Code Red capture files were provided by L. Christopher Paul and can also be downloaded from www.bofh.sh/CodeRed. This capture was lab-generated to show the various Code Red stages, so timestamps may not reflect the proper dates for the various stages. The worm spreads from the system 192.168.1.1 and infects the vulnerable target 192.168.1.105. The newly compromised system then begins scanning random IP addresses for open HTTP port 80. A definite giveaway in this capture is packet number 4, "GET /default.ida?NNNNNNNNN…", which is the exploit for Code Red. The random HTTP port 80 scanning that begins at packet number 12 should also alert you to something strange. This isn't typical web surfing because none of the targets are responding.

Figure 8.13 Code Red Stage 1 – Infection and Propagation

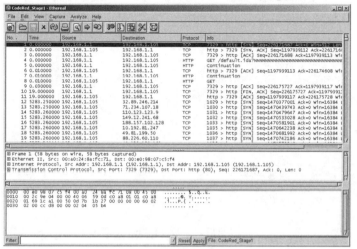

Figure 8.14 shows the "Follow TCP Stream" output of the initial exploit. Notice the exploit in the HTTP GET request at the beginning, and the checking of the of C:\notworm file, and web page defacement at the end.

Figure 8.14 Code Red Exploit Output

The CodeRed_Stage2 capture, Figure 8.15, shows the denial of service mode of the worm. The CodeRed_Stage2 capture file is located on the accompanying CD-ROM in the /captures directory. The infected server, 192.168.1.105 is attempting to flood the Whitehouse web server at 198.137.240.91. Since this was performed in a lab environment, the actual denial of service was not accomplished.

Figure 8.15 Code Red Stage 2 – Denial of Service

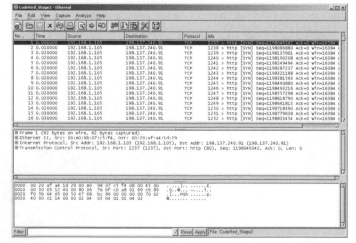

Ramen Worm

The Ramen worm is a collection of tools that can exploit several known vulnerabilities and can self-propagate. The original CERT Incident Note, posted on January 18, 2001, can be found at www.cert.org/incident_notes/IN-2001-01.html. Ramen targets Red Hat Linux 6.2 and Red Hat Linux 7.0 servers with vulnerable versions of the following:

- **wu-ftpd** This program runs on TCP port 21 and vulnerable versions contain a format string input validation error in the site_exec() function.

- **rpc.statd** This program runs on UDP port 111 and vulnerable versions contain format string input validation errors in the syslog() function.

- **Lprng** This program runs on TCP port 515 and vulnerable versions contain format string input validation errors in the syslog() function.

Once a host is compromised, the Ramen tools are copied into a directory called /usr/src/.poop. They are started and controlled by a series of shell scripts. Some of the important characteristics of the Ramen worm include the following:

- The webpage is defaced by replacing the index.html file. The new web page consists of the phrase "Hackers loooooooooooooooooove noodles" and a picture of a package of Ramen noodles.

- E-mail is sent to gb31337@yahoo.com and gb31337@hotmail.com with the text "Eat Your Ramen!".

- The tcpwrappers access control list (ACL) is disabled by removing the /etc/hosts.deny file.

- The file /usr/src/.poop/myip contains the IP address of the local system.

- The file /etc/rc.d/rc.sysinit is modified to include a startup script that initiates scanning and exploitation.

- A new program called *asp* is added, which creates a listener on TCP port 27374. This port is used to send the ramen.tgz toolkit file to other compromised systems. That is also the port that SubSeven uses. Coincidence? It is unclear why the author would want to use an already well-known port, since most IDSs should have been configured to alert activity on that port.

- The user names *ftp* and *anonymous* are added to /etc/ftpusers to disable anonymous FTP (File Transfer Protocol). By disabling anonymous FTP, this part of the worm code is actually fixing the vulnerability that it used to exploit the system!

- The rpd.statd and rpc.rstatd services are terminated and the /sbin/rpc.statd and /usr/sbin/rpc.statd files are deleted. However, there is no service called rpc.rstatd.

- The lpd service is terminated and the /usr/sbin/lpd system file is deleted.

Once the system has been modified, the Ramen worm begins scanning and exploiting the vulnerable systems that it finds. The worm generates random class B IP addresses to scan. It will then send packets with the SYN and FIN flags set and with a source and destination port of 21. Once a vulnerable system is compromised the following actions occur:

- The /usr/src/.poop directory is created on the victim.

- The ramen.tgz toolkit is copied to the new directory and to the /tmp directory. The /tmp directory is where the toolkit is stored so that it can be copied out to new vulnerable systems.

- The ramen.tgz toolkit is unarchived in the /usr/src/.poop directory and the initial shell script is started. The system is now fully compromised and will begin scanning for new vulnerable systems.

The ramenattack.gz packet capture was downloaded from www.whitehats.com/library/worms/ramen. Here you will find a very detailed analysis of the Ramen worm by Max Vision, called "Ramen Internet Worm Analysis" as well as the ramen.tgz source code. The ramen attack.gz capture file is also located on the accompanying CD-ROM in the /captures directory. Ethereal will automatically uncompress the file when you open it.

We will step through the various parts of the packet capture to show how the Ramen worm works.

1. In Figure 8.16, the infected system 192.168.0.23 is performing a SYN/FIN scan on the 10.0.0.0/24 Class B network. It receives a SYN/ACK from the target system at 10.0.0.23.

2. Next, in packet 26, the worm connects to the system to grab the FTP banner and determine if the system is a Red Hat 6.2 or 7.0 server. The banner that the Red Hat 6.2 server returns is as follows:

```
220 test2.whitehats.com FTP server (Version wu-2.6.0(1) Mon Feb 28
10:30:36 EST 2000) ready.
221 You could at least say goodbye.
```

Figure 8.16 Ramen Work Propagation Scanning

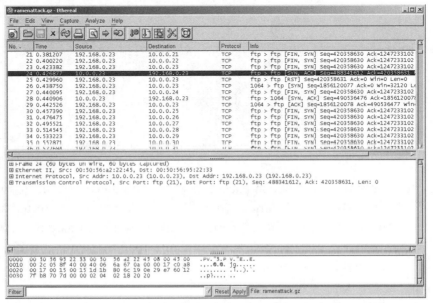

3. Next, the wu–ftp and rpc.statd exploits are launched against the potential target. The wu–ftp attempt begins at packet 137 and is unsuccessful, but the rpc.statd exploit succeeds. Figure 8.17 shows the payload of the rpc.statd exploit. Notice the padding of "90 90 90 90…" and the trailing "/bin/sh" that will execute a command shell. You will also notice in packet 289 that once the SYN/FIN scan is finished scanning the target 10.0.0.0/24 range it sends a SYN/FIN packet to 10.9.9.9 from port 31337. This represents the packet that is sent to www.microsoft.de when the scan is complete. Since the worm was activated and analyzed in a lab environment 10.9.9.9 was chosen to represent www.microsoft.de.

Figure 8.17 Ramen Worm rpc.statd Exploit

4. You will also notice in packet 290 that a connection is made with the port 39168 on the target system. The rpc.statd exploit created a backdoor on the victim on this port and it is now used to initiate the transfer of the worm and execute it. It also sends an e-mail to accounts at Hotmail and Yahoo. The output from this transfer is shown in Figure 8.18.

Figure 8.18 Ramen Worm Execution

5. The last connection you will see, beginning in packet 297 in Figure 8.17, is the actual transfer of the Ramen toolkit that was initiated in previous script. The new compromised system connects back to the attacker at port 27374 to download a copy of the worm.

6. The worm is now executing on the victim and will begin scanning for new vulnerable hosts.

Overall, the Ramen worm is easy to detect, especially since it uses a well-known Trojan port for the worm transfer. It contains unexplained and inefficient code and makes no attempt to be stealthy. There are also several places where its functionality could be optimized. However, this is a worm that exploits several different vulnerabilities and self-propagates. The security community should definitely watch out for more worms with these capabilities.

NOTE

A day-zero, or alternately a zero-day attack, is an exploit on a vulnerability that is not yet known about and for which there is no patch.

Summary

Analyzing real-world packet captures is both a science and an art. A high traffic network segment can present the analyzer with thousands of packets containing hundreds of connections, sessions, and protocols. Ethereal's built-in features such as TCP session reconstruction, display filters, and packet colorization help simplify the process of analyzing data. However, as with any skill, you must practice, practice, practice. Constantly analyzing network data will help you quickly assess what is normal and what is unusual behavior. If you don't have the ability to analyze your own network traffic data, participate in the Honeynet Project Scan of the Month challenges. These challenges cover network traffic analysis, as well as malicious code, exploits, and methodology.

You should also become familiar with reading and interpreting hexadecimal output. This will come in handy when you are analyzing day-zero attacks and you may have to implement your own custom signature. Intrusion detection systems often match a signature on the content of a packet in hexadecimal format.

In this chapter we presented several different types of packet captures and the processes used to analyze the data. You should have an understanding of the types of activity to look for in a packet capture and how to identify various types of network traffic. Combining this skill with the network troubleshooting methodology presented in Chapter 2 will help you to detect, analyze, and respond quickly to the next major worm outbreak.

Solutions Fast Track

Scanning

☑ Network scanning is used to detect open ports and services on systems.

☑ A TCP Connect scan completes the TCP 3-way handshake and is easily logged and detected.

☑ SYN scans were once used as stealthy scanning techniques; however most firewalls and IDSs can now detect these types of scans.

☑ Xmas scans are ineffective against Microsoft operating systems because they will respond with an RST from all ports, even if they are open.

☑ A Null scan sends packets with all flags turned off. Closed ports will respond with an RST/ACK and open ports will just drop the packet.

Remote Access Trojans

☑ Remote access backdoor programs are often delivered to unsuspecting users within a trojan program.

☑ Remote access backdoors operate in a client-server architecture, allowing the intruder complete control over the compromised system.

☑ SubSeven can notify the intruder, via IRC, e-mail, or some other method, that the victim computer is online.

☑ NetBus is an older Windows backdoor trojan that is easily detected by antivirus software, but like SubSeven, many variations exist.

☑ The RST.b trojan listens in promiscuous mode and will respond to UDP packets, containing the "DOM" payload, on any port.

Dissecting Worms

☑ Internet worms are becoming increasingly fast and complex.

☑ The SQL Slammer worm uses UDP to accomplish its fast propagation.

☑ The original Code Red worm operated in 3 stages: propagation, denial of service, and sleep.

☑ The Ramen worm is a collection of tools that can exploit several known vulnerabilities in the wu-ftpd, rpc.statd, and lprng utilities.

Frequently Asked Questions

The following Frequently Asked Questions, answered by the authors of this book, are designed to both measure your understanding of the concepts presented in this chapter and to assist you with real-life implementation of these concepts. To have your questions about this chapter answered by the author, browse to **www.syngress.com/solutions** and click on the **"Ask the Author"** form. You will also gain access to thousands of other FAQs at ITFAQnet.com.

Q: Why is it that when I right-click on some of my packets the "Follow TCP Stream" options is grayed out?

A: The underlying protocol that you are trying to reconstruct does not use TCP for its connection method. It may use the connectionless UDP method for its transmission.

Q: Can I use Ethereal to discover a trojan that is being sent to someone on my network?

A: No, Ethereal can only be used to discover the active use of the backdoor access program that the trojan installs. To Ethereal, or any network analyzer, the transmission of the trojan will appear to be a regular executable file.

Q: Can I use Ethereal to discover a virus that is being sent to someone on my network?

A: No, like a trojan, the transmission of a virus will look like a regular executable or some other type of file. Ethereal will not be able to tell that the file is infected.

Q: Are there network activities that will falsely resemble network scanning attacks?

A: Yes, there are lots of activities that will resemble network scans. A client program that is automatically searching for a server at startup may continue to send TCP SYN packets to the target address. Often multiple and rapid TCP connection that are associated with FTP and HTTP downloads also resemble network scan attacks and trigger alarms.

Chapter 9

Developing Ethereal

Solutions in this Chapter:

- Prerequisites for Developing Ethereal
- Ethereal Design
- Developing a Dissector
- Advanced Topics

☑ Summary
☑ Solutions Fast Track
☑ Frequently Asked Questions

Introduction

The fact that Ethereal is open source and distributed under the General Public License (GPL) allows many individuals to contribute to the overall success of the project. With developers throughout the world contributing for several years, Ethereal has become a viable tool for many organizations.

Ethereal developers have contributed new functionalities as well as features to the growing number of tools included in the Ethereal distribution. This includes the console-based version of Ethereal named Tethereal, as well as a number of other tools that are part of the Ethereal distribution.

The main Ethereal application is a Graphical User Interface (GUI) application utilizing components of GNU's Not UNIX (GNU) Image Manipulation Program called GIMP. The latest version of the GIMP Toolkit is now called GTK+. GTK+ is the official name of the toolkit but most developers refer to it as GTK. Although the name implies that GNU owns GTK, this is not the case. GTK is maintained as a separate entity at www.gtk.org. Ethereal uses the GTK library and functions for its GUI implementation. New features often require modifications to the GUI. This might include new menu items or modifications to existing menu selections. The core of the application includes the main window, menus, utility functions, etc.

The components of Ethereal that dissect packet structures are called *protocol dissectors*. These components are individual source code modules that instruct the main Ethereal application on how to dissect a specific type of protocol. The dissector can be complex or simple based on the protocol that is being dissected. Most of the contributions to the Ethereal project are either new dissectors or enhancements to existing ones.

By utilizing the concepts within this chapter, you should be able to grasp the basic steps to become a contributor to the Ethereal project. Many users and developers worldwide would benefit from your efforts and welcome anything you might want contribute.

Notes from the Underground…

Development Note

Because of the wide range of development on the Ethereal project, there may already be work in progress on a specific feature or protocol dissector. The Ethereal developer mailing list (ethereal-dev@ethereal.com.) is a good way to determine if work is already being done in a specific area. Questions can be posted to the ethereal-dev mailing list before you start work on a specific protocol dissector or feature. You can consult the Ethereal website for more information on the available mailing lists at www.ethereal.com.

Prerequisites for Developing Ethereal

The first step in the development process is to acquire the Ethereal source. You can download many different distributions from the Ethereal website, such as the currently released source code or the last nightly backup of the source code. You can also utilize the Concurrent Versions System (CVS) to keep up to date throughout your development process. CVS is the most risky, compared to released versions of Ethereal, because you are compiling code that hasn't been fully tested. Generally, however, the CVS code is of very high quality.

Even if you have an issue with the current CVS code, you can generally get one of the members of the Ethereal mailing list (ethereal-dev@ethereal.com) to make a quick change to resolve the issue. CVS gives you access to code changes as they are checked into the master build. It is the most up-to-date, but can contain unidentified bugs. Please keep in mind that the CVS distribution can be and is routinely updated as well. You might develop with the current released code and then find out that a specific function you are working with has changed. Instructions for utilizing the latest builds and CVS can also be found at the www.ethereal.com website.

Before you can add to or modify Ethereal, you must be able to build the application from source. To build from source you will need to acquire additional libraries and tools. Ethereal is a multiplatform application, meaning that it can run on many different operating systems. You will need to be able to build on the particular operating system that you will be developing on.

It is also important to understand that Ethereal is developed and built using a number of different programming languages. This includes many UNIX-based programs and shell scripts. For example, several modules within Ethereal are written in python and Perl. Although it may not be necessary for you to be proficient in each programming language, you might find times where you need to understand enough about the language to make a simple change. A majority of the code base for Ethereal is ANSI-C. The requirement for ANSI-C is due to the portability of the code to multiple operating system platforms. Special care should be taken when writing in C to use only those functions that are defined as ANSI-C and are portable. You should be able to use just about any C compiler with the Ethereal source. This would include GNU C Compiler (gcc) on Linux, as well as Microsoft Visual C++ on Windows.

Damage & Defense

Portability

Before starting any work you need to read the portability section 1.1.1 of the README.developer document contained in the doc directory of the source distribution. The word *portability* is used in reference to the steps a developer should take to ensure that Ethereal source can be compiled on all of the supported operating systems. For example, you wouldn't want to use a function that only exists on a win32 platform. This would cause Ethereal source to not compile or build correctly on the other supported operating systems. Typically, when a program is written to one operating system platform and then made to run on a different platform, the process is called *porting*. This is where the name portability is derived from.

Skills

To build a new dissector or modify the main application, you will need to be able to program in C. However, please keep in mind that modifications to existing dissectors may require you to be knowledgeable in another language.

Modifications to the Ethereal GUI will require some knowledge of GTK. The GTK website at www.gtk.org, contains online and downloadable tutorials for programming in GTK.

Contributions to the Ethereal project come from many different levels of developers. Some are novices while others might be considered to be experts. However, the overall Ethereal project is maintained by a group of highly experienced developers. New additions and or contributions are first reviewed by this group and then incorporated into the source distribution following any necessary changes. In some cases, the individual who reviews the changes might make a recommendation to the original developer for a specific change, or in other cases they may make the changes themselves.

Tools/Libraries

In most cases, you will need the developer kit for access to necessary libraries. A developer kit is different from the normal binary distribution. Generally, the developer package includes the compiled binaries for the operating system it was built for. For example, since Ethereal utilizes the GTK libraries for its GUI implementation, you will need to ensure that you have the developer kit for GTK. You will also need to make sure that you download the correct developer kit for the operating system that you are going to develop on. It is important to try to use the latest released version of the developer kit if possible. Although you might be able to build Ethereal with an older set of libraries, the results of the application running might not be as expected. However, in some cases this might not be an option. Some operating systems only support certain versions of support libraries. In general, you can consult the Ethereal developer mailing list or the developer section of the www.ethereal.com website.

Win32 ports of the required libraries are not necessarily located at their respective project site. For example, the win32 port for the libpcap library is called WinPcap. The following web pages list places where you can look for Win32 library ports. The www.ethereal.com/distribution/win32/development web page contains most of what you will need, but if you want to build with GTK 2.x you will need additional library packages not listed on the Ethereal website. Refer to the web pages located at www.gimp.org/~tml/gimp/win32.for GTK 2.x information and access to the Win32 ports.

When building Ethereal, you will need the GTK and GLIB libraries. Ethereal can be built using the older GTK 1.2, 1.3, or the newer GTK 2.x versions. The newer 2.x versions of GTK add more font control and have a better look and feel. These libraries can be downloaded from www.gtk.org. The installation chapter in this book identifies some of these issues when installing on Solaris and Red Hat distributions.

The console version of Ethereal, called Tethereal, only requires the GLIB libraries. If you will only be building the Tethereal application, you will not need GTK.

If you will be building with packet capture support in Ethereal or Tethereal, you will need to make sure that you have the libpcap libraries from: www.tcp-dump.org. Without packet capture support, users of the compiled program will only be able to view packet trace files. They will not be able to perform new packet captures. Win32 developers will need the WinPcap libraries instead of libpcap. These can be downloaded from http://winpcap.polito.it/.

The following is a list of libraries needed to build Ethereal. Remember that you will need to download the developer kit to acquire the necessary libraries for your operating system. Some packages are optional and can be linked to add additional features. UNIX/Linux operating systems will detect the installed libraries by the automake process. Automake will identify the library packages that can be included when you build Ethereal. On Win32 based computers the config.nmake file should be modified to define what libraries that you wish to include in the build process. These libraries will then be added to the final binary during the linker process of the build.

- **glib** Low-level core library for GTK (required).

- **gettext** GNU language conversion (required by glib).

- **libiconv** Character set conversion library (required by glib).

- **GTK** GIMP toolkit for creating graphical user interfaces (required for Ethereal build).

- **libpcap** Packet capture library for UNIX/Linux-based operating systems.

- **WinPcap** Packet capture library for Win32 based operating systems (optional).

- **ADNS** GNU Advanced DNS client library (optional) adds DNS lookup support.

- **net-snmp** Simple Network Management Protocol (SNMP) library (optional) adds SNMP support.

- **pcre** Perl Compatible Regular Expressions library (optional) adds Perl expression filters.
- **zlib** File compression library (optional) adds compressed file support.

If you will be building with GTK version 1.2 or 1.3, no additional libraries are needed for GTK. Otherwise, when building with GTK 2.*x* you will need the following additional libraries:

- **atk** Accessibility toolkit (required).
- **pango** Internalization of text (required).

Windows users must choose to either attempt to build from within cygwin using gcc or with a Win32-based compiler such as Microsoft's Visual C++ (MSVC++). They will also need to download a number of additional libraries. The default location specified in the Ethereal distribution for the libraries on Win32 is C:\ethereal-win32-libs. You should download and extract each required library to this location. Ethereal's scripts will then locate the libraries at build time. Otherwise, you will need to modify the config.nmake file located in the main distribution directory to point to the correct location for each library.

Tools that you might need are specific to the operating system in which you need them to run. The Ethereal compile and build process utilizes a number of script files. These scripts will require a number of tools to run successfully. Most of the tools have their roots in the UNIX/Linux operating systems. To compile and build Ethereal on non-UNIX-based operating systems you will need to have access to similar tools.

Windows users will also need to install cygwin. Cygwin is a Linux-like environment for Windows-based computers. It gives both a Linux Application Program Interface (API) emulator as well as a set of Linux-based tools. These tools are what allow the scripts utilized by Ethereal during the build process to work on Windows-based computers. Cygwin can be downloaded and installed from www.cygwin.com.

Windows users will also need to download Python. Python can be downloaded and installed from www.python.org/.

Most UNIX and Linux-based operating systems will include a C compiler and many of the required tools needed to build Ethereal.

The following is a list of tools needed to compile and build Ethereal:

- **Cygwin** Provides UNIX/Linux tools for Win32 developers. This is not needed for UNIX/Linux.

- **Perl** Needed for all operating systems.

- **pod2man** Part of Perl.

- **pod2html** Part of Perl.

- **Python** Needed for all operating systems.

- **Flex** Needed for all operating systems.

- **Bison** Needed for all operating systems.

Tools & Traps…

Building on UNIX and Linux-Based Operating Systems

Detailed instructions for building the Ethereal binaries from source are included in the INSTALL file, located in the main source directory. Chapter 3 of this book also outlines the build process on RedHat Linux.

Building on Windows-Based Operating Systems

Detailed instructions for building the Ethereal binaries from source are included in the file README.win32, located in the main source directory. This file includes instructions on building on both MSVC++ and Cygwin. It is also important to use **CMD.EXE** and not **COMMAND.COM** when attempting to build Ethereal. The program **CMD.EXE** provides long name support whereas the older **COMMAND.COM** is limited to 8.3 file naming conventions. Ethereal's source contains long named files and is not supported with command.com.

Windows users may need to update or change the default environment variables for their compiler to locate additional support libraries. For example, when building Ethereal, the wiretap source must include header files for winsock support. It is important that the build process can locate the correct include files. Validate that the following user environment variables are defined correctly:

- Include
- Lib

It's important to also make sure that cygwin is located in the user path environment variable to locate the necessary cygwin executables during the build process. These executables are the Windows equivalent of necessary UNIX/Linux binaries. For example **bison.exe** is the equivalent of its UNIX/Linux counterpart **bison**.

Ethereal Design

The Ethereal source distribution envelopes a main source directory and several subdirectories. The main source directory contains the following important source files:

- **config.nmake** This file instructs Ethereal where to locate libraries during the build.

- **Makefile.nmake** This is the script for making the Ethereal binaries on Win32.

- **Makefile.am** Automake configuration file for UNIX/Linux.

- **cleanbld.bat** File for switching between platforms.

- **configure** File for UNIX/Linux build and install.

- **idl2eth.sh** Shell script for creating Ethereal dissector for Interface Definition Language (IDL) files.

- **INSTALL** UNIX/Linux installation instructions.

- **make-xxx** Script files to build support modules.

- **packet-xxx** Protocol dissectors.

- **README** Associated readme files for multiple platforms.

- **tap-xxx** Protocol taps.

- **xxxx** Remaining files contain utility functions for Ethereal/Tethereal.

In Figure 9.1, you can see a breakdown of the directories contained in the Ethereal distribution.

Figure 9.1 Main Directory

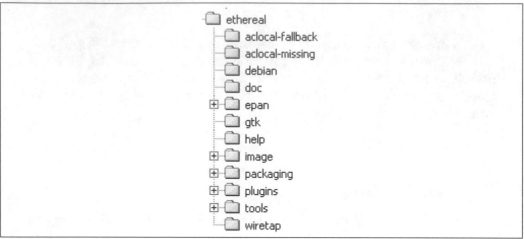

aclocal-fallback and aclocal-missing

The aclocal–fallback and aclocal–missing directories are used to store information used by automake on UNIX/Linux-based systems.

debian

The debian directory is used for compatibility with debian Linux-based operating systems. These files are not under packaging because the debian tools require that the debian directory to be at the top-level directory of a source package.

doc

Contained within the doc directory are many text documents to assist you in the development process. They are provided in the following list:

- **README.design** This document provides some useful information on the core structure of Ethereal.

- **README.developer** This is the main document to assist in the development of new protocol dissectors. Also included are helpful design pointers, a sample template and potential problems.

- **README.idl2eth** Refer to this document when you desire to build a dissector from an IDL file.

- **README.plug-ins** Documentation for utilizing the plug-in interface of Ethereal.

- **README.regression** Steps for testing and regressing new dissectors. This file provides a template with which you can test for regressions in packet decodes. The file is structured as a makefile that can be utilized after modifying the core Ethereal code or a dissector to ensure that Ethereal operates correctly.

- **README.tapping** Detailed information on the tapping system built into Ethereal.

- **README.tvbuff** Tvbuff is the main structure for dissectors to access and display data. It also performs checks on the data to trap for errors in the data stream to prevent stack and buffer overflows. This document describes the proper use of the tvbuff functions and data structure.

- **README.xml-output** Tethereal provides a mechanism to output data in XML/PDML (Product Data Markup Language) format. This document outlines what this capability provides.

epan

The epan directory contains most of the utility and global functions used within dissectors. The subdirectory dfilter contains source for display filter functionality. The ftypes subdirectory contains source that define the different data types that are utilized in the data type logic (see Figure 9.2).

Figure 9.2 epan Directory

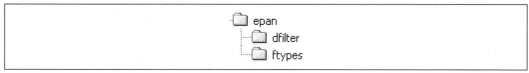

gtk

Contained within the gtk directory are the source files for the main Ethereal application. This includes the main GUI as well as the menu and toolbar. Basically, any of the Ethereal source that needs to access the GUI will reside within this directory.

help

The help directory will hold the source files that are used to build the content for the help menu dialogs. These are built during compile time and linked into the Ethereal binary file.

image

The icons and bitmaps linked into the Ethereal binary are stored in the image directory, as shown in Figure 9.3. The custom icons are stored in the toolbar subdirectory and are in X PixMap (XPM) format. The XPM file format is used to create icons and bitmaps for X-Windows-based operating systems.

Figure 9.3 Image Directory

Notes from the Underground…

Custom Icons

GTK 2.x allows you to change from stock icons to custom icons. When making your own custom icons, make sure you create them with the same physical dimensions as the other bitmaps contained in the toolbar subdirectory.

packaging

The packaging directory contains the necessary scripts and files to generate a binary distribution, as shown in Figure 9.4. Currently supported distributions include the Nullsoft Scriptable Installation System (NSIS) to generate a Windows installation package or the RedHat Package Manager (rpm) and System V Release 4 (svr4) to generate Linux and UNIX installation packages.

Figure 9.4 Packaging Directory

Notes from the Underground…

NSIS Package

To build the NSIS install package for Windows-based systems, you will need to download the NSIS compiler from www.nullsoft.com/free/nsis.

plugins

A number of dissectors have been written to interface with Ethereal through the plugin interface, as shown in Figure 9.5. For detailed information on how to create a plug-in, refer to the README.plugins document in the doc directory.

Figure 9.5 Plugins Interface

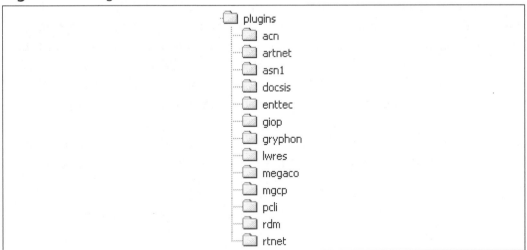

tools

Ethereal's source distribution contains several tools in this directory. In the tools directory the EtherealXML.py file is a python script to read Tethereal-generated PDML files. The lemon directory contains the *Lemon* tool, which will generate C source files based on a supplied template, as shown in Figure 9.6. Lemon is a parser generator for C or C++ that does the same job as bison and yacc, but Lemon provides more flexibility and does a better job of eliminating common errors. It also runs much faster then the other tools, is reentrant, and is thread-safe.

Figure 9.6 Lemon Directory

wiretap

The wiretap directory is the core capture file support library, which provides the support to read and write different capture file formats. For information on how to add or modify the capture file types supported by Ethereal, refer to the README.developer document located in the wiretap directory.

Developing a Dissector

A protocol dissector is most commonly written in C, although there are components of Ethereal that build C source from Python scripts, IDL files, and even Perl scripts. These files are named after the protocol they are meant to dissect. For example, a protocol dissector for a protocol called myprot would be named packet-myprot.c. These files are located in the main source directory. Some dissectors have been implemented as plug-ins. The advantage of a plug-in is that it does not require a complete recompile of the whole Ethereal source during development. However, even plug-ins start out as a packet-xxx.c source file. This section discusses the necessary steps for creating a standard packet-xxx.c dissector.

Notes from the Underground…

Before You Start

Before you start work on your dissector, open the README.developer file in the doc directory. Cut and paste the sample template. This will provide you with enough of a skeleton to get started.

Tools & Traps…

Source Editor Considerations

It is important that your editor saves files in the proper format. Ethereal source is composed of UNIX-style files. The source file should not contain lines that end in carriage return, line feeds (CR/LF). Lines of text should be terminated only by the line feed character. If you are programming on non-UNIX-based computers you will need to make sure that your editor supplies the correct end of line formatting. Otherwise, you will need to reformat the source files prior to submitting them back to the ethereal-dev mailing list.

Step 1 – Copy the Template

There are several steps that must be completed to integrate a new dissector into Ethereal. The first step is the comments, as seen in the following code. Remember that Ethereal is open source, so the main comment identifies not only that you did the work to create the dissector, but also includes information on the original contributor of Ethereal and the GPL.

```
/* packet-PROTOABBREV.c
 * Routines for PROTONAME dissection
 * Copyright 2000, YOUR_NAME <YOUR_EMAIL_ADDRESS>
 *
 * $Id: README.developer,v 1.86 2003/11/14 19:20:24 guy Exp $
```

```
*
* Ethereal - Network traffic analyzer
* By Gerald Combs <gerald@ethereal.com>
* Copyright 1998 Gerald Combs
*
* Copied from WHATEVER_FILE_YOU_USED (where "WHATEVER_FILE_YOU_USED"
* is a dissector file; if you just copied this from README.developer,
* don't bother with the "Copied from" - you don't even need to put
* in a "Copied from" if you copied an existing dissector, especially
* if the bulk of the code in the new dissector is your code)
*
* This program is free software; you can redistribute it and/or
* modify it under the terms of the GNU General Public License
* as published by the Free Software Foundation; either version 2
* of the License, or (at your option) any later version.
*
* This program is distributed in the hope that it will be useful,
* but WITHOUT ANY WARRANTY; without even the implied warranty of
* MERCHANTABILITY or FITNESS FOR A PARTICULAR PURPOSE. See the
* GNU General Public License for more details.
*
* You should have received a copy of the GNU General Public License
* along with this program; if not, write to the Free Software
* Foundation, Inc., 59 Temple Place - Suite 330, Boston, MA 02111-1307,
  USA.
*/
```

When working with the template, you need to replace certain text with your information. For example, for line 1, you would replace packet-PROTOAB-BREV.c to packet-myprot.c. Change line 2 (PROTONAME) to indicate the protocol your dissector is meant to decode. Line 3 should be modified with the copyright date, your name, and your e-mail address. Note that since Ethereal is open source, this is your claim to ownership of the submitted code. This doesn't keep other developers from modifying your code, but it does limit other people from taking ownership of your work. Once you contribute your code to the Ethereal project it becomes part of the GPL-licensed codebase and you will be added to the growing list of Ethereal contributors. Line 5 of the comment is important to the CVS system, as it identifies the current file ID and revision. This line is modified when source code is checked in and out of the CVS system. Make sure you do not remove this line. Finally, line 11 should be modified to document the source of your information used to build the dissector. If this information is not available or cannot be disclosed, then this section can be omitted. The rest of the comments should remain intact to reflect the original author, Gerald Combs, and the GPL information.

Step 2 Define the *Includes*

The next portion of the template, as seen in the following code, defines the *includes* for this source program. *Includes* are needed for global functions that this dissector calls. Ethereal defines a number of global functions that can be used within your protocol dissector. You might also need to include standard header files from your compiler or standard library. For example, string.h is a standard header file for string functions.

```
#ifdef HAVE_CONFIG_H
# include "config.h"
#endif

#include <stdio.h>
#include <stdlib.h>
#include <string.h>

#include <glib.h>

#ifdef NEED_SNPRINTF_H
# include "snprintf.h"
#endif

#include <epan/packet.h>
#include "packet-PROTOABBREV.h"
```

Output variables are set or passed to the C pre-processor to determine specific includes that might be needed to perform the build under specific conditions. For example, the HAVE_CONFIG_H include is only processed by *make* if this value is true. On Linux-based operating systems, autoconf generates output variables that may define even more output variables based on the build environment. Please refer to www.gnu.org/software/autoconf for more information.

Notes from the Underground...

Global Functions

Ethereal includes a large number of functions that can be used within your protocol dissector. To use these functions you must include the header file for the source that contains the defined function. One of the hard parts in utilizing the global functions provided by Ethereal is identifying the ones available for use. Let's say that you have an Internet Protocol (IP) address that you would like to display. You could manually format a display string or you could use the built-in global function. But where is the global function? The following list displays some of the most common includes that define the global functions that might be needed by your dissector:

- **prefs.h** Structure and functions for manipulating system preferences.
- **reassemble.h** Structure and functions for reassembly of packet fragments.
- **tap.h** Functions for utilizing the built-in tap interface.
- **epan/column-utils** Functions for manipulating the summary window column data.
- **epan/conversation.h** Functions for tracking conversations (Request to Reply).
- **epan/int-64bit.h** Functions for manipulating 64-bit integers.
- **epan/plugins.h** Functions for plug-in support.
- **epan/resolve.h** Functions for resolving addresses to names.
- **epan/strutil.h** Common string functions.
- **epan/to_str.h** Functions for string conversion.
- **epan/tvbuff.h** Testy Virtual Buffer (TVBUFF). A method used by dissectors to access packet data.

Continued

- **epan/value_string.h** Functions to locate strings based on numeric values.

The following structures may contain information important for your dissector.

- **epan/column-info.h** Structure of summary window column data.
- **epan/framedata.h** Structure of frame data.
- **epan/packet-info** Structure of packet information.

There are many more functions and structures defined in the Ethereal source. In some cases you will need to research available functions by analyzing other packet-xxx.c dissectors. Most of the utility functions you will need will be located in the epan directory.

Damage & Defense

Static Functions

It is strongly recommended that the functions you create within your dissector are declared as static. This will limit their scope to the current dissector and not conflict with any other functions that might be defined in another dissector or program. For example, if we create a function called dissect_my_protocol, we should create a function prototype like so:

```
static void dissect_my_protocol();
```

Step 3 Create the Function to Register

The next step in the development of a protocol dissector is to create the function to register your dissector with Ethereal.

```
/* Register the protocol with Ethereal
```

```
/* this format is required because a script is used to build the C
function
    that calls all the protocol registration.
*/


void
proto_register_PROTOABBREV(void)
{


/* Setup list of header fields  See Section 1.6.1 for details */
      static hf_register_info hf[] = {
              { &hf_PROTOABBREV_FIELDABBREV,
                    { "FIELDNAME",
"PROTOABBREV.FIELDABBREV",
                    FIELDTYPE, FIELDBASE, FIELDCONVERT, BITMASK,
                    "FIELDDESCR" }
              },
      };


/* Setup protocol subtree array */
      static gint *ett[] = {
              &ett_PROTOABBREV,
        };


/* Register the protocol name and description */
        proto_PROTOABBREV = proto_register_protocol("PROTONAME",
            "PROTOSHORTNAME", "PROTOABBREV");


/* Required function calls to register the header fields and subtree used */
        proto_register_field_array(proto_PROTOABBREV, hf, array_length(hf));
        proto_register_subtree_array(ett, array_length(ett));
```

It is important that the proto_register_xxx function is left justified as shown in the template. The scripts used to register protocol dissectors are make-reg-dotc and make-reg-dotc.py. These scripts parse all of the packet-xxx files to build a list of all dissectors to be registered with the Ethereal engine. If this function does not meet the proper syntax requirements, the scripts will fail to register your new dissector. The file that is generated by the scripts is called register.c and is located in the main Ethereal source directory. This file should not be edited manually since it is recreated each time you compile and build Ethereal.

The first part of the proto_register_myprot function sets up the hf array fields of the dissection. Although these are not required for packet dissection, they are recommended to take advantage of the full-featured display filter capabilities of Ethereal. Each item that is defined within the hf array will be an individual item that can be filtered upon within Ethereal. For example, ip.src is an element within the packet-ip dissector. A user can enter a display filter of **ip.src==10.10.0.1**. If the ip.src element was not defined, then this would be an invalid filter.

```
{ &hf_ip_src,
{ "Source", "ip.src", FT_IPv4, BASE_NONE, NULL, 0x0,
     "", HFILL }},
```

Tools & Traps...

hf Element Items

For a detailed description of each component of an element within the hf array, refer to the README.developer document located in the doc directory.

The next part of the registration process will be to define the array for the sub-tree called ett. The ett variables keep track of the state of the tree branch in the GUI protocol tree, for example, whether the tree branch is open (expanded) or closed. We register the protocols short and long names with Ethereal by calling the proto_register_protocol function (this causes the protocol to be displayed in the Enabled Protocols window). The final step is to register the hf and ett arrays with the proto_register_field_arry and proto_register_subtree_array

That's all it takes to register an available dissector with Ethereal. But, how would Ethereal know when to pass the data stream from a specific type of packet to this new dissector? Ethereal now needs to have the dissector instruct Ethereal when it should be called. For example, suppose we are writing a dissector to decode packets that are being transported on top of Transmission Control Protocol (TCP) with a port of 250. We need to instruct Ethereal to pass all packets that meet the criteria to our dissector.

Step 4 Instruct Ethereal

```
void
proto_reg_handoff_PROTOABBREV(void)
{
      dissector_handle_t PROTOABBREV_handle;

      PROTOABBREV_handle = create_dissector_handle(dissect_PROTOABBREV,
          proto_PROTOABBREV);
      dissector_add("PARENT_SUBFIELD", ID_VALUE, PROTOABBREV_handle);
```

The proto_reg_handoff_xxx function is used to instruct Ethereal when to call our dissector. The function create_dissector_handle passes the function that Ethereal will call to dissect the packets and the proto_xxx value that we registered as our protocol in the proto_register_protocol function. The dissector_add function allows us to specify the criteria that will trigger Ethereal to pass the packet to our dissector. PARENT_SUBFIELD allows us to specify the element within the parent dissector that we will trigger off of. For our example of TCP port 250, we would just set this value to tcp.port. We would then set the ID_VALUE to 250. Ethereal will then automatically pass data to our dissector by calling the function defined in create_dissector_handle if the value of tcp.port equals 250.

```
void
proto_reg_handoff_myprot(void)
{
      dissector_handle_t myprot_handle;

      myprot_handle = create_dissector_handle(dissect_myprot,
          proto_myprot);
      dissector_add("tcp.port", 250, myprot_handle);
}
```

Step 5 Create the Dissector

Now we must create our dissector. We will need to create the function that we registered with Ethereal for our packet dissection. In our example we called this function *dissect_myprot*. Ethereal will pass our function three data structures—tvb, pinfo, and tree. The tvb structure will be used to extract and decode the data contained in each element of the packet. The pinfo structure gives us specific information about the packet based on information that has previously been dissected by other processes. For example, the pinfo structure tells us which packet number this packet relates to. It also contains flags for processing fragmented packets or multiple dissections. Finally, the tree structure gives us a pointer to the memory location of the GUI displayed data in the decode window. For our example this would be a pointer to a memory location in the GUI display to the location of the data just below the TCP protocol section. This is the starting point where our dissected data will be displayed in the decode pane. See Figure 9.7

Figure 9.7 Dissector Data Displayed in the Decode Window

```
⊞ Frame 11 (62 bytes on wire, 62 bytes captured)
⊞ Ethernet II, Src: 44:45:53:54:42:00, Dst: 00:00:66:61:6b:65
⊞ Internet Protocol, Src Addr: 164.99.192.69 (164.99.192.69), Dst Addr: 137.65.80.178 (137.65.80.178)
⊞ Transmission Control Protocol, Src Port: cma (1050), Dst Port: ncp (524), Seq: 4077633585, Ack: 0, Len: 0
```

Our decode data will start immediately after the TCP section. We now can start decoding the packet. In some cases we want to grab information from the data stream into a local variable so that we can make logical decisions based upon its value. To acquire data from the packet we use tvb_get_xxx functions. For example, let's assume that the first byte in the packet is an unsigned integer that will contain the value of 0 for a request packet or a value of 1 for a reply packet. We can first define our variable and then use a tvb_get_guint8 function to get the data from the packet.

```
guint request_reply;
request_reply = tvb_get_guint8(tvb, 0);
```

The variable request_reply now contains the value of the first byte in the data stream. The parameters passed to the tvb_get_xxx functions vary but all will take the pointer to your local tvb and an offset. In many cases it makes sense to create a variable for the offset value and then increment that variable after making each tvb call.

```
guint request_reply, offset = 0;
request_reply = tvb_get_guint8(tvb, offset);
```

Notes from the Underground...

Variable and Function name Syntax

Ethereal utilizes a lower-case format for all syntax. The C language is case-sensitive and the variable RequestReply is a different variable than one named requestreply. The preferred syntax when writing source for Ethereal is to use all lower-case characters and separate words with the underscore character. For our example, it was request_reply. It is strongly recommended that you follow this requirement. It allows all of the Ethereal code to have the same look and feel.

tvb_get Functions

There are a number of tvb_get_xxx functions. These allow you retrieve data from the packet data stream based on the type of data you need to acquire. For example, you may need *x* number of bytes or you may need a 4-byte value. You may also find that the data in the data stream is in the wrong order. For example, you are expecting the value for a "long" to be returned as 0001 but instead it is returned as 1000. There are two types of each tvb_get_xxx function to allow you to get the data from the datastream in the endianess you need. Endianess refers to the pattern for byte ordering in native types, such as integers. There are only two main patterns, big endian and little endian, and these describe which end of a multibyte integer appears in the lowest address byte of the integer. Big endian means the most significant byte comes first, and little endian means the least significant byte comes first. The following illustrates each pattern for integer $0x87654321$. Please refer to the README.tvbuff and the README.developer documents located in the docs directory.

Value Types Used by Ethereal

Ethereal utilizes a number of common value definitions. These are defined in the README.tvbuff and the README.developer documents located in the doc directory. Different development environments will refer to value types by different names. Ethereal provides a common set

Continued

of value types to allow for easier portability between operating systems. The following is a brief listing of the most common:

guint8 (1-byte value)

guint16 (2-byte value)

guint32 (4-byte value)

guint64 (8-byte value)

guint8* (pointer to a byte value)

gchar* (pointer to a character string)

Now we want to display in the decode pane whether this is a request or reply packet. We do this with the proto_tree_add_xxx functions. In our example we only want to display in the decode window a message indicating if this is a request or reply packet.

```
if (request_reply==0)
        proto_tree_add_text(tree, tvb, offset, 1, "Request-(%d) ",
            request_reply);
else
        proto_tree_add_text(tree, tvb, offset, 1, "Reply-(%d) ",
            request_reply);
```

The proto_tree_add_text function requires the following parameters.

- **tree** Pointer to the protocol tree.
- **tvb** The tvbuff to mark as the source data.
- **offset** The offset in the tvb is where the data is located.
- **1** The length of the value, in bytes, in the tvb.
- **Request Packet (%d)** The printf type format for displaying the data.
- **request_reply** The data value to be displayed via the printf format.

> ## Notes from the Underground...
>
> ### proto_tree_add_xxx
>
> You might ask why the tvbuff information gets passed to the proto_tree_add_xxx function. We already have extracted the information into our variable request_reply. The tvbuff parameters tell Ethereal the portion of the data in the hex display pane to highlight when this value is selected in the decode pane. Also note that the tvbuff starts at the beginning of the data passed to your dissector. For example, when getting data from the tvbuff, the byte with an offset of 0 is the first byte of the packet data that is related to your protocol. The previous packet data that was decoded by a higher-level dissector is not accessible. This ensures that the data seen by your dissector only pertains to the protocol dissection you are attempting to accomplish.

There is one problem with this example. If we utilize the proto_tree_add _text function then this value is not a filterable element. So, if the user wanted to create a filter for all request packets in our dissector, they would not be able to. We could rewrite the example to utilize the hf array and make the request_reply value a filterable item.

```
if (request_reply==0)
        proto_tree_add_item(tree, hf_request, tvb, offset, 1, FALSE);
else
        proto_tree_add_item(tree, hf_reply, tvb, offset, 1, FALSE);
```

Although this example will now allow the user to filter on the request or reply condition, this is not the most efficient use of the proto_tree_add_xxx functions. Since the value is already stored there is no reason to force the dissector to reread the data. The proto_tree_add_uint function can be used to display the data already stored in our request_reply variable. If the value had not already been stored in a variable, the proto_tree_add_item function would be the most efficient to use.

```
if (request_reply==0)
                proto_tree_add_uint(tree, hf_request, tvb, offset, 1,
```

```
                       request_reply);
else
                   proto_tree_add_uint(tree, hf_reply, tvb, offset, 1,
                       request_reply);
```

If we change the proto_tree_add_text to proto_tree_add_item, then we utilize an hf element for displaying the data in the decode window. We now need to add the hf_request and hf_reply variables to the hf array.

You must first declare the hf variables at the top of the source file after your include statements.

```
static int hf_request = -1;
static int hf_reply = -1;
```

Now we just add the element information to the hf arrary.

```
{ &hf_request,
  { "Reqeust Packet", "myprot.request",
  FT_UINT8, BASE_DEC, NULL, 0x0,
  "", HFILL }},

{ &hf_reply,
  { "Reply Packet", "myprot.reply",
  FT_UINT8, BASE_DEC, NULL, 0x0,
  "", HFILL }},
```

With these changes, if the user would like to filter on all request packets in the myprot dissector, they enter the filter of myprot.request. Any packet that meets the request_reply value of 0 will contain an array element of myprot.request. Reply packets will contain an element of myprot.reply. Figure 9.8 shows an example of how a user might enter a display filter to force Ethereal to only display the packets for our new dissector.

Figure 9.8 Sample Display Filter

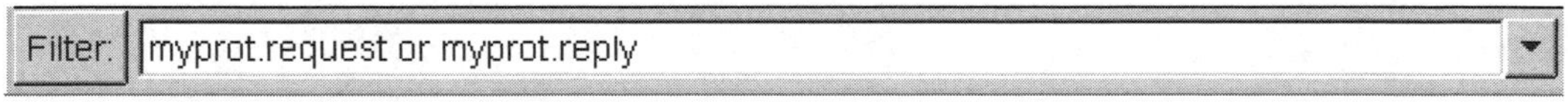

Filter: myprot.request or myprot.reply

Notes from the Underground…

proto_tree Functions

There are many variations of the proto_tree_add_xxx functions. The proto_tree_add_item is the most versatile because it allows the format of the data to be defined in the hf array. If you attempt to pass the wrong data types to any of the proto_tree_add_xxx functions, a runtime error will be displayed and Ethereal will halt. This error processing allows Ethereal to trap for errors instead of allowing memory to be overrun or corrupted. It is good practice to utilize the hf array even if you do not want the end user to be able to filter on a specific item in the decode. For these conditions you can specify that the element is hidden so that the end user will not know of its definition. For detailed information on all of the different proto_tree_add_xxx types and the format of the hf array, refer to the README.developer document in the doc directory.

The real work of the dissector begins here. You will need to go through the logic of each type of packet that the dissector will decode. You should utilize the tvb_get_xxx functions to get data you need to evaluate as well as the proto_tree_add_xxx functions to display information in the decode window.

But, there is one more important step that we have not considered at this point. The summary pane, as shown in Figure 9.9, allows the user to browse quickly through the packet trace without having to look at each packet decode. This window allows you to display brief but important information relative to the packet. Typically, most developers will provide summary data on request packets and only error information on reply packets. The col_set_str function allows you to set the value of the data within any of the displayed summary window columns.

Figure 9.9 Summary Pane

No..	Time	Source	Destination	Protocol	Info
11	22.720221	164.99.192.69	137.65.80.178	TCP	1050 > 524 [SYN] Seq=0 Ack=0 Win=16384 Len=0 MSS=1370
12	22.724357	137.65.80.178	164.99.192.69	TCP	524 > 1050 [SYN, ACK] Seq=0 Ack=1 Win=6144 Len=0 MSS=1370
13	22.724372	164.99.192.69	137.65.80.178	TCP	1050 > 524 [ACK] Seq=1 Ack=1 Win=16440 Len=0
14	22.724704	164.99.192.69	137.65.80.178	NCP	C Create Connection Service
15	22.729828	137.65.80.178	164.99.192.69	NCP	R OK
16	22.729856	164.99.192.69	137.65.80.178	NCP	C Get Big Max Packet Size - 65535
17	22.734531	137.65.80.178	164.99.192.69	NCP	R OK

In the following code example we see the check_col() and col_set_str() functions. These functions are just a subset of the column functions available.

```
if (check_col(pinfo->cinfo, COL_PROTOCOL))
    col_set_str(pinfo->cinfo, COL_PROTOCOL, "MYPROT");
```

Note that the first thing we do is to evaluate whether the column data exists. If it doesn't exist, then we cannot write to the column data structure. This is an important step since without this check you could potentially write to undefined memory. We then make the col_set_str function call to set the value of the protocol column "COL_PROTOCOL" to our protocol name "MYPROT".

```
if (request_reply==0)
{
    proto_tree_add_item(tree, hf_request, tvb, offset, 1, FALSE);
    if (check_col(pinfo->cinfo, COL_INFO))
        col_set_str(pinfo->cinfo, COL_INFO, "Request- ");
}
else
{
    proto_tree_add_item(tree, hf_reply, tvb, offset, 1, FALSE);
    if (check_col(pinfo->cinfo, COLINFO))
        col_set_str(pinfo->cinfo, COL_INFO, "Reply- ");
}
```

We now want to set the summary column to reflect if this is a request or reply packet. We do this the same way we did for the protocol column, by using the col_set_str function. Note that we still perform the check to validate that the column information is valid. Later in our dissector we can append information to the info column by using the col_append_str function.

> ### Notes from the Underground...
>
> ### Column Functions
>
> Ethereal includes a number of column functions to allow you to clear, set, and append to existing column data. These functions are defined in the epan/column-utils.h file as well as the README.developer document in the doc directory.

Step 6 Pass Payloads

The final thing your dissector should do is to pass on any payload that might be remaining to be dissected by additional dissectors. This handoff of the payload data is what each of the lower level dissectors performs to allow entry points for further dissection. For example, the TCP dissector decodes the TCP header information but the remaining payload is dissected by different higher-level dissectors. In some cases you may not need to pass on payload data, but it is recommended that your dissector look at the remaining data in the packet and pass it on if there is anything else to dissect. In some cases your dissector may contain a data payload that can't be actually dissected. In this case if you have remaining data in the packet structure that needs to be decoded by another dissector or as payload information, the remaining data should be displayed in some manner. The passing of the remaining payload back to Ethereal will automatically be displayed as [Data] if no further dissection can be performed. For example, there is no defined lower dissector to handle the decoding of the remaining data. If the remaining data is payload for your dissector then utilize the proto_tree_add_item and pass a -1 as the length parameter. Ethereal will then mark all of the remaining data in the packet as the defined proto_tree_add_item. The following information is extracted from the README.developer document located in the doc directory.

```
An example from packet-ipx.c -

void
dissect_ipx(tvbuff_t *tvb, packet_info *pinfo, proto_tree *tree)
{
```

```
tvbuff_t            *next_tvb;
int                 reported_length, available_length;

/* Make the next tvbuff */
next_tvb = tvb_new_subset(tvb, IPX_HEADER_LEN, -1, -1);

/* call the next dissector */
dissector_next(next_tvb, pinfo, tree);
```

You've just learned how to create a simple dissector. In the next section, we will discuss how to modify the files used to build Ethereal so that it can be compiled into the rest of the project. Before you start major work on your dissector you should first make sure that the build process will complete with your new dissector included. This will also validate that your registration is working and that Ethereal passes your dissector the packet data as expected. Under the "Advanced Topics" section of this chapter, we will explore some of the more complex issues you may encounter when creating a protocol dissector.

Running a Dissector

To add a new dissector to the Ethereal project you will need to modify some of the scripts used to manage the build process. The scripts that have to be changed will depend on the operating system that you are developing on. When developing on a UNIX/Linux-based operating system you will need to change the Makefile.am to add your new dissector. On Windows based operating systems you will need to modify the Makefile.nmake script.

```
DISSECTOR_SRC = \
    packet-aarp.c \
    packet-acap.c \
    packet-afp.c  \
    packet-afs.c  \
```

Both files contain the same structure to define the new dissector. Add your dissector to the DISSECTOR_SRC section of the file. When you build Ethereal this section is parsed and each dissector is compiled and linked into the main Ethereal binary.

Once you have successfully built Ethereal with your modifications you should go back and analyze your code. Places where you have not commented on what you are doing should be commented on if they are not obvious. This allows you and others to look at the code at a later date and determine what that particular section is doing. Also take note of any warnings reported by your compiler and try to resolve them. Generally, this might be improper data type casts or unused variable definitions.

After you have completed the cleaning up of the code and you are satisfied with its functionality, please contribute your changes back to the Ethereal project by sending a patch to the ethereal-dev mailing list. For changes to existing files it is recommended that the changes are sent as a patch to the existing file in CVS. It is also important that you consult with the proper individuals before you submit any proprietary information back to the Ethereal distribution. Remember that Ethereal is released under GPL and your submissions should be made under the same license agreement.

If you are working with a CVS distribution you can perform an update by issuing the following command:

```
cvs update -Pd
```

Then you should generate a patch with the command:

```
cvs diff -u packet-myprot.c >packet-myprot.c.diff
```

If the file you need to send is a new dissector, you should send the complete source file packet-myprot.c and a patch to both the Makefile.nmake and Makefile.am. Attempting to perform a CVS diff on your new dissector will not generate any information if your source does not exist in the CVS distribution. Your initial contribution will be a complete copy of the source. Future modifications should be submitted in patch form by generating a CVS diff file.

The Dissection Process

When does your dissector get called? When Ethereal reads a packet via the wiretap library it performs the following steps:

- The frame data is passed to the function epan_dissect_run().
- The function epan_dissect_run() defines the frame, column, and data pointers and calls the function dissect_packet().

- The dissect_packet() function creates the topmost tvbuff and then calls the dissect_frame() function.

- The dissect_frame() function dissects the frame data and displays in the decode pane of the GUI the frame information for the packet. For example, the arrival time, frame number, or frame length.

- The dissect_frame() funtion then calls the dissector_try_port() to see if there are any protocol dissectors to dissect the next part of the tvbuff. In the example shown in Figure 9.7, we see in the decode pane that we are passed to the Ethernet packet type dissector. This would be dissect_eth_common() function.

- The dissect_eth_common() function then decodes and displays the Ethernet header in the decode pane of the Ethereal GUI. Several different functions could be called at this point based on the Ethernet frame type. But once the Ethernet frame type has been decoded the remaining tvbuff is passed to the core Ethereal function dissector_try_port() again.

- The dissector_try_port() function again looks to see if there is another dissector registered for the remaining tvbuff.

- This process of decoding each layer of the packet continues, header by header, until we reach our protocol dissector. Ethereal calls each dissector, that dissector processes its data, then the dissector creates a new tvbuff and sends it back to dissector_try_port(). In our example we saw that myprot would eventually be the payload of a TCP packet. Ethereal would continue each dissection until the TCP dissector was processed. At this point dissector_try_port() would see that we are registered for TCP port 250.

- Finally, the dissector_try_port() function calls our dissector myprot.

- Once our dissector has completed its work it passes any remaining tvbuff back again. The process continues until either there is no more data or no more registered dissectors for the remaining data. Once this happens the next frame is read from the packet trace file.

Notes from the Underground…

When Ethereal Calls Your Dissector

It is important to realize that your dissector can be called multiple times. Every time a display or color filter gets applied to a packet trace, Ethereal will re-dissect the data again. When the user clicks on an item in the decode pane the dissector is again called to dissect that specific packet. Your dissector should evaluate the fd.flags.visited flag in the pinfo data structure to determine if it needs to perform work that has not been performed. Otherwise, you may overwrite data that is necessary to properly decode your packets, for example, adding new conversations into a conversation list that already exists. You should construct your dissector to take into consideration if the initial dissection has already been completed.

Advanced Topics

The previous section discussed the basic information necessary to create a simple dissector. But, as your dissector becomes more complex you will need to implement more advanced features. Ethereal provides many different mechanisms to assist you in making your dissector display and decode packet data in a more informative manner. In this section we will look at some of the more complex tasks that you may want to incorporate into your packet-xxx dissector.

We will also take a quick look at modifying the Ethereal GUI. This process will require you to acquire some knowledge of GTK and some of its features and mechanisms. Since Ethereal's GUI is generated by using the GTK libraries, you will find that it makes calls to functions that are not included in the Ethereal distribution. These functions are part of the GTK binaries that you downloaded in the GTK developer kit. Documentation on these functions are available at the GTK website at www.gtk.org.

Finally, this section includes a short description of the tap and plug-in implementations in Ethereal. Taps will allow you to build tools that acquire real-time data from Ethereal. The plugin interface will allow you to convert a packet-xxx dissector into a plug-in that can be loaded and unloaded.

Dissector Considerations

When you compose a dissector you may need to consider several factors. If the protocol that needs dissection runs on top of a connection-oriented protocol, you might need to track the request reply packets to ensure they match. Connection-oriented protocols generally guarantee delivery. The underlying protocol will retransmit packets if they are not acknowledged by their peer. So how do you handle retransmissions? Your dissector may also need to handle payloads that exceed the maximum packet size. The actual payload may span several packets and your dissector needs to defragment the data. There are also situations where you might want to store information either in the form of a memory value or across loading of the application. You will most likely encounter at least one of these conditions. This section is meant to provide some advanced topics to help you overcome and develop a way to handle these situations.

Creating Sub-trees

Many times the decoded data should be branched to a separate sub-tree. This practice allows users to see important summary information in the decode window and allow them to expand specific sections of the decode window to see more detail. For example, we may want to branch at a sub-level or a particular item that might contain more data or attributes then you want to normally display (see Figures 9. 10 and Figure 9.11).

Figure 9.10 Closed Item in Decode Pane

```
⊞ Communications Transports: 2
⊞ Tree Walker Transport Type: 2
```

Figure 9.11 Expanded Item in Decode Pane

```
⊟ Communications Transports: 2
     (TCP Protocol)
     (IPX Protocol)
⊟ Tree Walker Transport Type: 2
     (TCP Protocol)
     (IPX Protocol)
```

The user can now click on the **Entry Information** field within the decode window to expand the item and get more detailed information. Sub-trees are easily implemented with the proto_tree functions.

```
proto_item          *subitem;
proto_tree          *subtree;

subitem = proto_tree_add_text(tree, tvb, offset, -1, "Some Description");
subtree = proto_item_add_subtree(subitem, ett_myprot);
proto_tree_add_item(subtree, hf_myvalue, tvb, offset, 4, FALSE);
proto_item_set_end(subitem, tvb, offset);
```

The first step is to declare the proto_item and proto_tree variables.

The proto_tree_add_text function allows us to create a label. This is only one of many good uses of the proto_tree_add_text function. In this example, we pass the tree pointer that was given to us when our dissector was called. We also pass the tvb, offset, and length to the function so that when the user highlights the label in the decode window the remaining packet data will be highlighted. The -1 tells proto_tree_add_text that the length is all remaining data starting from the beginning offset. Finally, the label is passed to the function to describe what this sub-tree actually contains. We could branch from an actual element within the decode window as well instead of creating a label. To do this we could replace the proto_tree_add_text with a different proto_tree_add function. Once the label has been created in the original tree a new item pointer is returned in our sub-item variable.

The next function, proto_item_add_subtree, sets up the sub-tree in the display. It creates the sub-tree so that when we later perform another proto_tree_add function, we can reference the new sub-tree pointer.

The next call is to the proto_tree_add_item function. We pass the pointer for our new sub-tree in this function. This actually places the new element beneath the expandable label we created before. The value will not be viewable in the decode window until the sub-tree label is clicked on and expanded.

The final step in this example is to set the overall length of the proto_tree_add_item with the proto_item_set_end function. This is used when the length of the value being set is unknown. If you are working with items of known length, this function call is not necessary.

Many times you may want to create several branches of sub-trees. To do this, create multiple proto_items and proto_tree pointers. We would create sub-tree 1 and then sub-tree 2, but reference sub-tree 1 as the source tree. A visual display of the multi-level tree view can be seen in Figure 9.12.

```
item1 = proto_tree_add_text(tree, tvb, offset, -1,
```

```
        "Selector Option");
    tree1 = proto_item_add_subtree(item1, ett_myprot);
    number_of_items = tvb_get_ntohl(tvb, offset);
    proto_tree_add_uint(tree, hf_num_objects, tvb, offset, 4,
        number_of_items);
    foffset += 4;
    for (i = 1 ; i <= number_of_items; i++ )
    {
        item2 = proto_tree_add_text(tree1, tvb, offset, -1,
            "Option - %u", i);
        tree2 = proto_item_add_subtree(item2, ett_myprot);
    }
```

Figure 9.12 Visual Display of Multi-level Tree View

```
⊟ Selector Option
    Number of Options: 1
  ⊟ Option 1
    ⊟ Object ID Type: Printer Configuration Object ID (0x00000006)
        Printer Name: PUD_HP5Si_2 TEL
```

Bitfields

In some cases you may have a value that represents specific information based on what bits are set within the value. Bitfields give the user a visual display of each bit and whether they are enabled within the value, as shown in Figure 9.13.

Figure 9.13 Visual Display of Bits

```
⊟ Flags: 0x2062 - (Readable, Walk Tree, Dereference Alias, Prefer Referrals)
    .... .... .... ..1. = Readable: True
    .... .... ..1. .... = Walk Tree: True
    .... .... .1.. .... = Dereference Alias: True
    ..1. .... .... .... = Prefer Referrals: True
```

Bitfields are implemented through the use of the hf array elements. The following code is an example of the calling function that builds the subtree and summary data.

```
flags = tvb_get_guint8(tvb, offset);
strcpy(flags_str, "");
```

```
sep = " (";
if (flags & FLAG1) {
    strcat(flags_str, sep);
    strcat(flags_str, "Flag 1");
    sep = ",";
}
if (flags & FLAG2) {
    strcat(flags_str, sep);
    strcat(flags_str, "Flag 2");
    sep = ",";
}
if (flags_str[0] != '\0')
    strcat(flags_str, ")");
ti = proto_tree_add_uint_format(tree, hf_flags,
        tvb, offset, 1, flags, "Flags: 0x%04x%s", flags,
    flags_str);
flags_tree = proto_item_add_subtree(ti, ett_myprot);
```

The first step is to acquire the value from the tvbuff into the value flags. We then build our initial string and then compare the value of flags with our defined flag bits. If they match, we combine the string with the flag information. Once our summary string has been built we just create our sub-tree and display the data. We now need to display each of the valid bits in a bit view.

```
proto_tree_add_item(flags_tree, hf_flag_1,
        tvb, offset, 1, FALSE);
proto_tree_add_item(flags_tree, hf_flag_2,
        tvb, offset, 1, FALSE);


{ &hf_flag_1,
    { "Flag 1", "myprot.flag.1",
    FT_BOOLEAN, 8, NULL, FLAG1,
    "Is Flag one set? ", HFILL }},
{ &hf_flag_2,
    { "Flag 2", "myprot.flag.2",
    FT_BOOLEAN, 8, NULL, FLAG2,
    "Is Flag two set? ", HFILL }},
```

We display the bitfields by calling the proto_tree_add_item function with reference to our new sub-tree and the bitfield hf element names. Then, in the hf array, we define our new values. The key here is parameters 3, 4, and 6. Parameter 3 declares that this is a Boolean value. This means that we will evaluate this as a true or false condition. Parameter 4 declares that we will display 8 bits. Parameter 6 declares the actual value of the bitmask. You can substitute this value with the explicit mask. In our example, flag 1's value might be 0x01 and flag 2 might be 0x02.

Unicode Strings

Many times you will run into situations where the actual data contained in the packet might contain Unicode data. Unicode data is normally seen in the hex data window as a two-byte value. For example you might see:

```
57 00 6f 00 72 00 6b 00 73 00 74 00 61 00 74 00 69 00 6f 00 6e 00
W    o    r    k    s    t    a    t    i    o    n
```

When processing the data, most string conversion utilities will see the second byte of the multi-byte character as a terminating null. You might find that you need to parse the string to acquire single byte character strings. Many of the main string functions within Ethereal now perform this process for you but you might find that you have a situation that requires you to manually perform the conversion. Several dissectors include functions to convert multi-byte character strings to single byte strings. The following code is an example extracted from packet-ncp2222.inc:

```
static void
uni_to_string(char * data, guint32 str_length, char *dest_buf)
{
        guint32 i;
        guint16 c_char;
        guint32 length_remaining = 0;

        length_remaining = str_length;
        dest_buf[0] = '\0';
        if(str_length == 0)
        {
                return;
        }
}
```

```
            for ( i = 0; i < str_length; i++ )
            {
                    c_char = data[i];
                    if (c_char<0x20 || c_char>0x7e)
                    {
                            if (c_char != 0x00)
                            {
                                    c_char = '.';
                                    dest_buf[i] = c_char & 0xff;
                            }
                            else
                            {
                                    i--;
                                    str_length--;
                            }
                    }
                    else
                    {
                            dest_buf[i] = c_char & 0xff;
                    }
                    length_remaining--;

                    if(length_remaining==0)
                    {
                            dest_buf[i+1] = '\0';
                            return;
                    }
            }
            dest_buf[i] = '\0';
            return;
    }
```

Conversations

Ethereal conversations are a key component of many protocol dissectors. Each dissector that needs to track conversations will define and maintain their own conversation table. The conversation table gives the dissector the ability to track request and reply packets. You might ask why you would need to track the conversation. What if there is no information contained in the reply packets that identify which request the reply was for? In this case we would need to store the original request packet in memory so that when the reply packet is found we can decode it. For example, the NetWare Core Protocol (NCP) protocol only defines a sequence number on the request packet. But, each request reply sequence is a unique session. Running on top of TCP or Internetwork Packet Exchange (IPX), the request packet will be made from a specific address with a unique port/socket. If we match these conversation components then we can logically assume that the reply packet is a response to the original request. Unfortunately, these may not come in the proper order in a packet trace. The conversation list saves each request conversation within our conversation list. When we encounter a reply packet, we perform a lookup in the conversation list to determine which request the reply matches. If no originating request packet is found, we should display a message in the decode window that the packet could not be decoded due to no request packet being found. Section 2.2.7 of the README.developer document located in the doc directory provides basic skeleton code to setup a conversation table.

Some important steps should not be missed when using conversations lists. This includes the *initialization function* and the *cleanup function* that have to be placed in the protocol register routine. Many dissectors include conversation lists. If, after reviewing the section in the README.developer document, you still need a clearer example, refer to other dissectors that utilize this capability.

Packet Retransmissions

Packet retransmissions are common on busy networks. Your dissector should be able to handle such an occurrence if it is going to attempt to handle fragmented packets. If your dissector or protocol does not process fragmented packets, your dissector can treat these packets as normal packets. In most cases a simple conversation list can check for the occurrence of a request packet but if nothing triggers your dissector, it might be a duplicate entry. You may also find that you need to manage another memory table to track a retransmitted packet. However, in other cases, the lower-level protocol might have already detected the retransmissions.

The packet information structure pinfo can provide information for the status of the current packet being decoded. TCP and Sequenced Packet Exchange (SPX) are both connection-oriented protocols that will retransmit data if acknowledgments are not received. Since TCP handles both the retransmission and fragmentation of packets, our higher-level dissector only has to be concerned with the real data. However, in the case of SPX, the higher-level dissector has to trap for retransmissions if it is handling packet fragmentation. The next section discusses how the SPX dissector passes this information on to the higher-level dissectors. It is important for you to understand that a retransmission is a common occurrence on many networks. Your dissector should be able to determine if a packet is a retransmission or a normal packet. In some cases you may choose not to dissect retransmitted packets and just identify the original packet. Just remember that a retransmission can occur at any time. It may consist of a complete packet or an individual fragment.

Passing Data Between Dissectors

The pinfo->private_data element can be used to pass a pointer to a memory table with information regarding the specific packet being decoded. You should first define a structure in your lower level dissector that will hold the information. The following information was extracted from packet-ipx.h and packet-ipx.c:

```
/*
 * Structure passed to SPX subdissectors, containing information from
 * the SPX header that might be useful to the subdissector.
 */
typedef struct {
        gboolean eom;                   /* end-of-message flag in SPX header */
        guint8 datastream_type;       * datastream type from SPX header */
} spx_info;
```

Then we update the structure and save it to pinfo.

```
static void
dissect_spx(tvbuff_t *tvb, packet_info *pinfo, proto_tree *tree)
{
        spx_info        spx_info;


            /*
            * Pass information to subdissectors.
            */
            spx_info.eom = conn_ctrl & SPX_EOM;
            spx_info.datastream_type = datastream_type;
            pinfo->private_data = &spx_info;
```

Now, in the higher-level dissector we can retrieve this information. This information was extracted from the source file packet-ndps.c:

```
static void
ndps_defrag(tvbuff_t *tvb, packet_info *pinfo, proto_tree *tree)
{
    spx_info                *spx_info;

    /* Get SPX info from SPX dissector */
    spx_info = pinfo->private_data;
```

The higher-level dissector can now utilize the information from the lower level dissector to perform logical operations on the packet data.

Saving Preference Settings

It is often important for the user to determine how the protocol dissector might handle specific features of your dissector. For example, the packet fragmentation code can be enabled or disabled by the end user under the protocol preferences dialog. To implement a user configurable setting that will be either used during runtime or saved across multiple loads of Ethereal, you should add the ability to utilize the system preference file.

```
ldap_module = prefs_register_protocol(proto_ldap, NULL);
prefs_register_bool_preference(ldap_module, "desegment_tcp",
    "Desegment all LDAP messages spanning multiple TCP segments",
    "Whether the LDAP dissector should desegment message",
    &ldap_desegment);
```

This code goes into the proto_register_xxx routine. It creates a new entry in the preference files with the value of the referenced variable myprot_desegment. The following is an example of the entry created in the preference file. Figure 9.14 is an example of how the value will look to the end user when they go to the preferences option in Ethereal and select your protocol. We used the LDAP protocol dissector as our example.

```
# Whether the LDAP dissector should desegment messages
# TRUE or FALSE (case-insensitive).
ldap.desegment: TRUE
```

Figure 9.14 Example of LDAP Preference

Desegment all LDAP messages spanning multiple TCP segments:

In other cases you may need to keep information relating to a specific packet decode. It is best to utilize a conversation table to handle this type of condition.

Packet Fragmentation

Packet fragmentation can be handled at many different protocol layers. TCP already includes packet reassembly. If your dissector needs to do additional packet reassembly then you can utilize the reassembly functions defined in Ethereal. A good example of how to handle packet reassembly by TCP is located in section 2.7 of the README.developer document in the doc directory. It covers how to handle the packet reassembly when your dissector is running on top of TCP or User Datagram Protocol (UDP).

The files packet-ncp2222.inc, packet-atalk.c, and packet-clnp.c all give examples of how to defragment messages that are fragmented within the protocol you are dissecting. The logic involved in defragmented packets can be very complicated. You will find yourself spending many hours troubleshooting and fine-tuning the defragmentation function.

Value Strings

You will also find times when you read a specific value from the packet datastream that could be defined by many different descriptions based on the value. You will want to present a string to the user indicating what the value actually means. An example of this might be an error return value in a reply packet. The numerical value will indicate which error was being returned. The section 1.7.1 in the README.developer document located in the doc directory lists the match_strval and the val_to_str functions. The first step is to create the array of values.

```
static const value_string my_values[] = {
        { 0x00000000, "Value 1" ),
        { 0x00000001, "Value 2" },
        { 0x00000002, "Value 3" },
        { 0, NULL }
};
```

It is important to note the final line in the value string of [0, NULL]. This is the termination record for the value_string function. If this is omitted then Ethereal will continually scan memory and may possible generate a bounds error.

You can now utilize the match_strval or val_to_str functions to process the value.

```
valuestr = match_strval(value2, my_values);
```

But, you can simplify this process even further by utilizing the VALS capability of the hf arrary.

```
{ &hf_valuestr,
{ "This is my value", "myprot.valuestr",
    FT_UINT8, BASE_DEC, VALS(my_values), 0x0,
  "My value string", HFILL }}
```

This way we can just utilize the simple tvb_get and proto_tree_add functions.

```
value2 = tvb_get_guint8(tvb, 1);
proto_tree_add_uint(tree, hf_valuestr, tvb, 1, 1, value2);
```

The same feature can be utilized to display true or false value strings in the decode pane of the GUI, for example, if you wanted to display "Yes" or "No" based on a true or false value.

```
    typedef struct true_false_string {
        char    *true_string;
        char    *false_string;
    } true_false_string;
```

Value strings are very important for processing return values that might contain a large number of error codes. The value string gives you the ability to process all of the possible values and return a specific string to identify the actual error. Without this information the end user is forced to research the returned value to look up the return value. In some cases the value may not really indicate a problem, but by providing the string to the end user you will eliminate much frustration and make your dissector even more valuable. Figure 9.15 shows an example of data displayed in the decode pane when utilizing a value string to return a string based on the return value.

Figure 9.15 Example of Value String Display

```
NDS Completion Code: 0xfffffda5, (-603) No Such Attribute
```

The Ethereal GUI

The Ethereal GUI is created through calls to the GTK library. When you develop for the Ethereal GUI you must consider compatibility issues for other builds of Ethereal. This means that you must program for both GTK version 1.2 and versions 2.x. Some of the GTK functions work in both versions but others need to be programmed specifically for the version that Ethereal is built with. The README.developer document located in the doc directory does not contain any information on the modifications to the GUI. As a reference you should use the GTK website at www.gtk.org as well as other GUI code located in the GTK directory.

The Item Factory

The main menu for Ethereal is created via a GTK item factory. The following information is extracted from the gtk/menu.c source file included in the Ethereal source distribution:

```
/* This is the GtkItemFactoryEntry structure used to generate new menus.
        Item 1: The menu path. The letter after the underscore indicates an
                accelerator key once the menu is open.
        Item 2: The accelerator key for the entry
        Item 3: The callback function.
        Item 4: The callback action.  This changes the parameters with
                which the function is called.  The default is 0.
        Item 5: The item type, used to define what kind of an item it is.
                Here are the possible values:

                NULL                    -> "<Item>"
                ""                      -> "<Item>"
                "<Title>"               -> create a title item
                "<Item>"                -> create a simple item
                "<ImageItem>"           -> create an item holding an image
                                           (gtk2)
```

```
    "<StockItem>"           -> create an item holding a stock
                               image (gtk2)

    "<CheckItem>"           -> create a check item

    "<ToggleItem>"          -> create a toggle item

    "<RadioItem>"           -> create a radio item

    <path>                  -> path of a radio item to link
                               against

    "<Separator>"           -> create a separator

    "<Tearoff>"             -> create a tearoff separator (gtk2)

    "<Branch>"              -> create an item to hold sub items
                               (optional)

    "<LastBranch>"          -> create a right justified branch
        Item 6: extra data needed for ImageItem and StockItem (gtk2)
  */
```

The set_menu_sensitivity function enables and disables the availability of
menu items based on a specified condition. Generally, you will only need to
modify the Ethereal menu if you are creating a tool or making a change to some
other portion of the GUI.

When the item factory option is selected, the function listed in Item 3 will
be called. In GTK, callback functions are what get called when an item is
selected.

Using GTK

When an item is selected, GTK passes a handle to the active selection. These are
called widgets in GTK.

```
void
my_widget(GtkWidget *w _U_, gpointer d _U_)
{
    GtkWidget      *main_vb
    GtkTooltips    *tooltips;
#if GTK_MAJOR_VERSION < 2
    GtkAccelGroup *accel_group;
#endif
```

Notes from the Underground…

Development Note

Note the _U_ value being defined in the my_widget function. The use of _U_ is to represent an undefined parameter. These values are not used within the function. The process of defining them as _U_ allows the compiler to not fail on the function due to undefined variables. This also eliminates the use of memory for values that you do not intend to use.

When our menu item is selected, GTK passes us the GTK widget pointer and data structure. We then create a new GTK widget for our window.

The GtkTooltips is a value that allows us to store information that will be displayed when the user places his or her mouse pointer over a GTK widget. For example, suppose that we have a button on our window that (when clicked) will change the current display filter to one of our choosing. Although the size of the button only allows us to label it as "Filter", we can define a tool tip that provides a more detailed description of the button's function.

The GtkAccelGroup is necessary for GTK version 1.2. It allows for accelerator keys to be used on the keyboard to access menu items.

```
if (mywindow_w != NULL) {
  /* There's already a "My Window" dialog box; reactivate it. */
  reactivate_window(mywindow_w);
  return;
}

mywindow = dlg_window_new("Ethereal: My Window");
SIGNAL_CONNECT(mywindow_w, "destroy", mywindow_destroy_cb, NULL);

tooltips = gtk_tooltips_new ();

#if GTK_MAJOR_VERSION < 2
  /* Accelerator group for the accelerators (or, as they're called in
    Windows and, I think, in Motif, "mnemonics"; Alt+<key> is a mnemonic,
```

```
      Ctrl+<key> is an accelerator). */
  accel_group = gtk_accel_group_new();
  gtk_window_add_accel_group(GTK_WINDOW(mywindow_w), accel_group);
#endif
```

We first check to make sure our window is not already open. If it is, then we reactivate it. If it is not, then we create a new dialog window. When you create the new window you should create a callback handler to take care of the window being closed by the user clicking the exit button in the upper right-hand corner of the dialog box. The SIGNAL_CONNECT function tells GTK what to do when the specified signal occurs. In this case it is the destroy signal that we are trapping for.

Finally, we initialize the tooltips. Notice that we only perform the accelerator group from GTK version 1.2. Accelerator keys in GTK 2.x are defined when creating the item. We will see this later.

```
  /* Container for each row of widgets */
  main_vb = gtk_vbox_new(FALSE, 3);
  gtk_container_border_width(GTK_CONTAINER(main_vb), 5);
  gtk_container_add(GTK_CONTAINER(mywindow_w), main_vb);
  gtk_widget_show(main_vb);
```

The first step is to create our main window. Next, we create a box on the new window. The gtk_vbox_new creates the new box that we will add to our window. The gtk_container_border_width defines the border for our window. The gtk_container_add now adds our new box to the main window. Finally, the gtk_widget_show forces GTK to paint the information to the screen. The following demonstrates the creation of an **OK** button on the main_vb window.

```
  /* Button row: OK button */
  bbox = gtk_hbutton_box_new();
  gtk_button_box_set_layout (GTK_BUTTON_BOX (bbox), GTK_BUTTONBOX_END);
  gtk_button_box_set_spacing(GTK_BUTTON_BOX(bbox), 5);
  gtk_container_add(GTK_CONTAINER(main_vb), bbox);
  gtk_widget_show(bbox);

#if GTK_MAJOR_VERSION < 2
  ok_bt = gtk_button_new_with_label ("OK");
#else
```

```
  ok_bt = gtk_button_new_from_stock(GTK_STOCK_OK);
#endif
  SIGNAL_CONNECT(ok_bt, "clicked", capture_prep_ok_cb, cap_open_w);
  GTK_WIDGET_SET_FLAGS(ok_bt, GTK_CAN_DEFAULT);
  gtk_box_pack_start (GTK_BOX (bbox), ok_bt, TRUE, TRUE, 0);
  gtk_widget_grab_default(ok_bt);
  gtk_widget_show(ok_bt);
```

The first section of this code creates a new horizontal button box, adds it to the main_vb window, and forces GTK to paint the new box.

We then check the GTK version and create the new button depending on the version of GTK. Note that GTK version 2.*x* allows us to specify the icon used for this button. This is how you can create custom icons and incorporate them into Ethereal. We register the callback function for GTK to use when the button is clicked, register the button as the default button, and finally paint the button on the screen.

You can also register widget data to a widget so that when it is selected then the data associated to the widget gets passed to the calling function. For example, in the gtk/find_dlg.c file, a number of defines are set to identify the buttons within the find window.

```
/* Capture callback data keys */
#define E_FIND_FILT_KEY        "find_filter_te"
#define E_FIND_BACKWARD_KEY    "find_backward"
```

Next, the keys are registered as data to the dialog with the object_set_data function.

```
  OBJECT_SET_DATA(find_frame_w, E_FIND_FILT_KEY, filter_text_box);
  OBJECT_SET_DATA(find_frame_w, E_FIND_BACKWARD_KEY, backward_rb);
```

Finally, when the find_frame_w is selected, the callback function can access the values of the attached buttons by calling the object_get_data function.

```
  filter_te = (GtkWidget *)OBJECT_GET_DATA(parent_w, E_FIND_FILT_KEY);
  backward_rb = (GtkWidget *)OBJECT_GET_DATA(parent_w,
E_FIND_BACKWARD_KEY);
```

The GTK website contains many examples and a window builder tool that you can download and experiment with. To program in GTK you must know the static defines for predefined items like GTK_STOCK_XXX and GTK_CAN_DEFAULT. All of this information is available from the GTK website.

TAPS

Ethereal implements a tap system to allow for real-time statistics during packet captures. These can also be used by tools that register to the tap interface and command Ethereal to redissect a saved packet capture file. The tap system is documented in the README.tapping document located in the doc directory. Also in the main source directory you will find a number of tap-xxx files you can use for a reference on the tap interface. The file gtk/endpoint_talkers_table.c can be used for an example of how to implement a TAP inside of an included tools menu option.

You implement the tap interface in two steps. The first step is to install the tap into the protocol dissector you would like to get information from. The second step is to add the tap listener to your application. Many of the protocol dissectors included in Ethereal already contain taps. Most likely you will only need to create your tap listener and perform the work you need to do. If you find that a tap is not installed in the protocol you need, the process is simple through the use of only a few lines of code. Please refer to the README. tapping for more information.

Plug-ins

Ethereal also supports the implementation of protocol dissectors as plug-ins. Plug-ins are preferred by some developers because they can be developed and debugged without having to rebuild the whole Ethereal distribution. You can compile and build your plug-in and then copy the binary to the plugins directory under the name of your plug-in. Ethereal ships with a number of plug-ins and each can be loaded or unloaded depending on whether they are installed prior to launching Ethereal. The plugin interface mimics the dissector interface. In fact, plug-ins are first developed as a normal dissector. Then, additional code is added to make the dissector a plug-in. The key part of developing a plug-in is the plugin_init and plugin_address_table_init functions to register the plug-in with Ethereal. The file README.plugins located in the doc directory outlines the steps you need to take to generate a plug-in dissector for Ethereal.

Summary

This chapter has outlined some of the most important parts of developing in Ethereal. There are several kinds of components to which you can contribute:

- Protocol Dissectors
- Plug-ins
- The Ethereal GUI
- Tools

This chapter went into great detail documenting the proper steps to take when creating a dissector. By consulting the README.developer document in the doc directory, you can cut and paste a template to help you get started. However, since the document does not clearly define each step necessary in the development process, this chapter attempts to provide these steps in a logical order. You first modify the header and the *include* statements. We then register the protocol dissector. Finally, create the dissector code to actually decode the data. The important factor in the decode section is to utilize the hf array in the register function so that elements can be filtered upon.

This chapter also covered several advanced topics including a basic guide to GTK programming. Many of the topics covered will be experienced by someone creating a protocol dissector. Handling of the advanced topic issues correctly can eliminate many hours of unnecessary work and research. After debugging your work, make sure you go back and cleanup as much of the code as possible. Insert comments to make the code clear. In addition, make sure you remove unused variable definitions. If possible, clean up any remaining warnings displayed in the compile process by your compiler. Finally, please contribute your modifications back to the Ethereal project by e-mailing a patch to the ethereal-dev mailing list. Again, make certain that any information that you contribute back to Ethereal is not going to violate any proprietary claims. Ethereal is released under the GPL and all contributions should be consistent with this licensing agreement.

Solutions Fast Track

Prerequisites for Developing Ethereal

☑ The Ethereal source must be obtained before you can start any new development. You have the option of downloading different types of download packages. The Ethereal website, www.ethereal.com, has links to download previous versions, the current version, nightly backups, and CVS code.

☑ The requirements for Windows based computers are different from UNIX/Linux based computers. Windows based computers require additional tools to emulate the UNIX/Linux environment.

☑ To build Ethereal, a number of libraries and tools will need to be used. There are several libraries that are optional depending on whether you decide to add a specific feature.

☑ Ethereal can be compiled and run on a number of operating systems. For this reason you must ensure that you program in ANSI C for portability between all of the supported platforms.

☑ Before you start any work on Ethereal, make sure you can compile and link Ethereal into its executable binary form.

Ethereal Design

☑ The main directory of the source distribution is the primary location of protocol dissectors, protocol taps, and dissector code.

☑ The GTK directory is used to store the GUI source used in Ethereal. You will find the main application as well as the toolbar and menu source in this directory.

☑ Most of the utility functions for Ethereal are located in the epan directory. These functions include conversion functions as well as tvb and column functions.

☑ The doc directory of the distribution is where you will locate most of the documentation that is shipped with the Ethereal source. This is a great resource to anyone wanting to develop in Ethereal.

Developing a Dissector

☑ Before you start any Ethereal development, make sure you can build the Ethereal executable.

☑ The first step in developing a dissector is to utilize the template provided in the README.developer document.

☑ It is important to consider the GPL and other factors when modifying the header comments from the template. Note that this is where you need to add your personal information so you can receive credit for your work.

☑ Global Ethereal functions are provided to ease the development of dissectors.

☑ Registering your protocol dissector is a necessary process so that Ethereal knows when to pass packet data on to your dissector.

☑ The hf array provides the mechanism to incorporate display and color filters.

☑ Using tvb_get_xxx functions to access data for the frame. The data passed to your dissector does not include the data that has already been decoded by other dissectors.

☑ Using the proto_tree functions allow you to print to the decode pane of the Ethereal GUI.

☑ One of the most important steps a dissector should do is to pass any remaining packet data back to Ethereal. This way future dissectors can be written to dissect the remaining packet data.

Advanced Topics

☑ Creating sub-trees allows you to display data in a more informative way in the decode pane of the GUI. Users needing more detailed information can expand the item to view the details.

☑ Ethereal provides a mechanism to display bitfields in a graphical view. This allows the user to see from the bit display what the actual fields represent.

☑ Many dissectors must be able to handle unicode strings. Unicode strings present a challenge to normal string processing because of their 2 byte width.

☑ There are situations that require you to have the ability to track request and reply packet pairs. Ethereal provides the conversation list functions to keep specific information of a source packet so that it can be matched to a reply packet.

☑ Packet retransmissions are a normal occurrence on most networks. It is important that Ethereal protocol dissectors can handle this type of condition. The use of conversation lists can help in this process.

☑ Users should have the ability to configure different components in Ethereal. This includes the ability to turn on or off a feature within your protocol dissector. The preference files give you a place to store values so your dissector can retrieve them the next time Ethereal is active.

☑ During the processing of data within a packet, you may need to know certain information from another dissector. Ethereal provides a mechanism to pass data between dissectors with the pinfo->private_data pointer.

☑ Fragmentation occurs when the payload of a packet exceeds the actual size of the packet. The protocol will break the payload into pieces and then send each one within a fragment. The destination device will then collect all of the fragments and reassemble the original payload. Dissectors need to have the ability to process these packet fragments. Ethereal utilizes several de-fragment functions to track and reassemble fragmented data.

☑ There are many times within the packet data that the number displayed is a user-friendly string to define the value. Most gerror codes are returned as numerical values but the number itself means little to the end user. Value strings give you the ability to convert numerical values to a meaningful message.

☑ Ethereal's GUI utilizes the GTK item factory for creating and manipulating its menu items. Adding a new menu item is a quick process by adding new items to the item factory.

☑ If you plan to develop or modify any of the Ethereal GUI you will need to become familiar with GTK programming and its rich set of functions. The GTK website provides documentation and examples on proper ways of writing to the GTK library: www.gtk.org.

☑ Ethereal provides a mechanism to receive real-time data. Tools can utilize the tap system to gather information from a live capture or from an existing packet trace.

☑ Packet dissectors do not have to be compiled into the Ethereal source. The plugin interface provides a mechanism to convert your dissector from the packet-xxx type source to a plugin. Plugins can be compiled quicker and can be added and removed prior to launching the Ethereal executable.

Frequently Asked Questions

The following Frequently Asked Questions, answered by the authors of this book, are designed to both measure your understanding of the concepts presented in this chapter and to assist you with real-life implementation of these concepts. To have your questions about this chapter answered by the author, browse to **www.syngress.com/solutions** and click on the **"Ask the Author"** form. You will also gain access to thousands of other FAQs at ITFAQnet.com.

Q: How does Ethereal know when a dissector should be called?

A: The dissector_add function defines the condition in which the dissector should be called.

Q: Where do you locate the design document for developing Ethereal?

A: There really isn't a design document, but the README.developer document and the other documents contained in the doc directory contain useful information.

Q: How do you pass information from one dissector to another?

A: By using the pinfo->private_data to pass a pointer to the other dissectors data.

Q: How do I know what functions are provided by Ethereal?

A: We have tried to list many of the common ones within this chapter, but for a complete listing you should look at the header files of the source for all *exports*. Exports are the mechanism that allows you to define the public functions that will be available to the rest of the application. Functions that are not exported are limited in visibility to the module in which they are defined. Although they may be limited in their visibility, it is important that you do not create a function within your dissector that might conflict with a public function that has been exported. This is one of the reasons why you should declare your private functions as static unless you plan to export the function for use with other Ethereal modules.

Q: Can I build Ethereal with Microsoft Visual C++?

A: Yes, you just need to make sure you have all of the required libraries and tools. It is important to realize that building under Microsoft Visual C++ does not include using the visual studio environment. Building Ethereal utilizes the command line interface and you build Ethereal.exe with nmake.exe. Ethereal does not include any visual studio workspace or configuration files to be used with the visual studio GUI. To build Ethereal under Microsoft Visual C++ you open a CMD window and then navigate to the main source directory of Ethereal. Finally you execute nmake with the syntax – **nmake –f makefile.nmake**.

Q: Where can I find more information on programming the GUI?

A: The GTK website has development tutorials and examples at www.gtk.org

Supported Protocols

This section lists the 400+ protocols, by description, that are supported by Ethereal protocol decoders. The display fields, field values, and elongated descriptions of each protocol can be found on the accompanying CD-ROM in the /filters folder of Chapter 5.

Ethereal 0.10.0a provides 483 protocol keywords. This list shows the protocol names and descriptions.

aal1 ATM AAL1

aal3_4 ATM AAL3/4

aarp AppleTalk Address Resolution Protocol

acap Application Configuration Access Protocol

acn ACN

afp AppleTalk Filing Protocol

afs Andrew File System (AFS)

ah Authentication Header

aim AOL Instant Messenger

ajp13 Apache JServ Protocol v1.3

alcap AAL type 2 signaling protocol – Capability set 1 (Q.2630.1)

ans Intel ANS probe

ansi_637_tele ANSI IS-637-A (SMS) Teleservice Layer

ansi_637_trans ANSI IS-637-A (SMS) Transport Layer

ansi_683 ANSI IS-683-A (OTA (Mobile))

ansi_a_bsmap ANSI A-I/F BSMAP

ansi_a_dtap ANSI A-I/F DTAP

ansi_map ANSI Mobile Application Part

aodv Ad hoc On–demand Distance Vector Routing Protocol

arcnet ARCNET

arp Address Resolution Protocol

artnet Art-Net

asap Aggregate Server Access Protocol

ascend Lucent/Ascend debug output

asf Alert Standard Forum

asn1 ASN.1 decoding

asp AppleTalk Session Protocol

atm ATM

atp AppleTalk Transaction Protocol packet

atsvc Microsoft Task Scheduler Service

auto_rp Cisco Auto-RP

bacapp Building Automation and Control Network APDU

bacnet Building Automation and Control Network NPDU

bacp PPP Bandwidth Allocation Control Protocol

bap PPP Bandwidth Allocation Protocol

beep Blocks Extensible Exchange Protocol

bfdcontrol Bi-directional Fault Detection Control Message

bgp Border Gateway Protocol

bicc Bearer Independent Call Control

bofl Wellfleet Breath of Life

bootp Bootstrap Protocol

bootparams Boot Parameters

bossvr DCE/RPC BOS Server

brdwlk Boardwalk

browser Microsoft Windows Browser Protocol

bssap BSSAP/BSAP

bssgp BSS GPRS Protocol

budb DCE/RPC BUDB

butc DCE/RPC BUTC

bvlc BACnet Virtual Link Control

cbcp PPP Callback Control Protocol

ccp PPP Compression Control Protocol

CCSDS CCSDS

cdp Cisco Discovery Protocol

cdpcp PPP CDP Control Protocol

cds_clerkserver CDS Clerk Server Calls

cds_solicit DCE/RPC CDS Solicitation

cflow Cisco NetFlow

cgmp Cisco Group Management Protocol

chap PPP Challenge Handshake Authentication Protocol

chdlc Cisco HDLC

cldap Connectionless Lightweight Directory Access Protocol

clearcase Clearcase NFS

clnp ISO 8473 CLNP ConnectionLess Network Protocol

cltp ISO 8602 CLTP ConnectionLess Transport Protocol

comp_data PPP Compressed Datagram

conv DCE/RPC Conversation Manager

cops Common Open Policy Service

cosine CoSine IPNOS L2 debug output

cotp ISO 8073 COTP Connection-Oriented Transport Protocol

cpfi Cross Point Frame Injector

cpha Check Point High Availability Protocol

cprpc_server DNS Control Program Server

cups Common Unix Printing System (CUPS) Browsing Protocol

data Data

dccp Distributed Checksum Clearinghouse Protocol

dce_dfs DCE DFS Calls

dce_update DCE/RPC UpServer

dcerpc DCE RPC

ddp Datagram Delivery Protocol

ddtp Dynamic DNS Tools Protocol

dec_stp DEC Spanning Tree Protocol

dfs Microsoft Distributed File System

dhcpv6 DHCPv6

diameter Diameter Protocol

distcc Distcc Distributed Compiler

dlsw Data Link SWitching

dns Domain Name Service

dnsserver Windows 2000 DNS

docsis DOCSIS 1.1

docsis_bpkmattr DOCSIS Baseline Privacy Key Management Attributes

docsis_bpkmreq DOCSIS Baseline Privacy Key Management Request

docsis_bpkmrsp DOCSIS Baseline Privacy Key Management Response

docsis_dsaack DOCSIS Dynamic Service Addition Acknowledge

docsis_dsareq DOCSIS Dynamic Service Addition Request

docsis_dsarsp DOCSIS Dynamic Service Addition Response

docsis_dscack DOCSIS Dynamic Service Change Acknowledgement

docsis_dscreq DOCSIS Dynamic Service Change Request

docsis_dscrsp DOCSIS Dynamic Service Change Response

docsis_dsdreq DOCSIS Dynamic Service Delete Request

docsis_dsdrsp DOCSIS Dynamic Service Delete Response

docsis_map DOCSIS Upstream Bandwidth Allocation

docsis_mgmt DOCSIS Mac Management

docsis_regack DOCSIS Registration Acknowledge

docsis_regreq DOCSIS Registration Requests

docsis_regrsp DOCSIS Registration Responses

docsis_rngreq DOCSIS MAP Messages

docsis_rngrsp DOCSIS Ranging Response

docsis_tlv DOCSIS Appendix C TLV's

docsis_uccreq DOCSIS Upstream Channel Change Request

docsis_uccrsp DOCSIS Upstream Channel Change Response

docsis_ucd DOCSIS Upstream Channel Descriptor

docsis_vsif DOCSIS Vendor Specific Endodings

drsuapi Microsoft Directory Replication Service

dsi Data Stream Interface

dtsprovider DCE Distributed Time Service Provider

dtsstime_req DCE Distributed Time Service Local Server

dvmrp Distance Vector Multicast Routing Protocol

eap Extensible Authentication Protocol

eapol 802.1x Authentication

echo Echo

edonkey eDonkey Protocol

eigrp Enhanced Interior Gateway Routing Protocol

els FC Extended Link Svc

enc OpenBSD Encapsulating Device

enip EtherNet/IP (Industrial Protocol)

enttec ENTTEC

epm DCE/RPC Endpoint Mapper

epm4 DCE/RPC Endpoint Mapper4

esis ISO 9542 ESIS Routing Information Exchange Protocol

esp Encapsulating Security Payload

eth Ethernet

etherip Ethernet over IP

fc Fiber Channel

FCdNS Fiber Channel Name Server

fcct Fiber Channel Common Transport

fcip FCIP

fcp Fibre Channel Protocol for SCSI

fcs FC Fabric Configuration Server

fcsp Fiber Channel Security Protocol

fddi Fiber Distributed Data Interface

fix Financial Information eXchange Protocol

fldb DCE/RPC FLDB

fr Frame Relay

frame Frame

ftp File Transfer Protocol (FTP)

ftp-data FTP Data

ftserver FTServer Operations

fw1 Checkpoint FW-1

FZS Fibre Channel Fabric Zone Server

giop General Inter-ORB Protocol

giop-coseventcomm Coseventcomm Dissector Using GIOP API

giop-cosnaming Cosnaming Dissector Using GIOP API

gmrp GARP Multicast Registration Protocol

gnutella Gnutella Protocol

gprs_ns GPRS Network service

gre Generic Routing Encapsulation

gryphon DG Gryphon Protocol

gsm_a_bssmap GSM A-I/F BSSMAP

gsm_a_dtap GSM A-I/F DTAP

gsm_a_rp GSM A-I/F RP

gsm_map GSM Mobile Application Part

gsm_sms GSM SMS TPDU (GSM 03.40)

gss-api Generic Security Service Application Program Interface

gtp GPRS Tunneling Protocol

gvrp GARP VLAN Registration Protocol

h1 Sinec H1 Protocol

h225 H225

h245 H245

h261 ITU-T Recommendation H.261

h263 ITU-T Recommendation H.263 RTP Payload header (RFC2190)

h4501 H4501

hclnfsd Hummingbird NFS Daemon

hpext HP Extended Local-Link Control

hsrp Cisco Hot Standby Router Protocol

http Hypertext Transfer Protocol

hyperscsi HyperSCSI

iapp Inter-Access-Point Protocol

ib Interbase

icap Internet Content Adaptation Protocol

icl_rpc DCE/RPC ICL RPC

icmp Internet Control Message Protocol

icmpv6 Internet Control Message Protocol v6

icp Internet Cache Protocol

icq ICQ Protocol

igap Internet Group Membership Authentication Protocol

igmp Internet Group Management Protocol

igrp Cisco Interior Gateway Routing Protocol

ilmi ILMI

imap Internet Message Access Protocol

initshutdown Remote Shutdown

ip Internet Protocol

ipcomp IP Payload Compression

ipcp PPP IP Control Protocol

ipfc IP Over FC

ipmi Intelligent Platform Management Interface

ipp Internet Printing Protocol

ipv6 Internet Protocol Version 6

ipv6cp PPP IPv6 Control Protocol

ipx Internetwork Packet eXchange

ipxmsg IPX Message

ipxrip IPX Routing Information Protocol

ipxsap Service Advertisement Protocol

ipxwan IPX WAN

irc Internet Relay Chat

isakmp Internet Security Association and Key Management Protocol

iscsi iSCSI

isdn ISDN

isis ISO 10589 ISIS InTRA Domain Routing Information Exchange Protocol

isl Cisco ISL

isns iSNS

isup ISDN User Part

iua ISDN Q.921-User Adaptation Layer

jabber Jabber XML Messaging

kadm5 Kerberos Administration

kerberos Kerberos

klm Kernel Lock Manager

kpasswd MS Kpasswd

krb5rpc DCE/RPC Kerberos V

l2tp Layer 2 Tunneling Protocol

lacp Link Aggregation Control Protocol

lane ATM LAN Emulation

lanman Microsoft Windows Lanman Remote API Protocol

lapb Link Access Procedure Balanced (LAPB)

lapbether Link Access Procedure Balanced Ethernet (LAPBETHER)

lapd Link Access Procedure, Channel D (LAPD)

laplink Laplink

lcp PPP Link Control Protocol

ldap Lightweight Directory Access Protocol

ldp Label Distribution Protocol

llap LocalTalk Link Access Protocol

llc Logical-Link Control

lmi Local Management Interface

lmp Link Management Protocol (LMP)

lpd Line Printer Daemon Protocol

lsa Microsoft Local Security Architecture

lsa_ds Microsoft Local Security Architecture (Directory Services)

lwapp LWAPP Encapsulated Packet

lwapp-cntl LWAP Control Message

lwapp-l3 LWAPP Layer 3 Packet

lwres Light Weight DNS RESolver (BIND9)

m2pa MTP2 Peer Adaptation Layer

m2tp MTP 2 Transparent Proxy

m2ua MTP 2 User Adaptation Layer

m3ua MTP 3 User Adaptation Layer

mailslot SMB MailSlot Protocol

malformed Malformed Packet

mapi Microsoft Exchange MAPI

mbtcp Modbus/TCP

mdshdr MDS Header

megaco MEGACO

messenger Microsoft Messenger Service

mgcp Media Gateway Control Protocol

mgmt DCE/RPC Remote Management

mip Mobile IP

mipv6 Mobile IPv6

mmse   MMS Message Encapsulation

mount   Mount Service

mp   PPP Multilink Protocol

mpeg1   RFC 2250 MPEG1

mpls   MultiProtocol Label Switching Header

mplscp   PPP MPLS Control Protocol

mrdisc   Multicast Router DISCovery protocol

msdp   Multicast Source Discovery Protocol

msnip   MSNIP: Multicast Source Notification of Interest Protocol

msnms   MSN Messenger Service

msproxy   MS Proxy Protocol

mtp2   Message Transfer Part Level 2

mtp3   Message Transfer Part Level 3

mtp3mg   Message Transfer Part Level 3 Management

mysql   MySQL Protocol

nbdgm   NetBIOS Datagram Service

nbipx   NetBIOS over IPX

nbns   NetBIOS Name Service

nbp   Name Binding Protocol

nbss   NetBIOS Session Service

ncp   NetWare Core Protocol

ndmp   Network Data Management Protocol

ndps   Novell Distributed Print System

netbios   NetBIOS

netlogon   Microsoft Windows Logon Protocol

nfs   Network File System

nfsacl   NFSACL

nfsauth   NFSAUTH

nisplus   NIS+

nispluscb   NIS+ Callback

nlm   Network Lock Manager Protocol

nlsp   NetWare Link Services Protocol

nmpi   Name Management Protocol over IPX

nntp   Network News Transfer Protocol

nspi   NSPI

ntlmssp   NTLM Secure Service Provider

ntp   Network Time Protocol

null   Null/Loopback

oamaal   ATM OAM AAL

ospf   Open Shortest Path First

oxid   DCOM OXID Resolver

pap   PPP Password Authentication Protocol

pcli   Packet Cable Lawful Intercept

pcnfsd   PC NFS

per   Packed Encoding Rules (ASN.1 X.691)

pflog   OpenBSD Packet Filter log file

pflog-old OpenBSD Packet Filter log file, pre 3.4

pgm Pragmatic General Multicast

pim Protocol Independent Multicast

pipe SMB Pipe Protocol

pop Post Office Protocol

portmap Portmap

ppp Point-to-Point Protocol

pppmux PPP Multiplexing

pppmuxcp PPPMux Control Protocol

pppoed PPP-over-Ethernet Discovery

pppoes PPP-over-Ethernet Session

pptp Point-to-Point Tunneling Protocol

prism Prism

q2931 Q.2931

q931 Q.931

q933 Q.933

qllc Qualified Logical Link Control

quake Quake Network Protocol

quake2 Quake II Network Protocol

quake3 Quake III Arena Network Protocol

quakeworld QuakeWorld Network Protocol

radius Radius Protocol

ranap Radio Access Network Application Part

raw Raw packet data

raw_sip Session Initiation Protocol (SIP as raw text)

rdm RDM

remact DCOM Remote Activation

rep_proc AFS (4.0) Replication Server call declarations

rip Routing Information Protocol

ripng RIPng

rlogin Rlogin Protocol

rmcp Remote Management Control Protocol

rmi Java RMI

rmp HP Remote Maintenance Protocol

roverride Remote Override interface

rpc Remote Procedure Call

rpc_browser RPC Browser

rpc_netlogon Microsoft Network Logon

rpl Remote Program Load

rpriv Privilege Server Operations

rquota Remote Quota

rs_acct DCE/RPC RS_ACCT

rs_attr Registry Server Attributes Manipulation Interface

rs_bind DCE/RPC RS_BIND

rs_misc DCE/RPC RS_MISC

rs_pgo DCE Name Service

rs_plcy RS Interface Properties

rs_prop_acct DCE/RPC RS_PROP_ACCT

rs_repadm Registry server administration operations.

rs_replist DCE/RPC Repserver Calls

rs_unix DCE/RPC RS_UNIX

rsec_login Remote sec_login preauth interface.

rsh Remote Shell

rstat RSTAT

rsvp Resource ReserVation Protocol (RSVP)

rsync RSYNC File Synchroniser

rtcfg RTCFG

rtcp Real-time Transport Control Protocol

rtmp Routing Table Maintenance Protocol

rtnet RTNET

rtp Real-Time Transport Protocol

rtpevent RFC 2833 RTP Event

rtsp Real Time Streaming Protocol

rwall Remote Wall Protocol

rx RX Protocol

sadmind SADMIND

samr Microsoft Security Account Manager

sap Session Announcement Protocol

sb3 Fiber Channel Single Byte Command

sccp Signaling Connection Control Part

sccpmg Signaling Connection Control Part Management

scsi SCSI

sctp Stream Control Transmission Protocol

sdlc Synchronous Data Link Control (SDLC)

sdp Session Description Protocol

sebek SEBEK - Kernel Data Capture

secidmap DCE Security ID Mapper

serialization Java Serialization

ses ISO 8327-1 OSI Session Protocol

sflow InMon sFlow

sgimount SGI Mount Service

short Short Frame

sip Session Initiation Protocol

skinny Skinny Client Control Protocol

slarp Cisco SLARP

slimp3 SliMP3 Communication Protocol

sll Linux cooked-mode capture

smb SMB (Server Message Block Protocol)

smpp Short Message Peer to Peer

smtp Simple Mail Transfer Protocol

smux SNMP Multiplex Protocol

sna Systems Network Architecture

sna_xid Systems Network Architecture XID

snaeth SNA-over-Ethernet

snmp Simple Network Management Protocol

socks Socks Protocol

sonmp Nortel SONMP

spnego Spnego

spnego-krb5 SPNEGO-KRB5

spoolss Microsoft Spool Subsystem

spray SPRAY

spx Sequenced Packet eXchange

srvloc Service Location Protocol

srvsvc Microsoft Server Service

sscop SSCOP

ssh SSH Protocol

ssl Secure Socket Layer

stat Network Status Monitor Protocol

statnotify Network Status Monitor CallBack Protocol

stp Spanning Tree Protocol

stun Simple Traversal of UDP Through NAT

sua SS7 SCCP-User Adaptation Layer

svcctl Microsoft Service Control

swils Fiber Channel SW_ILS

syslog Syslog message

t38 T38

tacacs TACACS

tacplus TACACS+

tapi Microsoft Telephony API Service

tcap Transaction Capabilities Application Part

tcp Transmission Control Protocol

tds Tabular Data Stream

telnet Telnet

teredo TEREDO Tunneling IPv6 over UDP through NATs

tftp Trivial File Transfer Protocol

time Time Protocol

tkn4int DCE/RPC TokenServer Calls

tns Transparent Network Substrate Protocol

tpcp Alteon – Transparent Proxy Cache Protocol

tpkt TPKT

tr Token-Ring

trmac Token-Ring Media Access Control

tsp Time Synchronization Protocol

tzsp Tazmen Sniffer Protocol

ubikdisk DCE/RPC FLDB UBIK TRANSFER

ubikvote DCE/RPC FLDB UBIKVOTE

ucp Universal Computer Protocol

udp User Datagram Protocol

udpencap UDP Encapsulation of IPsec Packets

unreassembled Un-reassembled Fragmented Packet

v120 Async data over ISDN (V.120)

vines_arp Banyan Vines ARP

vines_echo Banyan Vines Echo

vines_frp Banyan Vines Fragmentation Protocol

vines_icp Banyan Vines ICP

vines_ip Banyan Vines IP

vines_ipc Banyan Vines IPC

vines_llc Banyan Vines LLC

vines_rtp Banyan Vines RTP

vines_spp Banyan Vines SPP

vj PPP VJ Compression

vlan 802.1q Virtual LAN

vrrp Virtual Router Redundancy Protocol

vtp Virtual Trunking Protocol

wap-wsp Wireless Session Protocol

wap-wsp-wtp Wireless Transaction Protocol

wap-wtls Wireless Transport Layer Security

wbxml WAP Binary XML

wccp Web Cache Coordination Protocol

wcp Wellfleet Compression

whdlc Wellfleet HDLC

who Who

winreg Microsoft Registry

wkssvc Microsoft Workstation Service

wlan IEEE 802.11 wireless LAN

wlan_mgt IEEE 802.11 wireless LAN management frame

wlancap AVS WLAN Capture header

x.25 X.25

x.29 X.29

x11 X11

xdmcp X Display Manager Control Protocol

xot X.25 over TCP

xyplex Xyplex

yhoo Yahoo Messenger Protocol

ymsg Yahoo YMSG Messenger Protocol

ypbind Yellow Pages Bind

yppasswd Yellow Pages Password

ypserv Yellow Pages Service

ypxfr Yellow Pages Transfer

zebra Zebra Protocol

zip Zone Information Protocol

About the CD

This CD-ROM contains the installation, reference, and packet capture files that are used in various chapters of this book. The files for each chapter are located in the directory from which they are referenced in the book.

Chapter 3 contains the Ethereal 0.10.0 installation files for Windows, Red Hat Linux 9.0, Solaris 9, and the Ethereal source code. All files are provided in uncompressed .tar, .exe, .rpm, or Solaris package format. This chapter also includes prerequisite and supporting programs for the Ethereal installation. These directories are: adns, ethereal, gtk+_glib, gzip, pcap, pcre, perl, snmp, and zlib. Newer versions of Ethereal may have been released since the creation of the CD-ROM, so please check the Ethereal website at www.ethereal.com.

Chapter 5 contains an extensive Ethereal display filter reference. It is located in the /filters directory.

Chapters 4 and 8 contain several packet capture examples. These are located in the /captures directory. The packet captures range from large network scans to trojan backdoor activity. Some of these packet captures were obtained from the Honeynet Project while others were lab generated. Taking time to analyze these packet captures will give you valuable hands-on experience with Ethereal and its features.

Index

A

aarp (Appletalk Address Resolution Protocol), 213
About Plugins dialog box, 196–197
absolute time, 230, 239–240
Accellent
  Ethereal compatibility, 44
  as format for reading capture files, 305
  as format for saving capture files, 307
ÄCK flag, 354, 355–356
aclocal-fallback directory, 388
aclocal-missing directory, 388
Address Resolution Protocol, 25–26, 29, 213, 217, 511
ADNS (Asynchronous DNS) library, 205, 384. *See also* GNU adns
AG Group, 43, 305
ah keyword, 213
AiroPeek, 43, 305
AIX iptrace, 44, 305
Analyze menu
  Contents of TCP Stream window, 179–181
  Decode As dialog box, 177–179
  Edit Display Filter List dialog box, 172–175
  Enabled Protocols dialog box, 176–177
  illustrated, 171
  list of options, 171–172
  Match submenu, 175–176
  overview, 171
  Prepare submenu, 175
  Protocol Hierarchy Statistics dialog box, 192–193
  Statistics submenu, 194
  Summary dialog box, 192
  TCP Stream Analysis submenu, 181–192
Analyzer sniffer, 10–11

and operator, 212–213, 244
ANSI-C code, 382
AntiSniff, 30
Appletalk, 213, 217
application layer, Open Systems Interconnection (OSI) model, 16
Apply Color Filters dialog box, 156–160
arithmetic operators, 218
ARP (Address Resolution Protocol), 25–26, 29, 213, 217, 511
ASCII strings, 235
Asynchronous DNS (ADNS) library, 205, 384. *See also* GNU adns
atalk keyword, 213, 217, 511
atk library, 385
atmsnoop program, 43, 304
Authentication Header, 213
automount feature, 81

B

back doors, 7–8, 359–363
Background Color dialog box, 157
Biondi, Philipe, 348
Bison, 386
bitfields
  displaying, 417, 432
  dissector considerations, 415–417, 432
  in tcpdump syntax, 221–223
bitwise operators, 218, 221–223
Black Orifice, 7
Boolean fields, 230, 233–234
Boot Protocol (BOOTP), 19
broadcast domains, 22, 23
buffers, as network analyzer component, 4
byte sequences, 230, 236–237, 241, 242–243
bzip2 files, 79

C

C language, 382, 435
cable taps, 21–22, 27
capture drivers, 4, 78, 121–122. *See also*
    libpcap
capture files
    command-line options, 201
    File menu options, 136–147
    large, 168–169
    opening, 138, 305–306
    printing, 141–147
    reading (*See* reading capture files)
    saving, 140–141, 306–307, 350
Capture Filter dialog box, 251
capture filters
    adding to list in Capture Filter dialog
        box, 252
    deleting from list in Capture Filter
        dialog box, 253
    vs. display filters, 48, 206, 208–209, 260
    examples, 224–227
    exchanging with others, 254
    language manual, 260
    saving, 252, 253, 259
    testing, 224
    user interface, 249–254
    writing, 209–227, 257–258
Capture menu
    Capture Options dialog box, 162–169
    Edit Capture Filter List dialog box,
        169–170
    illustrated, 161
    list of options, 162
    overview, 161
Capture Options dialog box, 162–169
Carnivore, 11, 12–13
carriage return, line feed (CR/LF), 393
Carrier Sense Multiple Access/Collision
    Detection (CSMA/CD) protocol,
    20–21
CD-ROM, mounting, 81

cd00r sniffer, 8
Century Tap cable taps, 21
Check Promiscuous Mode (CPM) tool,
    31
Cinco Networks, 43, 305
Cisco, 25, 305
cleanbld.bat file, 387
clnp keyword, 214
Code Red worm, 367–370
col_append_str function, 407
collision detection, 21
collision domains, 22, 23, 37
color filters, 156–160
Coloring Rules option, 246
col_set_str function, 406–407
column functions. *See* column-utils.h file
column-utils.h file, 308, 396
column_info.h file, 397
Combs, Gerald, 41
command-line options
    editcap, 283–284
    Ethereal, 200–202, 204
    HP-UX nettl, 343–344
    vs. menus, 200–202
    mergecap, 289–290
    snoop, 328
    Snort, 322
    TCPDump, 314
    Tethereal, 263–267, 309–310
    text2pcap, 295–297
    WinDump, 317–318
company policies, 33
comparison operators, 230–231
compression utilities, 79
Concurrent Version System (CVS),
    51–52, 117, 381, 410
config.nmake file, 387
configure file, 117–120, 387
Connect scans, 355–356
Connectionless Network Protocol, 214
contains operator, 237, 241, 259

Contents dialog box, Help menu, 195

Contents of TCP Stream window, 179–181

context-sensitive menus, 197–200

conversation.h file, 396

conversations, 418–419, 433

copyleft, 42

CoSine L2 debug, 44, 305

CSMA/CD (Carrier Sense Multiple Access/Collision Detection) protocol, 20–21

custom icons, 390

CVS (Concurrent Version System), 51–52, 117, 381, 410

Cygwin, 385, 386

D

DARPA (Defense Advanced Research Projects Agency), 18

data link layer, Open Systems Interconnection (OSI) model, 17

Data View Window
  defined, 47, 128
  illustrated, 133, 134
  overview, 132–134
  pop-up menu, 200
  using with Protocol Tree Window, 133

DBS Etherwatch, 44, 305

DCS100 network analyzer, 11–14

debian directory, 388

decnet keyword, 214, 217

Decode As dialog box, 177–179

decodes, as network analyzer component, 4

Defense Advanced Research Projects Agency (DARPA), 18

denial of service (DoS) attacks, 16

Department of Defense, 18

dependencies, 81–82, 99, 100–101, 102, 103, 104, 108, 109–114

developer kits, 383–386

developer mailing list, 381

Digital Equipment Corporation, 214, 217

directories, 388–392

directory path, 124

discovery. *See* scanning

Display Filter dialog box, 251

display-filter fields
  address, 230, 237–239
  boolean, 230, 233–234
  byte sequence, 230, 236–237, 241, 242–243
  expressions in, 229–249
  floating point, 230, 234
  frame-number, 230, 233
  glossary of names, 248–249
  hidden, 247
  integer, 230, 231–233
  list of field types, 230
  list of operators, 230–231
  and logical operations, 244
  logical operators in, 244
  multiple protocol occurrences, 244–246
  overview, 229
  ranges, 241–243
  ranges functionality, 241–243
  string, 230, 234–236
  time, 230, 239–240

display filters
  adding to list in Display Filter dialog box, 252
  vs. capture filters, 48, 206, 208–209, 260
  constructing in Filter Expression dialog box, 254–256
  deleting from list in Display Filter dialog box, 253
  exchanging with others, 254

Internet Protocol, 49–50
language manual, 209
overview, 48–49
saving, 252, 253, 259
vs. tcpdump filters, 227
user interface, 249–254
using to select packets, 246
writing, 227–256, 258
Display Options dialog box, 155–156
dissector_add function, 434
dissectors
    and bitfields, 415–417
    considerations, 413–424
    and conversations, 418–419
    copying templates, 393–395
    creating, 401–408
    creating sub-trees, 413–415
    defining include files, 395–397
    developing, 392–412, 432
    displaying data in decode, 408
    how they work, 410–412
    list of plugins, 391
    naming, 392
    and packet fragmentation, 422, 433
    and packet retransmissions, 419–420,
        433
    passing data between, 420–421
    passing on payloads, 408–409
    as plug-ins, 429, 434
    registering, 397–400
    role in Ethernet history, 41–42
    running, 409–410
    saving preference settings, 421–422
    and unicode strings, 417–418
DNS (Domain Name System)
    asynchronous-capable, 77
    lookups, 29, 205
    reverse lookups, 139
    and TCP, 19
    and UDP, 19
doc directory, 388–389

DoD (Department of Defense) model,
    18
Domain Name System (DNS)
    asynchronous-capable, 77
    lookups, 29, 205
    reverse lookups, 139
    and TCP, 19
    and UDP, 19
DoS (denial of service) attacks, 16
downloading Ethereal, 75, 126–127, 203
Dsniff, 10, 25, 78
Dynamic Host Configuration Protocol
    (DHCP), 19

E

e-mail
    and Carnivore, 13
    Ethereal information resources, 52–53
    protecting, 32–33
EBCDIC strings, 235
Edit Capture Filter List dialog box,
    169–170
Edit Color Filter dialog box, 156–158
Edit Display Filter List dialog box,
    172–175
Edit menu
    Find Packet option, 148, 149–150
    Go To Packet option, 148, 151
    illustrated, 148
    list of options, 148–149
    overview, 147
    Preferences option, 148, 153–154
    Time Reference submenu, 148,
        151–152
editcap
    command-line options, 283–284
    examples, 284–287
    filter capability, 301
    overview, 57, 281, 300
    vs. Tethereal, 301

usage output, 281–283

Enabled Protocols dialog box, 176–177

Encapsulating Security Payload, 214

encryption, as resource-intensive, 37

End System-to-Intermediate System, 214

Endace Measurement Systems, 44, 305

enumeration. *See* scanning

epan directory
  column-utils.h file, 308, 396
  column_info.h file, 397
  conversation.h file, 396
  defined, 389
  framedata.h file, 397
  int-64bit.h file, 396
  packet-info.h file, 397
  plugins.h file, 396
  resolve.h file, 396
  strutil.h file, 396
  to_str.h file, 396
  tvbuff.h file, 396
  value_string.h file, 397

Equal To operator, 218

esis keyword, 214

esp keyword, 214

ether keyword, 211, 217

Ethereal
  command-line options, 200–202, 204
  command-line version (*See* Tethereal)
  compatibility with other programs, 43–44, 308–349
  defined, 9
  developer mailing list, 381
  developer tools and libraries, 383–386
  development prerequisites, 381–387, 431
  directory path, 124
  display windows, 3, 46–48, 228, 229
  displaying list of installed plugins, 196–197
  displaying list of supported protocols, 196
  downloading, 75, 126–127, 203
  enabling and disabling features, 117–120
  glossary of protocol and field names, 248–249
  GUI overview, 3, 46–48, 424–429, 433, 434
  Help menu, 194–197
  history, 41–42
  information resources, 52–54
  installation log, 94, 95–98
  installing from Red Hat Linux, 108–117
  installing from source code, 108–120
  installing on UNIX-based systems, 99–120, 122
  installing on Windows platforms, 91–99, 122
  launching, 127, 203
  list of needed libraries, 384–385
  list of source directories, 388–392
  list of source files, 387
  list of supported protocols, 44–46
  Main Window, 127–134, 203–204
  network architectural configurations, 49–64, 70
  obtaining software, 52, 75, 117, 121, 126–127, 203
  overview, 40–41, 69
  portability issues, 382
  reading files overview, 304–306, 350
  reading files with HP-UX nettl, 347
  reading files with Netasyst, 341–342
  reading files with snoop, 330–333
  reading files with Snort, 325–326
  reading files with TCPDump, 316–317
  reading files with Tethereal, 312–313
  reading files with WinDump, 319–320
  role in discovering trojan problems, 378
  setting preferences, 153–154
  source distribution, 387–392

starting, 127, 203
supporting programs overview, 54–59, 69–70
syntax, 402
system requirements, 77
upgrading to new version, 123
user interface, 3, 46–48, 424–429, 433, 434
using to troubleshoot networks, 64–68, 70
version issues, 52, 117, 123, 381
Web site, 54, 75, 126–127
Ethereal User's Guide, 54
EtherealXML.py tool, 279–280
Ethernet
  addresses in field expressions, 236–237
  CSMA/CD protocol, 20–21
  MAC addresses, 15–16
  overview, 14–16
EtherPeek
  capturing and saving data with, 336–338
  defined, 10, 43
  overview, 336
  reading Ethereal files with, 305, 338–339
Ettercap, 10, 78
exis keyword, 214
exporting files, 308–349
expressions
  in display-filter fields, 229–249
  Ethernet addresses in, 236–237
  Filter Expression dialog box, 172–173, 233, 254–256

F

FBI, 11
fddi keyword, 211, 215, 217
Federal Bureau of Investigation (FBI), 11
Fiber Distributed Data Interface, 211, 215, 217

fields
  address, 230, 237–239
  boolean, 230, 233–234
  byte sequence, 230, 236–237, 241, 242–243
  display-filter types, 229–249
  expressions in, 229–249
  floating point, 230, 234
  frame-number, 230, 233
  glossary of names, 248–249
  hidden, 247
  integer, 230, 231–233
  and logical operations, 244
  multiple occurrences, 244–246
  ranges, 241–243
  string, 230, 234–236
  time, 230, 239–240
file compression, 79
file formats, 304–307, 393
File menu
  illustrated, 137
  list of options, 137
  Open option, 137, 138
  overview, 136
  Print option, 137, 141–147
  Save As option, 137, 140
  Save option, 137, 140
File Transfer Protocol (FTP), 7, 8–9, 19
filename extensions, 352
files
  command-line options, 201
  exporting, 308–349
  importing, 308–349
  opening, 138
  printing packets, 141–147
  reading (See reading capture files)
  saving, 140–141
Filter Bar, 128, 134–136
Filter Expression dialog box, 172–173, 233, 254–256
filtering packets, 48–52, 134–136, 301

filters. *See also* capture filters; display filters
  capture *vs.* display, 48, 206, 208–209, 260
  color, 156–160
  command-line options, 202
  creating, 50–52
Find Packet dialog box, 149–150
Find Packet menu option, 148, 149–150
Flex, 386
floating point numbers, 230, 234
flooding switches, 25, 37
formats, file, 304–307, 393
fragmentation, packet, 422, 433
frame-number fields, 230, 233
frame pseudo-protocol, 237
framedata.h file, 397
frames, defined, 17
Free Software Foundation, 42
FTP (File Transfer Protocol), 7, 8–9, 19
functions
  creating, 397–400
  global, 396–397, 435
  static, 397

G

gettext library, 384
GIMP Toolkit, 77, 158. *See also* GTK
GLIB libraries, 77, 109–110, 383, 384
global functions, 396–397
glossary of protocol and field names, 248–249
Gnome RPM package, 100, 101, 102
GNU adns, 77, 111
GNU Project, 42–43
Go To Corresponding Frame menu option, 233
Go To Packet menu option, 148, 151
Graph Control dialog box
  Cross tab, 191

Graph type tab, 191–192
  Magnify tab, 189–190
  Origin tab, 190–191
  overview, 188–189
  Zoom tab, 188, 189
graph windows
  choosing type to display, 191–192
  and Graph Control dialog box, 188–192
  RTT graphs, 187–188, 192
  Stevens' time-sequence graphs, 182–183, 192
  tcptrace time-sequence graphs, 183–187, 192
  throughput graphs, 187, 192
Greater Than operator, 218, 223
Greater Than or Equal To operator, 218
GTK
  creating Ethereal GUI, 424–429
  custom icons, 390
  defined, 77, 383, 384, 385
  how it works, 425–429
  installing, 109, 110
  item factories, 424–425
  overview, 158–159
  Web site, 435
gtk directory, 389
gzip files, 79, 301

H

hardware, as network analyzer component, 4
hardware addresses, 230, 239
Harris, Guy, 41
header files, list of global functions, 396–397
help directory, 389
Help menu
  Contents dialog box, 195
  illustrated, 194

list of options, 195
Supported Protocols dialog box, 196
hexadecimal output
    and Data View Window, 47, 132, 204
    reading, 376
    and Text2pcap, 58, 59, 70, 293, 297, 300
hf arrays, 399
hidden fields, 247
Honeynet Project, 354, 366
honeypots, 29–30
host-to-host layer, DoD model, 18
hosts, 30, 210–211
HP-UX nettl
    capturing and saving data, 345–347
    command-line options, 343–344
    Ethereal compatibility, 44
    as format for reading capture files, 305
    overview, 342–343
    reading Ethereal files with, 347
    usage output, 343
HTTP (Hypertext Transfer Protocol)
    headers, 240, 241
    hiding traffic, 245–246
    and TCP, 19
    vulnerability to sniffers, 7
hubs, 22, 29

I

icmp keyword, 214, 217, 218
ICMP ping packet layout, 218, 219, 220–221
ICMP Redirects, 26
ICMP router advertisements, 26
icons, stock vs. custom, 390
idl2eth.sh file, 387
IDQ.DLL file, 367
Ifstatus tool, 31
igmp keyword, 214, 217
igrp keyword, 214, 217

image directory, 389
IMAP (Internet Mail Access Protocol), 7
importing files, 308–349
includes
    defining in dissectors, 395–397
    list of global functions, 396–397
Information field, 128, 132, 136, 204, 205
INSTALL file, 387
installation log, 94, 95–98
installing Ethereal
    mixing installation methods, 123
    platform availability, 76
    from RPMs, 99–102
    software downloads, 75, 126–127, 203
    from Solaris package, 104–108
    from source code, 108–120
    system requirements, 77
    on UNIX-based systems, 99–120, 122
    on Windows platforms, 91–99, 122
installing libpcap, 80–87
installing WinPcap, 87–91, 124
instructing Ethereal, 400
int-64bit.h file, 396
integer fields
    frame number type, 233
    overview, 231
    possible values, 230, 231–233
    representation examples, 231
    signed vs. unsigned, 230
Interior Gateway Routing Protocol, 214
Intermediate System-to-Intermediate System, 214
International Standards Organization (ISO), 16, 214
Internet Control Message Protocol. See icmp keyword
Internet Group Management Protocol, 214
Internet layer, DoD model, 18

Internet Protocol. *See* IP (Internet Protocol)

Internet service providers (ISPs), 33

Internetwork Packet eXchange. *See* IPX (Internetwork Packet eXchange)

intruders, use of sniffers, 6–8, 352

IP addresses
  capturing traffic, 210–211
  and Carnivore, 13
  as fields, 230, 237–238, 259

IP display filters, 49–50

IP (Internet Protocol), 18, 49–50

ip keyword, 214, 217

IPSec (IP Security), 32

iptrace, 44, 305

IPX (Internetwork Packet eXchange), 214, 230, 237, 238–239

isis keyword, 214

ISO (International Standards Organization), 16, 214

item factories, 424–425

J

jabber, 5

jitter, 5

L

large capture files, 168–169

lat keyword, 214, 217

law enforcement. *See* FBI

Layer 3 protocols, 18

Lemon tool, 392

Less Than operator, 218, 223

Less Than or Equal To operator, 218

libcrypto, 103

libiconv, 384

libpcap
  defined, 77, 384
  filtering engine, 227

  as format for saving capture files, 306
  installing from source files, 85–87
  installing from Sun packages, 83–85
  installing using RPM, 80–83
  overview, 78
  and promiscuous mode, 37
  ways to install, 80

libraries. *See also* libpcap; WinPcap
  Asynchronous DNS, 205, 384
  developer kits, 383–386
  GLIB, 77, 109–110, 383, 384
  libcrypto, 103
  list needed to build Ethereal, 384–385
  Tethereal tools, 384
  Win32, 383
  Zlib, 77, 111–112, 385

line feeds, 393

link keyword, 217

Linux-based systems. *See also* Red Hat Package Manager (RPM)
  building Ethereal on, 386–387, ch3
  installing Ethereal, 108–117
  list of needed libraries for Ethereal, 384–385

Linux Bluez Bluetooth, 44, 305

Local Area Transport, 214, 217

logical operators, 212–213, 244

lower case, 402

Lrk5 rootkit, 7

Lucent/Ascend, 43, 305

M

MAC (Media Access Control) addresses
  and ARP Redirect, 25–26
  flooding, 25, 37
  name resolution, 139
  overview, 15–16
  spoofing, 26
  and switches, 23

mailsnarf, 13

Main Window, Ethereal
  Data Tree Window, 128, 132–134
  Filter Bar, 128, 134–136
  illustrated, 127
  Information field, 128, 132, 136, 204,
    205
  list of components, 128
  Menu Bar, 128, 136
  overview, 127, 203–204
  Protocol Tree Window, 128, 130–132
  Summary Window, 128–130
  Tool Bar, 128
Maintenance Operation Protocol, 214,
  217
make-xxx file, 387
Makefile.am file, 387, 409
Makefile.nmake file, 387, 409
man pages, 209
manuf file, 117, 118
Match submenu, Analyze menu, 175–176
matches operator, 235
Media Access Control. *See* MAC (Media
  Access Control) addresses
Menu Bar, 128, 136
menus
  Analyze menu, 171–194
  Capture menu, 161–170
  vs. command-line options, 200–202
  context-sensitive, 197–200
  Edit menu, 147–154
  File menu, 136–147
  Help menu, 194–197
  overview, 136, 204
  pop-up, 197–200
  View menu, 154–161
mergecap
  command-line options, 289–290
  and gzip, 301
  overview, 57–58, 287, 300
  usage examples, 290–292, 352
  usage output, 287–289
Microsoft Desktop Engine (MSDE), 365
Microsoft Network Monitor
  capturing and saving data, 334–335
  defined, 10
  Ethereal compatibility, 43
  as format for reading capture files, 304
  as format for saving capture files, 307
  Frame View window, 334, 335
  main window, 333, 334
  overview, 333
  reading Ethereal files with, 336
Microsoft Visual C++, 435
mirroring ports. *See* ports, spanning
modified libpcap, as format for saving
  capture files, 306
mopdl keyword, 214, 217
moprc keyword, 214, 217
mounting CD-ROM, 81
MSDE (Microsoft Desktop Engine), 365
msnchat tool, 279–281

N

name resolution
  command-line options, 202
  and DNS lookups, 29, 205
  overview, 139–140
  repeated addresses, 205–206
NCP (NetWare Core Protocol), 233, 236
negative numbers, 243
Net Optics cable taps, 21
Net-SNMP, 77, 100, 111, 384
Netasyst
  capturing and saving data with,
    340–341

overview, 339
reading Ethereal files with, 341–342
netbeui keyword, 214
NetBIOS Extended User Interface (NetBEUI), 214
NetBus trojan, 361–363
NetWare Core Protocol (NCP), 233, 236
network access layer, DoD model, 18
network analysis, 2, 35–37. *See also* sniffing, defined
network analyzers. *See also* Ethereal; sniffers
  basic parts, 4
  buffer component, 4
  capture driver, 4, 78, 121–122
  decode component, 4
  examples, 9–11
  hardware, 4
  how they work, 35–36
  intruder use, 6–8
  list of sniffer products, 9–11
  overview, 2–3
  policy issues, 33, 36–37
  real-time analysis feature, 4
  reasons for using, 5–11, 35
  who uses, 35
Network Associates Sniffer, 9, 43, 304, 307, 339, 342. *See also* Netasyst
Network File System (NFS), 19
Network Instruments Observer, 44, 305, 307
network interface cards (NICs)
  capturing traffic, 211, 352
  hardware addresses, 211
  promiscuous, 15, 27–29
network intrusion detection system (NIDS), 320. *See also* Snort
network layer, Open Systems Interconnection (OSI) model, 17
Network Monitor. *See* Microsoft Network Monitor
network name resolution, 139, 205

Network News Transfer Protocol (NNTP), 19
Network Promiscuous Ethernet Detector (Neped), 30
network scanning. *See* scanning
networks
  scanning (*See* scanning)
  sniffing traffic, 6–8
  troubleshooting with Ethereal, 64–68
NetXRay, 43, 305
NFS (Network File System), 19
NICs. *See* network interface cards (NICs)
NIDS (network intrusion detection system), 320. *See also* Snort
Nmap, 8, 78
NNTP (Network News Transfer Protocol), 19
non-disclosure agreements, 33
Not Equal To operator, 218
not operator, 212–213, 244
Novell LANalyzer, 43, 304, 307
NSIS install package, 391
Null scans, 358–359

O

One-time Passwords In Everything (OPIE), 32
one-time passwords (OTP), 32, 38
Open dialog box, 138
Open menu option, 137, 138
open source software, 42–43
Open Systems Interconnection (OSI) model
  application layer, 16
  data link layer, 17
  vs. DoD model, 18
  list of layers, 16–17
  network layer, 17
  overview, 16

physical layer, 17
presentation layer, 16
session layer, 17
transport layer, 17
opening files, 138
OpenSSL, 103
operators
  arithmetic, 218
  bitwise, 218, 221–223
  comparison, 230–231
  Equal To operator, 218
  Greater Than operator, 218, 223
  Greater Than or Equal To operator, 218
  Less Than operator, 218, 223
  Less Than or Equal To operator, 218
  logical, 212–213, 244
  matches operator, 235
  Not Equal To operator, 218
  not operator, 212–213, 244
  and operator, 212–213, 244
  or operator, 212–213, 244
  order of precedence, 213, 259
OPIE (One-time Passwords In Everything), 32
or operator, 212–213, 244
OSI model. *See* Open Systems Interconnection (OSI) model
OTP (one-time passwords), 32, 38

P

package management tools. *See* Red Hat Package Manager (RPM)
packaging directory, 390–391
packet-info.h file, 397
packet size, 223–224
packet sniffers. *See* sniffers
packet-xxx file, 387
packets. *See also* capture drivers; capture filters
  Ethernet overview, 15

filtering, 48–52
filtering Summary Window display, 134–136
fragmentation, 422, 433
vs. frames, 17
printing, 141–147
retransmission, 419–420, 433
viewing in Data View Window, 132–134
viewing in Protocol Tree Window, 130–132
viewing in Summary Window, 128–130
Packetyzer, 11
pango library, 385
path, 124
payloads, passing, 408–409
pcre library, 385
PDML format, displaying Tethereal output in, 278–281
Perl, 77, 112, 386
physical layer, Open Systems Interconnection (OSI) model, 17
PIM (Protocol Independent Multicast) protocol, 214, 217, 244
pinfo data structure, 401, 434
pkgadd command, 83, 104, 108, 123
pkginfo command, 108
pkgrm command, 108, 123
platforms
  installing Ethereal on Red Hat Linux, 108–117
  installing Ethereal on UNIX-based systems, 99–120, 122
  installing Ethereal on Windows platforms, 91–99, 122
  list for installing Ethereal, 76
  portability issues, 482
plug-ins
  About Plugins dialog box, 196–197
  displaying installed list, 196–197
  dissector list, 391

epan/plugins.h file, 396
  plugins directory, 391
  protocol dissectors as, 429, 434
plugins.h file, 396
pod2html, 386
pod2man, 386
Point-To-Point Protocol. *See* ppp
      keyword
Point-To-Point Protocol Daemon (pppd)
      logs, 44, 305
pop-up menus, 197–200
POP3 protocol, vulnerability to sniffers,
      7
port keyword, 212
port mirroring. *See* ports, spanning
portability, 382
ports
  capturing traffic, 212
  spanning, 24, 25, 27
ppp keyword, 217
pppd logs, 44, 305
Preferences menu option, 148, 153–154
prefs.h file, 396
Prepare submenu, Analyze menu, 175
presentation layer, Open Systems
      Interconnection (OSI) model, 16
Print menu option, 137, 141–147
printing
  help information, 202
  packet information, 141–147
  protocol trees, 143–146
  version information, 202
process layer, DoD model, 18
programming languages. *See* C language;
      Perl; Visual C++
PromiScan, 30
Promisc.c tool, 31
promiscuous mode, 30, 31, 206
protocol dissectors, 240, 241, 245
protocol fields, 215–221, 230, 241

Protocol Hierarchy Statistics dialog box,
      192–193
Protocol Independent Multicast (PIM)
      protocol, 214, 217, 244
Protocol Tree Window
  illustrated, 131, 132
  overview, 128, 130–132
  role of Information field, 128, 132,
      136, 204, 205
  using with Data View Window, 133
protocol trees
  and no-value fields, 240–241
  printing, 143–146
  Protocol Tree Window overview, 128,
      130–132
  Tethereal display output, 267–269
protocols. *See also* Ethernet
  displaying list, 196
  Ethereal-supported, 44–46
  glossary of names, 248–249
  multiple occurrences per packet,
      244–246
  name resolution, 139–140
  Supported Protocols dialog box, Help
      menu, 196
  TCP/IP overview, 18–19
  as tcpdump keywords, 213–214, 215,
      217–218
  vulnerability to sniffers, 7
proto_tree functions, 413–414
proto_tree_add functions, 404–406, 417
Python, 385, 386

R

r0rns sniffer, 7
RADCOM, 43, 305
Ramen worm, 371–375
Ramirez, Gilbert, 41
ranges, 241–243
rarp keyword, 214, 217

RAT (Remote Admin Trojan), 7
reading capture files
  with HP-UX nettl, 347
  with Netasyst, 341–342
  overview, 304–306, 350
  with snoop, 330–333
  with Snort, 325–326
  with TCPDump, 316–317
  with Tethereal, 312–313
  with WinDump, 319–320
README files
  defined, 387
  developer document, 388, 434
  doc directory list, 388–389
real-time analysis, as network analyzer
      component, 4
reassemble.h file, 396
Red Hat Linux
  installing Ethereal, 108–117
  libpcap as format for saving capture
      files, 306
  and Ramen worm, 371–375
Red Hat Package Manager (RPM)
  installing Ethereal from, 99–102
  installing libpcap, 80–83
  list of versions, 99–100
  overview, 81–83
relative time, 230, 239–240
remote access trojans, 359–363, 377
Remote Admin Trojan (RAT), 7
resolve.h file, 396
retransmitting packets, 419–420, 433
Reverse Address Resolution Protocol
      (RARP), 214, 217
reverse lookups, DNS, 29
ring buffer captures, 165–167
rlogin protocol, 7
rootkits, 7, 8
Routing Information Protocol (RIP), 19
RPMs. See Red Hat Package Manager
      (RPM)

RST.b trojan, 363
RTT graphs, 187–188, 192

S

Sapphire worm, 365
Save As dialog box, 140–141
Save As menu option, 137, 140
Save menu option, 137, 140
saving
  capture files, 140–141, 306–307, 350
  capture filters, 252, 253, 259
  display filters, 252, 253, 259
sca keyword, 214, 217
Scan3.log file, 366
scanning
  Null scans, 358–359
  overview, 354, 376–377
  similar-appearing activities, 378
  TCP Connect scans, 355–356
  TCP SYN scans, 356–357
  XMAS scans, 357–358
sctp keyword, 214, 218
ISDN4BSD project, 44, 305
Secure Shell (SSH), 32
Secure Sockets Layer (SSL), 32
Sentinel tool, 30
Server Message Block (SMB) protocol,
      233
session layer, Open Systems
      Interconnection (OSI) model, 17
Sharpe, Richard, 41, 54
Shomiti/Finisar Surveyor, 43, 304
Show Packet in New Window menu
      option, 160–161
signed integers, 230
Simple Network Management Protocol
      (SNMP). See SNMP (Simple
      Network Management Protocol)
Slammer worm, 365–366, 367

SMB (Server Message Block) protocol, 233

SMTP (Simple Mail Transfer Protocol), 7, 19

Sniffer, 3, 9, 43, 304, 307, 339, 342. *See also* sniffers

Sniffer Technologies, 342. *See also* Netasyst

sniffers. *See also* network analyzers
   backdoor, 7–8, 359–363
   detecting, 27–31, 36
   FTP session example, 8–9
   how they work, 35–36
   intruder use, 6–8
   list of products, 9–11
   permission to use, 33
   policy issues, 33, 36–37
   protecting against, 31–33, 36
   reasons for using, 5–11, 35
   session capture, 8–9
   vs. Sniffer, 3
   tools for detecting, 30–31
   ways to use, 6–8
   writing programs, 19–20

sniffing, defined, 2

Sniffit, 10

SNMP (Simple Network Management Protocol)
   Net-SNMP package, 77, 100, 111, 384
   and UDP, 19
   vulnerability to sniffers, 7

snoop
   capturing and saving data, 329–330
   command-line options, 328
   defined, 10
   Ethereal compatibility, 43
   as format for reading capture files, 304
   as format for saving capture files, 307
   overview, 326
   reading Ethereal files with, 330–333
   usage output, 327

viewing capture files together with tcpdump capture files, 352

Snort
   capturing and saving data, 322–325, 352
   command-line options, 322
   defined, 10
   overview, 78, 320
   and promiscuous mode, 206
   reading Ethereal files with, 325–326
   usage output, 320–322

Solaris. *See also* snoop
   installing Ethereal from, 104–108
   installing libpcap from, 83–85

spam prevention, 68

spanning ports, 24, 25, 27

Spanning Tree Protocol, 214

spoofing, 15–16, 26

SQL Server, 365

SQL Slammer worm, 365–366, 367

SSL (Secure Sockets Layer), 32

Stallman, Richard, 42

static functions, 397

Statistics submenu, Analyze menu, 194

stealth scans, 356–357

Stevens' time-sequence graphs, 182–183, 192

stp keyword, 214

Stream Control Transmission Protocol, 214, 218

strings
   in fields, 230, 234–236, 241
   matches operator, 235
   types, 235

strutil.h file, 396

sub-trees, 413–415, 432

SubSeven, 7, 360–361

Summary dialog box, Analyze menu, 192

Summary Window
   filtering display, 134–136
   overview, 128–130
   pop-up menu, 197–198

Sun Microsystems. *See also* snoop
  installing Ethereal from Solaris
      packages, 104–108
  installing libpcap from Solaris packages,
      83–85
Supported Protocols dialog box, Help
      menu, 196
SuSE Linux libpcap, 306
switches
  defeating, 25–27
  failing closed, 25
  failing open, 25
  flooding, 25, 37
  vs. hubs, 22
  and MAC addresses, 23
  overview, 22–23
  port mirroring feature, 24
  reconfiguring port spanning, 27
SYN flag, 354, 355–356
syntax, Ethereal, 402
system requirements, 77
Systems Communication Arcitecture,
      214, 217

T

tap systems, 429, 434
tap-xxx file, 387
tap.h file, 396
TAPS. *See* tap systems
Taps. *See* Test Access Points
tar archive format, 79, 85–86
tarballs, 85–87
TCP Connect scans, 355–356
TCP flags field, 221–223
TCP header, 215, 216
TCP/IP protocols, 18–19
tcp keyword, 214, 215, 217, 218
TCP Stream Analysis submenu, Analyze
      menu, 181–192. *See also* Contents
      of TCP Stream Window
TCP SYN scans, 356–357

TCP (Transmission Control Protocol),
      18–19, 354
TCPDump
  capturing and saving data, 314–316
  command-line options, 314
  defined, 10
  vs. display filters, 227
  ether keyword, 211
  Ethereal compatibility, 43
  as format for reading capture files, 304
  and hardware addresses, 211
  and host names and addresses, 210–211
  logical operations, 212–213
  malicious code in, 79
  overview, 78, 313
  and ports, 212
  and protocol fields, 215–221
  protocol names as keywords, 213–215
  reading Ethereal files with, 316–317
  syntax, 209–224
  usage output, 313
  viewing capture files together with
      snoop capture files, 352
  vs. WinDump, 317
tcpflow, 78
TCPIPtrace utility, 44, 305
TCPstat, 78
tcptrace time-sequence graphs, 183–187,
      192
Telnet, 7, 19
Test Access Points, 21
testing capture filters, 224
Tethereal
  –z (statistics) option, 267, 271–278
  capturing and saving data, 310–312
  command-line options, 263–267,
      309–310
  displaying output in PDML format,
      278–281
  displaying packets to screen, 267
  vs. editcap, 301
  filter capability, 301

glossary of protocol and field names, 248–249

overview, 54–56, 262, 299, 308

reading Ethereal files with, 312–313

tools and libraries, 384

usage examples, 267–271, 310–312

usage output, 262–263, 308–309

using display filters on capture, 206

writing captures to files, 267

text2pcap

command-line options, 295–297

overview, 58–59, 293, 300

usage examples, 297–298

usage output, 294–295

throughput graphs, 187, 192

time fields, 230, 239–240

Time Reference submenu, Edit menu, 148, 151–152

time-sequence graphs

Stevens', 182–183, 192

tcptrace, 183–187, 192

TLS (Transport Layer Security), 32

TokenPeek, 43, 305

Tool Bar, 128

tools directory, 392

TOrnKit, 7

Toshiba, 43, 305

to_str.h file, 396

Transmission Control Protocol/Internet Protocol (TCP/IP), 18–19

transport layer, Open Systems Interconnection (OSI) model, 17

Transport Layer Security (TLS), 32

transport name resolution, 140

tree data structure, 401

trojans

defined, 364

and Ethereal TCP Stream feature, 361, 362

NetBus, 361–363

overview, 359–360, 377

remote access, 359–363, 377

RST.b trojan, 363

SubSeven trojan, 360–361

vs. viruses and worms, 364–365

troubleshooting networks with Ethereal, 64–68

trr keyword, 218

tvb data structure, 401

tvb_get functions, 402, 406

tvbuff.h file, 396

U

_U_ value, 426

udp keyword, 214, 218

UDP (User Datagram Protocol), 18, 363, 366

Unicode strings, 235, 417–418, 433

UNIX-based systems. See also Linux-based systems

building Ethereal on, 386, ch3

installing Ethereal from RPMs, 99–102, 122

installing Ethereal from Solaris package, 104–108, 122

installing Ethereal from source code, 108–120, 122–123

list of needed libraries for Ethereal, 384–385

unmounting CD-ROM, 81

unsigned integers, 230

upgrading Ethereal, 123

U.S. Department of Defense, 18

U.S. Federal Bureau of Investigation (FBI), 11

User Datagram Protocol (UDP), 18–19, 214, 218, 363, 366

V

value strings, 422–423, 433

values, field type, 230

value_string.h file, 397

versions, Ethereal. *See also* Concurrent
    Version System (CVS)
  command-line, 54–56
  issues, 52, 117, 123, 381
  latest, obtaining, 52, 117
  printing information, 202
  upgrading to latest, 123
View menu
  Apply Color Filters dialog box,
    156–160
  Display Options dialog box, 155–156
  list of menu options, 154–155
  overview, 154
  Show Packet in New Window option,
    160–161
virtual private networks (VPNs), 31, 38
Virtual Router Redundancy Protocol,
    214, 218
viruses
  benign *vs.* malignant, 364
  defined, 364
  vs. trojans and worms, 364–365
  types, 364
Visual C++, 435
Visual Networks, 307
Visual UpTime, 43, 305
VMS, 305
vrrp keyword, 214, 218

W

W32.Slammer worm, 365
W32.SQLExp. Worm, 365
Web site, Ethereal, 54, 75, 126–127
WildPackets, 43, 305, 336–339
Win32 libraries, 383
Windows 2000
  and Code Red worm, 367
  installing Ethereal, 91–99, 122
  Network Monitor, defined, 10
Windows NT, 10, 367
Windows platforms

installing Ethereal, 91–99, 122,
    386–387
  list of needed libraries for Ethereal,
    384–385
Windows sniffing, 7
Windows XP, 367
WinDump
  capturing and saving data, 318–319
  command-line options, 317–318
  defined, 9
  overview, 78, 317
  reading Ethereal files with, 319–320
  vs. TCPDump, 317
  usage output, 317
WinPcap
  defined, 384
  installing, 87–91, 124
  overview, 78
  running after installation, 94
  upgrading to new version, 123
wiretap directory, 352, 392
worms
  Code Red worm, 367–370
  defined, 365
  overview, 365, 377
  Ramen worm, 371–375
  SQL Slammer worm, 365–366, 367
  vs. trojans and viruses, 364–365
writing
  capture filters, 209–227, 257–258
  display filters, 227–256, 258

X

Xmas scans, 357–358
xxxx file, 387

Z

-z (statistics) option, Tethereal, 267,
    271–278
Zethereal, 348–349
Zlib library, 77, 111–112, 385

Version 2, June 1991

Copyright (C) 1989, 1991 Free Software Foundation, Inc.
59 Temple Place - Suite 330, Boston, MA 02111-1307, USA

Preamble

The licenses for most software are designed to take away your freedom to share
and change it. By contrast, the GNU General Public License is intended to guarantee your freedom to share and change free software—to make sure the software
is free for all its users. This General Public License applies to most of the Free
Software Foundation's software and to any other program whose authors commit
to using it. (Some other Free Software Foundation software is covered by the
GNU Library General Public License instead.) You can apply it to your programs,
too.

When we speak of free software, we are referring to freedom, not price. Our
General Public Licenses are designed to make sure that you have the freedom to
distribute copies of free software (and charge for this service if you wish), that you
receive source code or can get it if you want it, that you can change the software
or use pieces of it in new free programs; and that you know you can do these
things.

To protect your rights, we need to make restrictions that forbid anyone to deny
you these rights or to ask you to surrender the rights. These restrictions translate
to certain responsibilities for you if you distribute copies of the software, or if you
modify it.

For example, if you distribute copies of such a program, whether gratis or for a
fee, you must give the recipients all the rights that you have. You must make sure
that they, too, receive or can get the source code. And you must show them these
terms so they know their rights.

We protect your rights with two steps: (1) copyright the software, and (2) offer
you this license which gives you legal permission to copy, distribute and/or
modify the software.

Also, for each author's protection and ours, we want to make certain that
everyone understands that there is no warranty for this free software. If the software is modified by someone else and passed on, we want its recipients to know
that what they have is not the original, so that any problems introduced by others
will not reflect on the original authors' reputations.

Finally, any free program is threatened constantly by software patents. We wish to
avoid the danger that redistributors of a free program will individually obtain
patent licenses, in effect making the program proprietary. To prevent this, we have

made it clear that any patent must be licensed for everyone's free use or not licensed at all.

The precise terms and conditions for copying, distribution and modification follow.

TERMS AND CONDITIONS FOR COPYING, DISTRIBUTION AND MODIFICATION

0. This License applies to any program or other work which contains a notice placed by the copyright holder saying it may be distributed under the terms of this General Public License. The "Program", below, refers to any such program or work, and a "work based on the Program" means either the Program or any derivative work under copyright law: that is to say, a work containing the Program or a portion of it, either verbatim or with modifications and/or translated into another language. (Hereinafter, translation is included without limitation in the term "modification".) Each licensee is addressed as "you".

Activities other than copying, distribution and modification are not covered by this License; they are outside its scope. The act of running the Program is not restricted, and the output from the Program is covered only if its contents constitute a work based on the Program (independent of having been made by running the Program). Whether that is true depends on what the Program does.

1. You may copy and distribute verbatim copies of the Program's source code as you receive it, in any medium, provided that you conspicuously and appropriately publish on each copy an appropriate copyright notice and disclaimer of warranty; keep intact all the notices that refer to this License and to the absence of any warranty; and give any other recipients of the Program a copy of this License along with the Program.

You may charge a fee for the physical act of transferring a copy, and you may at your option offer warranty protection in exchange for a fee.

2. You may modify your copy or copies of the Program or any portion of it, thus forming a work based on the Program, and copy and distribute such modifications or work under the terms of Section 1 above, provided that you also meet all of these conditions:

a) You must cause the modified files to carry prominent notices stating that you changed the files and the date of any change.

b) You must cause any work that you distribute or publish, that in whole or in part contains or is derived from the Program or any part thereof, to be licensed as a whole at no charge to all third parties under the terms of this License.

c) If the modified program normally reads commands interactively when run, you must cause it, when started running for such interactive use in the most ordinary way, to print or display an announcement including an appropriate copyright notice and a notice that there is no warranty (or else, saying that you provide a warranty) and that users may redistribute the program under these conditions, and telling the user how to view a copy of this License. (Exception: if the Program itself is interactive but does not normally print such an announcement, your work based on the Program is not required to print an announcement.)

These requirements apply to the modified work as a whole. If identifiable sections of that work are not derived from the Program, and can be reasonably considered independent and separate works in themselves, then this License, and its terms, do not apply to those sections when you distribute them as separate works. But when you distribute the same sections as part of a whole which is a work based on the Program, the distribution of the whole must be on the terms of this License, whose permissions for other licensees extend to the entire whole, and thus to each and every part regardless of who wrote it.

Thus, it is not the intent of this section to claim rights or contest your rights to work written entirely by you; rather, the intent is to exercise the right to control the distribution of derivative or collective works based on the Program.

In addition, mere aggregation of another work not based on the Program with the Program (or with a work based on the Program) on a volume of a storage or distribution medium does not bring the other work under the scope of this License.

3. You may copy and distribute the Program (or a work based on it, under Section 2) in object code or executable form under the terms of Sections 1 and 2 above provided that you also do one of the following:

a) Accompany it with the complete corresponding machine-readable source code, which must be distributed under the terms of Sections 1 and 2 above on a medium customarily used for software interchange; or,

b) Accompany it with a written offer, valid for at least three years, to give any third party, for a charge no more than your cost of physically performing source distribution, a complete machine-readable copy of the corresponding source code, to be distributed under the terms of Sections 1 and 2 above on a medium customarily used for software interchange; or,

c) Accompany it with the information you received as to the offer to distribute corresponding source code. (This alternative is allowed only for noncommercial distribution and only if you received the program in object code or executable form with such an offer, in accord with Subsection b above.)

The source code for a work means the preferred form of the work for making modifications to it. For an executable work, complete source code means all the source code for all modules it contains, plus any associated interface definition files, plus the scripts used to control compilation and installation of the executable. However, as a special exception, the source code distributed need not include anything that is normally distributed (in either source or binary form) with the major components (compiler, kernel, and so on) of the operating system on which the executable runs, unless that component itself accompanies the executable.

If distribution of executable or object code is made by offering access to copy from a designated place, then offering equivalent access to copy the source code from the same place counts as distribution of the source code, even though third parties are not compelled to copy the source along with the object code.

4. You may not copy, modify, sublicense, or distribute the Program except as expressly provided under this License. Any attempt otherwise to copy, modify, sublicense or distribute the Program is void, and will automatically terminate your rights under this License. However, parties who have received copies, or rights, from you under this License will not have their licenses terminated so long as such parties remain in full compliance.

5. You are not required to accept this License, since you have not signed it. However, nothing else grants you permission to modify or distribute the Program or its derivative works. These actions are prohibited by law if you do not accept this License. Therefore, by modifying or distributing the Program (or any work based on the Program), you indicate your acceptance of this License to do so, and all its terms and conditions for copying, distributing or modifying the Program or works based on it.

6. Each time you redistribute the Program (or any work based on the Program), the recipient automatically receives a license from the original licensor to copy, distribute or modify the Program subject to these terms and conditions. You may not impose any further restrictions on the recipients' exercise of the rights granted herein. You are not responsible for enforcing compliance by third parties to this License.

7. If, as a consequence of a court judgment or allegation of patent infringement or for any other reason (not limited to patent issues), conditions are imposed on you (whether by court order, agreement or otherwise) that contradict the conditions of this License, they do not excuse you from the conditions of this License. If you cannot distribute so as to satisfy simultaneously your obligations under this License and any other pertinent obligations, then as a consequence you may not distribute the Program at all. For example, if a patent license would not permit royalty-free redistribution of the Program by all those who receive copies directly or indirectly through you, then the only way you could satisfy both it and this License would be to refrain entirely from distribution of the Program.

If any portion of this section is held invalid or unenforceable under any particular circumstance, the balance of the section is intended to apply and the section as a whole is intended to apply in other circumstances.

It is not the purpose of this section to induce you to infringe any patents or other property right claims or to contest validity of any such claims; this section has the sole purpose of protecting the integrity of the free software distribution system, which is implemented by public license practices. Many people have made generous contributions to the wide range of software distributed through that system in reliance on consistent application of that system; it is up to the author/donor to decide if he or she is willing to distribute software through any other system and a licensee cannot impose that choice.

This section is intended to make thoroughly clear what is believed to be a consequence of the rest of this License.

8. If the distribution and/or use of the Program is restricted in certain countries either by patents or by copyrighted interfaces, the original copyright holder who places the Program under this License may add an explicit geographical distribution limitation excluding those countries, so that distribution is permitted only in or among countries not thus excluded. In such case, this License incorporates the limitation as if written in the body of this License.

9. The Free Software Foundation may publish revised and/or new versions of the General Public License from time to time. Such new versions will be similar in spirit to the present version, but may differ in detail to address new problems or concerns.

Each version is given a distinguishing version number. If the Program specifies a version number of this License which applies to it and "any later version", you have the option of following the terms and conditions either of that version or of any later version published by the Free Software Foundation. If the Program does not specify a version number of this License, you may choose any version ever published by the Free Software Foundation.

10. If you wish to incorporate parts of the Program into other free programs whose distribution conditions are different, write to the author to ask for permission. For software which is copyrighted by the Free Software Foundation, write to the Free Software Foundation; we sometimes make exceptions for this. Our decision will be guided by the two goals of preserving the free status of all derivatives of our free software and of promoting the sharing and reuse of software generally.

NO WARRANTY

11. BECAUSE THE PROGRAM IS LICENSED FREE OF CHARGE, THERE IS NO WARRANTY FOR THE PROGRAM, TO THE EXTENT PERMITTED BY APPLICABLE LAW. EXCEPT WHEN OTHERWISE STATED IN WRITING THE COPYRIGHT HOLDERS AND/OR OTHER PARTIES PROVIDE THE PROGRAM "AS IS" WITHOUT WARRANTY OF ANY KIND, EITHER EXPRESSED OR IMPLIED, INCLUDING, BUT NOT LIMITED TO, THE IMPLIED WARRANTIES OF MERCHANTABILITY AND FITNESS FOR A PARTICULAR PURPOSE. THE ENTIRE RISK AS TO THE QUALITY AND PERFORMANCE OF THE PROGRAM IS WITH YOU. SHOULD THE PROGRAM PROVE DEFECTIVE, YOU ASSUME THE COST OF ALL NECESSARY SERVICING, REPAIR OR CORRECTION.

12. IN NO EVENT UNLESS REQUIRED BY APPLICABLE LAW OR AGREED TO IN WRITING WILL ANY COPYRIGHT HOLDER, OR ANY OTHER PARTY WHO MAY MODIFY AND/OR REDISTRIBUTE THE PROGRAM AS PERMITTED ABOVE, BE LIABLE TO YOU FOR DAMAGES, INCLUDING ANY GENERAL, SPECIAL, INCIDENTAL OR CONSEQUENTIAL DAMAGES ARISING OUT OF THE USE OR

INABILITY TO USE THE PROGRAM (INCLUDING BUT NOT LIMITED TO LOSS OF DATA OR DATA BEING RENDERED INACCURATE OR LOSSES SUSTAINED BY YOU OR THIRD PARTIES OR A FAILURE OF THE PROGRAM TO OPERATE WITH ANY OTHER PROGRAMS), EVEN IF SUCH HOLDER OR OTHER PARTY HAS BEEN ADVISED OF THE POSSIBILITY OF SUCH DAMAGES.

END OF TERMS AND CONDITIONS

<u>How to Apply These Terms to Your New Programs</u>

If you develop a new program, and you want it to be of the greatest possible use to the public, the best way to achieve this is to make it free software which everyone can redistribute and change under these terms.

To do so, attach the following notices to the program. It is safest to attach them to the start of each source file to most effectively convey the exclusion of warranty; and each file should have at least the "copyright" line and a pointer to where the full notice is found.

one line to give the program's name and an idea of what it does.
Copyright (C) *yyyy name of author*

This program is free software; you can redistribute it and/or
modify it under the terms of the GNU General Public License
as published by the Free Software Foundation; either version 2
of the License, or (at your option) any later version.

This program is distributed in the hope that it will be useful,
but WITHOUT ANY WARRANTY; without even the implied warranty of
MERCHANTABILITY or FITNESS FOR A PARTICULAR PURPOSE. See the
GNU General Public License for more details.

You should have received a copy of the GNU General Public License
along with this program; if not, write to the Free Software
Foundation, Inc., 59 Temple Place - Suite 330, Boston, MA 02111-1307, USA.

Also add information on how to contact you by electronic and paper mail.

If the program is interactive, make it output a short notice like this when it starts in an interactive mode:

Gnomovision version 69, Copyright (C) *year name of author*
Gnomovision comes with ABSOLUTELY NO WARRANTY; for details
type `show w'. This is free software, and you are welcome
to redistribute it under certain conditions; type `show c'
for details.

The hypothetical commands 'show w' and 'show c' should show the appropriate parts of the General Public License. Of course, the commands you use may be called something other than 'show w' and 'show c'; they could even be mouse-clicks or menu items—whatever suits your program.

You should also get your employer (if you work as a programmer) or your school, if any, to sign a "copyright disclaimer" for the program, if necessary. Here is a sample; alter the names:

Yoyodyne, Inc., hereby disclaims all copyright
interest in the program `Gnomovision'
(which makes passes at compilers) written
by James Hacker.

signature of Ty Coon, 1 April 1989
Ty Coon, President of Vice

This General Public License does not permit incorporating your program into proprietary programs. If your program is a subroutine library, you may consider it more useful to permit linking proprietary applications with the library. If this is what you want to do, use the GNU Library General Public License instead of this License.

Syngress: *The Definition of a Serious Security Library*

Syn·gress (sin–gres): *noun, sing.* Freedom from risk or danger; safety. See *security*.

Check Point Next Generation Security Administration
Cherie Amon and Doug Maxwell

The Check Point Next Generation suite of products provides the tools necessary for easy development and deployment of Enterprise Security Solutions. Check Point VPN-1/FireWall-1 has been beating out its competitors for years, and the Next Generation software continues to improve the look, feel, and ease of use of this software. *Check Point NG Security Administration* will show you the ins and outs of the NG product line.

ISBN: 1-928994-74-1

Price: $59.95 USA $92.95 CAN

Special Ops: Host and Network Security for Microsoft, UNIX, and Oracle
Erik Pace Birkholz

"Strap on the night vision goggles, apply the camo pain, then lock and load. *Special Ops* is an adrenaline-pumping tour of the most critical security weaknesses present on most any corporate network today, with some of the world's best drill sergeants leading the way."
—Joel Scambray, Senior Director, Microsoft's MSN

ISBN: 1-928994-74-1

Price: $69.95 USA $108.95 CAN

Stealing the Network: How to "Own the Box"
Ryan Russell, FX, Joe Grand, and Ken Pfiel

Stealing the Network: How to Own the Box is NOT intended to be an "install, configure, update, troubleshoot, and defend book." It is also NOT another one of the countless Hacker books out there now by our competition. So, what IS it? *Stealing the Network: How to Own the Box* is an edgy, provocative, attack-oriented series of chapters written in a first hand, conversational style. World-renowned network security personalities present a series of chapters written from the point of an attacker gaining access to a system. This book portrays the street fighting tactics used to attack networks.

ISBN: 1-931836-87-6

Price: $49.95 USA $69.95 CAN

SYNGRES